*f*P

Sophia Tolstoy

A Biography

Alexandra Popoff

FREE PRESS

New York London Toronto Sydney

Free Press
A Division of Simon & Schuster, Inc.
1230 Avenue of the Americas
New York, NY 10020

First Free Press hardcover edition May 2010

FREE PRESS and colophon are trademarks of Simon & Schuster, Inc.

For information about special discounts for bulk purchases,
please contact Simon & Schuster Special Sales at 1-866-506-1949
or business@simonandschuster.com

The Simon & Schuster Speakers Bureau can bring authors to your live event.
For more information or to book an event contact the Simon & Schuster Speakers Bureau at 1-866-248-3049 or visit our website at www.simonspeakers.com.

All photographs courtesy the L. N. Tolstoy State Museum, Moscow,
unless otherwise specified.

Book design by Ellen R. Sasahara

Manufactured in the United States of America

1   3   5   7   9   10   8   6   4   2

Library of Congress Cataloging-in-Publication Data

Popoff, Alexandra.
Sophia Tolstoy : a biography / Alexandra Popoff. — 1st Free Press hardcover
ed.
p. cm.
Includes bibliographical references and index.
1. Tolstaia, S. A. (Sofia Andreevna), 1844–1919. 2. Tolstaia, S. A. (Sofia
Andreevna), 1844–1919—Marriage. 3. Authors' spouses—Russia—Biography.
4. Tolstoy, Leo, graf, 1828–1910. 5. Wives—Russia—Biography.
6. Women—Russia—Biography. I. Title.
PG3390.P67 2010
891.73'3—dc22
[B]
2009047615

ISBN 978-1-4165-9759-9
ISBN 978-1-4165-5990-0 (ebook)

To my husband, Wilfred

Contents

Acknowledgments

THIS BOOK WAS written with grants from the Canada Council for the Arts and the Saskatchewan Arts Board, and I am indebted to them for supporting my project.

Many people helped me during the six years of research and writing of this biography. I am grateful to Vitaly Remizov, director of the L. N. Tolstoy State Museum in Moscow, for permission to publish the photographs. The museum trustees and curators gave me exclusive access to Sophia Tolstoy's unpublished memoir, prose, and correspondence. I am particularly thankful to the deputy director, Natalia Kalinina, and curators Olga Golinenko, Tatyana Nikiforova, Marina Loginova, and Tamara Polyakova (of the Tolstoys' home in Moscow), who facilitated my research over the years. The Yasnaya Polyana curator, Tatyana Komarova, shared her insights and her great love of the subject; she also gave me a wealth of information.

I am indebted to my husband, Wilfred, for his faith, great patience, encouragement, and unfailing support during all stages of my writing. His editing of this book and suggestions were vital. I want to thank my perceptive literary agents Susan Arellano and Rose Marie Morse for their support. I am grateful to Dr. Julie Buckler from Harvard's Davis Center for Russian and Eurasian Studies, who first gave me the idea to write this biography.

My special thanks go to my parents, from whom I inherited my love of literature. I am particularly grateful to my father, with whom I had discussed this book. My father gave me his rare ninety-volume edition of Tolstoy's collected works, which was the prize of his library. I consulted this edition among many other sources.

I am thankful to translator and author Antonina Bouis and biographer Robert Calder for reading portions of my manuscript. For assistance with the description of Sophia Tolstoy's Lutheran upbringing I consulted Pastor James Dimitroff; I am thankful to him for the information he provided, and for inspiring conversations.

This project would have been impossible without the help of the many librarians at the University of Saskatchewan, the L. N. Tolstoy State Museum, and the Russian State Library.

A Note on Russian Names

I N THE RUSSIAN language, a formal address requires the use of first name and patronymic (derived from the father's first name). However, in this book I have used only first names, which will be more familiar to a Western audience.

Sophia Tolstoy's name in Russian is Sophia Andreevna Tolstaia. But I have used the masculine form of her family name, Tolstoy, so as not to create confusion. I refer to Tolstoy by his family name, but in quotations I have preserved his name and patronymic, Lev Nikolaevich.

Russians commonly use a diminutive of the first name among family and friends; for example, Tanya for Tatyana, Masha for Maria, Sasha for Alexandra, Seryozha for Sergei, Misha for Mikhail, Andryusha for Andrei, Alyosha for Alexei, and Vanya (or Vanechka) for Ivan. Sophia called Tolstoy by his diminutive, Lyovochka. He called her Sonya.

Translations of Sophia Tolstoy's letters, prose, and memoir are my own, unless otherwise specified. I also translated some of Tolstoy's letters and diary entries not included in the editions of his *Letters* and *Diaries* edited by R. F. Christian.

Prelude

Only my childhood did not belong to him—and even that belonged to him. My fondest memories are of my first childish love for him . . .

—Sophia Tolstoy, "My Life"

I N 1906, WHEN Sophia had emergency surgery at the family estate, Yasnaya Polyana, to remove a fibroid tumor from her womb, Tolstoy awaited the outcome in the woods. He asked to have the bell rung once if the surgery was successful and several times if it was not. He told her while she was convalescing: "You are in bed; I cannot hear your steps through the house, and I find it difficult to read or write."[1] While researching *War and Peace* in 1867, he wrote Sophia from Moscow, "I am sitting alone in my room upstairs, having just read your letter . . . For God's sake, don't stop writing daily to me . . . I am a dead man without you."[2]

Tolstoy admired Sophia's inexhaustible energy—he called it "the force of life." She charged him with the emotion essential to his writing. During his brilliant literary period, when he created *War and Peace* and *Anna Karenina,* she was his muse, assistant, and first reader.

Upon marrying him at eighteen, Sophia began assisting Tolstoy in all his undertakings, even farming and social work. And there were her own duties: nursing and homeschooling their thirteen children, running a large household, and managing all business affairs. Like her husband, she loved work "of every kind—intellectual, artistic and physical."[3] Tolstoy is photographed in blouses she had sewn; her family and visitors slept under blankets she knitted.

Tolstoy's expectation that she could handle anything inspired her energy and boldness. She copied out his voluminous novels, along with his corrections, in the days when only she could read his scrawl and they lived a solitary life, without secretaries. During the Russian famine of the 1890s, she participated in a relief effort with Tolstoy and their older children. She organized fund-raising—writing a passionate appeal to the nation that was carried by newspapers across the country and the world—personally received donations, purchased supplies, and hired volunteers.

Sophia was as multifaceted as her genius husband. Unlike other noblewomen of her day, she transcended class boundaries: she met with the tsar on publishing business and assisted peasant women in labor. Living in the country without a district doctor, she practiced medicine with skills learned from her father, a court physician. She also treated her family and servants, and nursed Tolstoy through several life-threatening illnesses.

In 1886, she became Tolstoy's publisher and produced eight editions of his collected works as well as individual volumes, handling all stages of the process herself. She began to collect his archive right after their marriage: the priceless drafts and manuscripts of *War and Peace* would not have survived without her. Generations of scholars could thank her for recording Tolstoy's pronouncements when he intimated to her his intentions for his novels.

Clearly, Sophia's contribution was great, but it has been consistently denied. It's been written that she had published Tolstoy's works, managed their estate, hired servants, and summoned doctors for him against his will. Yet she has become known for opposing her husband, not for supporting him. The Tolstoys' marriage is still believed to be one of the unhappiest in literary history. She was even accused of "murdering" her husband.

To this last charge, she retorted that it took her a long time to "murder" him. Tolstoy lived to eighty-two, producing ninety volumes of writings, almost all written during their marriage. It is unlikely that the genius could have created more and that someone else would have safeguarded Tolstoy's peace of mind better.

A century ago, Tolstoy's religious followers branded Sophia evil. Their accounts depict Tolstoy as a saint whose martyrdom was suffered at home. The idea was concocted by his disciple Vladimir Chertkov, who had led a smear campaign against Sophia. In *The Last Days of Tolstoy,* he compared Sophia's treatment of her husband with acts of torture practiced during the Spanish Inquisition. To portray Tolstoy as a martyr necessitated making Sophia evil. But despite the absurdity of the accusations, Chertkov's biased book and similar biographies from that period have not been dismissed, leaving Sophia's name to be publicly cleared.

Misconceptions about Sophia have penetrated most biographies, shaping our knowledge of Tolstoy. These all have one source: Chertkov. For decades, he suppressed favorable information about Sophia and exaggerated his own role in Tolstoy's life. In Soviet days, Chertkov edited Tolstoy's most comprehensive edition of collected works, a project that took a team of scholars many years to produce. Directing their efforts, Chertkov had the authority to rewrite history. He created so much controversy around Sophia's name that her contribution to Tolstoy was dismissed. Her memoir, "My Life," was rejected as irrelevant and remained unpublished. It seemed that almost everyone who met Tolstoy, even briefly, published a book about him, but his wife's memoir was confined to the archives for eight decades. Sophia's papers were also unavailable for research and without these documents her true story could not be told. I was fortunate to receive access to her archive and to read her unpublished memoir, prose, and letters.

Sophia's memoir chronicles her eventful life, beginning with her childhood, when she first met Tolstoy. This voluminous work depicts the writer as she alone knew him, with all his weaknesses and contradictions. Perhaps her candid account might affect Tolstoy's reputation. But her accuracy and logic are undeniable. Another major source to help understand Sophia's life and contribution is the couple's correspondence. Although it has been marginally published, biographers have ignored this rich source.

Sophia handled more than the complexities of marriage to a writer of genius. In the early 1880s, after his religious conversion, Tolstoy gave up literature. Determined to live by the Gospels, he renounced his former achievement and life of privilege. In his confessional, religious, and philosophical works he made sweeping renunciations, rejecting all social institutions, the government, and the official Church. His contradictions were equally unfathomable: while he renounced property, his life was unchanged—he remained with the family, at their estate. All of this created unique problems in the family's life, making Sophia's relationship with Tolstoy enormously difficult.

When Tolstoy insisted that she follow him on his path of worldly renunciation, Sophia said she could not. She told him that while his spiritual quest was genuine, for her it would be a poor imitation and detrimental to the family. In her memoir, Sophia explains that she saw Tolstoy's ideas as unworkable, especially because he offered no guidance for the family's practical life. But while she didn't share his nihilism and couldn't follow him, she continued to make it possible for Tolstoy to live and work as he chose and shielded him from all material responsibilities.

Beginning in the 1880s, the couple lived practically separate lives. Tolstoy wrote at Yasnaya Polyana, the only place on earth that gave him inspiration. Sophia, in Moscow, handled the children's education and supported the family with her publishing proceeds. As she worked to accommodate Tolstoy's needs and those of their large family, her life became "a tangle of toil and haste."

When Tolstoy renounced property, he shifted it to her shoulders, enabling her to assume responsibility for their estate. She became the sole breadwinner of their large family. But the harder she worked as a mother, estate manager, and publisher, the more their practical life contradicted Tolstoy's new beliefs. Her position was complex: Tolstoy himself gave Sophia power of attorney and permission to produce his collected works but would later criticize her for selling his books. Tolstoy lived by choice, while Sophia's life was ruled by necessity. As a publisher, Sophia fought battles with censors, lifting the ban on Tolstoy's nonfiction and his novella *The Kreutzer Sonata*. This achievement left him indifferent because his popularity did not depend on publication. Tolstoy's reputation was such that even his excommunication could not undermine it; on the contrary, it was the authority of the Orthodox Church that suffered. Sophia's letter to the Holy Synod, in which she protested her husband's excommunication, elicited only an ironic response from him. But despite his putting her down, the significance of her effort and contribution remains.

In the later years, when it was assumed that the couple had drifted apart, Tolstoy continued to rely on Sophia for all practical affairs. His charities and causes needed a cash flow. Sophia helped to raise funds and handled transactions on his behalf. Contrary to what has been written, she sympathized with the plight of the Doukhobors, religious sectarians who were one of Tolstoy's causes. And she had her own charities, serving a Moscow orphanage as a trustee. But these facts, which reveal her contribution, were never publicized.

Having translated Tolstoy's philosophical treatise *On Life* into French, Sophia understood his idea of relinquishing one's material being for the spiritual life. At Tolstoy's request, she also translated a biography of St. Francis of Assisi by Paul Sabatier into Russian. The book about the Italian medieval friar who established a religious order was important for Tolstoy at the time he was establishing his own following. Her translation of this work appeared unaccredited.

Sophia disliked her husband's followers, describing them as "a mixed lot of people."[4] They had renounced careers, money, sex, and entertainment and were mostly idle. Their main business in life was Tolstoy; however, they did not know him as a novelist. The majority were familiar only with his religious and philosophical tracts.

When crowds of these followers gathered in Moscow and in Yasnaya Polyana to listen to Tolstoy preach, Sophia had to lodge and feed them. Yet she put aside her annoyance and pleaded with the authorities on behalf of younger followers persecuted for refusing military service. She also protested the exile of his disciple Chertkov in a letter that was published by many newspapers.

Although Sophia did not follow Tolstoy blindly, she shared important values with him: "We both believe in God, in goodness, and in submitting to God's will. We both hate war and capital punishment . . . We both dislike luxury."[5] While many assumed the family lived in luxury, this is simply another myth. The Tolstoy estate in Yasnaya Polyana and their Moscow residence continue to impress visitors with their simplicity.

With Tolstoy's fame growing, Yasnaya Polyana became flooded with visitors from Russia and abroad. They had read his works and were now disappointed to find that Tolstoy did not practice his principles of self-denial. Although he had renounced property, he continued living on his estate, which his wife managed. Sophia continued to bear their children, even after he repudiated sexual love. And she published and earned profits from the very books in which Tolstoy denounced money and property. Correspondents and visitors persistently pointed out these contradictions. So, it was convenient to shift the blame to Sophia. Her position, in which she bore total responsibility for the family, was vulnerable. The frequent criticism inspired this diary entry: "I am sick and tired of eternally acting as a screen for my husband to hide behind."[6] But perhaps the most damaging and lasting criticisms of her were made in Tolstoy's diaries, which he allowed Chertkov to read and copy. And although Tolstoy would later destroy some of the disparaging entries, enough remained for the disciples to harass Sophia.

Recognizing her contribution, Tolstoy wrote to her in 1897, "I remember with love and gratitude the long 35 years of our life together . . . You gave me and the world what you were able to give; you gave much maternal love and self-sacrifice, and it's impossible not to appreciate you for it."[7] Her contribution to his literature cannot be denied: Tolstoy's great novels draw from their family's life. Sophia's labor as a copyist and editor went into *War and Peace* and *Anna Karenina*. She created the best conditions for his writing and her support was indispensable to Tolstoy, who constantly struggled with depression.

Tolstoy wrote 839 letters to Sophia. He called these letters their "little encounters," sharing his feelings and thoughts with her spontaneously. She replied in the same way, on impulse; her love shines through the letters she wrote to reassure him during his periods of despair. Her willingness to serve him and her capacity to understand him as an artist did not lessen in the later years when he wrote fiction only occasionally.

After three decades of marriage, Tolstoy wrote her, "We are bound together by the past, and the children, and the awareness of our faults, and compassion, and an irresistible attraction. In a word, we are wrapped up and tied together well and truly. And I'm glad."[8]

Their family's life remained a source of inspiration for Tolstoy and continued to provide ideas and themes. Tolstoy observed Sophia during the painful moments when their children were born. It was through her suffering that he perceived "the divine essence of love, which constitutes our soul." Upon the death of their youngest son, Vanechka, he noted in his diary, "But she astonishes me . . . by her amazing power of love."[9] Sophia gave her love to Tolstoy and, through him and his work, to the world. But while Tolstoy was universally admired, she would meet with prejudice and criticism.

Her personal achievement has been silenced and we are only now beginning to discover it. She was artistically gifted, but not until midlife did she have the time to explore her talents. As a photographer, she documented family life and produced an album of pictures, published during her lifetime. In her sixties, she began to study painting on her own: it was late to take instruction. She was also a prolific writer, having produced several novellas, stories for children, and voluminous diaries. But she considered her memoir, "My Life," to be her major literary work: she read chapters of it to Tolstoy and had his approval. In the end, however, her effort was discounted and her life was defined by the final and most trying year with Tolstoy.

By 1910, Yasnaya Polyana became a crowded place, with Tolstoy's disciples and guests recording his every word. Alienated from Tolstoy by a wall of people, Sophia was made to feel superfluous in her own house. But it did not end there: Chertkov launched a struggle for control of Tolstoy's literary legacy, driving her to hysteria with his secrecy and scheming.

He imposed a secret will on the ailing Tolstoy. Chertkov's final redaction to it appointed him as Tolstoy's literary executor. Signing this document triggered dramatic events leading to the writer's flight from home and his death.

Tolstoy's flight was anticipated by his followers who wanted him to prove his teaching. When on the freezing night of October 28, 1910, Tolstoy left his ancestral estate, he was congratulated by Chertkov, who wrote: "I cannot express in words the joy I feel in hearing that you have gone away."[10] Yet the disciple would publicly blame Sophia for Tolstoy's departure. For Sophia, her separation from Tolstoy was a tragedy: they had been a part of each other's existence for fifty years. Tolstoy was recuperating from several strokes and suffering heart and lung problems; Sophia remarked that he had fled to die. Within days of his departure, Tolstoy was dying of pneumonia in a small railway station in Astapovo, an event covered by reporters from around the world. Sophia was photographed on the platform, peeking at her husband through a shuttered window. Chertkov and other disciples surrounding Tolstoy during his final days did not allow her to bid farewell to her husband. She was admitted only after he had slipped into a coma. For the rest of her life Sophia suffered from the agonizing thought that Tolstoy had died in her absence and wondered whether he heard the words of love she whispered to him.

As a widow, Sophia lived at Yasnaya Polyana, preserving the estate as her husband left it in 1910. She cataloged Tolstoy's library, helped his biographers, and toured visitors through the house. And she was still copying Tolstoy's fiction, to fathom, relive, enjoy it, and to communicate with her husband beyond the grave.

Chapter One

Childhood

S OPHIA KNEW TOLSTOY her entire life: he was her mother's childhood friend. But the relationship between the two families went back even further. Sophia's maternal grandfather, Alexander Islenev, was a neighbor and hunting companion of Tolstoy's father, Nicholas, who lived on the family estate, Yasnaya Polyana, near Tula. The Islenevs and the Tolstoys visited each other during holidays, name days, and birthdays, attended by a throng of servants, cooks, and lackeys.[1] In his first novel, *Childhood,* which brought him recognition, Tolstoy portrayed both families.

Sophia's maternal grandmother was the daughter of a well-known statesman, Peter Zavadovsky, a favorite of Catherine the Great. The empress showered Zavadovsky with promotions and awards, appointing him minister of education, senator, and count of the Holy Roman Empire. Zavadovsky's palace, Lyalichi at Ekaterinodar,[2] in southern Russia, was designed on the empress's orders by a renowned Italian architect.[3] Zavadovsky's palace, comprising 250 rooms, was a desolate place: he complained it felt like an aviary for crows. He asked Catherine's permission to marry Countess Vera Apraksina, later appointed a lady-in-waiting. The couple's only surviving daughter was Countess Sophia Zavadovsky.

The countess's story was often heard in the family: in her teens she was first married off to Prince Kozlovsky, soon discovering he was an alcoholic. A divorce was unfeasible, but she left her husband for a common-law union with Islenev, whose estate neighbored the Tolstoys'. The countess secretly married Islenev in a parish church, but the bigamy was discovered and the couple's six children were declared illegitimate. They received the improvised name Islavin and were assigned to the merchant class. Lyubov Alexandrovna Islavin, Sophia's mother, was one of the children. She danced with Tolstoy on his birthdays and was his sister's best friend. In *Childhood* Tolstoy described something akin to first love toward the girl who would become his mother-in-law. He once pushed her from a low balcony for talking to another boy; the fall nearly crippled her. When Tolstoy became a celebrated writer, Lyubochka,[4] as he called her, still talked down to him even though she was only two years his senior.

Like all the Islavin children, Lyubov Alexandrovna was painfully aware of her illegitimacy and semiaristocratic origin. At sixteen, she married a physician of German descent, Andrei Yevstafievich Behrs, twenty years her senior. The marriage was seen by her family as a misalliance: the nobility looked down on the medical profession, equating it with that of musicians, the very bottom.

Although Sophia's parents met under adverse circumstances, these proved ideal for romance. Her mother was dangerously ill when Behrs, a Moscow physician stopping in the provincial city of Tula, was summoned to examine her. Behrs was actually heading to Turgenev's estate in the neighboring Oryol when he treated Lyubochka and proposed to her. The meeting was destined to link two of the greatest novelists, Tolstoy and Turgenev.

Sophia's ancestors on her father's side were German Lutherans. Her great-grandfather Ivan Behrs (Johann Bärs), a cavalry captain in the Austrian army, was invited to Russia as a military instructor by Empress Elizabeth I. He died shortly after, in 1758. Behrs's immediate family knew little about his wife, Maria. Their only son, Evstafy, raised and educated by a German foster family, became a successful apothecary. By the time he married Elizaveta Wulfert, a descendant of Westphalian nobility, Evstafy owned two stone houses in Moscow. The couple's sons, Alexander and Andrei,[5] born in 1807 and 1808, were baptized Evangelical Lutheran.

Sophia's father, Andrei Behrs, was four when Napoleon invaded and his family fled the burning Moscow. Evstafy stayed behind hoping to save his property but could only helplessly watch the destruction of his drug-store and the stone houses. Fleeing in disguise, with a servant and two pistols, he was captured by the French but managed to escape; these events were later woven into *War and Peace.*

After the war, Evstafy reopened a drugstore, but things were never the same. He entered government service and his wife embroidered purses, all to make ends meet. The couple's two sons were educated as charity boys in a private boarding school. Brilliant and ambitious, Alexander and Andrei entered the medical school at Moscow University, aged fifteen and fourteen. The careers of Sophia's uncle and father were similar: both attained high rank in the civil service, earning them hereditary noble titles and identical promotions and awards.

While still a medical student, Andrei Behrs was invited to accompany the Turgenev family on a journey abroad. His family knew Varvara Petrovna Turgenev, née Lutovinova, heiress to an enormous fortune.[6] Behrs would later reminisce about their travel through Europe, medical lectures, and performances of the Italian opera in Paris featuring the legendary Maria Malibran.[7]

According to Tolstoy, Behrs was "a very straightforward, honest and quick-tempered man" and "a big womanizer."[8] As a bachelor, he sired several children and had a daughter by Varvara Turgenev in 1833.[9] In childhood, Sophia met Lizanka René, her father's daughter by a French governess, and fearing that she also might be illegitimate, she compelled Behrs to produce her birth certificate.[10]

After his marriage to Lyubov Alexandrovna in 1842, Behrs, already court physician, was also appointed a supernumerary doctor of Moscow theaters. Behrs was rarely seen at home, juggling two jobs, a private practice, and an extensive social life. The children inherited his deep sense of duty and almost religious devotion to work, attributed to his Lutheran upbringing. For Sophia, daily toil was essential; to feel virtuous she would list a multitude of chores to be performed during the day.

The family lived in a Kremlin apartment, adjacent to the ancient Poteshny (Amusement) Palace, a three-story mansion of white stone with carved jambs. Originally used as a court theater by the first Romanov tsars, the palace was later utilized as an ordnance house in the mid-nineteenth century and was remodeled to accommodate apartments for Kremlin staff. The rooms were modest, like those of rank-and-file officials. The windows faced the Troitsky Tower by the main entrance to Red Square. Illuminated at night, it glowed "from top to bottom, as if made of diamonds."

The house in the Kremlin where Sophia grew up, by the Troitsky Tower and the main entrance to Red Square. Photo by the author.

Every summer, the family retreated to their government dacha, or country house, in Pokrovskoe-Streshnevo, near Moscow. In her novella "Song without Words" Sophia depicts the beginning of the summer season and the exodus from Moscow, then a provincial city:

> A procession of carts laden with furniture, featherbeds, baby carriages, plants, and trunks; cows tied by their horns; the belongings of city residents moving to the dachas stretched along the Moscow streets to the city gates.[11]

Sophia was born at the dacha on August 22, 1844, the second of thirteen children, five of whom died in infancy. The four older children, born a year apart, were Liza, Sophia, Tanya, and brother Sasha. After an interval came four younger boys, Petya, Vladimir, Stepan, and Vyacheslav, still a baby when Sophia married. Her happiest memories were of the summers at the dacha and of her freedom there, enjoyed to the full when compared with their more restricted city life. In Moscow, the girls had to be escorted on their walks by their father's batman, in military uniform and helmet.

Much of the summer was spent with their father's hunting dogs, black setters and white pointers with reddish yellow spots. Behrs trained the valuable setter pups and sent them as gifts to his friends and to the tsar. By then, their father was an old man: the children remembered him as "tall and erect, with large blue eyes and a long grey beard." At the dacha, he drove in his charabanc or walked with a gun over his shoulder and a setter by his side.[12]

Sophia's father, Andrei Behrs, in 1862.

Their dachas were built on land that had belonged to the old Streshnev clan for more than two centuries. The last heir, an old, semiparalyzed man, permitted the Behrs children to raid his garden and roam in the woods. From their second-floor bedroom window, the girls had a view of the old noble mansion and its ponds, the winding road, and the Pokrovskoe church with its green cupolas. Tolstoy would later remember how he used to drive along this winding road to Sophia's dacha after he had fallen in love with her. The two of them would also drive on the same road at the sundown of their lives, taking their youngest son to the cemetery.

Sophia's uncle Konstantin Islavin, a childhood friend of Tolstoy and a frequent guest at their dacha, sparked her interest in music. A talented pianist, Islavin impressed Nikolai Rubinstein, founder of the Moscow Conservatory, with his interpretation of Chopin; yet he failed his examination. As an illegitimate son, he had neither property nor a family of his own; his insecurity became an obstacle to a career of any kind. He lived through the charity of relatives. In childhood, his stays were a delight for Sophia and her siblings: "He introduced us to all the arts and for the rest of my life I maintained . . . a strong desire for learning, eager to understand every type of creativity." They danced to his piano improvisations. "I remember the delight I experienced in childhood when Uncle Kostya played Chopin on the piano, and my mother sang in her high soprano, with a pleasant timbre, Alyab'ev's 'The Nightingale' or a gypsy song 'Aren't You My Soul, Fair Maiden.'" Once, he called at their dacha with Tolstoy, when the cook was having his midday nap. Sophia and her sister Liza heated up the stove and made dinner for their guests. Tolstoy praised them: "What sweet girls . . . How well they fed us."

Turgenev also visited her family whenever he was in Russia. At dinners he told of his hunting adventures, describing masterfully "the beautiful scenery, the setting of the sun, or a wise hunting dog."[13] He was very tall and Sophia, nearsighted, could only see his face when he bent over to pick her up. "He would lift us into the air with his large hands, give us a kiss, and always tell something interesting."

The Behrs lived in the part of Moscow that had witnessed the Napoleon invasion. In *War and Peace,* which Sophia would later copy out, Napoleon looks through his binoculars at the Kremlin towers, expecting a delegation with the keys to the city. Those medieval towers could be seen from her window and she dreamt of an excursion through them and the Wall Walk, a fighting platform atop the walls.

Behrs obtained special permission for his children to go on a tour of the towers, with two grenadiers as guides. Troitsky Tower, the closest to their home, was known for its notorious prison cells. They examined the mysterious passages and the narrow stone staircases, and heard stories of how the criminals were walled up there. As they climbed the staircase of the Spassky Tower to see the mechanism of the big clock, it began to hiss, roar, and ring; "the sound was deafening."

When Nicholas I drove by their Kremlin home, the Behrs children bowed from their windows; he smiled and saluted back. As children of a court official, they did gymnastics in the Great Kremlin Palace and amused themselves by running through the corridors, which were adorned with paintings by Bacciarelli, Titian, Rubens, and others. While standing on the balcony overlooking his chamber, they watched the new emperor Alexander II dine, and once heard him rebuke his lackey, "Fool! I ordered you to bring me beer!"

Despite their noble upbringing, the Behrs children were assigned chores, took turns in the kitchen, sewed, and taught their younger siblings. Their Petersburg cousins, the children of Uncle Alexander and his Scottish wife, Rebecca Pinkerton, were raised the same way. Sophia and her siblings were told that they would have to earn their living because they had no fortune and the family was large. She was eager to help with various chores, becoming her mother's right hand: "If something had to be lifted, moved, carried . . . or my father's or mother's room had to be tidied up—they would choose me as the healthiest, strongest girl who didn't care much for learning."

The Behrs were lavishly hospitable: their relatives and friends came to stay for months. The house staff, consisting of ten or twelve, also lived in the apartment. The coachman and the housekeeper, Stepanida Trifonovna, with whom Tolstoy would stop to talk, were treated as part of the family. The housekeeper, in charge of all holiday baking and preparations, was remembered for her enormous Easter cakes.

The family attended services at the Church of the Virgin Birth, the chapel for the grand dukes and tsaritzas. The church's main entrance had been walled up and could only be entered through the winter garden, adjacent to the Great Kremlin Palace. At Easter, the sisters ran through the palace corridors and the garden, anticipating the magnificent choir and the whooping toll from the Ivan the Great Bell Tower, answered by festive pealing across Moscow. Orthodox services in the Kremlin were solemn and beautiful, inspiring a mood for prayer and tears of ecstasy. At home, Sophia liked to pray in solitude, kneeling for hours before an icon. The stable world of her childhood, with its ancient faith and customs, remained a stronghold through the many trials of her marriage. Her memory would bring her back to the world that had inspired her belief "in the importance of life."[14]

Her father's German Lutheran culture influenced her less, although her grandmother Elizaveta Wulfert lived with the family. Every Sunday, the girls went to her bedroom to play with the fabulous dolls she ordered from Petersburg, along with garments and toy furniture. Sophia, however, preferred musical toys, which she herself assembled. She was also a passionate collector of stones and herbaria, a hobby she would resume in old age.

Sophia's sister Liza, diligent and bookish, was nicknamed "the professor" in the family. She was in charge of policing her siblings, which made her unpopular. Tanya, the youngest and everyone's favorite, was Sophia's confidante. She would describe Sophia as a spirited girl with red cheeks, dark braids, and dark eyes with a "touch of sentimentality which easily changed into sadness."[15]

Sophia believed she inherited her father's quick temper and her mother's good looks. Lyubov Alexandrovna was attractive and serene, with a noble bearing. Alien to her husband's broad circle of acquaintances, she was always at home, nursing a baby, or helping the older children with their homework. Their first foreign language was German; French was introduced by their mother.

> I can see, as if today, a notebook with French words, written in her hand and beginning with God—*dieu*, father—*le père*, mother—*la mère*, etc. Most distinctly I imagine my mother either teaching us, or lying down on a short divan with a book to hear our homework. The divan was of quilted cherry-colored satin. I remember feeling sorry for her when she gazed at me with her large, black, weary eyes, swallowing small pieces of coal. Perhaps it was during her pregnancies ... These pieces I collected for her in the stoves where I could fit my little body, inspecting curiously its inner walls and passages.

When governesses took over supervising the children's studies and Sophia neglected her assignments, she was caned. Lyubov Alexandrovna admin-

Sophia's mother, Lyubov Behrs, in 1862.

istered the punishment in Grandmother Wulfert's bedroom. "I took off my clothes and crossed myself. Clasping my bare arms above the elbow, my mother began to hit me with a rod. I jumped, screamed, and trembled of cold." That Sophia was caned for laziness in her childhood is surprising; in adult life her energy was unmatched.

Tolstoy, a casual guest, would do gymnastics with the children and participate in their charades. Once, he composed a mini-opera. It had a conventional plot: a jealous husband suspects a knight of courting his wife and kills him in a duel. Sophia and her siblings had to think up their own lines. The words had to sound Italian, he directed, but the meaning could be compromised. Tolstoy's intent was to poke fun at libretti, although he always found the theme of jealousy compelling. It would reemerge in *Anna Karenina* and in *The Kreutzer Sonata,* a novella about a husband who kills his wife. Later, Sophia would receive prominent roles in his fiction. But in childhood, when he conducted his mini-opera, she was simply part of the choir.

At Christmas, Sophia and the other children played various games.

One involved baking a pie with a small bean in it. The guest who found the bean would become tsar and choose a tsarina. Then they would sit on makeshift thrones to perform their roles. When Sophia was chosen tsarina, she was a natural, giving orders to her loyal subjects. One summer, she played the game with her siblings when Tolstoy visited the family's dacha.

> I remember we were once feeling very happy and playful, and I kept repeating the same foolish sentence: "When I am Tsarina I'll do such and such," or "When I am Tsarina I'll order such and such." Just beneath the balcony stood my father's cabriolet, from which the horse had been unhitched. I hopped inside and shouted, "When I am Tsarina I'll drive around in a cabriolet like this!" Lev Nikolaevich immediately stepped into the horse's place, seized the shafts and pulled me along at a brisk trot. "And I'm going to take my Tsarina for a drive!" he said . . . "Do stop, please! It's much too heavy for you!" I cried, but I was loving it, and was delighted to see how strong Lev Nikolaevich was, and to have him pull me around.[16]

When in the winter of 1854 Tolstoy left for the Crimean War, Sophia was ten. His departure upset her and she decided that she would join him at the front as a nurse. After Tolstoy went to the Crimea, Sophia read his novel *Childhood* and cried over it, memorizing the passage, "What times could be better than the times in which the two highest virtues, innocent gaiety and boundless need for love, were the sole impulses in life?"[17] Later, as Tolstoy's publisher, Sophia would read the novel numerous times; yet her first emotional response to it never lessened.

When she was eleven, several major events took place. Her German grandmother died in Petersburg during a cholera epidemic. The emperor died. The Crimean War continued and the sisters had to wear mourning dresses and gray jackets, nicknamed "patriotic coats." They were the color of soldiers' uniforms and had brass buttons with imperial eagles. Everyone read Tolstoy's *Sebastopol Stories,* his realistic accounts from the battlefield: he was Russia's first war correspondent. The children also felt patriotic. They attended Glinka's opera *A Life for the Tsar,* as it was their mother's favorite. Sophia knew the score by heart and played it at home on the piano.

In August 1856, the Kremlin was preparing for the coronation of Alex-

Sophia around the time she met Tolstoy.

ander II. Sophia and Liza were given tickets by a wealthy patient of their father's and watched the ceremony from the balcony overlooking Uspensky Cathedral, where tsars were anointed. They saw the new emperor and his empress, Maria Alexandrovna,[18] wearing ermine-lined mantles under a baldachin of gold brocade:

> The moment was tremendously celebratory. Through the loud cheers of the crowd, the canon shots, the orchestra played "God, Save the Tsar" . . . I was choking of excitement, prepared to do anything for the tsar, to give my life for him.

The royal parade along the central Tverskaya Street became etched in her memory as "a vivid picture of gold, uniforms, beautiful carriages, dresses, sounds of music, drums, and people shouting 'hurrah.'" Impressive in his gold-embroidered uniform, the youthful heir, about Sophia's age, was riding by the emperor's side. Decades later, as Tolstoy's publisher, she would be granted an audience by Alexander III.

From her early teens, Sophia participated in amateur theatricals, popular at the time. The family staged vaudevilles, with their mother directing. Sophia got a male role as a social climber in *A Crow in Peacock Feathers*[19] and sang her couplets dashingly: "That's what wealth does, that's what a million does." In one theatrical, Mitrofan Polivanov, her brother Sasha's friend from the cadet corps, had the role of Sophia's husband. Polivanov was a tall and phlegmatic youth, two years Sophia's senior. They were "childishly in love with each other" and agreed to get married when Polivanov made a career. He graduated from the military academy and was eventually promoted to the general staff; Sophia broke her word by marrying Tolstoy.

In 1860, Sophia and Liza prepared for university exams, which would certify them as governesses. Sophia studied at the home of a friend, a daughter of the Moscow University inspector Zaikovsky. In the evenings, students gathered there to discuss Turgenev's recent novel *Fathers and Sons,* the nihilists, and the woman's question. As other girls of the sixties, Sophia dreamt of dedicating herself to a cause larger than family: "I longed to live for others: I yearned with all my soul for the joys of renunciation, even asceticism."[20] It was also a time of great expectations, dreams about liberty and Russia's future. During the winter of 1861, Alexander II signed the long-awaited Emancipation Act. Slavery was abolished.

The student discussions at the Zaikovskys were followed by troika rides and dancing. The night before her exam in divine law, Sophia danced at the house of the dean of medicine. She got an excellent mark, while Liza, despite preparation, failed her exam. Sophia's essay on music was the best of the year. When she was already married, her professor told Tolstoy she had "a great flair for literature . . . That's just the wife you need."

Completion of exams marked the end of Sophia's and Liza's home education and girlhood: their daily schedule was removed from the classroom wall.[21] The sisters were given watches, allowed to plan their leisure, tailor long dresses, and put up their braids. The interval between Sophia's childhood and marriage lasted only one year, a time marked by intense introspection: "That brilliant light that illuminated the world for me would dim later on . . . And how good it felt! The world seemed boundless." She read a great deal and engaged herself in writing, painting, music, and photography, forms of creativity that fascinated her for the rest of her life.

There would be no time for art instruction later on, but at the age of seventeen she took drawing lessons, learning to work with pencil and India ink. The lessons ended before she moved on to watercolors. Still, on her own, she copied paintings from an album of reproductions from the Dresden and Berlin galleries. Curious about photography, she learned the craft from a Greek student named Kurkuli, a strange, taciturn boy and friend of her brother Sasha. It was with his camera that Sophia took her first pictures on a walk along the Moscow River. She would resume this hobby in midlife, becoming an expert photographer.

At sixteen, she had written a novella titled "Natasha," about three sisters and their falling in love. She read chapters to Tanya, who was delighted to recognize herself in Natasha, the youngest character. The novella did not survive: Sophia burned it along with her youthful diaries before her wedding. She would regret it later because Tolstoy used the story as an inspiration for *War and Peace*: "When Lev Nikolaevich depicted [Natasha Rostova] in *War and Peace* he drew on my novella and borrowed the name for his heroine . . . he read it a month before our wedding and praised me for *pure demands on love.*"

Tolstoy recognized himself in her character Prince Dublitsky, a seasoned bachelor, whose name implied duplicity: "I read it all without a sinking heart . . . but 'unusually unattractive appearance' and 'fickleness of opinions' touched me on the raw." When Sophia asked Tolstoy about her story, he said that he had skimmed through it; however, in his diary he admitted: "She gave me a story to read. What force of truth and simplicity!"[22]

In the novella, Prince Dublitsky marries the eldest sister, just as Tolstoy was expected to marry Liza. His attraction to the middle sister, in whom Sophia portrayed herself, is implied. The middle sister marries an ideal young man, like Polivanov. As Tanya observed, Sophia's novella "pictured the conflict in her own heart."[23]

Sophia was moved to write it after a revelation by her older cousin Lyuba Behrs, who told her about the "mysteries of matrimony." Information on sexual love would, it was believed, corrupt a virgin, and was therefore kept secret. Obtaining the knowledge surreptitiously from her cousin made Sophia feel guilty: "I became hysterical, flung myself on the bed and sobbed until my mother came in running." The ideal of chastity became rooted in her heart after Tolstoy read aloud Turgenev's novella *First Love* at their house. The sisters were impressed with his comment that the feeling of the sixteen-year-old youth was pure and genuine, while his father's physical passion was "an abomination and a perversion." She decided that if she would ever marry "it must be only with a man equally chaste as I. My novella described such *pure* first feelings between my hero and heroine."

During Sophia's last winter at home, her family lived through a crisis. At night, Behrs would burst into Lyubov Alexandrovna's bedroom and make jealous scenes. Waking to their mother's pleas for help, the sisters had to sit in her bedroom. Behrs, forgetting himself, shouted at his wife and daughters. By morning, worn out, he kissed their hands, cried, and asked for forgiveness. "This perpetual expectation of our father's nocturnal visits to our mother's bedroom . . . darkened our young souls. We loved our mother a great deal . . . and felt extremely sorry for her." In her own marriage, Sophia would experience Tolstoy's jealousy and recall these haunting nights of her youth.

In the spring, as the family packed for their dacha, Tolstoy visited Behrs, asking him to examine his lungs, as he feared consumption. Tolstoy also asked Behrs whether he believed he was healthy enough to marry. He had already mentioned to his sister, Maria Nikolaevna, that he liked the Behrs family particularly well, and "if I ever marry, I will only marry in that family."[24] As Tolstoy would imply in *Anna Karenina,* when depicting himself in Levin, Sophia's family had replaced his own:

> Strange as it may seem, Konstantin Levin was in love precisely with the house, the family, especially the female side of it. He did not remember his own mother, and his only sister was older than he, so that in the Shcherbatskys' house he saw for the first time the milieu of an old, noble, educated and honorable family, of which he had been deprived by the death of his father and mother."[25]

Over the summer, Lyubov Alexandrovna took the girls to their grandfather's estate and the neighboring Yasnaya Polyana. For the first time, Sophia visited her grandmother's grave, saw the parish church where she married Islenev, and even met the priest who had wed them secretly. Standing by her tombstone, Sophia imagined "what misery she must have endured with her first husband, Kozlovsky, a drunkard, to whom she was married against her will, then with her unlawful second husband, Alexander Mikhailovich Islenev, my grandfather, living in this country place, bearing an endless annual succession of children." Despite fear of inheriting her grandmother's fate as well as her name, she found the story irresistible: "Everything seemed fantastic, full of beauty and magic."[26]

At Yasnaya Polyana, Sophia visited the house she would soon enter as mistress. The Behrs sisters and their maid were lodged in the vaulted room downstairs, a former larder, where the furniture consisted of a few sofas and a chaise longue. Just as they were getting the beds ready, Tolstoy walked in. He helped arrange a bed for Sophia, pushing a stool against the chaise longue, and covered it with a sheet. "I felt embarrassed but there was also something lovely and intimate about making up the beds together." Later that evening, Tolstoy joined Sophia on the balcony.

> I shall never forget that mood I was in . . . I don't know if it was the effect of nature, real untamed nature and wide open spaces; or a premonition of what would happen a month and a half later . . . perhaps it was simply a farewell to my girlhood freedom; perhaps it was all these things, I don't know. But there was something so significant about my mood that evening, and I felt such happiness and such an extraordinary sense of boundlessness. The others were all going in to supper and Lev Nikolaevich came out to call me too . . . I just remember him saying to me: "How simple and serene you are," which pleased me very much. I had such a good sleep in the long chair which Lev Nikolaevich had made up for me . . . I fell asleep with a new feeling of joy in my young soul.[27]

At Ivitsy, their grandfather's estate, Tolstoy unexpectedly turned up during a dance. When the guests were leaving, he asked Sophia to stay with him on the terrace and read what he would write. "He brushed the games scores off the card table, took a piece of chalk and began writing. We were both very serious and excited. I followed his big red hand, and could feel all my powers of concentration and feeling focus on that bit of chalk and the hand that held it. We said nothing."[28] He only initialed the words of his long sentences but she readily deciphered them: "Your youth and need for happiness too vividly remind me of my age and incapacity for happiness." Tolstoy also wrote that her family was wrong about his intention to marry Liza, the eldest. "Our elation was such that we soared high above the world and nothing could possibly surprise us." In *Anna Kar-*

enina, Tolstoy would recount this episode as a proposal scene, though he did not actually propose to Sophia at Ivitsy.

When the sisters returned to their parents' dacha, Tolstoy visited frequently and took her for walks. "Those last days of my girlhood were extraordinarily intense, lit by a dazzling brightness and a sudden awakening of the soul . . . 'Mad nights!' Lev Nikolaevich would say as we sat on the balcony or strolled about the garden. There were no romantic scenes or confessions. We had known each other for so long. Our friendship was so simple and easy. And I was in a hurry to end my wonderful, free, serene, uncomplicated girlhood. Everything was wonderfully simple, I had no ambitions, no desires for the future."[29]

Sophia at seventeen when Tolstoy courted her. This was his favorite photo of her.

On August 28, 1862, Sophia congratulated Tolstoy on his thirty-fourth birthday: "When I am tsarina, I'll issue a benevolent decree, but as I am a simple mortal, I *simply* congratulate you on having seen God's world on one beautiful morning, and I wish you see it as long as possible, the way you see it now."[30] Liza wrote that she expected something important to happen on the twenty-eighth. Whenever Tolstoy came for dinner Liza would be seated next to him. In his diary, Tolstoy admitted he was "beginning to hate Liza as well as pity her."[31]

Upon their return to Moscow, Tolstoy continued to visit, carrying a proposal letter in his pocket. He gave it to Sophia on September 16, the day before her and her mother's name day, celebrated together. Tolstoy awaited her reply in her mother's bedroom. "I flew up the stairs on wings . . . Lev Nikolaevich stood in the corner, leaning against the wall, waiting for me. I went up to him and he seized both my hands. 'Well, what's the answer?' he asked. 'Yes—of course,' I replied."[32]

On the name day, Sophia and Liza, dressed identically, in light mauve and white *barège* gowns, greeted guests. When Lyubov Alexandrovna announced her daughter's engagement, everyone assumed that Liza was the bride. Their former French tutor later remarked that he was disappointed Tolstoy did not propose to Liza: she was a better student.

The betrothal lasted only one week (in *Anna Karenina* Tolstoy changes it to a month, to make it more believable). Sophia was entering a mad pace of life, which she would maintain for forty-eight years. During that frantic week, Tolstoy visited daily but their meetings were no longer a joy: "I felt crushed." Out of an excess of honesty, Tolstoy gave her his bachelor diaries, informing her of his sexual past and his liaison with the peasant Aksinya, by whom he had a son. The first diary opened with an entry at nineteen when he was treated for gonorrhea, contracted from a prostitute. "I remember how shattered I was by these diaries . . . It was very wrong of him to do this; I wept when I saw what his past had been."[33] Tolstoy was disappointed with her reaction, expecting understanding from his bride.

A few days before the wedding they drove to the Bolshoi Theatre to see *Othello*. A famous tragedian of the day, the black American actor Ira Aldridge, was on tour in Russia and his performance in Moscow was not to be missed. (Aldridge was the first black actor in the world to play Othello.)[34] Lyubov Alexandrovna, already at the theater with her other daughters, sent a carriage for Tolstoy and Sophia. On the way, Tolstoy was ominously silent and Sophia "a bit afraid of him."

Chapter Two

Family Happiness

O N SEPTEMBER 23, 1862, their wedding day, Tolstoy visited the house of his bride, contrary to convention. Sophia, along with Tanya and a maid, was downstairs packing her trunks for Yasnaya Polyana. The newlyweds were to leave in Tolstoy's new *dormeuse* immediately after supper. Entering unannounced, Tolstoy took all by surprise. When he asked to talk to Sophia in private, she sensed the worst. "We sat down together on our valises and he started tormenting me, questioning me and doubting my love for him. The thought occurred to me that he wanted to run away, and that he might have sudden fears of marriage. I started to cry."[1] In *Anna Karenina* Tolstoy relives his last-minute doubts:

> "I've come to say that we still have time. It can all be cancelled and corrected." . . . "I don't understand," she replied fearfully. "You mean that you want to take back . . . that we shouldn't?" "Yes, if you don't love me." "You're out of your mind!" she cried, flushing with vexation. But his face was so pathetic that she held back her vexation.[2]

Lyubov Alexandrovna, alerted by Tanya, came and reproached Tolstoy: "Well, you've chosen a fine time to make her cry. Today is her wedding day, it's hard enough for her as it is, and she's got a long journey ahead of her." Looking penitent, Tolstoy left.

The wedding was appointed for eight o'clock in the evening at their parish Church of the Virgin Birth. "Just before seven that evening, my sisters and friends began to dress me. I begged them not to call the hairdresser, as I wanted to do my own hair, and the girls pinned on the flowers and the long tulle veil. The dress was also tulle, and in the current fashion—very open at the neck and shoulders. It was so thin, light and airy, it seemed to envelop me like a cloud." Sophia and her family waited at their home for Tolstoy's best man to announce that the groom was in the church. But the messenger was an hour late and Sophia, recalling her morning conversation with Tolstoy, fretted that he "had run away."

However, the reason for the delay was trivial: Tolstoy forgot to leave out a clean white shirt when he packed and because it was Sunday, all stores were closed. He had to send his valet to Sophia's house to unpack the *dormeuse* and find the shirt. "Another age elapsed while they took the shirt back to the bridegroom and he put it on and got to the church. Then began the farewells, the tears and the sobs, and I felt utterly distraught." In *Anna Karenina* Tolstoy depicts the events of the wedding intact, including the episode with the shirt, which he found irresistible.

Tolstoy in 1862 as a groom.

Sophia's parents did not attend. Behrs was unwell and still upset that Tolstoy had proposed to his middle daughter. Liza looked grim and Sophia was avoiding her. When Sophia entered her father's study to bid farewell, he was moved by the sight of her in her bridal dress and they both had a cry. For the wedding supper Lyubov Alexandrovna prepared a small feast for several friends and relatives of fruit, sweets, and champagne: Tolstoy insisted the reception be private. Finally came the blessings: "Maman took down the icon of St. Sophia the martyr, and with her brother, my uncle Mikhail Alexandrovich Islenev, standing beside her, she blessed me with it." Her mother's choice of icon would have significance for Sophia.

The Palace Church was "just a moment away" from their house but the drive seemed longer, especially with Polivanov and Sophia's brother Sasha accompanying her on the ride. Sophia sobbed uncontrollably as they sat across from her "in solemn silence." Her brother Petya, thirteen, escorted her to the doors of the Kremlin Palace, holding the icon.

Tolstoy waited in the winter garden, unusually elegant in white shirt and tails. He took Sophia's right hand and they walked through the palace corridors to the church, where the priest met them. When they entered the church, the guests, many of whom were palace employees, stared at the bride, thinking she was the cause of the delay. Sophia heard them whisper about her "extreme youth" and "tear-stained eyes."

The priest "took both our hands in his and led us to the lectern. The palace choir was singing, two priests conducted the service . . . Lev Nikolaevich has described our wedding beautifully . . . in his novel *Anna Karenina*." The ceremony barely registered with her after the eventful day. "I experienced absolutely nothing as I stood there at the altar. I just felt as though something obvious and inevitable was happening . . . The ceremony ended, everyone congratulated us, and then Lev Nikolaevich and I drove home together, just the two of us. He was very affectionate to me and seemed happy."

After a quick supper, Sophia changed into a dark blue traveling dress and the family observed the custom of sitting down before a journey. Sophia approached every household member in turn and all wished her well, each saying something memorable; everyone cried. Tolstoy said they sounded as if they were burying Sophia.

The church in the Kremlin where Sophia and Tolstoy were wed.

She would describe this autumn night in Gothic colors: it was cold and rain was pouring down. Tolstoy "was impatient to be off," while she dreaded their intimacy. "I had an agonizing lump in my throat and was choking with misery. For the first time I suddenly realized that I was actually leaving my family and everyone I had ever loved in my life *forever*." Her family assembled on the porch and when the horses took off, Lyubov Alexandrovna, usually composed, uttered a piercing cry. "Lev Nikolaevich slammed the carriage door shut . . . I sat crouched in one corner, wretched and exhausted, and wept uncontrollably." They drove silently beyond the city gates onto the unlit country road.

Their first stop to change horses was at Biryulevo station. The rooms were "large, bare, and cheerless, with red damask furniture." Tolstoy

Sophia in 1862 as a bride.

asked her to be hostess and serve tea, and she obeyed—not cheerfully, as he had anticipated, but as though she were "condemned to death."

> And how was I not to fear? After Biryulevo, and even back at the station, the torment began, which every bride must go through. Not to mention the agony, what an embarrassment it was! How painful, dreadfully humiliating! And what sudden new passion, unconscious, irresistible, was awakened, dormant until then in a young girl. Mercifully, it was dark in the carriage, so that we couldn't see each other's face. I could only hear . . . his breath, hasty, frequent, passionate. Conquered by his power and intensity, I was obedient and loving, although crushed by the agonizing physical pain and unbearable humiliation. And again, again, all night, the same attempts, the same sufferings.[3]

Tolstoy made a crude entry in his diary: "She was in tears. In the carriage. She knows everything and it's simple. At Biryulevo. Her timidity. Something morbid."[4] Sophia would never forgive his impatience: three decades later, she described their first night as a rape. "Violence had been committed; this girl was not ready for marriage; female passion, recently awakened, was put back to sleep."[5] The rest of the journey to Yasnaya Polyana vanished from her memory: she could remember neither conversations, nor where and when they made further stops. The new diary, begun upon her marriage, reveals her confusion and disappointment. "I always dreamt of the man I would love as a complete whole, new, *pure* person . . . Since I got married I have had to recognize how foolish these dreams were, yet I cannot renounce them."[6] Her ideals were inspired by Tolstoy's novel *Childhood,* which she continued to love. She had yet to learn to separate the man from his works.

On the following evening, the couple arrived at the white gatehouse of Yasnaya Polyana. Tolstoy's aunt Tatyana Ergolskaya and his brother Sergei Nikolaevich greeted them with traditional bread and salt at the mansion. The aunt blessed Sophia with an icon of the Virgin Mary. Sophia bowed to her feet, as custom required, and kissed the icon and her new relatives. She was entering the house where she would spend most of her life.

The gate to the Yasnaya Polyana estate.

Her new family was small: Tolstoy and his two old aunts. The main house of the originally larger manor, in which Tolstoy was born, had been dismantled and carted away in 1854, to pay Tolstoy's gambling debts. The family now lived in one of the remaining wings. Sophia had never seen the original house, but it would be described in *War and Peace:* "The enormous house, on the old stone foundations, was built of wood and plastered only inside. The big, roomy house with its bare plank floors was furnished with the simplest hard sofas and armchairs, tables and chairs, fashioned from their own birches by their own joiners."[7]

Unlike other noblemen's nests, the Yasnaya house was austere and modestly furnished. The couple used plain iron forks and knives at the table until Sophia's trousseau arrived. The old park was neglected: paths through it looked untidy without sand; weeds grew in flower beds and around the house where the servants dumped garbage. Sophia did not dare introduce changes for two years; she then ordered the place cleaned thoroughly and the paths sanded.

Just days into her marriage, Sophia, confused about her new experiences, wrote to her sister Tanya, signing her letter "Countess Tolstoy." She boasted she had a "delightful" room of her own, spacious, bright, with high ceilings. "Everything is cozy and beautiful. I am not yet completely settled, there are still a few trifles to take care of. It is very pleasant to unpack little by little."[8] She asked her to send some powder and a pair of warm boots, hoping they would arrive with her trousseau.

> Yesterday we had our first tea upstairs around the samovar, as it should be in a happy family. Auntie is so pleased, Seryozha[9] is so nice, and as for Lyovochka, I have no words. I am frightened and abashed that he loves me so much, Tatyana; why should he, tell me? What do you think? Could he stop loving me? I am afraid to think of the future. This is no mere idle dream as in my maiden days—I know well what life has in store for me and am only afraid that something might go wrong.

In a postscript to Sophia's letter, Tolstoy wrote to his sister-in-law, "Do me a favor. Read this letter and send it back to me. Do you feel how wonderful and touching it all is—the thoughts about the future and the powder." Sophia was delightful in her new role, he wrote, acting as "grown-up and mistress of the house—and she did it brilliantly, very much like the real thing."

Tolstoy wrote to introduce Sophia to Alexandrine, a maid of honor in the royal family as well as his relation and confidante: "I've lived to the age of 34 and I didn't know it was possible to be so much in love and so happy."[10] He added in another letter, which he wrote in Sophia's presence: "Living together is such a frightening responsibility . . . She is reading this . . . and doesn't understand a thing and doesn't want to understand, and there's no need for her to understand." Sophia added in a postscript: "He's mistaken; I understand everything, absolutely everything that concerns him."[11] She wished Tolstoy would treat her like Alexandrine, whose opinions he valued.

Days after arriving at Yasnaya Polyana, Tolstoy took her to a village wedding and suggested going on foot. Sophia agreed, unaware of the distance; it turned out that the place was eighteen kilometers away. Walking in her city shoes, she earned painful blisters by the time they arrived. The simple ceremony disappointed her, after the glamour of the Kremlin Palace Church. Tolstoy took her home in a springless cart used by peasants: he liked to live simply and Sophia was to adjust to his way of life.

Yasnaya Polyana was then isolated: the railroad had yet to come to Tula and there were few visitors.[12] Autumn rains turned roads into mud, confining Sophia to the house for weeks; the sky from her window looked gray with rain, and the leafless park was gloomy. Late fall was to become her hated time of year: "I am used to a more boisterous life, while there is nothing here but deathly silence. But . . . one can get used to anything. And in time I shall turn this into a cheerful noisy house and live for my children. I shall make a serious and purposeful life for myself and enjoy my young ones."[13]

Pregnancy, which she discovered in October, depressed her. Although depression would haunt her with each pregnancy, sixteen in all, she thought her first experience the most trying. She was then still but a growing child herself, physically and emotionally unprepared for the change.

When Sophia and Tolstoy first quarreled she blamed her inadequacy: "Lyovochka is a wonderful man and I feel that absolutely everything is my fault . . . Why have I ruined this dear man, whom everybody loves so much?"[14] "Today there was *a scene*," Tolstoy noted in his diary, left open

Rear view of the house on the Yasnaya Polyana estate. Photo by Sophia Tolstoy.

on his desk for her. "I was sad that we behave just the same as other people. I told her she had hurt me with regard to my feelings for her, and I wept. She's charming. I love her even more. But is it all genuine?"[15]

Tolstoy would go on hunting trips, leaving her in the company of the two aunts, whose main interests were cards and dinner. For Sophia, bursting with energy, they were poor companions. She missed Moscow, her large family, especially her mother, and sister Tanya. "Please let Mama read my letters," she begged, "I am writing to both of you, as you are inseparable in my thoughts and I am open with you as before . . . Dear Mama, she is always so understanding, so kind, and so wonderful . . . My sweet Lyovochka, it will be a while before he becomes my 'mama.' And this will happen because I love him more every day."[16]

Before October 29, Tanya's sixteenth birthday, Sophia wrote that she was beginning to assist Tolstoy, hand-copying his novellas: "We live seriously, sensibly . . . I . . . read Lyovochka's *Cossacks,* which will be published soon, and copy his novella *Polikushka,* which we will also send to publish. We are playing duets, Lyovochka gets angry that I fail to observe the tempo but promises to teach me."

Copying became part of her routine, which also included mending Tolstoy's clothes and rolling his cigarettes. Tolstoy remarked that no one could roll cigarettes so flawlessly and Sophia carried on, although the smell of tobacco made her sick. He went for walks, leaving his manuscript for her to copy and his diary on his desk, an invitation to read and learn: "I love her more and more, although with a different love; there have been difficult moments."[17]

After the couple had several rows, Tolstoy rationalized: "(1) because I was rude and (2) because of her n[erves]." He was irritable after being unable to deliver his novellas on time to the *Russian Herald* and asked Katkov, the editor, to extend his deadline. "I'm still annoyed with my life, and even with her. *I must work.*"[18] Reading this, Sophia felt guilty that their family happiness distracted him.

"I am copying for Lyovochka days on end," she reported to Tanya.[19] She read both his correspondence and drafts to better understand her husband. In the evening, her copying and house chores over, Sophia napped on the floor on a large bearskin. She used the bear's brown head as a pillow, while Tolstoy read aloud *Les Misérables.* It was the bear that nearly killed him during a hunt: she was already gnawing at his forehead when a peasant, Arhip Ostashkov, chased her away with just a branch. The scar on Tolstoy's forehead was a reminder. Sophia would one day paint Ostashkov's portrait in watercolors: the hunter, impressive in cowhide coat and fur hat, brandishes the legendary branch.[20]

From Moscow, her sisters wrote about a ball they were to attend at Christmas where the tsar would make an appearance. "Maidens, don't entice the tsar," Sophia replied to them lightly on November 11. "Don't sin, he is a married man. I know, Tatyanka, you will be making your google eyes. Never mind, you are still a child, God will forgive." She was confiding in her sisters that Tolstoy planned to include them all in a new novel. And she chatted about her pregnancy: "I am amused and somewhat scared. Got caught so soon! Welcome to the christening; there will be a good feast. But where the little squashed frog will arrive is still a mystery, hopefully in Moscow, so that the new relation could properly introduce himself to your respectable family . . . So, maidens, I am a proper lady. I'm still behaving mischievously, upsetting the auntie who follows me around with her 'Easy, easy!' And I surprise her with my *entrechats.*"

Months into her stay in Yasnaya, Sophia met Tolstoy's former mistress, Aksinya Bazykina, and their son, Timofei. Tolstoy promised to send Aksinya away but she continued to live on the estate. His journal, which Sophia reread, revealed that he once was passionately in love with the woman. After seeing Aksinya, who came with other village women to scrub the floors at their mansion, Sophia made a desperate entry: "One of these days I think I shall kill myself with jealousy. 'In love as never before!' he writes. With that fat, pale peasant woman—how frightful!"[21] A month later, she had a dream: Aksinya comes to work in their garden with the peasant women. She is in a black silky dress, one of those Sophia had brought with her from Moscow. Sophia, with a sudden fury, grabs Aksinya's child and begins to tear him to pieces, but then Tolstoy enters, picks up the torn legs and arms, and tells her it was only a doll.

Tolstoy read this entry and responded with a story, told in a letter to Tanya. It describes his dream of Sophia's transformation into a china doll, the adventure taking place in their bedroom. "I heard her coming out from behind the screen and walking towards the bed. I opened my eyes . . . and saw Sonya—but not the Sonya that you and I knew—a Sonya made of *china!* . . . My fingers made no impression on her cold, china body and, what surprised me even more, she had become as light as a glass phial." The doll is pregnant, like Sophia, her belly "protruding upwards like a cone, and rather unnatural for a china doll." The dream continues with Dora, their yellow setter (a present from Sophia's father to Tolstoy), grabbing the doll and threatening to smash it. Tolstoy rescues the doll and wraps her warmly, "on the outside with morocco and on the inside with crimson velvet, then puts it in a wooden box with a clasp."[22] Tolstoy transformed Sophia's nightmare into a joke.

Before Christmas, the couple drove in a sleigh through Moscow's snow-covered streets. Tolstoy later mused that when Sophia saw the Kremlin towers, familiar to her since childhood, she "almost died of excitement."[23] They stopped at the central Shevrie Hotel and visited friends separately: Sophia was then too shy to accompany Tolstoy and meet his worldly aquaintances. "I . . . feared that Lyovochka might be ashamed of me for something." Sophia was a child wife and, as some told her, was "so youthful and so touching with her belly."[24]

But she did accompany Tolstoy to concerts and exhibitions, always fascinated by Moscow's cultural life. Tickets to Nikolai Rubinstein's concert were sold out but the pianist made an exception for Tolstoy, also placing a chair for Sophia in the front row. Rubinstein was a friend of both Tolstoy and her uncle Konstantin Islavin, a pianist. She would later remark how embarrassed she was with Rubinstein's attention: "Not a shadow of vanity did I have in my heart back then; I did not have something that spoiled me later on—that serene, triumphant, and habitually self-assured tone that, yes, I am honored . . . because I am the wife of Leo Nikolaevich Tolstoy and deserve these honors."[25]

In January, still in Moscow, Tolstoy noted: "I love it when she sits close to me . . . and she says: 'Lyovochka,' and stops—'why are the pipes in the stove so straight?' or 'why do horses live such a long time?' . . . I love it when she is a girl in a yellow dress and sticks out her lower jaw and tongue; I love it when I see her head thrown back and her serious and frightened and childlike and passionate face."[26]

Their lengthy stay was beginning to weigh on Tolstoy, who was yearning to resume work at Yasnaya. He admitted in his journal, "I suppose a great deal has boiled up inside me unnoticed; I feel that she is depressed, but I'm more depressed still."[27] Sophia attributed his annoyance to her pregnancy. A kind word from Tolstoy would revive her: "My husband . . . is everything to me; he is responsible for all that is good in me, because I love him deeply and care for nothing in the world but him."[28] He told her that their quarrels, even the trivial ones, were "a scar on love."[29] To demonstrate this, he picked up a sheet of paper and tore it in half. Impressed, Sophia replied in her diary, "It is hard to live together without quarrelling, but I must try not to all the same, for he is right, our quarrels make a *cut*." When they quarreled, yet again, she felt "like a devil in the presence of a saint." His many talents and virtues inspired her awe: "I am afraid to talk to him or look at him . . . A man like this could make one die of happiness and humility."[30]

After two months in Moscow, Sophia concurred with Tolstoy that "Kremlin life is oppressive" and that "one cannot be satisfied merely with one's family . . . but that one needs . . . a larger cause."[31] Tolstoy was amused with her diary entry, making a postscript: "I need nothing but you. Lyovochka talks a lot of nonsense sometimes."

In February, when the couple left for Yasnaya Polyana, Sophia's family again assembled on the porch. As their sleigh began to move, Tolstoy shouted to Tanya, inviting her to visit, "You shall come to us with the swallows!"[32]

He noted in his diary, "Tanya—sensuality." But he concluded the entry with a tribute to Sophia: "I will always love her."[33] Tanya had a lovely voice, taking instruction from Rosalie Laborde, a French opera singer, who taught at the Moscow Imperial Theatre School. Tanya's family expected her to have a stage career and Tolstoy called her Madame Viardot. (A great French singer, Pauline Viardot was also Turgenev's rumored lover. For Sophia's family, who met Viardot on her visit to Russia, her name was a household word.) Although Tanya never made it to the stage, Tolstoy described her singing in his first great masterpiece, *War and Peace*. Tanya was vivacious, graceful, easygoing, and apparently irresistible.

Back at Yasnaya, Sophia felt that Tolstoy belonged to her almost exclusively: "There is me and his work—nothing else matters to him . . . I am glad he is writing . . . I feel that my life and *my duty* is here, and I want nothing more."[34] At the end of February 1863, she wrote Tanya that Tolstoy "has begun a new novel. I'm so glad."[35] It was the first mention of what was to become *War and Peace*.

The novel demanded his complete concentration and the couple's relationship grew harmonious. Tolstoy noted: "She is everything . . . She is transforming me—incomparably more so than I her."[36] Sophia echoed: "I read *his* diary and it made me happy."[37] As long as his writing flowed uninterruptedly ("the basis of everything is work"),[38] the idyll lasted. But in a bout of melancholy, Tolstoy would desert his family happiness: "I am puny and insignificant. And I've been like that since I married the woman I love."[39]

Later, Sophia would analyze their first year: "Lev Nikolaevich was very changeable with me. From passion he turned to coldness; from the highest opinion of me . . . he went to another extreme, claiming . . . he was the most unfortunate man in the world . . . Then I cried thinking that I was silly and uneducated and that he regretted marrying the girl incapable of appreciating him."[40]

But he did appreciate her. In spring, taking his usual break from writing to work on the farm, Tolstoy reported to Afanasij Fet, his friend and neighbor: "Sonya is working with me too. We have no steward; I have people to help with field-work and the building, but she manages the office and the cash by herself. I have bees, sheep, a new orchard and a distillery. Everything progresses little by little, although of course poorly compared with the ideal."[41] He managed the farm with the help of a student, while Sophia walked to the barns to watch over milking and record butter production. She told her sister of her new responsibilities: "We have become quite the farmers: we are buying cattle, fowl, piglets, and calves. We are purchasing bees."[42]

The beehives came from her grandfather Islenev's estate. Near the end of her confinement, Sophia walked two miles daily, carrying lunch to her husband in the field. There she watched Tolstoy at the apiary with a net over his head and heeded his lecture on the life of bees, although she understood little why beekeeping fascinated him. However, when copying *War and Peace,* she would understand his metaphors. In the novel, he likens a queenless beehive to Moscow deserted by its dwellers before it was occupied by Napoleon. The city seemed alive and breathing when Napoleon looked at it through his binoculars, but everything that constituted its life was already gone. Moscow was populated only by looters in a way a queenless hive is overtaken by robber bees.

In Sophia's family history, bees were also linked with Napoleon's invasion: on the Behrs coat of arms was an image of a swarm of bees attacking a bear. During the War of 1812, their property and documents were burned. Her father applied to reinstate the emblem but was allowed only a beehive with bees, no bear. (In German, Behrs means "bear.")

That spring, Sophia wrote her sister: "Here everything is farming, farming till the end of time ... Lyovochka, once he starts something, throws his heart and soul into it. This is very praiseworthy yet a little boring."[43] Tolstoy wanted to purchase a Japanese breed of pigs and wrote Behrs asking to introduce him to the seller: "There is a certain Baron Sheping in Moscow who owns these Japanese pigs . . . I feel that I cannot be happy in life until I get some of my own."[44] When the pigs arrived, Tolstoy hired a retired officer, a drunkard, to care for them: he wanted to reform the man. Sophia saw this experiment fail: the drunkard starved the pigs to death. Tolstoy, ever the idealist, refused to accept her explanation. He suspected an epidemic and read volumes researching what the problem might be.

Their neighbor Fet used to liken a typical honeymoon to a team of un-broken oxen trying to pull their load uphill. However, he was impressed with the young countess. When in May, Fet was driving into the main alley at Yasnaya, he saw Tolstoy casting a fishnet over a pond, with the help of village lads. Sophia, despite her pregnancy, was running at her husband's summons with a bundle of heavy barn keys attached to her belt. Greeting Fet on the run, she jumped over a palisade and continued to the pond. "The life of the young countess jumping over the poles, in her condition, must have been inspired with the most blissful expectations. The count himself, who spent his entire life keenly searching for novelty, was living through a period when he was discovering a world still unknown to him, in which he believed with all the enthusiasm of a young artist."[45]

Fet soon visited again and had tea with the couple near the apiary. So-phia remembered, "It was a lovely evening in June, the glowworms in the grass shone with iridescent green. Lev Nikolaevich promised to buy me emerald earrings if we had money, like the ones my sister Tanya had. So he picked up two beetles from the ground, as a prank, and put them against my ears: 'Here are the emerald earrings, aren't they good?'" Fet liked the joke and wrote a poem, concluding with the lines: "My hand is in your hand, what marvel! And on the ground are two glowworms, two emeralds."[46] Fet would spoil Sophia with his attention, sending a poem dedicated to her after every visit: "And, behold, enchanted by thee . . . I understand, bright creature, all the purity of thy soul."[47] Sophia replied to him in doggerel. Fet would also visit with his kindly and hospitable wife, neé Maria Petrovna Botkin, who came from the wealthy family of a tea merchant.[48]

Although Sophia's father could secure the attention of medical experts in Moscow, her child was to be born at Yasnaya. Sophia had premonitions of dying in labor and imagined a widowed Tolstoy: "How sad and ter-rible it would be to leave him."[49] She was also affected by Tolstoy's state of mind, which he described in his diary as "depressing and without hope."[50] She looked forward to her sister's arrival to cheer her up: "I have not seen gay and carefree people for such a long time . . . Nightingales are singing, the night is marvelous, warm; Tanya, please reply to me quickly. I will be so glad to have you here when the little Tolstoy is born."[51] Sophia also in-quired about the latest fashions in Moscow: "Tell me more about the cloth, the color, and the hats. This spring I should be sewing anyway and so it's better to make it fashionable . . . Come, cheer up my soul."[52]

Tolstoy wanted their first child to come into the world on the twenty-eighth day of the month—he believed it was his providential number. And, in fact, Sophia did give birth to their son Seryozha on June 28, 1863. When her pangs began, Tolstoy rushed to fetch midwife Marya Ivanovna Abramovich, who would become a frequent attendant, delivering all their children.

Preparation for the birth was filled with symbolism: Tolstoy arranged for a leather couch to be brought in, the same one on which he had been born. In his diary Tolstoy grasped the agony of the day:

> The darling, how beautiful she was with her expression of serious-ness, honesty, strength and emotion. She was wearing a dressing-gown which was open, and a little embroidered jacket; her black hair was untidy—with a feverish, blotchy red face and big burning eyes she walked about and looked at me . . . She kissed me simply and calmly. While people were swarming about, the pangs started again . . . There were a few more pangs, and each time I held her and felt her body trembling, stretching and contracting; and the impression her body made on me was quite, quite different from previously, both before and during our marriage. In between times I ran about, arranging for the sofa on which I was born to be moved into her room.[53]

(The atmosphere of that night traveled into *War and Peace,* where Tolstoy describes preparations for the birth in the Bolkonsky house. When the little princess begins to have pangs, the servants bring in a leather sofa with a "solemn and quiet"[54] expression on their faces.) Sophia gave birth at two in the morning; Tolstoy looked distraught, his eyes red from weeping. Everyone in the house celebrated with champagne. However, within days the spirit of jubilation gave way to unhappiness. Sophia was making a slow recovery, yet Tolstoy insisted she must suckle the baby and care for him without assistance. In *War and Peace* he would describe the birth of their first child and the commotion that followed, and discuss at length the advantages of breast-feeding and "the unnaturalness and harmfulness of wet nurses."[55]

Sophia's nursing did not go well: she developed mastitis and her fissures were causing severe pain.[56] When blood and pus began to emerge instead of milk, a wet nurse had to be engaged. Tolstoy avoided the nursery with an expression of "morose animosity"[57] on his face. Sophia felt that he blamed her for failing to live up to his Rousseauian ideal of a healthy mother and wife. On July 23, 1863, Sophia noted in her diary: "I am in agonizing pain. Lyova is murderous. He wants to wipe me from the face of the earth because I am suffering and am not doing my duty, I want not to see him at all because he is not suffering but just goes on writing."[58]

Tolstoy read this and was overcome with remorse: "Sonya, forgive me, I have only just realized that I am to blame and have wronged you greatly." But his repentance was short-lived: he lost his temper and crossed out the note. In the meantime, the baby became dangerously ill. In the midst of the crisis Sophia's father addressed the couple with his sobering medical advice:

> You think you are a thoroughly unhappy mother because you found yourself forced to engage a wet nurse; the husband comforts his wife by promising not to enter the nursery because its atmosphere disgusts him . . . I see that you have both gone out of your minds . . . Can it be unknown to you, good husband, that mental suffering has a harmful and injurious effect on the organism and especially on a woman after a recent confinement . . . Stop acting foolish, dear Sonya . . . Is it such a disgrace that you could not manage to breastfeed your baby, and whose fault is it? Your own and especially your husband's, who, without considering his wife's condition, forces her to do things which can only prove injurious to her . . . He is a great master of words and of writing but when it comes to deeds, it is a different matter. Let him write a story about a husband who tortures his sick wife and wants her to continue nursing her baby; all the women will stone him.[59]

The family's confrontation over nursing continued through the summer. In September, days before their first wedding anniversary, Tolstoy announced he was going off to war.[60] At first, Sophia thought he was joking; when it turned out to be the truth, she was appalled: "What sort of behavior is that? Is he unbalanced? No, I think not, merely erratic . . . One day they decide to get married, enjoy it, and produce some children—next day it's time to leave it all behind and go off to war . . . His inconsistency and cowardice have made me respect him less. But his talent is almost more important to him than his family . . . What despotism! 'This is what I want,' he says, 'don't you dare say a word!' . . . And I love him, that's the worst of it, when I see him he looks so depressed, forever morosely searching his soul."[61]

But Tolstoy soon abandoned his idea of going to war and resumed his novel. For seven years, while he wrote *War and Peace,* Sophia heard his chapters and endlessly copied his revisions, admiring the novel that would captivate the world.

Chapter Three

Natasha

I N THE FALL OF 1863, the Tula gentry held a ball to honor heir to the throne Nikolai Alexandrovich. Sophia dreamt of attending but it was decided that Tolstoy would escort her younger sister Tanya. "When Lev Nikolaevich put on his dress coat, he and Tanya left for Tula and the ball; I started to cry bitterly and wept all evening. We were living a monotonous, secluded, dull life, and suddenly such an opportunity comes up and I (just nineteen) am deprived of it."[1] His expedition with Tanya would inspire Natasha Rostova's first ball in *War and Peace*.

Tolstoy "mixed" Sophia with her sister to create his Natasha. Tanya was the model for the heroine's youth and Sophia, who never had a chance to be carefree, was used for her motherhood. Sophia and Tanya made an amazing team, Tolstoy liked to say: "If you were horses, a breeding plant would pay dearly for such a team."[2]

Tanya went snipe shooting with Tolstoy, while Sophia stayed home with her high temperature caused by mastitis. Tolstoy would describe his trip with Tanya in an enchanting chapter about hunting with the Rostovs. Sophia accepted his pursuit of inspiration: "I remember, Lev Nikolaevich called me to his study downstairs and read this chapter to me, after he had just written it, and together we laughed and were happy."[3] The heroine's name, Natasha, came from Sophia's early novella, which she had burned shortly before her marriage. Tolstoy liked it and borrowed the idea of her story to depict the Rostov family and the three sisters.

While still a bachelor outlining his family ideal, Tolstoy wrote that his wife would take interest in his work, as well as his hobbies, and give up her love of entertainment. Driving by a lighted mansion with him and hearing Strauss waltzes, she would suppress her urge to dance: "This pleasure will never really be hers to experience."⁴ Upon reading this at eighteen, Sophia sensibly remarked: "Poor man, he was still too young to realize that happiness can never be planned in advance, and you will inevitably be unhappy if you try to do so. But what noble splendid dreams these were nevertheless."⁵ She would work hard to implement his ideal of family life.

Decades later, when asked to describe the literary house in which *War and Peace* was written, Sophia told a biographer, "There was no such 'house'; surely, I was quite a young girl . . . when I married, and only vaguely realized the great importance of the husband whom I adored."⁶ She looked forward to the evenings when Tolstoy would bring her newly written or revised chapters. Some parts had to be copied many times, for he kept revising them. Sophia loved copying *War and Peace,* work she did for seven years, remarking, "The idea of serving a genius and great man has given me strength to do anything."⁷

Tolstoy wrote daily, at his regular hours, and went for walks; this routine would remain over the years. In the evenings, he read to her, either his new chapters, Molière comedies, or *Our Mutual Friend* by Dickens. Sophia copied at night, when there was nothing to distract her. The novel was a vast world, which she had not had a chance to experience, and she invested her "entire soul" to understanding what she was copying. Tolstoy made many drafts of the novel's opening, set in a political salon in 1805 at the start of the European conflict with Napoleon. He wrote slowly, "with difficulty," perfecting his prose: when he wrote, there was nothing but deadly silence at home. Sophia was young and had to restrain her impulses: "At this moment I should love to go to a *dance* or do something amusing."⁸ But compared to his needs, her own seemed insignificant. She learned to endure solitude: they lived at Yasnaya uninterruptedly, traveling to Moscow when Tolstoy needed to do research.

Sophia's father helped find historical materials for the novel. Among the first to learn about *War and Peace,* Behrs wrote Tolstoy enthusiastically: "You have chosen a great subject for the novel—may God give you success."[9] At Tolstoy's request, he obtained from his acquaintance Maria Volkova, a lady-in-waiting, her correspondence with Countess Varvara Lanskaia, from the years 1812 to 1818. Tolstoy used the letters in the novel. Behrs also arranged for interviews with friends who remembered the invasion and the great fire of Moscow.

Christmas of 1863 was spent with Sophia's family. Tolstoy conducted research, while Sophia consulted doctors about her mastitis. Behrs had arranged appointments with several medical professors. Their stay was brief because Tolstoy was in a hurry to resume work. Sophia soon wrote from Yasnaya that she was glad to return to their purposeful life in the country: "When I recall the Kremlin, a large animated picture presents itself—the many beloved faces, the long table, the bright lights, and one face after another with such distinctive and charming expressions. Here it's solitude, peace, and quiet. I am so used to it that I have quite forgotten my former life."[10] Behrs replied that her letter radiated happiness.[11]

As Sophia would remark, she banished her own aspirations as threatening to her commitment to Tolstoy and his work.[12] Since childhood she had a great desire to study art, a longing that would return. Once, in Tolstoy's absence, she was writing to him when his sister, Maria Nikolaevna, began playing Schubert. She described her sensation to Tolstoy:

> I'm sitting in your study, writing to you and crying . . . The music I haven't heard for so long took me away from my sphere of the nursery, diapers, children . . . to a distant, unfamiliar place . . . I've long stifled these strings that music and nature set quivering and causing pain within me . . . I feel them now, it hurts and feels good. But it's better for us, mothers and mistresses of the household, to stay away from all this . . . I'm listening to the music, my nerves are taut, I love you terribly, I see the gorgeous sunset through the windows of your study; the Schubert melodies, which left me indifferent before, are now turning my soul over and I cannot hold back my tears . . . The candles will be soon lit, I will be called to nurse . . . and my sentiment will pass, as if I never had it.[13]

Tolstoy replied, "My soul, I understand your tears, they fill me with joy, and I love them very, very, very much."[14] He sympathized with Sophia's desire to study art but in the coming years, pregnancies prevented her from realizing her dream.

During *War and Peace* her life was entirely consumed with her husband and his work: "I felt so much a part of him, loved him so passionately, that my life seemed to me trivial and unnecessary without him."[15] His writing fascinated her: she sat in his study when he wrote, sewing in silence. When Tolstoy went hunting for diversion, she organized his papers, filed his drafts, and read his letters and diaries. "I look around your study and remember everything: how you used to dress for the hunt by the gun cabinet, how Dora would jump happily around you; how you used to sit at the desk writing and I would approach the door and open it timidly, afraid to disturb you, and you, noticing that I hesitated, would say, 'Come in.' That's all I wanted."[16]

In spring and summer, when the beauty of the world won over Tolstoy's urge to write, he farmed. He was passionate about farming but lacked the patience and practicality to succeed, so farm losses were ongoing. For Sophia, his state of mind mattered more. She described to her sister how Tolstoy despaired over his failures and, to distract him, she took him for a drive with his favorite horse, Mighty: "We drove at great speed, and it was so jolly that we soon forgot all about the farming troubles."[17] The farm provided a diversion for Tolstoy and allowed him to observe nature. Yasnaya became part of his creative laboratory: metaphors in *War and Peace* often evolve from the worlds of farming and hunting.

In 1863, Tolstoy admitted to many people that he considered himself extremely fortunate. Making progress with the novel, he wrote his relative Alexandrine, "I am a husband and a father, who is fully satisfied with his situation . . . I only *feel* my family circumstances, and don't think about them. This condition gives me an awful lot of intellectual scope. I've never felt my intellectual powers, and even all my moral powers, so free and so capable of work . . . Now I am a writer with *all* the strengths of my soul, and I write and I think as I have never thought or written before."[18] Vladimir Sollogub, a man of letters, visiting Yasnaya during *War and Peace,* told Sophia she was "the perfect wife for a writer" and a nursemaid of her husband's talent. She vowed in her diary to become "an even better nursemaid of Lyovochka's talent from now on."[19]

Tolstoy, then an advocate of marriage, explained he felt transformed, his state of mind allowing greater productivity: "I imagine myself an apple tree, which used to grow with water sprouts in every direction, and which became pruned in the course of life; now that it's trimmed, tied, and supported, its trunk and roots can grow without hindrance. And that's how I grow."[20] A few decades later, Tolstoy would renounce his artistic achievement, insisting, with the same passion, that his marriage did not matter at all.

In August 1864, while Tolstoy traveled and hunted, the couple corresponded daily. Sophia supervised the farm in his absence and he sent instructions for harvesting clover and planting winter crops. She asked him to report about his trip in detail: "Write to me, like a diary."[21] What a joy it would be for her to travel along, "just the two of us, like a young couple."[22] Tolstoy wrote tenderly, "You say I forget you. Not for a minute, especially with others. I can forget you on a hunt, when it's the snipe alone that I remember, but with people, every situation, every word reminds me of you, and I want to tell you what I cannot tell anyone, but you alone."[23]

In her letters to Tolstoy, Sophia described life at home in his absence: baby Seryozha had the croup: "If you could only see how pathetic he was. He was crying, suffocating; when the mustard burned him, he jerked his little feet, grabbed my hair, pulled at my earrings and my collar, as if he was trying to crawl inside me and was begging to be saved . . . How many thoughts I thought last night; how much I loved you." She described how she made poultices and rubbed Seryozha with warm oil to make him sweat. In the morning, when the doctor arrived, she went outside for the first time in several days. The grass was glistening in the sun. Sister Tanya returned from a ride, looking "smart, fresh, and charming in her velvet jacket and motley-feathered hat. I envied her, thinking that you would be impressed, and this frightened me a bit. For I am unattractive, tired-looking, and too inelegant."[24] But Tolstoy did not want her elegant: he imagined her in a gray robe, nursing the baby behind a screen. In the epilogue of *War and Peace,* he would use that letter to depict Natasha in Pierre's absence. He asked Sophia to keep a separate diary when he hunted, saying he would read it upon his return. It was a pleasure for her to write the three-day diary, conversing with Tolstoy.

The previous summer, sister Tanya became involved with Tolstoy's brother Sergei Nikolaevich, who was twenty-five years her senior. Caught by a thunderstorm while visiting, she had to spend the night at his estate. The two fell in love, describing the occasion to Tolstoy as their most "poetic" experience. But marriage was impossible: Sergei Nikolaevich had a common-law wife, Masha Shishkina, and children by her. The affair left Tanya heartbroken: she became depressed and gave up singing. In the novel Tolstoy describes a vivacious Natasha losing her love of life.

Checking on his brother's estate in his absence, Tolstoy spent a night in that same house. In a letter to Sophia he said that he fell asleep on the couch where Tanya had slept and dreamt "of various characters in my novel."[25] Tolstoy wrote of several things at once: his brother and her sister in love, his attraction to Tanya (he trusted Sophia to understand his complex emotions), and his intent to use her sister's experience in the novel. He would speak of his inspiration casually, and only later, realizing the importance of it all, would Sophia regret not having recorded more.

In September 1864, just before their second wedding anniversary, Tolstoy wrote that their relationship had grown stronger and firmer: "We love each other, i.e., we are dearer to each other than all other people in the world . . . No secrets, and nothing to be ashamed of. Meanwhile I've begun a novel . . . but I'm in the stage of correcting and revising." By then, Sophia had copied innumerable revisions and knew some parts by heart, admitting to Tolstoy that occasionally "it would seem that it's not your novel that is so good, but that I am so clever."[26]

That fall, Tolstoy had an accident while hunting on an untamed horse: he smashed his right arm and dislocated his shoulder. He was afraid to alarm Sophia, who was again pregnant, and asked a peasant to drive him to his village. When Sophia found out, she drove to fetch him, discovering Tolstoy in a crowded hut, a peasant setting his arm. At home, he was attended to by a local practitioner and then a doctor from Tula, who set his bone unsuccessfully.

Days after, on October 4, Sophia gave birth to a daughter, Tanya. While recuperating and nursing, she also had to care for Tolstoy, who was in great pain from the fracture. Despite sleepless nights, the couple enjoyed an idyll. Tolstoy wrote sister Tanya that Sophia was "nice with her fledglings," handling her duties simply and cheerfully.[27]

In November, still unable to use his right arm, Tolstoy went to Moscow and stayed with his in-laws while consulting doctors. The couple kept in touch with telegrams and letters. Sophia wrote, "You are in my world and I am in yours. And who was this Sonechka[28] Behrs in the Kremlin, only a shadow remains."[29] When apart, they idealized each other: "Yesterday, when I did not write to you, my darling Lyovochka, I felt as I had in childhood when failing to say my prayers."[30] Tolstoy replied from her parents' apartment with her childhood portraits, at four different ages, before him; he could not sleep unless he had written to her.

He had asked her to copy the first installment of the novel, twenty-eight chapters. As he was leaving for Moscow, he told her, "You are my helper." In her letter, Sophia reminded him of this episode: "And I'd be happy to help you and copy for you, from morning till night."[31]

> How good is everything you left for me to copy. How I like Princess Marya! You can see her clearly. What a splendid sympathetic character. I will also criticize you. Prince Andrew, I think, is still unclear. You can't say what kind of person he is. If he is clever, then why can't he understand and explain to himself his relationship with his wife? The old prince is also very good. But I liked him more in the first draft, which has dissatisfied you . . . It was such a pleasure for me to copy. Are you writing in Moscow?[32]

(In Princess Marya, Tolstoy depicted his mother, whom he knew only from collected accounts: she died when he was a baby. Sophia's mother and sisters were portrayed in the Rostovs, spontaneous and warm. These two families are central to the novel—islands of stability in a sea of war.)

In Tolstoy's absence, Sophia had his family—his brother, his sister, and their children—staying at Yasnaya. With the house full of people, she lived downstairs, copying the novel in his vaulted study. Around her in-laws, who were much older, she felt like their "adopted child," she wrote Tolstoy. When alone with him, she was a tsarina. "I am still downstairs, here's my kingdom, my children, my occupations, and my life."[33]

Tolstoy wanted to publish the novel in installments in the *Russian Herald*, but Sophia advised him to wait because he could lose his wealthy readers—potential book buyers—who also subscribed to the magazine. Publishing the book was more profitable, she reckoned. Tolstoy preferred magazine publication because it would save him the trouble of dealing with printers and censors.[34] However, *War and Peace* was not a good novel for serialization: when the first installments appeared, the reception was lukewarm.

Sophia wrote to "remind" Tolstoy of his own words: "Don't read your novel to anyone who can judge it. Remember, they have misled you before, and now it's risky; someone might say a stupid thing and you'd take it close to heart."[35] He replied that her letter affected him like "good music . . . it was gay and sad and pleasant, and I wanted to cry. What a clever woman you are, telling me not to give the novel to anyone to read."[36] Later, Tolstoy did read it to several friends successfully, writing Sophia that praise can never hurt a writer; it's only dangerous not to be praised.

Despite pain in his arm, Tolstoy spent two hours with magazine editors negotiating royalties: he wanted an exorbitant three hundred rubles per printer's page.[37] And yet, selling his work was repulsive to him, Sophia knew. She alone could understand and explain this contradiction: "It's awful, to sell your ideas, your feelings, your talent, your very soul!"[38] Tolstoy replied that she understood precisely how he felt and that this was the best proof of her love.

In the meantime, he had to undergo surgery on his arm. It was performed at his in-laws' apartment on November 28. (He chose his providential number for the date of the surgery.) Sophia's mother and sister Tanya assisted while Tolstoy, under chloroform, had his arm rebroken and reset. Sophia was informed by a telegram that it went well. Tanya also wrote a letter, describing how, before the chloroform took effect, a delirious Tolstoy got up from his armchair and addressed everyone in the operating room: "My friends, we cannot live like this."[39] First, they all were frightened, then amused.

A letter from Sophia arrived while Tolstoy was still recovering from the chloroform: he cried when it was read to him. He dictated a reply to Tanya but found it awkward to be intimate. As soon as he could hold a pen, he scribbled a note. Sophia replied, "What a joy it is for me to make out your scrawl."[40]

She finished copying the parts of *War and Peace* Tolstoy left for her and dispatched them to Moscow. Upon rereading the manuscript, he became depressed, writing her that his talent "disappointed" him. Away from home, he lost his mental balance and confidence: "I lose my '*équilibre*' without you."[41] He continued, in another letter, that a great "misfortune" had befallen him: he was "beginning to cool off to his novel."[42] He felt the few chapters he had dictated in Moscow were flat and unexciting, "and without emotion a writer's work cannot flow."[43]

His despair growing, he continued: "As a good wife, you think about your husband as you do about yourself, and I remember your saying to me that all the military and historical side over which I'm taking such pains will turn out badly, but the rest—the family life, the characters, the psychology—will be good. That couldn't be more true."[44]

Sophia knew that he occasionally "doubted his powers, denied his talent."[45] She urged him on: "Prepare, prepare some work for me."[46] It was the "nasty" chloroform that had upset his nerves. "Don't surrender to your nerves, my darling Lyovochka, they are playing a trick on you. And you cannot judge your talent, why would it disappear all of a sudden? . . . Just wait, it will come back. And if you are not in the mood for writing, we will go and look at the pigs, the sheep, the cows . . . we will walk on the freshly fallen snow and enjoy the scenery; we will read aloud and romp with the children."[47] She wrote again, to reassure him:

> Why have you lost heart and courage? . . . Haven't you the strength to get up? Remember how many joys your novel gave you, how well you were thinking it over, and now you don't like it! No, Lyovochka, it's wrong. Just come back and instead of the dirty, stone Kremlin house you will see our Chepyzh[48] shining in the bright sun . . . you will remember our happy life here . . . and again, with a happy face, you will share your writing plans with me . . . And you will dictate to me.[49]

In the novel, Pierre's doubts disappear not because Natasha answers his difficult questions "but because her image immediately transferred him to a different, bright realm of inner activity . . . into a realm of beauty and love for which it was worth living."[50] For Pierre, the world is divided "into two parts: one is she, and there is all happiness, hope, light; the other is where she is not, and there everything is dejection and darkness."[51]

Sophia's letters raised his spirits. "My dear heart," Tolstoy wrote. "Only love me as I love you, and nothing else counts for me, and everything is fine."[52] At Yasnaya, preparing for his return, Sophia decorated the house and padded the floor of the nursery with oilcloth. She slept on the floor when nursing, for fear of dropping the baby. Tolstoy received her letter when he was about to leave for Yasnaya and replied, "The day after, after tomorrow, on the oilcloth floor of the nursery, I will embrace you, my slender, quick, my dear wife."[53]

Remembering the elation of their meetings, Sophia would write, "A woman cannot possibly love stronger than I loved Lev Nikolaevich. He was neither handsome nor young, with only four bad teeth in his mouth. But the joy that would rise in me when I met him . . . that joy illuminated my life for a long, long time."[54]

Tolstoy's homecoming after surgery was celebrated with two magnificent masked balls. On the eve of the Epiphany, the couple made elaborate preparations. Thrones for the king and queen—two armchairs with golden eagles' heads—were placed on a table in the drawing room. Tables and benches were draped with green cloth and a white palanquin was spread over the chairs. Flowers, bay trees, and orange trees were brought from their greenhouse, creating a "superb" impression. A pie was baked with a bean inside. In childhood, when Sophia received the bean and was chosen queen, Tolstoy pulled her around in a cabriolet.

Family, friends, and servants arrived in costume: there was an old major, a dancing giant ("the effect was extraordinary"), and a real dwarf, "absolutely tiny," whom Sophia hired. When the musicians came, the procession entered "to a deafening noise of little bells, crackers, and cymbals." The bean pie was cut, the king and queen chosen and seated on their thrones. "After that the racket we set up was indescribable. Songs, dances, games, bladder fights, firecrackers, ring-around-the-roses, refreshments, a collation, and to end up with, Bengal lights. After which we all had headaches and tummyaches the whole of that night and next day."[55] The fun continued for two more days, with feasting and racing on troikas.

Tolstoy was the soul of the party, having regained his spirits a month after his surgery. Carnival scenes with the Rostovs and troika racing in *War and Peace* were written by a happy man. His family life was the air he breathed; it nourished his craft. In January 1865, Tolstoy wrote Alexandrine that his family happiness was getting "smoother and deeper" every day. "And the materials that make up this happiness are of the very plainest: the children who (excuse me) soil themselves and scream, my wife who nurses one child and leads the other along and reproaches me every minute for not seeing that they are both on the edge of the grave, and paper and ink, by means of which I describe events and the feelings of people who have never existed."[56] In the novel, there are no secondary subjects: family affairs and global events are woven together.

In 1865, large portions of the novel were completed and installments began to appear in the *Russian Herald*. During the summer, when Tolstoy visited neighboring estates and hunted, Sophia and the children stayed with his sister, Maria Nikolaevna. Wanting privacy, Sophia settled into an unused bathhouse with her children and Tatyana Filippovna, the nanny who had nursed Tolstoy.

In the daytime, when Sophia was copying, the place was hot and buzzed with flies: "Just as I begin to copy, the children distract me, flies are biting, or I get carried away and read on."[57] The novel absorbed her: "I am surrounded by many parts of you, e.g., the children, and your writing."[58] He wrote, in a simultaneous letter, that he looked forward to seeing her and the children and recalled her smile, happy and serene.

While Sophia was copying a war part—the surrender of the Austrian army near Ulm in 1805—she began to appreciate the military and the historical side in the novel, writing this to Tolstoy. She was moved when "the unfortunate General Mack," after losing his entire army to Napoleon, arrives at the Russian camp to admit defeat "and the inquisitive aides-de-camp stand around him, and he is almost crying, and his meeting with Kutuzov . . . I liked it terribly."[59] When her sister-in-law would invite her to the main house, she would continue copying in a corner of the drawing room.

By winter, Tolstoy decided to refresh his impressions of society, which had become "too abstract" after living in the country for years.[60] He missed theater, music, libraries, and stimulating conversation. Early in 1866, the family went to Moscow for two months, staying in a downtown apartment. Tolstoy used to say that once they had enough money they would spend their winters in Moscow. He dreamt of buying a house in the Arbat neighborhood, settled by scholars and professors. A decade later, when they could afford it, his attitude changed.

But that winter, Tolstoy indulged in the arts and took classes in sculpting at the School of Painting, Sculpture, and Architecture. Sophia observed him modeling a statuette of a horse from red clay and later tried sculpting as well, making a miniature bust of Tolstoy. Among people they met in Moscow was her mother's cousin, the artist Mikhail Bashilov, who was the school inspector. At Tolstoy's request, Bashilov made splendid drawings for a separate edition of *War and Peace*. Tolstoy sent him sister Tanya's youthful portrait to sketch Natasha in girlhood. But because Bashilov worked slowly, Tolstoy eventually gave up the idea of an illustrated edition.

In Moscow, Tolstoy read parts of the novel to a gathering of friends; he read "exceptionally well" when not nervous.[61] His listeners were thrilled, while Sophia dozed off: she knew these chapters by heart. Besides, a third pregnancy made her lethargic.

When they returned to Yasnaya, she began sewing for the baby due that summer. On All Saints' Day, May 22, she took Seryozha and Tanya for their first communion, proud of the way they looked in their white dresses. It was warm and sunny, and upon returning from church, the family drank chocolate in the garden. That day, Sophia gave birth to son Ilya, their third child.

On September 17, it was "with special joy" that Sophia celebrated her name day. To surprise her, Tolstoy invited a military band, and the Dyakovs and other neighbors danced on the veranda, lit with candles and lanterns. "I shall never forget the young ladies darting about in their white muslin dresses . . . but it is Lyovochka's sweet cheerful face I remember most clearly . . . I do not believe that any two people could be closer than we are. We are terribly fortunate, in every way—in our children, our relationship, our life."[62]

In November, Tolstoy was in Moscow, researching Masonic documents for the novel. He wrote Sophia daily, of his progress with the novel and of his love for her. "I am not remembering you, but I am always aware of you. This is not just a phrase."[63] Dispatching the manuscript to Tolstoy, Sophia wrote, "I am beginning to feel that this is your child and so it is mine, and sending this batch of sheets to Moscow, I feel like I'm letting the child go out into the world, afraid someone might hurt him."[64] She had begun to understand the novel on a new level:

Sophia in 1866 during War and Peace *with Tanya (left) and Seryozha.*

As I copy I experience a whole new world of emotions, thoughts and impressions. Nothing touches me so deeply as his ideas, his genius . . . Whether it is because I have changed or because this novel really is extraordinarily good, I do not know. I write very quickly, so I can follow the story and catch the mood, but slowly enough to be able to stop, reflect upon each new idea and discuss it with him later . . . For some reason he listens to what I have to say (which makes me very proud) and trusts my opinions.[65]

Tolstoy worked with great intensity, hoping to complete the novel by the end of the following year, an unrealistic goal. The pressure increased when on top of the magazine deal, he signed a contract to publish the book. Rarely pleased with his work, he put in long hours to perfect it. In early winter 1867, overworked and suffering severe headaches, he was examined by Dr. Grigory Zakharin in Moscow, who found his nerves "seriously upset." As Sophia had remarked, "At times, his nerves were so strained that he broke into tears when reading certain passages."[66] Fet, who visited that winter, compared Tolstoy to a large crystal bell, which rang from even a tiny quiver: he was bursting full of ideas.[67]

Sister Tanya, then staying at Yasnaya, witnessed one of Tolstoy's angry spells. A pregnant Sophia was sitting on the floor, sorting the contents of her chest drawer. Tolstoy walked in and told her to get up immediately. When she refused, he shouted at her and stormed out of the room. Sophia followed to ask what was wrong, but Tolstoy screamed "Get out!" and threw a tray of china and a barometer on the floor. Tanya entered his study when Sophia fled. Standing in the middle of the room, Tolstoy was pale, his lips trembling; he stared at one spot. "I was sorry for him and was frightened—I've never seen him like this before. Without saying a word to him, I ran to Sonya's room. She was very pitiable and kept repeating, like a mad woman: 'Why? What's the matter with him?'"[68] When, after the incident, Sophia had a miscarriage, Tolstoy promised to control his anger.

Tolstoy was exhausted with his work, unable to compromise quality, and Sophia had to share the tension. She wrote in her diary: "Lyovochka has been writing all winter, irritable and excited, often with tears in his eyes. I feel this novel of his will be superb. All the parts he has read to me have moved me almost to tears too."[69] That same winter, the children contracted scarlet fever. Little Tanya was unconscious for several days and Sophia was afraid of losing her. She nursed the children back to health. Drained by worry and sleeplessness, on top of copying for Tolstoy, she was "in a terrible state of agitated depression."[70]

Despite his deadlines, Tolstoy insisted on several sets of proofs and Sophia kept copying his corrections. Only infrequently, when proofs were dispatched and the children asleep, would the two have an evening of recreation. They would stay up late, playing duets. "Lev Nikolaevich was particularly fond of Haydn's and Mozart's symphonies. At that time I played rather badly, but I tried very hard to improve."[71] Their work on the novel united them: the bond established during *War and Peace* would prove indestructible.

In September 1867, Tolstoy traveled with Sophia's younger brother Stepan to visit the site of the Battle of Borodino. On this village field in

September 1812, a quarter million troops clashed during the largest and bloodiest single-day battle of the Napoleonic campaign. Tolstoy wished to "write a battle of Borodino, the like of which there has never been before." He promised to tell Sophia about his trip; meantime, he wanted her to write him more often: "Your letters made me feel good at heart, because there is *you* in them. And you put all the best of you into your letters and your thoughts about me . . . Your letters are an enormous pleasure to me, darling."[72]

Upon his return, Tolstoy related his impressions of the trip to Sophia. He often gave such talks before settling down to write. In the novel, he depicts Natasha as a perceptive listener, heeding Pierre's account of the war. "Not only her gaze, but her exclamations, and the brief questions she asked, showed Pierre that she understood precisely what he meant to convey . . . It was clear that she understood not only what he was telling, but also what he would have liked to but could not express in words."[73] Having an interested listener helped bring out his hero's best.

There were two weddings at Yasnaya in 1867. Sister Tanya married her cousin Sasha Kuzminsky. A young lawyer who would later have a brilliant career as a statesman, Kuzminsky was then a court investigator in Tula. However, at the age of twenty-three, he was considered too young to marry and Sophia's family was unenthusiastic.[74] The recently widowed Dyakov, a wealthy landowner, was believed a better match, even by Tolstoy. Tanya's wedding to Kuzminsky was in July and as her parents did not attend, Tolstoy was the proxy father of the bride. Shortly after, Tolstoy's brother Sergei Nikolaevich, with whom Tanya was in love, married his longtime partner, Masha.

Liza, the eldest Behrs sister, was the last to marry. She was twenty-five in January 1868, when Tolstoy and Sophia attended her wedding. It was cheerless because Behrs was gravely ill: only weeks earlier, he had suffered a stroke, which left him paralyzed on one side.

Liza's husband, Gavriil Pavlenkov, was a colonel in the Guards and a landowner. As Sophia remarked, he was "kind and rich but shouldn't have married because my sister remained a virgin." Eight years later, Liza divorced him to marry her cousin Alexander Behrs.[75] In *War and Peace,* Liza is depicted in the rational and insensitive Vera Rostov. In life, Liza was brilliant and ambitious, publishing many articles as well as a book on

Chapter Four

A Shadow Passed between Us

WITH THE PUBLICATION of *War and Peace,* Tolstoy established himself as the greatest living writer. But he and Sophia did not enjoy his success. At the height of eminence, Tolstoy became depressed; he frequently spoke of death. His hopelessness began to affect Sophia. As he traveled to Penza province, south of Moscow, to buy more land, she wrote him, "I am alone with my dark thoughts, suppositions, and fear. It's so hard to live in the world without you . . . Everything seems so shallow and petty without the best part, and the best—is you, only you, you alone, forever."[1]

In a simultaneous letter on September 4, 1869, Tolstoy wrote that "something extraordinary" happened to him when he spent a night in Arzamas. "I was terribly tired, I wanted to go to sleep and I felt perfectly well. But suddenly I was overcome by despair, fear and terror . . . I'll tell you the details of this feeling later: but I've never experienced such an agonizing feeling before and may God preserve anyone else from experiencing it."[2]

He gave up the idea of buying land and cut short his trip, later describing the troubling incident and his agonizing fear of death in his novella *Notes of a Madman.* Tolstoy had suffered bouts of despair before and had to be "constantly busy" to escape this condition. Sophia noted in her diary, "Sometimes (but only when he is away from his home and his family) he imagines that he is going mad, and so great is his fear of madness that I am terrified whenever he talks about it."[3] After the happy years when Tolstoy wrote *War and Peace,* he entered a period of mental inactivity and doubt, "the deadliest time."[4] Lying in bed during the day and staring emptily at one spot, he would growl at Sophia if she disturbed him: "Leave me alone, you can't let me even die in peace."[5]

Later, as he searched for a new theme to inspire him, his gloom receded and he gave Sophia talks on various subjects. She began to record his pronouncements in her journal. Before, she had been too busy to keep consistent records but "now is a good time to start." In February 1870, she wrote in "Notes for Future Reference": "*War and Peace* is finished and no major new work has been embarked upon yet." Tolstoy told her of plans to write a comedy "but I am sure this is not his real work."[6] Then he gave her a talk "about various Russian historical characters" from the epoch of Peter the Great. Simultaneously, he had a plot for a contemporary novel "about a married woman of noble birth who ruined herself."[7] This was a first mention of *Anna Karenina,* the novel he would begin three years later.

That winter, his cheerfulness returned sporadically. During happy days they skated on a pond at Yasnaya and Tolstoy amused himself with "all sorts of tricks, skating on one leg, then on two, skating backwards, going round in circles, and so on."[8] Sophia, a tireless skater, enjoyed the simple sensation of gliding. Occasionally, the family assembled in the drawing room for readings: Tolstoy read Jules Verne's *Twenty Thousand Leagues under the Sea* in French and illustrated the novel for the children. Other personal events were mostly erased from Sophia's memory that year. In June, she weaned son Lev and, soon after, became pregnant again.

At year's end Tolstoy began to study Greek with a theology student. He said he was living in Athens; life was only enjoyable when he learned "some new Greek word or phrase." Three months later, he was reading the *Odyssey* and the *Iliad,* rarely consulting a dictionary. Sophia checked his oral and written translations against Gnedich's standard and was amazed with his progress. Tolstoy told her he wanted to write a book as pure and elegant in style "as classical Greek literature, or Greek art."[9]

In February 1871, Sophia prematurely bore a sickly girl, Masha, and soon after, she contracted puerperal fever, which put her at death's door. A desperate Tolstoy telegraphed her pulse and other medical data to their family doctor in Moscow. In *Anna Karenina,* he would convey the actual drama: "The doctor and his colleagues said it was puerperal fever, which in ninety-nine cases out of a hundred ends in death. All day there was fever, delirium and unconsciousness. By midnight the sick woman lay without feeling and almost without pulse."[10] His heroine's survival is based on fact: Sophia's robust health pulled her through.

Sophia and sister Tanya (standing) in 1871. Sophia's hair was shaven after she'd had puerperal fever.

A month later, she made her first walk through the house, wearing a cap over her shaven head. During high fever, cold compresses had to be applied to her head and the hair had to go. Without time to recover, she had to look after Tolstoy, who suffered a new bout of depression and took to bed. He also developed arthritic pain in his knee, which made him shriek. It was during this difficult winter, with both of them ill, that Sophia felt "Lyovochka . . . is no longer the person he was. He says it's old age, I say it's illness." Family happiness was eclipsed: "A shadow seems to have passed between us . . . Now I am permanently beset by fears that something will happen."[11] Several months later, in Tula, Sophia had her picture taken, a portrait in a bonnet; Tolstoy said she looked like a martyress in it, "aged and thin, and pitiful."[12] In *Anna Karenina,* he gave her features to Dolly, exhausted after childbirth and illness, "her face pinched and thin, her big frightened eyes protruding on account of that thinness."[13]

When in spring Tolstoy developed a cough, Sophia persuaded him to take a rest in the Samara prairies. He dreaded consumption, which killed his two older brothers, and traveled there to drink the curative *kumis,* fermented mare's milk. Tolstoy left in June with Ivan Suvorov, his old manservant. Sophia's brother Stepan, a seventeen-year-old law student, would also join them. Stepan carried a small icon of Raphael's *Madonna della Sedia,* which Sophia was sending to Tolstoy. It was a present from Tolstoy's aunt Ergolskaya, who blessed him with it before he left for the Crimean War. Tolstoy was supposed to take the icon everywhere he traveled. Sophia wrote in her accompanying letter: "For God's sake, do not allow yourself to slip into fear, despair, and anxiety. Everything you do for your own calm and amusement—I will approve of it."[14]

She stayed at Yasnaya in the company of relatives who had assembled for the summer. Sister Tanya lived in her separate wing of the house with Sasha Kuzminsky and their two infant daughters. Varya and Liza, Maria Nikolaevna's daughters, also came. Tolstoy gave each of the nieces ten thousand rubles as dowries after publishing *War and Peace;* Sophia approved because the nieces were penniless. Liza, recently married, arrived with Leonid Obolensky, treasurer for the city of Moscow. Varya was being courted by Nikolai Nagornov, another Moscow government official.

Sophia wrote Tolstoy that the family had gathered around her and that she was happy to be at the center: "I'm asked questions on every subject, my opinion is respected, everyone is nice to me, and I'm so pleased."[15] Her mother was also at Yasnaya with Sophia's youngest brother, Vyacheslav. After Behrs died, Lyubov Alexandrovna had to vacate their Kremlin apartment and settled in Petersburg with her son.

The family drove for picnics to the edge of the old Zaseka forest, taking sweets and a samovar. From their spot in a clearing they watched peasants make hay and cook meals by their shelters. Sophia wrote Tolstoy, "Hay is fragrant, people are cheerful, the evening is fine and warm, the mist is beginning to rise . . . old oaks and the dazzling sunset. I haven't felt so good in a long time."[16] They went mushrooming, swimming, and riding; in the evenings, Tanya sang romances, accompanying herself on the guitar.

There was a new sport at Yasnaya—giant stride (*Pas de Géants*). It involved a type of maypole, with ropes attached to a swiveling top; the players used the ropes to take giant circular strides. Tolstoy ordered it from Poiret, the owner of a gymnastic school in Moscow. Sophia was delighted when, at her suggestion, Tolstoy purchased the contrivance. The pole was installed on the lawn and children and adults alike learned to leap around it. They amused themselves until dark, telling Sophia her idea was ingenious.

Tolstoy's first letters from Samara were cheerless: "I've begun to get a feeling of depression like a fever at 6 o'clock every evening . . . the sensation of which I can't convey better than by saying that soul and body part company."[17] He felt like crying when his depression robbed him of an ability to perceive the world, so vital to him: "I only feel 1/10 of what exists . . . I look at everything as though I were dead."[18] Sophia asked Tolstoy to stop learning "the hateful" Greek, which she blamed for his depression. No wonder they call it a "dead" language: it apparently inspires a "dead" outlook.

But Tolstoy's apathy slowly waned and his interest in life returned. He read little and enjoyed his "nomadic" existence, walking and hunting with Stepan in the prairie and living in a *kibitka*.[19] Invited to the Bashkir villages, the two participated in daylong feasts, eating roast mutton with their hands and drinking huge quantities of *kumis,* reminding Tolstoy of prehistoric times. Sophia asked whether he was writing in his nomad's tent, "with visions of the prairie, herds of horses . . . and the setting sun."[20] But he became absorbed in his new idea of buying an estate in Samara.

He wrote Sophia that the land there was cheap and he anticipated huge returns, despite drought. Having witnessed his farming fiascos at Yasnaya, she was skeptical. "What can I say to you about purchasing an estate there? . . . If you think it's profitable, it's your business, then I don't have an opinion. But living in the prairie without a single tree for hundreds of miles around—only extreme necessity would drive you there, one could never go voluntarily, particularly with five children . . . Finally, my opinion is expressed. Don't be cross, my dear; if I contradict you, do as you wish."[21] Tolstoy then made such practical decisions in their family.

He bought 6,750 acres, originally granted by the tsar to General Tuchkov, for twenty thousand rubles. In his acquisitions, as with all his projects and hobbies, Tolstoy loved his dream, and at this time was passionately interested in breeding and farming. He wanted to enlarge the family's fortune "in the shrewdest way" and already calculated future income from this new estate. Commenting on his projections, Sophia would later write, "Lev Nikolaevich imagined mountains of wheat and other goods, he pictured herds of amazing sheep and new breeds of horses born from Kirgizian mares and English stallions. But for all this, Lev Nikolaevich lacked patience and practical skill. Everything he acquired would soon go to waste."[22]

Tolstoy returned in time for their birthdays in August and they were reunited with the joy that had brightened their marriage. On August 28, Tolstoy's birthday, Sophia hosted a big reception with music, a special supper, and champagne. When in fall all the guests departed, happiness gave way to gloom. Their niece Varya noted in her diary: "Sonya is cheerless . . . I understand her. Lyovochka is irritable, ill, which is sad. I noticed that without him Sonya is calmer and happier."[23] The couple had tensions. After Masha's birth, when Sophia nearly died from puerperal fever, she did not want more children. Because Tolstoy objected to contraception, she avoided intimacy.

She also dreaded the return of Tolstoy's depression, particularly when he shared his dark thoughts: "He constantly drags me down into his own hopeless melancholy."[24] Having her sister around to discuss things was essential for her to cope.

In August, sister Tanya, who had been living in Tula, moved to Kutais,[25] in Georgia, where Kuzminsky was transferred. He was making a successful career as a government official; his postings would take them to several cities in the Caucasus, Kharkov, Kiev, and eventually Petersburg.

Tanya's letters described her journey through the Caucasus, along the Black Sea coast, and her engaging social life in Kutais. Yasnaya in October was cheerless, and looking at the dark clouds from her window, Sophia wrote her sister, "I often think, it must be warm and beautiful [in the Caucasus] and that geography and climate affect a person a great deal . . . Here it's muddy, nasty, and gloomy."[26] She became pregnant again—and as with each one of her pregnancies, she was emotionally and physically unwell, particularly in the first months.

But she summoned her energy when Tolstoy needed her help with his pedagogical project. He was absorbed in writing his own curriculum, primer, arithmetic, and readers, in his belief that "two generations of *all* Russian children, from tsars' to peasants', will study with the aid of this primer alone."[27] Sophia copied his numerous revisions, until she developed "disgust to paper and ink."[28] (As with his novels, he revised his primer many times.) At Tolstoy's request, she contributed her original stories for various reading levels. These were unpretentious but engaging episodes from her life: how her mother taught her to sew when she was six, and how she later taught her own daughter. A story about a tamed sparrow had traces of Turgenev's influence: she had heard his hunting tales in childhood. Her contribution would appear without credit in Tolstoy's collection.

Tolstoy was composing the school texts "with pride, confidence and the firm conviction that he was doing good and useful work."[29] Sharing this sentiment, Sophia praised the books to sister Tanya, promising to send copies upon publication: "We are now busy with children's books . . . You'll be glad we wrote them when you'll be teaching your own children."[30] As often happened in their marriage, Sophia did not know whether she liked the project because of its merits or because of Tolstoy's elation.

That year, a large addition to the Yasnaya house was built to accommodate their growing family. Before Christmas, when the addition was completed, Sophia hosted a masquerade and the usual tree party for the village children: her goal was "to keep everyone happy." She composed a magic tale for a puppet show; Varya added decorations and light effects.

Several evenings were spent dressing skeleton dolls. Sophia bought bare wooden dolls in bulk and had her children sew costumes from remnants. Each year, they designed new costumes: soldiers in red and blue uniforms, Scotsmen in kilts, a Russian nurse in a headdress, a gypsy with a red shawl, a tsarina, and whatever else their fantasies and fashion magazines inspired. These were given to the village children with other presents. Sophia would tell this story in her collection *Skeleton Dolls*.

The Dyakovs, Uncle Kostya, Liza with Obolensky, and Sophia's brother Sasha, as well as others, arrived for the holidays. Twenty people sat down for the feast, crowned by an enormous plum pudding made by their English governess. "After the dinner we all, big and little alike, played cat and mouse, blind man's buff, etc. Everything was so jolly."[31] The children, Tanya and Seryozha, were dressed as French marquises, Varya as a clown, and Liza as a muzhik, all in costumes Sophia had sewn. On Christmas Day, during a masquerade, with Uncle Kostya playing the piano, Sophia, dressed as a peasant, danced the Russian *trepak*. Dyakov was an animal trainer, leading a dancing goat—Tolstoy. Celebrations went on for three days: family and guests tobogganed, skated, and raced on troikas.

"It has been a happy winter," noted Sophia, "our souls have been in harmony again, and Lyovochka's health has not been bad."[32] Tolstoy wrote Alexandrine: "My life is just the same, i.e. I couldn't wish for anything better . . . The great joys are a family which is terribly fortunate, children who are fit and well, and, I'm almost certain, intelligent and unspoiled, and work."[33]

That same winter, he opened a school for peasant children in their house and engaged everyone to teach, even their older children and guests. Thirty-five children came regularly for classes. Tolstoy taught a large group of boys in his study; Sophia instructed eight girls and two boys in another room. Seryozha, Tanya, and even six-year-old Ilya taught pupils in the hall and played with them after classes. Within a week, the students grasped the alphabet and rudiments of spelling; after a month, everyone could read. Sophia wrote sister Tanya that there was a "crying need" to teach these children who worked "with such enjoyment and enthusiasm."[34] Teachers were equally motivated, proud of their students' success and boasting about it. "Every evening such a crowd comes in, noisy, reading aloud, storytelling—your head spins sometimes."[35] The project was useful for the family: their own children were well engaged and learned from the students. Tolstoy was occupied with pedagogy, work he loved, and Sophia supported his undertaking: "It would be a pity to give up now . . . A bit longer and they'll have it for the rest of their lives."[36] The school continued until summer.

In April, when proofs of the *ABC* arrived, Sophia helped Tolstoy meet his deadline: the books had to come out in time for a May pedagogical exhibition in Moscow. They proofread until four in the morning with windows open, hearing nightingales in the park.

Upon publication, the primers' poor reception disappointed Tolstoy: "If my novel had been such a failure I would readily have believed them and simply accepted that it was no good. But I feel quite convinced that my *ABC* is unusually good and they just didn't understand it."[37] Tolstoy, passionate about his projects and easily distraught if any one of them failed, would dismiss former achievements. He wrote Alexandrine that *War and Peace* was "repulsive" to him and he could not read some parts without shame.

On June 13, 1872, Sophia gave birth to son Petya, their sixth child, and soon admired his huge appetite and cheerfulness. To keep Sophia company, sister Tanya arrived from the Caucasus with children and staff, a journey made despite her late pregnancy. Tolstoy soon left to inspect their Samara estate, sending detailed letters to Sophia. The house was small and shabby, which upset him; he sent a floor plan with suggestions on how to remodel two large rooms. It was where the family would later spend several summers. He could not live there alone: "And to work without you—without a sense that you are around, I think I can't."[38]

In his absence, a bull gored a herdsman to death at Yasnaya. The Tula investigator charged Tolstoy with criminal negligence. Upon his return, he was put under house arrest until the end of an inquiry. Annoyed, he considered selling Yasnaya and moving to England with his family. He wrote Alexandrine, "My wife views the prospect with pleasure—she loves everything English . . . Our plan is to settle at first near London, and then to select a beautiful and healthy spot by the sea, wherever there are good schools, and buy a house and some land."[39] But upon receiving a letter from the local court, in which the investigator's mistake was acknowledged, Tolstoy gave up this idea. (The following year, another herdsman was gored to death at Yasnaya, which Tolstoy believed was an "incredible coincidence.")[40]

Now twenty-nine, Sophia wanted to travel and experience society, admitting to her sister that at Yasnaya she was occasionally bored and lonesome. "Only in work I can escape this cowardly boredom."[41] Over the years, Tolstoy had talked of living in Moscow, England, or by the Black Sea, where he considered buying land. This idea also never materialized because Tolstoy preferred to live and work at Yasnaya and Sophia's life was subordinated to his needs.

Sophia invested her energy in teaching their children. Although they had regular teachers, she and Tolstoy supplemented instruction. (Tolstoy was still in charge of their education, himself interviewing and hiring teachers and governesses. A decade later, his views would change drastically.) Sophia taught music, languages, and history; trying to be thorough, she compiled and illustrated her own Russian grammar books. She also attempted to write a popular history to replace the banal textbooks. The project interested her and promised satisfaction but she did not complete it: "Again my endeavors would be upset with my new pregnancy, nursing, or simply lack of time and fatigue."[42]

In the fall, when Tolstoy resumed his research for a historical novel set in the period of Peter the Great, Sophia observed him with interest, reporting to her brother Stepan: "Lyovochka is surrounded by a pile of books, portraits, paintings; he is absorbed in reading and taking notes. In the evenings . . . he shares his plans with me, tells me what he wants to write; occasionally, he is disappointed and despairs, as he thinks that nothing will come of it; sometimes, he is very close to begin to write with great enthusiasm."[43]

Tolstoy had earlier described this particular period to Fet; he was writing nothing "but working painfully. You can't imagine how difficult I find this preparatory work of plowing deeply the field which I'm *compelled* to sow."[44] During this time of doubt and research, Sophia tried to chronicle what route his inspiration would take.

As he told Sophia, before he began a historical novel he needed to know intimately the lives of ordinary people. But despite reading a mass of materials on the eighteenth century, he said he still lacked detail. Tolstoy occasionally read his research notes to her, which she found fascinating. "He jots down in various little notebooks anything that might come in useful for an accurate description of the manners, customs, clothes, houses, and the general way of life in this period . . . Elsewhere he jots down any ideas he may have about the characters, plot, poetic passages, and so on. It's like a mosaic . . . He is still reading documents, and one by one the characters are all coming to life before his eyes. He has written about ten different opening chapters, but isn't happy with any of them. Yesterday he said: 'The machine is all ready, now it must be made to work.'"[45] She was already looking forward to reading, copying, and discussing it but he put aside the project: his characters from Peter the Great's time had to wait. "They may begin to move and breathe, but not now."[46]

Tolstoy suddenly became immersed in another project. A year earlier, there was an incident in their neighborhood, reported in the local newspaper: an unknown young woman, well dressed, jumped under the passing freight train and was cut in half. Tolstoy attended the postmortem and the spectacle had "a terrible effect on him," he told Sophia. The woman's skull was "smashed in and her naked body frightfully mutilated." The victim was Anna Pirogova, the mistress of their neighbor Alexander Bibikov; she had committed suicide in a fit of jealousy.

In March 1873, when Tolstoy told Sophia that he had written a page and a half and was pleased with it, she assumed it was another beginning for his historical novel. But it turned out he was writing a contemporary work, "about a married woman of noble birth who ruined herself,"[47] which would become *Anna Karenina*. By the time he embarked on it, Sophia had nearly forgotten about the occurrence in their neighborhood. The novel would employ Anna Pirogova's suicide in its ending. "So strange, the way he just pitched straight into it," she wrote in "Notes for Future Reference."

The opening of the novel was inspired by Pushkin's *Tales of Belkin*. Sophia prepared this book for Seryozha and left it in the drawing room; Tolstoy opened it while having coffee, read the first paragraph, and "went into ecstasies."[48] He praised Pushkin's concise, matter-of-fact style: "How good and simple. Straight to the point. That's how one should write." That same evening, he wrote the famous opening of *Anna Karenina* and read to Sophia the celebrated lines about happy and unhappy families and the confusion in the Oblonsky household. She entered the date in her diary: March 19, 1873. It was the brightness and simplicity of Pushkin's prose that inspired him: "I have learned so much from Pushkin . . . He is my father, and one must always be guided by him."[49]

And so, after studying Greek, devoting himself to pedagogy, and developing a plot for a historical novel, Tolstoy settled down to write *Anna Karenina*. As soon as he began writing, Sophia resumed her "responsibilities of copying and keenly sympathizing with his work."[50]

Chapter Five

Observing the Artist

I N MARCH 1873, Tolstoy became absorbed with *Anna Karenina,* completing the plot outline by the end of the month. Sophia happily remarked in her diary, "Lyovochka is writing his novel, which is going well."[1] However, his enthusiasm did not last: spring, as always, brought Tolstoy fear of consumption. He wanted to go to their new Samara estate for another *kumis* cure, which helped restore his strength in the past. Once he expressed this wish, Sophia knew that she had to travel with him. He did not like to part from her, and besides, she felt responsible for practical arrangements, the side of life Tolstoy found frustrating. It was then decided the entire family would go.

Tolstoy went to Moscow to buy forty-three items on Sophia's shopping list. Despite his simple tastes, he patronized the most reputable stores, making quality purchases and overspending, habits he ascribes to Pierre in *War and Peace.* Meanwhile, to save, Sophia was sewing clothes for the children: "I am simply swamped with sewing."[2] They needed spare clothing for the arid prairie over the summer because water was in short supply and doing laundry would be difficult.

A considerable part of their luggage and provisions were sent in advance. Sophia spent hours kneeling before huge trunks, packing linen and clothing. Ahead of her was a long journey with six children and overnight stops at dirty stations. They would travel by rail to Nizhny Novgorod, by boat on the Volga, and finally from Samara, in a caravan of horse-drawn carriages over the dusty prairie.

In the middle of preparations, the family received a letter from sister Tanya. Tolstoy told Sophia there had been "a great, great misfortune"; she guessed correctly that Dasha, Tanya's eldest daughter, and the family's favorite, had died. Although Sophia's intuition was well known, Tolstoy was still impressed: "How could she know this?"[3]

Dasha had died from typhus at four. Tanya's letter described the girl's final days in detail; reading it, Sophia imagined every moment. She suffered along with her sister, to "lift some grief from your soul," as she wrote. "How many times, Tanya, we spoke with each other that our children might die and always quickly chased away these thoughts." But despite her grief, Sophia sensed that comfort was to be found in their strong faith that Dasha was in a better world: "Thy will be done!"[4] Tolstoy, in his letter, wrote that "only religion can bring comfort."[5]

The Tolstoys, along with their staff, were leaving for Samara in early June; in all, the group consisted of sixteen people. During their last night at home, Sophia sat down to paint travel books to amuse her children during the long journey. Over the years, she made dozens of such books for her family and to give away: the children preferred them to store-bought ones. These picture books, none of which survives, told amusing stories. Daughter Tanya recalls:

> The things she managed to cram into those pictures! There were terrifying wolves carrying off little children into dark woods; a scene of mushroom gathering, another of swimming in a river; a fire with figures of children carrying buckets of water; hares stealing cabbages and carrots; a Christmas tree decorated with gingerbread, apples and candles . . . Mama's drawings displayed scant respect for the rules of perspective, proportion, or verisimilitude . . . the results were naïve. But what a wealth of content![6]

In the morning, Tolstoy assigned everyone to various carriages. Sophia was in a barouche with Petya, whom she still nursed at twelve months. On the train, she slept with him on the floor of their crowded compartment, which she covered with a spread. It was her first journey through the vast country and her first time sailing on the Volga, which impressed her with its calm and majesty.

From Samara, the family had to drive for about 130 miles through arid prairie: "It was very windy, dusty, and wearingly hot." A country inn, where they stopped for the night, was infested with parasites, so the family slept outside: the children in carriages, Tolstoy and Sophia on a haystack.

Eight days after leaving home, the family arrived. The house consisted of four small bedrooms; the men's quarters were still being renovated, so Tolstoy and the boys slept in a shed. Sophia promptly took charge of the kitchen and because of an ongoing threat of cholera in the region imposed strict hygiene. When flies and poor sanitation caused stomach upsets, she treated family and staff with remedies she had brought from home. Tolstoy wrote sister Tanya that their Samara vacation surpassed his expectations: Sophia "understood" the subtle beauty of the prairie and adapted to a Spartan life.

"It's been two weeks since we have settled on the farmstead in the middle of the infinite steppe," Sophia wrote Tanya. "We use water from the well for drinking and washing. There's nowhere to swim or hide from the heat. We sit either in the shade of the veranda . . . or in a room with closed shutters."[7] During the hottest time of day, she sat in the shade with *Othello,* reading it in English to better grasp the work.

Her letters described herds of wild horses, oxen plowing fields, the prairie with its infinite space and inescapable sun. This area, once populated by the Scythians, was settled by many ethnic groups, including the Bashkirs, Kirgiz tribesmen, Mordovians,[8] Chuvashi,[9] Cossacks, and Tartars. Perhaps nowhere else could so many different cultures be found in one place, where Christians and Muslims lived together in perfect harmony. The Tolstoys enjoyed the hospitality of Russians, Cossacks, and Bashkirs when touring their villages.

The Bashkir women, in their long, flowing garments of striped cotton, prepared the *kumis* in their *kibitkas,* the women's quarters separated from the men's by a curtain. Sympathetic to the Muslim women "condemned to perpetual seclusion inside their *kibitkas,*"[10] Sophia would sit with them, sew, and watch them prepare the brew. It was fermented in horsehide containers and stirred with long sticks. Tolstoy would sit with the men, drinking his *kumis* from a wooden bowl. While he consumed huge quantities, Sophia detested its foul smell.

They went for rides and walks in the prairie to watch sunsets and observed new and interesting life. "The steppe lost most of its beauty because of drought, but at night there is something lovely and alien in the upturned bowl of the heavens and in the limitless expanse of land; sometimes you hear men playing their pipes in the distance or oxen tinkling their bells. Ten oxen pull a plough here; everything is so unfamiliar and gigantic, with those plowmen, mowers, and other laborers staying in the field for the night with lights you can see here and there... *Stipa,* the white silky grass in the fields, is really beautiful, particularly in the sunset: it's so clear and light, as though floating above the land."[11]

In July, the prairie was burned by the sun; the locals could not remember such a severe drought in the past fifty years. Crops at the Tolstoys' farm were meager, but elsewhere, around distant villages, fields were bare and there was not enough water for the cattle. "Here there was no rain since the holy week, so we've been living for a month and watching the infinite space gradually wither before our eyes and horror descending on the local people who struggle for the third year in a row to feed themselves and to sow again." Another crop failure was anticipated, and compared to this calamity Sophia felt their financial losses were secondary. Their family was fortunate, and while some bad luck was inevitable, "so let it be with the money."[12]

Their farmstead became a center for the locals, with class and cultural differences practically nonexistent. "You won't believe, Tanya, how close we are here with the people: today we drank tea with a Russian muzhik and a Bashkir; they are like friends of ours, and are very useful with their practical advice and help."[13] For their part, the Tolstoys provided employment to many during harvest, which cost them more than it yielded. But for people whose crops had failed, it was a chance to feed themselves, their families, and their livestock.

The Tolstoys refused no one: several hundred laborers "set up their tents in the field, grazed the oxen, and harvested wheat." Some families camped in the yard, sleeping near the barns, in or underneath their carts. They arrived with "cows, dogs, and even hens" because of food and water shortages. Although the harvest of 1873 was meager, a multinational, colorfully dressed mass of reapers in the field presented a grand spectacle.

The family hired local cooks to bake bread and make porridge to feed the workers. While it was becoming apparent that people would not survive another winter without help, the authorities refused to recognize the crisis. Sophia wrote an article about the Samara famine, with an appeal for help, and showed it to Tolstoy. He read it: "But who will believe you without facts?"[14] He promptly set out with Sophia's brother Stepan to survey the province and assess one in every ten households.

Upon his return, Tolstoy wrote a report about the famine, which was published in the *Moscow Gazette.* As her article remained unpublished, Sophia would refer to "our article."[15] Tolstoy also wrote Alexandrine, who had close ties to court, asking her to appeal to "the good and the mighty in this world."[16] The aid began to pour in and, although unevenly distributed, many benefited. As Sophia remarked in her memoir, "It was not in vain that God sent us that year to live in the Samara steppes; our presence may have saved many people from starvation."[17] Two decades later, the Tolstoys would organize another relief operation on a much larger scale.

When the family returned to Yasnaya, Sophia weaned her robust baby and lived through the trial of separation she had experienced with each child: "I blessed him, and cried and prayed for him. It is very hard, this first separation from one's baby."[18] Without a chance to regain her strength, she became pregnant the following month. "I am so weak, I am bent over."[19] But her pregnancy was not only a strain on her body, it was also unwanted. Sophia conceived when she dreamt of a respite, wanting to regain her spirits. She was emotionally unprepared to nurture new life. "People who never experienced this maternal, utterly physiological life cannot imagine what a difficult, unbearable toil this is."[20] Tolstoy depicts her incessant motherhood in *Anna Karenina,* where he also makes a reference to contraception. (It was marginally practiced in their day, although discussed clandestinely. Tolstoy was the first Russian writer to raise the issue.) But practicing contraception was against Tolstoy's beliefs.

After the summer break, Tolstoy resumed writing *Anna Karenina.* At this time, the famous portraitist Ivan Kramskoy arrived. He had been commissioned by the Tretyakov Gallery to paint prominent Russians and persuaded Tolstoy to sit. Sophia was able to observe two creative giants at work. "I remember entering the small drawing room, observing both artists: one is painting Tolstoy's portrait, the other writing his novel *Anna Karenina*. Both serious and absorbed, both genuine artists of great magnitude; I felt admiration for them."[21] Sophia asked Kramskoy to make a copy of that portrait, to which he replied that it was easier to paint another original, so he painted two portraits simultaneously.

Kramskoy's painting captured the magnetic power of Tolstoy's gaze. Daughter Tanya recalls the expressiveness and changeability of her father's deep-seated blue eyes, "sometimes gentle and caressing, sometimes merry, sometimes severe and inquisitorial."[22] In 1904, when Sophia became obsessed with painting, she copied Tolstoy's portraits by various artists, including Kramskoy. She executed this task with surprising boldness, given that she never studied art. But Kramskoy's technique was beyond her and she could not capture that all-penetrating gaze. Instead, she depicted the expression in Tolstoy's eyes she knew and loved, "smiling and kind, and excited."[23]

Tolstoy did not have the patience to sit through Kramskoy's entire session and left on a hunting trip just as the painter finished his head and hands. The rest of the portrait was completed in Tolstoy's absence. Sophia found it incomprehensible that Tolstoy had no time to sit for a portrait that would last forever. She watched Kramskoy stuff Tolstoy's gray blouse with rags and place the headless dummy onto a chair to model the torso. Because Sophia knew how Kramskoy finished the portrait, Tolstoy's torso in the painting always appeared artificial to her.

In November, baby Petya died of a throat infection. Sophia, again pregnant, was devastated: "I had fed him for fourteen and a half months. What a bright, happy little boy—I loved my darling too much and now there is nothing. He was buried yesterday. I cannot reconcile the two Petyas, the living and the dead; they are both precious to me, but what does the living Petya, so bright and affectionate, have in common with the dead one, so cold and still and serious?"[24] Petya was buried in the Kochaki family cemetery, near the ancient Nikolsky church, behind the tomb of Tolstoy's parents. Sophia was stunned when she saw him exposed to snow and frost, lying in an open coffin in a white dress: "I nursed him . . . I shielded him from drafts, I dressed him warmly . . . now he is frozen solid."[25] Tolstoy would use her experiences to depict a mother's grief at the loss of her child in *Anna Karenina:*

> And again there came to her imagination the cruel memory, eternally gnawing at her mother's heart, of the death of her last infant boy, who had died of croup, his funeral, the universal indifference before that small, pink coffin, and her own heart-rending, lonely pain before the pale little forehead with curls at the temples, before the opened, surprised little mouth she had glimpsed in the coffin just as it was covered by the pink lid with the lace cross.[26]

Sophia had a premonition that the family was going through "a patch of grief" and the worst was not over. Indeed, in their house alone there would be five deaths within three years. (The couple's three children and Tolstoy's old aunts died during this time.) Tolstoy wrote Alexandrine, "When burying Petya I was concerned for the first time about where I am to be laid . . . It had the same effect on Sonya, despite her youth."[27] Sophia fenced the plot around Petya's grave, reserving a place for herself: "It's my best and most rightful spot; until then everything is temporary."[28]

Her way out of hardship was to lose herself in work. She lived by the needs of the day, running the house, dealing with staff, rehearsing piano duets with Seryozha and Tanya, and sewing shirts for all of her children. On top of this, she was coping with a difficult pregnancy: "My back hurts so much that I want to cry sometimes; I am weak and short of breath."[29] At the end of her long day, she would copy for Tolstoy, a task she never considered burdensome.

Having completed the first part of *Anna Karenina,* Tolstoy was preparing it for publication. "You will like Lyovochka's new novel," Sophia reported to sister Tanya, "it will be very good, as to when he completes it—God knows."[30] Tolstoy made continual revisions; she copied with no end in sight.

Tolstoy took the completed part to the printers, deciding to publish it himself. Sophia, in his absence, copied chapters of the second part. When proofs began to arrive, she helped Tolstoy meet his deadlines. Then they would sit until one o'clock in the morning, talking and reading, and have a late supper, which Sophia warmed up on a spirit lamp.

Sophia was overdue when on April 22 she gave birth to their seventh child, Nikolai. In the absence of her regular midwife, a village woman assisted. The couple expected a girl "but a boy was born, just like the other we lost."[31] Sophia was painfully tender with the newborn, loving him "for Petya who died and for the baby himself."[32]

In the summer of 1874, when sister Tanya visited Yasnaya with her family, Sophia felt rejuvenated. They all went for picnics, made jam outside, played lawn games, went mushrooming, and enjoyed their children's company, that "wild but sweet and cozy little world, their . . . interests, their joys, and sorrows."[33] Their summer fun went into the novel where Tolstoy portrays Sophia as Dolly, "surrounded by all her bathed, wetheaded children."

> To touch all those plump little legs, pulling stockings on them, to take in her arms and dip those naked little bodies and hear joyful and frightened shrieks; to see the breathless faces of those splashing little cherubs, with their wide, frightened and merry eyes, was a great pleasure for her.[34]

Tolstoy's old aunt Tatyana Ergolskaya died in June. Later that summer Tolstoy traveled to Samara with their eldest, Seryozha, to inspect the estate. He soon reported that there was another crop failure in Samara. That year, the harvest was abundant elsewhere in the province and "the only place . . . that was missed by the rain was my estate . . . I went there and couldn't believe my eyes, and felt hurt."[35] Against his expectations, the Samara estate did not produce revenue; in fact, he estimated the family lost twenty thousand rubles in two years, a considerable sum by his standards and a humbling experience.

And there was more trouble to come. Tolstoy lost interest in the novel and directed the printers to stop typesetting. Instead, he became preoccupied with elementary education, passionately advocating his particular method of teaching literacy. He opened schools and dreamt of organizing colleges to train peasant teachers. While touring the new schools, he was struck by the sight of "ragged, dirty, skinny children with their bright eyes" and wanted to rescue them from drowning in darkness. Real people started to interest him more than fictional ones.

In October, Sophia reported to sister Tanya that work on the novel had come to a halt and Tolstoy was spending his time "either teaching in school or hunting or sitting in his study downstairs with the teachers, whom he instructs about how they should teach."[36] He said the novel was repulsive to him and he wanted to give it up.

As he revised his *ABCs*, Sophia complained to her brother Stepan: "Lyovochka became immersed in *public education* . . . and this occupies him morning and night. I watch it all in bewilderment, regretting that his energies are being wasted on such pursuits instead of writing the novel; and I fail to understand the usefulness of all this, for his activities concern only a small corner of Russia, the Krapivensky district."[37] To her sister, she admitted she could not sympathize with his educational projects: "If he were writing his novel, it would be a lot better."[38]

> There isn't much to tell about myself. I teach and nurse, like a machine, from morning till night. And I copied the *ABCs*; but when I felt that the end was not near, all these little words and phrases, "Masha ate her kasha," etc., began to annoy me so much that I dropped it altogether; let a scribe do this work. My task was to copy out the immortal *War and Peace* and *Anna [Karenina]*."[39]

At the time he put aside *Anna Karenina,* they were "swamped with letters from editors offering ten thousand in advances and five hundred silver rubles per printer's page." Tolstoy refused even to discuss the matter, although the family was under financial strain following losses in Samara. Some forest near the border of Yasnaya had to be sold to settle debts. But as Sophia explained to her sister, it was not the money she regretted: Tolstoy had abandoned his writing.

> Never mind the money, it's his vocation, writing the novels, which I love, value, and feel so enthusiastic about, while these *ABCs*, arithmetics, and grammars I despise . . . What's lacking in my life now is Lyovochka's work, which I always enjoyed and admired. You see, Tanya, I am a true writer's wife, so close to my heart do I keep our creative work.[40]

(With her family Sophia often used the collective "we" when referring to Tolstoy's projects.)

By the end of the year Tolstoy returned to the novel, although reluctantly and still lacking inspiration. He promised it to the *Russian Herald,* which had published *War and Peace.* This put Sophia in a mood to celebrate and she made elaborate preparations for Christmas. She hosted a masquerade and put on a show, with the family, guests, and servants acting scenes from a folk play. Stepan, Tolstoy's favorite among her brothers, made a surprise visit; Sophia was so happy to see him, she "squealed with joy."[41] Sister Tanya sent a large Oriental carpet from the Caucasus, to cover the slippery parquet in the drawing room. Sophia and Tolstoy spread it out, remembering their older daughter's dreadful accident in November. While sliding in her shoes on the floor, Tanya had fallen, broke her collarbone, and struck her head. For two days she lay semiconscious, as cold compresses were applied to her head and leeches to her ears. Tolstoy took her for a consultation in Moscow and the couple was relieved by the doctors' reassurances.

In January 1875, Nikolai developed meningitis. Sophia watched her baby go "through all the stages of this hopeless disease."[42] As Tolstoy wrote his editor and friend Nikolai Strakhov, she spent three weeks by the boy's bedside, despairing "one minute that he will die, and the next that he will live and be an idiot."[43] She would forever remember the boy's frenzied look during the illness, his insatiable appetite when she nursed him, and her own sense of helplessness. "His death was different from Petya's, who was taken away from us unexpectedly . . . this little one was dying for almost a month and we were in torment watching him suffer."[44]

On February 22, the day of Nikolai's funeral, Sophia and Tolstoy stood in the family cemetery. It was -20°C and windy; the couple worried over each other's health. The wind was ripping the baby's muslin blanket and wreath; filled with foreboding, Sophia fled. She poured out her grief to sister Tanya: "I look at my children and I ponder, 'Why do I have to teach them, torment them, scold them, while, perhaps, they won't live.'"[45] In *Anna Karenina,* Tolstoy captures this sense of futility in a mother's monologue:

"Then the children's illnesses, this eternal fear; then their upbringing . . . education, Latin—all of it so incomprehensible and difficult.
And on top of it all, the death of these same children . . . And all that for
what? What will come of it all?"[46]

Their family's grief had a sudden effect on Tolstoy: during his son's
illness "his mental valve" became unblocked. As he wrote Strakhov,
"It's strange: I feel the need and the joy of work as never before."[47] He
repeated to Fet, with the same surprise, that he experienced a rush of
creative ideas "at the very worst time of the child's illness."[48] Sophia felt
alone in her grief but when copying Tolstoy's new chapters, she was
happy and spiritually alive.

Anna Karenina began to appear in installments. In mid-February,
during their grieving, Strakhov wrote that readers were ecstatic and the
reception nearly exceeded that of *War and Peace.* The news left Tolstoy
almost "indifferent." Sophia wrote listlessly, "Lyovochka's novel is being
published, people say it's frightfully successful, and I feel so strange: we
have such grief, and everyone there is celebrating us."[49]

Tolstoy was working intensely, revising completed parts for publication and adding chapters; Sophia was copying daily. Daughter Tanya,
then ten, would recall Sophia settling down at her desk in the evenings.
Although behind her was a long day, it was clear "from the expression of
concentration on her face, that for her the most important time . . . was
just beginning." Occasionally, Tolstoy approached her as she was copying
and looked over her shoulder. "Then my mother would take his big hand
and kiss it with love and veneration, while he tenderly stroked her dark,
shining hair then bent to kiss the top of her head."[50]

Only a few months after Nikolai's death, Sophia was pregnant again.
It was spring, a time of apathy for Tolstoy; he looked forward to another
summer in Samara. Sophia, lacking strength, dreaded the difficult journey. She had a nervous collapse and spent several days in bed. Tolstoy became deeply concerned when she developed a cough and began spitting
blood. He took her to Moscow to consult their family physician, Grigory
Zakharin. During his examination Sophia shrieked from pain in her right
shoulder and arm. Zakharin forbade physical work, copying, and even

teaching, and prescribed "a regimen of silence."[51] The doctor's verdict was that "my health, particularly my nerves, were in a bad shape . . . that I over-exerted myself." He admonished Tolstoy, "But you did not spare her."[52]

With Tolstoy and everyone at home now treating her considerately, Sophia summoned her strength. She had the capacity to bounce back quickly, and within weeks was packing for Samara. She had been looking forward to a relaxing summer at Yasnaya with her mother and brothers, but had to cancel their visit. Her selflessness was the bane of her life.

Tolstoy wrote *Anna Karenina* with long interruptions, cooling off to his work at times, then declaring his intention to drop it. Their Samara vacation did not help. The fall of 1875 was particularly difficult: Tolstoy was forcing himself to resume the "dull, commonplace *Anna Karenina*" and get it out of the way.[53] Unable to make progress, he hunted obsessively.

In October, the children caught whooping cough. Sophia, tending to them while pregnant, contracted the disease for the second time in her life. On November 1, she prematurely bore a girl, Varya, who died soon after. After giving birth, Sophia developed peritonitis and suffered excruciating pain during paroxysms of coughing. Again, she was at death's door. Treatment consisted of leeches applied to her womb to reduce inflammation, and bromides, opium, and ice packs to control pain.

During the "two tormenting weeks" when Sophia fought for her life, doctors and nurses were constantly present, a source of annoyance to Tolstoy, who eschewed medicine. In a letter to Fet, Tolstoy described family life during this bout of grief: "Fear, horror, death, the children's merriment, eating, haste, doctors, falsehood, death, horror."[54] As before, death's proximity stimulated his thought, he admitted: "All this time—2 weeks—I've been looking after a sick wife who gave birth to a stillborn child and has been at death's door. But it's a strange thing—I've never thought with such vigor about the problems which interest me as at this time." He was reading Wilhelm Wundt, the German psychologist, and again abandoned his novel: "My God, if only someone would finish *A. Karenina* for me! It's unbearably repulsive."[55]

While Sophia was recovering, Tolstoy's old aunt Pelageya Yushkova became bedridden. Sophia had to supervise care for the immobile patient. The aunt's death in December affected Tolstoy more than the deaths of his children. He had lived with her as a student; she was the last link to his parents. That winter, he frequently complained of depression, writing to his brother that it was time for him to die. With Tolstoy's love of life, which he depicted with greater reality than the actual world, it was painful for Sophia to see him so depressed, perennially talking about death.

Despite Tolstoy's melancholy weighing on her, Sophia found strength to carry on. In her memoir, she recalls, "I was lonesome, working beyond strength . . . while Lev Nikolaevich would often tell me that his life is over, it's time to die, and he can enjoy nothing."[56] Watching Tolstoy struggle with depression, "despondent and dejected for days and weeks on end," she waited patiently and with hope "that God will light the spark of life in Lyovochka and he will be once more the person he used to be."[57]

Sophia hoped he would return to the novel. Although she did not talk to him directly about it, he read this in her eyes. Once, he surprised her by saying: "Don't nag me that I'm not writing, my head is heavy!" To sister Tanya, Sophia explained that she had not said anything: she did not dare. His readers across the country were waiting for Tolstoy to complete the novel—but even this did not matter. She continued, "How can I nag? What right do I have?"[58]

Before Christmas, when Tolstoy resumed writing, she broke the news: "Lyovochka is working very assiduously on *Anna Karenina* and if it were not for the sad story with the aunt, I would have been copying it already and the new chapters would appear in January."[59] But his writing did not flow as before. When the chapters appeared in the *Russian Herald* Sophia felt they were somewhat "dry"; this was also Tolstoy's opinion.

However, both were pleased with the following installment, which contained the chapters that describe Levin's proposal to Kitty, drawn from their own betrothal. The installment also contained a chapter of Anna Karenina's near-death experience when she contracts puerperal fever after the birth of her daughter. All this was only too familiar to Sophia.

In the spring of 1876, when Sophia suffered a miscarriage, her condition deprived Tolstoy of his peace of mind. "My wife has been dangerously ill," he admitted to writer Pavel Golokhvastov. "Now she is in bed again, and you tremble every moment lest the situation should get worse."[60] Sophia described their state of affairs to her sister: "Lyovochka is troubled with my illness and this distracts him from writing."[61]

Tolstoy was obsessively revising galley proofs, undeterred by telegrams from the *Russian Herald* with pleas to speed up proofreading. The phrase "Anna Karenina" became commonplace in the household and the older children observed "both *papa* and *maman*" at work. Sophia copied Tolstoy's corrections and insertions, despite being unwell:

> She would sit up all night making a fresh copy of the whole thing. In the morning the new pages, covered with her small clear handwriting, would be neatly piled on her table, ready to be sent back by post "when Lyovochka gets up." But first *papa* had to take them to his study to look over them "for the last time," and by evening it was the same thing all over again: everything had been rewritten and scribbled over ... Publication of the novel in *The Russian Herald* was held up more than once because of this rewriting, and sometimes months passed before the next installment appeared.[62]

Sophia dreamt of a holiday abroad when the novel was completed. Her mother was traveling in Italy; Sophia longed for picture galleries and the sea, which she had never seen. Tolstoy promised to consider a European vacation but was clearly reluctant: "It's very likely that we shall go abroad soon, and probably to Italy, which is so repulsive to me, but less so than Germany. In Europe it seems to me that I could only live in England, but people go away from there for their health, and there is no point in going there."[63] The final argument against the travel was the expense.

But cost was not a problem when in September Tolstoy traveled to Samara to oversee the arrival of a shipment of purebred English stallions. He bought them in Orenburg, southeast of Samara, by the Urals. Several steeds mysteriously disappeared en route and were said to have drowned (or sold for vodka, as Sophia cynically observed). Tolstoy then owned herds of wild horses, which he wanted to cross with the English purebred steeds. A team of keepers and grooms was engaged for his stud farm. Several years later, when he cooled off to the project, the expensive stallions went to waste.

As he traveled to Samara, Tolstoy wrote to thank Sophia for letting him pursue his hobby. He knew it was difficult for her. "I've seen the effort you made to overcome yourself, as not to hinder me ... and I love you even more for doing it." He also wrote that he was imagining her the way he loved her most—the girl in a lilac dress at her parents' dacha in Porkovskoe; the vision excited and softened him.[64] It was an indirect way to thank her for sacrificing her European holiday, as well as a reference to the novel where he depicts her in her youth.

During Tolstoy's absence, Sophia reread his diaries and drafts and suddenly felt "a great desire to write his biography."[65] She had a wealth of material but realized there was a serious obstacle: she could not be impartial. Two years later, Sophia would interview Tolstoy for a biographical essay, which he said was excellent. It was well written, utterly factual, and excluded any interpretation on her part.

Tolstoy's trip to Samara did not lift his depression, as they both had hoped: he told Sophia his brain was asleep. He went hunting and played the piano for hours; as he observed, "perhaps, in music, as well as in hunting, he looked for relief from the questions and doubts which tormented him."[66] He despaired over his creative ability. One November day, he told her that he had some ideas for the novel: he was sitting in his study, examining his dressing gown. "And suddenly this piece of embroidery on my sleeve suggested a whole chapter to me. Anna is cut off from all the joys of this side of a woman's life, for she is alone, other women spurn her, and she has no one to talk to about all the ordinary, everyday things that interest women."[67] It was at moments like this, when Tolstoy intimated his ideas to Sophia, that she felt involved "in serious and purposeful work."[68] His writing gave her a sense of mission.

Sophia soon reported to her sister, "At last we are writing *Anna Karenina* in earnest, i.e., without interruptions. Lyovochka is excited and absorbed, adding a whole chapter every day; I am copying for him eagerly; there are freshly copied pages of the chapter, written yesterday, underneath this letter."[69]

During the winter and spring of 1877, *Anna Karenina* was making an "astonishing, wild success" with the public.[70] The chapters produced an "explosion" in literary circles and reviews were ecstatic. Every installment was an event anxiously anticipated by the public. Tolstoy's editor, Strakhov, quipped that each piece was announced in the press with an urgency similar to reporting a war.

In January, while Tolstoy was completing the novel, Sophia went to Petersburg on her own. She had been unwell for two years and Tolstoy (although he did not believe in medicine) wanted her to be examined. He insisted that she consult celebrity clinician Sergei Botkin, a close friend of Alexandrine.[71]

On the train a lady in her compartment was reading *Anna Karenina* in the *Russian Herald,* and Sophia enjoyed her husband's public success for the first time. Katkov, the editor of the *Russian Herald,* was also on the train. Newspapers were full of reviews of the serialized novel and she saved them to take home. In Petersburg, Sophia met Alexandrine, her husband's confidante. Once intimidated by this worldly woman, dreaming to be like her, Sophia was now her equal.

Later, describing to Tolstoy her first meeting with Sophia, Alexandrine suggested Sophia carried some of his aura and resembled his likable heroines: "First of all, I feel I've long known her, and even her appearance is *precisely* what I have pictured from far away. Moreover, she is nice from head to toe, modest, intelligent, sincere, and cordial . . . She made a warm impression, such that I cannot possibly convey; I am all saturated with her and with you . . . In her voice there is something from you, some of your intonations, and I also liked that."[72] Sophia's friendship with Alexandrine would last longer than did Tolstoy's. When he rebelled against the Church, both women, deeply religious, were offended.

Professor Botkin found "nothing serious" with Sophia's health, except for her nerves. His prescriptions were commonplace, as she informed Tolstoy: potassium arsenite, or arsenic, and kali bromide to calm the nerves. (It was not yet known that side effects of potassium arsenite included nervous disorders: the cure was worse than the illness.)

During her brief stay in Petersburg Sophia attended a performance of Verdi's *Aida* and visited the Hermitage, where she was fascinated with Raphael, Rubens, and Murillo. She would have liked to go back and view the art again, but had to hurry home. Tolstoy wrote that he missed her badly: "I'm trying not to think about you. Yesterday, I approached your desk and jumped away as if burnt, so as not to visualize you."[73]

Soon she was back to her routine at Yasnaya, copying Tolstoy's final installments to meet deadlines. She was now with another child. As the end of the novel was near, Sophia asked Tolstoy to buy her a present for helping him. From Moscow, where he went on business, he brought her a ring with a ruby and two diamonds. The family nicknamed it "Anna Karenina."

In March, Tolstoy told Sophia what was making him happy: "First of all you do, and secondly my religion." She had already noticed a great spiritual change taking place. "After a long struggle between lack of faith and the longing for faith, he has suddenly become much calmer . . . He has been observing the fasts, going to church, and saying his prayers." In summer, Tolstoy made a pilgrimage to a monastery with Strakhov, who was at Yasnaya to help edit *Anna Karenina.* (The novel was soon to appear in book form.) Upon his return from the Optina Monastery, Tolstoy talked about the monks' way of life, deciding "to obey all the commands of the Church."[74] To accommodate him, Sophia introduced to the household strict observance of all Orthodox customs.

Commenting on his spiritual transformation, Sophia would remark, "One could already sense some anxiety rising within Lev Nikolaevich, his dissatisfaction with life, his search for more meaning, and the need of a more spiritual, religious life for himself." But in the days when he completed *Anna Karenina* "nothing yet upset our happiness and love. We were in agreement on every issue, in the children's upbringing and education . . . in our various beliefs, religious and worldly."[75]

That fall, Nikolai Rubinstein gave a concert in Tula. Sophia, although practically immobile during the final months of her pregnancy, traveled to hear the performance. Heavy and embarrassed by her looks, she did not appear in public after this occasion. Her belly was so big that she could barely move around the house. The remaining two months she spent at home, embroidering a large woolen carpet in the Persian style. "Thus the maidens in olden times would sit in towers and work their endless needlework to amuse themselves in solitude."[76] Tolstoy was either in his study or hunting, and Sophia's only company was his sister Maria Nikolaevna.

On December 6, she gave birth to a son, Andrei. Her nerves were taut, she was constantly on the verge of tears, and was "painfully tender" with the newborn. Tolstoy, observing her during the birth, was, as always, moved and excited, "although it's an old thing for me."[77] The event made him more cheerful, as fear that Sophia would die in labor was lifted. At the end of the month, as she was recuperating, Tolstoy told her his thoughts for future works, which she recorded. He wanted to write a historical novel about Russian settlers in Samara. Another idea, equally fascinating, was for a book where he would "demonstrate the absolute necessity for religion."[78]

Chapter Six

At a Crossroads

I N JANUARY 1878, Tolstoy told Sophia "he was experiencing something rather similar" to the days of *War and Peace*.[1] What now absorbed him was his earlier idea for a historical novel about the
Decembrists. Sophia learned about this plot a year into their marriage,
when Tolstoy became fascinated with the rebel aristocrats who protested
slavery. They had demanded a constitution and abolition of serfdom, but
their standoff with the government, on December 14, 1825, ended in mass
arrest and exile. Tolstoy was inspired by their selflessness and idealism.

But first he wanted to tell the story of their youth and participation in
the war with Napoleon. Thus, *War and Peace* emerged, a novel depicting these men's glorious past defending Russia. *The Decembrists* would
describe their postwar fight against despotism in their own country. To
Tolstoy, the new novel was a natural sequel. For Sophia, it recalled the
blissful days when he wrote his first masterpiece.

Over the winter, Tolstoy conducted research in Tula, Moscow, and Petersburg, interviewing former Decembrist exiles and their families. Their
stories moved him; in a letter to Sophia, he promised to tell her about his
encounter with Anastasia Pushchina, the daughter of the executed Decembrist and poet Kondraty Ryleev.[2] Sophia replied she wanted to know
more about Ryleev's daughter. Stories of the Decembrists and their families had inspired Sophia's generation.

Tolstoy wrote from his mother-in-law's house in Petersburg. His schedule was packed and in telegraphic style he listed his meetings, chores, and a visit to the Peter and Paul Fortress where the Decembrists had awaited their sentences. When he returned to Yasnaya, he piled a mass of historical materials on his desk. Sophia observed him "moved to tears," reading Decembrists' memoirs.[3] As the plot for the novel grew, Tolstoy prayed that he could accomplish at least part of it. When in late October, he finally read one of the drafts to her, Sophia felt it was "an immense, interesting and serious undertaking."[4] There was even more hope when he picked up a volume of Dickens: he turned to English literature for inspiration when "about to start writing himself."[5] But their hopes for this novel would remain unfulfilled: Tolstoy never completed it. Years later, Sophia would publish the drafts for *The Decembrists* in his collected works.

Back when he was doing research in Petersburg, Tolstoy finalized the purchase of another estate, 10,800 acres in Samara for forty-two thousand rubles, making a 50 percent down payment in cash. He was impatient to inspect the property and show it to the family. For Sophia, who was expected to undertake the journey willingly, it offered more hardships. As she wrote Tanya, "I'm expecting a direction from God . . . and the return of my energy."[6]

In April, their youngest son, Andryusha, became ill with meningitis and she relived the nightmare of baby Nikolai, who had died from the disease. Tolstoy described the events to Alexandrine: "The child is wasting away, Sonya torments herself and the child gets even worse."[7] Andryusha survived, but according to Sophia the meningitis compromised his character and ability to learn.

Tolstoy left for Samara with the older boys, Ilya and Lev. It was agreed that he would decide whether Sophia should join him with the other children. From Samara, he sent a telegram describing their new homestead: "Lodging, water, horses, carriages—good; but manure, hordes of flies, drought; advise coming."[8] Sophia set out in July, determined to make the place livable and introduce hygiene because of the ongoing dysentery and cholera in the region.

It would be their last trip to the prairies as a family: Tolstoy's worldview was about to change; he would renounce their property and expected her to see things his way. But that summer he was enthusiastic about the estate. Tolstoy organized a race and made announcements far and wide;

the prizes he bought included a foreign-made gun and a silver watch. Fans assembled on a hill near the homestead: it was strewn with carts, horses, and bonfires from top to bottom. Sophia described the spectacle as "strikingly beautiful and characteristic." When the race began at Tolstoy's signal, the crowd of several hundred cheered and yelped. The Kirgizian boys rode bareback; they had to circle a track five times, twenty-five kilometers in all. Later there were melodious Bashkirian throat songs, folk dances, and a feast, about which Sophia remarked: "For two days the Russian and the Bashkirian guests were eating and drinking and in two days they ate two horses, fifteen sheep, and drank several barrels of *kumis.*"[9] The locals remembered that race and feast at the count's house for years.

When the family returned to Yasnaya, a telegram from Turgenev announced his visit. Tolstoy never met him after their quarrel in 1861, which started over trifles but nearly ended in a duel. Growing more religious, Tolstoy did not want to have enemies and wrote to Turgenev: "Please let us extend our hands to each other."[10] From Paris, Turgenev replied he would eagerly shake the extended hand.

Sophia's previous memory of the great novelist was of his visit to her parents' home when she was fourteen; he had kissed her hand and said, "What a pity that the girls have grown."[11] The quarrel had prevented her from meeting Turgenev for many years, until her own children were teenagers. But Sophia always remembered him with special warmth, and in 1903, she published reminiscences of her early impressions and of his visits to Yasnaya.

To welcome Turgenev, she ordered his favorite meals, including semolina soup sprinkled with dill, and a round chicken pie, which, as he would say, only the Russian chefs knew how to make.

> Turgenev, a gentle man with grey hair, enchanted us with the eloquent and picturesque way he described both the simplest and the most sublime of subjects. He first described Antakolskii's statue of Christ in such a way as to bring it to life before our eyes, and then told us about his beloved dog Pegasus with exactly the same descriptive mastery.[12]

She recalls an occasion when there were thirteen seated at the table and they joked about this unlucky number, "wondering who was fated to die first and who was afraid of death." Turgenev said it was impossible not to be afraid and first raised his hand: *"Que celue craint la mort lève la main."*[13] Tolstoy was next: *"Eh bien, moi aussi je ne veux pas mourir."*[14] In the company of two writers aspiring for immortality no one else dared raise a hand. (Turgenev died on September 3, 1883, at his estate in Bougival, near Paris. Sophia would receive his warm farewell letter and autographed picture.)

When in the spring of 1880, Turgenev visited Yasnaya again, it was a splendid May evening and Tolstoy invited their guest and the family to shoot snipe. Standing beside Turgenev in the forest and watching him load his gun, Sophia asked why he stopped writing. He smiled at her and said, "Nobody can hear us, my soul. So, I will tell you that every time I wanted to write something new, I shook in fever of *love*. Now, it's all over, I am old; and I can neither love nor write any more."[15] It was the time when Tolstoy also had given up writing fiction, although for a different reason. Tolstoy wanted to promote morals and no longer believed that his fiction served this higher purpose. He also rejected entertainment, so when Turgenev showed them "a sort of Paris cancan" that evening, Tolstoy was annoyed.

Still, in 1879, after abandoning *The Decembrists,* Tolstoy undertook laborious research for a historical novel set in eighteenth-century Russia. Sophia watched in disbelief, writing sister Tanya: "Lyovochka reads, reads, reads ... and writes very little. Sometimes, he utters, 'Now I can see it more clear!' or, 'Ah, with God's help, something I am going to write will be very important!' But the epoch that he chose for his work stretches for a hundred years! That means there will be no end to this."[16] This novel was left unfinished when he became absorbed in religion.

Around this time, Sophia had a telling dream. She comes to the Cathedral of Christ the Savior in Moscow; while she stands before it with the children, the crucifix comes alive. The Savior raises his right hand and points to Heaven. The dream made a lasting impression on her mind and soul: overawed, she wrote Tolstoy, "The Lord sends me my *cross to bear— patience.*"[17] She could already sense their lives were changing and there would be more hardship.

In the summer of 1880, they could still spend time together as a happy family. And although Tolstoy eschewed entertainment, he participated in it. Sister Tanya, daughter Tanya, and the nieces staged funny skits, which

Tolstoy had composed for them, and vaudevilles. The entertainment had them "laughing to hysterics." Thirty people would stay overnight in Yasnaya during these theatricals, which, as Tolstoy wrote Fet, "everybody, including myself, enjoyed."[18] Tolstoy would sit down with Sophia and their guests to play a card game called *vint*. Thinking back to these days, Sophia would exclaim, "How simple and clear our life was then, and all our relationships!"[19] But this period was ending: the mood in Yasnaya was that of gloom.

They lived through a time when Tolstoy became a devout Orthodox Christian, determined to obey all the commands of the Church. Their family observed a strict Lenten fast to accommodate him. Sophia even gave up eating fish, her diet consisting of water and rye bread. In the evenings, the entire family read the Gospels. They lived so righteously that Sophia could not avoid some sarcasm in letters to her sister: "We keep strict fasts, we are studying and living as prescribed in the Holy Scriptures; that is, we love goodness, labor, piety, and so forth."[20] Sister Tanya, about to move to Kharkov, where Sasha Kuzminsky was promoted, discussed social engagements, spiritualism (a new fad), the latest fashions, and gossip. Sophia wrote that she had nothing interesting to report, "because I am fasting and I live very piously."[21]

Tolstoy's period of piety would end as abruptly as it began. During Lent, when the family was having a vegetarian dinner, he asked for the meat cutlets, reserved for the children's tutor, an atheist. Sophia reminded him it was a fast day, to which Tolstoy replied, "I don't intend to fast anymore, and please don't order any more Lenten meals for me." He ate the cutlets with relish, with the children watching. Several of them would have no religion at all as adults, which did not surprise Sophia: they were morally confused. She knew that Tolstoy had a great need for religion but was unsatisfied with their traditional faith. His spiritual search was complex but his conversions were sudden.

Strakhov, an old friend, was stunned when on his regular visit to Yasnaya he found Tolstoy "in a new anti-Church phase."[22] Only recently they had made pilgrimages to churches and monasteries. Now, Tolstoy vehemently criticized the official Church for its alliance with authority and described its history as a series of "lies, cruelties, and deceptions."[23]

Tolstoy was becoming more aloof, his mood darkening; occasionally he seemed unaware of Sophia's existence. When he did join her for tea, "a rare event nowadays," they discussed death, religion, and the meaning of life. He had already distanced himself from their past: in his major non-fictional work of the time, *A Confession,* he depicted their previous life as a series of mistakes. His literary achievement, fame, wealth, and family were now irrelevant. There was no returning to their old way of life: the past held fear of death, madness, and suicide. He was seeking salvation from his tormenting doubts in strong faith. Sophia would not read this work until later, but she realized that Tolstoy's mood had changed greatly over the years.

She reported the new developments to sister Tanya: Tolstoy was writing articles and working eight to ten hours a day. "Lyovochka is working, or so he says, but alas! He is writing religious tracts, reads and thinks until his head aches, and all this to prove how inconsistent the Church is with the teaching of the Gospels. There will be hardly ten people in Russia interested in this. But there is nothing to be done. I only wish . . . this passes as a malady."[24] But Tolstoy felt he was on a mission: his religious writings would occupy him for years. He would criticize dogmatic theology and undertake his own translation of the four Gospels in order to grasp the genuine messages of Christ. And yet, Sophia was accurate in her prediction that these works would be read least of all.

Tolstoy's attacks on traditional religion offended her deeply, creating a rift between them: "No argument would force me to separate from the Church. I could not accept Lev Nikolaevich's view of Christianity and religion in general . . . I felt that Lev Nikolaevich was right, but only on the matter of his personal self-perfection . . . His renunciations of the Church and the existing social order I could not accept . . . my soul could not take it."[25] Unable to sympathize with his nonfiction ("it pains me, but I cannot change myself"),[26] she resigned as Tolstoy's copyist.

His angry denial of Orthodoxy and the Church, his abuse of the clergy . . . were unbearable. Back then I still copied for him all of his writings and corrections. But once, I remember, it was in 1880, I wrote and wrote till blood rushed to my head . . . anger rose in my heart, I collected the sheets and carried them to Leo Nikolaevich, saying that I will no longer copy for him because I feel bitter and uneasy. So, he had to hire a scribe for himself . . . But until then . . . what an immense enjoyment I felt copying his artistic works countless times."[27]

By 1879, the couple had six living children. The eldest, Seryozha, was expected to enter university. Tanya had to come out in society. But Tolstoy's ideas about their children's future had changed: he now disapproved of their education and social success. According to daughter Tanya, it was Tolstoy who took her to her first ball and introduced her to his many acquaintances. A short while later he condemned entertainment, criticized people of their class, the aristocracy, and everyone else who was rich.

Sophia feared that she would have to raise their children on her own, at the time when the boys needed their father to guide them and she was soon to give birth to another child. That fall, late in her pregnancy, she accompanied Tolstoy on his walks. She would usually end up frustrated, as she was short of breath and could not keep up; she watched him walk away from her. The walks were evocative of their relationship, with his restlessness and need to move on, her futile attempts to catch up, and the growing gap between them.

There was no sense of togetherness now that Tolstoy had left his literary vocation behind. His literature gave her purpose and joy; without it, there was a void. She would spend days nursing, teaching, sewing, and doing other chores, but an essential part was missing. As she noted in her diary, "I feel like a machine. I should so like a little time for myself, but that's out of the question, impossible."[28] In fact, she loaded herself with more chores than necessary: keeping busy every minute of the day allowed her to overcome a sense of uncertainty. She would work herself into a stupor: "I sew and sew, till I get nauseous, desperate, suffocated, headachy, miserable, and still sew."[29]

That year, children were continually ill; Sophia had nursed daughter Masha through diphtheria. She was emotionally drained and lived in perennial fear "that someone else would get sick."[30] The thought of a new baby filled her with gloom: "My horizons have become so narrow, and my world is such a small and dismal place."[31] Heavy, suffering from a toothache and neuralgia, she was a sorry sight.

On December 20, 1879, Sophia bore their seventh child, Mikhail. Painful nursing, more worry, and sleepless nights lay ahead. She wrote

Tanya: "Lord, how hard are these long, cold nights, when you go to breast-feed."[32] She could only endure it this one last time: after ten births, she had no more capacity for motherhood.[33] Yasnaya felt "just like a prison, although it's bright, morally and materially superior, but I feel I'm locked up here . . . and I want to knock down the walls, push everything aside, and set myself free."[34] At thirty-five, Sophia wanted to experience society and travel, like other women of her class.

During this difficult time Sophia escaped in philosophy. As she would remark, "I was simply *learning* wisdom from various philosophers."[35] Prince Leonid Urusov, the vice-governor of Tula and Tolstoy's chess companion, introduced Sophia to Seneca, Plato, and the Stoic philosophers Epictetus and Marcus Aurelius. The time formerly reserved for copying Tolstoy's manuscripts she now spent preparing for discussions with Urusov. Sophia enjoyed his attention and sense of courtship, ordering a special dinner and putting on a festive dress when he visited. This relationship helped fill a spiritual void: Urusov treated her with chivalry and admiration. He never failed to bring flowers, chocolates, and gifts for the children. It made Tolstoy jealous and he attempted to restrict his visits; however, Urusov remained his and Sophia's friend. When Urusov translated Tolstoy's religious work *What I Believe* into French, Sophia helped to verify it. Urusov sparked her interest in Tolstoy's philosophy and predicted his views would spread around the world.

In 1880, Turgenev wrote from Paris that *War and Peace* had been translated into French and was a sensation. He himself read it five times. As well, he reported that Gustave Flaubert was impressed with the novel's artistry and psychology and screamed with delight as he read it![36] Turgenev asked Tolstoy to return to literature. Describing how Tolstoy's change of vocation affected her, Sophia remarked: "Certainly, it was impossible not to regret the end of activity by such a great artist as Lev Nikolaevich, and I could not but regret the end of my happiness."[37] Tolstoy wrote religious tracts and his new style and tendency to moralize were "insufferably boring" to her.[38]

For Tolstoy, his literary work was a thing of the past. To an acquaintance who admired *Anna Karenina,* he replied, "I assure you that this vile thing no longer exists for me."[39] He referred to himself as a writer in the past tense: "I *was*[40] a writer, and all writers are vain and envious—I at least was that sort of writer."[41] As well, he criticized Shakespeare and called Goethe's *Faust* the "trashiest of trash."[42] His old friends Strakhov and Fet were astonished to learn he had left fiction for religious work and was immersed in *A Translation and Harmony of the Four Gospels,* a project they believed irrelevant.

In June, there was a Pushkin festival with the unveiling of his monument in Moscow. The event drew rapturous crowds: Pushkin was the national poet and everyone's pride. Besides, Dostoevsky and Turgenev were among the speakers. Tolstoy dismissed the event's importance and refused to participate, even though he had called Pushkin his "teacher." His absence generated gossip, which Dostoevsky shared in a letter to his wife, Anna. People were saying that Tolstoy no longer wrote fiction and that he had gone mad.

It was a time when Tolstoy asserted his religious views with the zeal of a convert, insisting that everybody "can and must" agree with him.[43] In Petersburg he quarreled with Alexandrine, who was stunned by his abuse of Orthodoxy. He called it a bunch of lies; when she protested, he left Petersburg without saying good-bye. Strakhov was appalled when Tolstoy shouted at him during their religious discussion at Yasnaya, and later wrote him: "I felt as if you were reading me out of the Church!"[44] Tolstoy would later soften this intolerant tone, but in the early 1880s, when he was formulating his religious views, he had to destroy established ones. When Sophia refused to accept his criticism of traditional religion she had to face his disapproval: "He was either silent with me for days or attacked me and criticized everything."[45] Moreover, he criticized their entire way of life as not austere enough.

Before his birthday in August, Tolstoy traveled to Moscow on business. This was the first time they were spending his birthday apart from each other. Sophia was seeing him to the station; they drove in silence. It was a sad farewell. Their past could not be discussed, for it did not matter to him anymore. And they could not talk about his fiction. Two scribes were now copying his articles on religion, so he did not need her assistance. Their family's practical affairs did not interest him. For Sophia, their alienation was painful. In her letter to Tolstoy on August 28, 1880, when he turned fifty-two, she wrote: "Yesterday, as I was driving with you, I thought to myself, what I wouldn't give to read your heart, to know what you are thinking? It hurts me that you share your thoughts with me so little. Morally, it would be good for me, even essential. You must think I am stubborn, whereas I think that slowly but surely much that is good in you finds its way into me. And this makes life easier for me."[46] In fact, she wanted time to adjust: his ideas were advancing too fast for her. She was looking for the compromise she had been able to find in the past.

In October the couple attended Rubinstein's concert. Sitting beside Tolstoy, Sophia noticed he was overcome with emotion, his face and eyelids twitching. The music and Rubinstein's superb playing continued to move him as in the past. For Sophia, this was a rare chance to appear in society with her husband and daughter Tanya. She wore a coral necklace and a black silk dress, "which I reworked and decorated with black and lilac satin. I pinned on pansies, which Mama had sent."[47] Daughter Tanya in her white cashmere gown was a success. Friends invited them for tea but Sophia had to rush home to nurse baby Misha.

The concert was a ray of sun breaking through the clouds that fall. Tolstoy, occupied with religious work, was gloomy and irritable. The couple frequently quarreled. Sophia wrote her sister that she was "badly divided" in her heart:

> Everything here goes as before, even blissfully on the surface, but with Lyovochka it's cold and remote. At home either nothing interests me anymore or provokes heartache, suffering, pity, extreme tenderness for the children, and a desire to die . . . I have been lonesome in the past but never so lonesome as now. For it's become so obvious to me . . . that I'm of no interest to anyone. Yet, it's now, more than ever before, that I need someone's kindness.[48]

Determined to practice his new religious beliefs, Tolstoy visited prisons, courts, and houses of detention. Sophia observes in her memoir:

> It was as if he was intentionally looking for places where he could see human suffering and abuse; he heatedly denounced the existing social order, condemned everything, suffered himself, and sympathized with only those oppressed. His disapproval and condemnation turned also against me, our family, and everyone who was rich and not unhappy.

It was depressing to see that Lev Nikolaevich suddenly began to suffer for all of humanity, becoming extremely morbid as a result. It seemed that he turned away from everything in the world that was joyful and bright in order to see the opposite.[49]

Religious writing depressed him, in contrast with fiction writing, which had enlivened and invigorated him. Although Sophia recognized that his new ideals of serving humanity were "undoubtedly good and lofty," she could not measure up to them.

Her life had become more restricted: visitors to Yasnaya were now rare. When Sophia mentioned having guests over Christmas, Tolstoy protested that they would disturb his work. Her idea to go out on her own was met with scorn. "So, I stayed without diversion in my hard life. I sensed my own pettiness beside my husband and the meanness of my desire to amuse myself."[50] In addition, the weather was nasty, the small children were ill, and Tolstoy was in poor health. But even more unsettling was his perennial disapproval of her and lack of interest in her life.

Tensions escalated when she refused intimacy. In a letter to sister Tanya, on December 8, 1880, Sophia wrote she had a nervous breakdown, which under the circumstances was a blessing: "Fortunately, I became very ill, developing severe pains on my right side, in the pit of my stomach, and in my back. I screamed and rolled for seven hours, became petrified, and frightened everyone. God knows what it was, but it came back this week, twice, and now it's gone without a trace. Lyovochka feared I would die and returned his affection. You probably understand why he was cold, as do I."[51] Since then, the ice melted, she continued, and Tolstoy began to treat her more kindly.

It was Sophia's first hysterical fit, eighteen years into her marriage. She had married a writer whose art was at the center of her life. When he rejected his art he also discounted her contribution. He pressed her to comply with his new religious beliefs and way of life. As this pressure increased, her hysteria became recurrent. In her day there was a stigma against the disease, and with prevailing superstitions she would have been seen as evil.[52]

Although Tolstoy loved humanity, he could be insensitive to individuals. For Sophia, the opposite was the case. She did not care for the suffering of humanity as an abstraction; she sympathized with real people. Over the years she had provided free medical help at Yasnaya. Although she was helping the very poor, Tolstoy ignored her efforts: "In all this I was alone because Lev Nikolaevich rejected medicine; not only did he have little sympathy for my work, he mocked it, which upset me terribly."

Her knowledge of medicine came from observing her father in childhood and from Florensky's *Family Medicine*. First, she treated her household: family, guests, servants, and teachers. Later, because infections were rampant in nearby villages and there was no medical help, people drove from afar to see her about intestinal troubles, rheumatism, eye diseases, and so on. They crowded near the porch, where she examined them. Sophia was also summoned to help with difficult labors: "Call the countess, she has a magic touch."

> Perhaps I was just lucky, but my recovering patients gave me a lot of joy. I remember, particularly in summer, just as you enter the porch, the women are already waiting for me, some with their children; and there are carts with the sick driven here. I would talk to each one, examine, and give medicine. And how many times I had to assist with difficult labor![53]

She considered enrolling in a medical course in Moscow or Petersburg and mentioned this to Tolstoy, but he showed no support. Years later, when a peasant came to Yasnaya in Sophia's absence, looking for her medical help, Tolstoy learned from him that she was a good healer. He wrote Sophia that he "felt flattered."[54]

Although Sophia could not disagree with Tolstoy about helping one's neighbor, a discord between them soon ensued. This happened when he became determined to practice every commandment of Christ literally and wanted the family to live by the Scriptures.

In January 1881, as Tolstoy was immersed in the Gospels, Sophia described the change in his views and mood in "Notes for Future Reference." Her insightful record would inform his many biographers tracing his spiritual conversion.

He has begun to study, translate, and interpret the Gospels. He has seen the *light* (in his words), and this light has illuminated his whole view of the world. His attitude to people has changed too, according to him, for whereas before he had just a small circle of *intimates,* people like *him,* he now has millions of men as his brothers. Before, his wealth and his estate were his *own*—now if a poor man asks for something he must have it. His soul is undoubtedly in a state of calm clarity, but he suffers deeply for all the human misery and poverty he sees about him, for all those in jail, for all the hatred, injustice and oppression in the world— and this deeply affects his impressionable soul and undermines his life.[55]

When Tolstoy discovered a new way to live, he passionately believed it was the only way. He wanted Sophia to follow him on his new spiritual path, but it was practically impossible for her to do so with the family. The change occurred at the peak of Tolstoy's fame and affected his views, char- acter, work, and lifestyle. It was about to turn Sophia's life upside down.

Chapter Seven

Life with a Religious Philosopher

I N THE SPRING OF 1881, Tolstoy began to give away his property and cash. Pilgrims and peasants poured into Yasnaya, asking for, among other things, livestock and seed for planting. When Sophia tried to restrain distribution, Tolstoy quoted from the Gospels: "Give to him that asketh thee!" He even gave money to a village drunk, with deplorable results: the man started a brawl and beat his wife senseless. Sophia feared Tolstoy had lost his mind. She observed, in a letter to her family, that this religious-philosophical mood was "most dangerous."[1]

Tolstoy did not care how his money was used: his goal, in fact, was not to help the poor. He felt it was necessary to give away what he had "not in order to do good but in order to become less guilty." As his daughter Tanya remarked, "Giving away everything he possessed meant freeing himself from a sin—the sin of ownership."[2] Tolstoy knew it was impossible to satisfy the needs of the multitudes that besieged Yasnaya. Money and property had become intolerable, as he revealed in his treatise *What I Believe*.

Tolstoy had never before labored with such intensity as he did in his fifties while working on the *Union and Translation of the Four Gospels*.[3] He conducted "an investigation of the teachings of Christ" based not on the Church's interpretation but "simply on what has come down to us" from Jesus.[4] His goal was to recapture the "authentic" messages, which he translated from the Greek. He focused his attention on the Sermon on the Mount and the Ten Commandments. "And no matter how strange it is to say this after 1,800 years, it was my lot to discover these rules as if they were something new. Only when I understood these rules—only then did I understand the significance of Christ's teaching," he wrote.[5] Eventually he reduced Christianity to five moral imperatives, of which the principle of nonresistance[6] was the most important. He argued it was the key to understanding Christianity. It was only possible to attain peace by forsaking the old law of "an eye for an eye." The message of Christ was not to resist evil by force, yet this principle was not being practiced by Christians, a failing he was determined to correct.

Tolstoy's doctrine of nonresistance had far-reaching consequences. It led him to renounce property, since it had to be protected by the law. This in turn called for renouncing the governments, courts, police, prisons, and the military. He argued that no physical force must be used to compel any human being.[7] But even his future followers could not understand how to apply these principles.

That spring, Tolstoy tried to convince family and friends of the need to practice his doctrine. "A talk with Fet and my wife. The Christian teaching is impracticable. So, it's stupid? No, but it's impracticable. But have you tried to practice it? No, but it's impracticable."[8] Frictions with his family and friends arose when Tolstoy ardently insisted that his interpretation of the Gospels must be followed in daily life. It is tragic and ironic that his passion for the Gospels, which he believed would save the world, was generating discord, not unity and peace. That same spring, he began to criticize Sophia and the family in his diary because they disagreed. He stopped corresponding with Fet as well.

Son Ilya remembered a sudden change in Tolstoy: "He became taciturn, morose, and irritable, and our former jovial buoyant companion and leader was transformed before our eyes into a stern and censorious preacher."[9] Their neighbor Dmitry Dyakov, whom Tolstoy met as a student, was appalled when he began to preach about how people should live: "I used to speak with Lyovochka . . . and this is God Jehovah."[10] Sophia sensed the change more intensely than others, remarking that she was happy with Tolstoy when he was an artist. Since he had become a religious thinker and moralist, her happiness had tarnished.

Tolstoy was trapped by his religious maxims, his diary reveals: "One's family is one's flesh. To abandon one's family . . . is to kill yourself." It was impossible for him to serve the family because of his new beliefs and his desire to serve only God: "Serve not the family but the one God."[11] But Tolstoy could not abandon his family and continued to live with them, while torn by conflict. Before, family was his ideal; now it was a burden.

As he became further withdrawn from family and estate matters, Sophia had to take on more responsibilities. He wanted her to ponder global issues, but she had no time to listen to him now. In the course of a day she dealt with practical and financial matters on top of nursing, teaching, and sewing.

In February, she weaned their baby Mikhail, and in March, she discovered a new pregnancy. Tolstoy created a crisis, objecting to the family's move to Moscow when Sophia was in the midst of preparations. She wrote her sister about quarreling with Tolstoy: "I even wanted to leave home. That's because we started to live like Christians. In my view, before this so-called Christianity, life was a lot better."[12]

It was around this time that Tolstoy announced his intention to give their land to the peasants. According to his plan, the family would retain a small plot with a cottage and support themselves through physical work. In his unfinished play *And the Light Shineth in Darkness* Tolstoy describes the actual drama that took place between him and Sophia when he made this decision.[13] Drawn from their conversations, it is believed to be his most autobiographical work.

> This is my plan: we will give our land to the peasants, keeping for ourselves fifty acres, the entire orchard, the vegetable garden, and the flooded meadow. We will try to work ourselves, but we will not force each other, or the children. What we keep should still bring us about five hundred rubles. (Act 2, scene 2)

Tolstoy wanted Sophia to willingly renounce their property, either persuaded by his argument or out of love for him. (Applying pressure would contradict his doctrine of nonresistance.) Sophia dismissed the plan as unfeasible. She was not young and strong anymore, nor was Tolstoy. Their children, raised as nobles, would be utterly confused:

How could Seryozha, in whom we instilled, since his beginning, the idea of . . . university education, suddenly believe that his efforts were futile, and pick up an axe and a plough? How could Tanya, with her love of art, society, theater, gaiety, and smart dresses, give this up, and stay in the country to farm? And finally, how could I, with my eight children . . . give up my usual life for the sake of an ideal, created not by me but forced upon me? . . . And so, the painful discord has ensued.[14]

Tolstoy's play reveals the impossibility of his demands and the moral dilemma they created for Sophia: "How cruel you are—is this Christianity? . . . I cannot take away from my children and give to strangers."[15] His clear mission, as he now perceived it, was to serve God according to the Gospels: "Take no thought for your life, what ye shall eat, or what ye shall drink." Sophia, however, had to think how their family would live.

Tolstoy's idea to give up his property was not unique in prerevolutionary Russia. Alexei Bibikov, the manager of their Samara estate, was formerly a landowner. He gave up his land, married a peasant, and lived with her on a small plot he reserved for himself. Tolstoy was impressed by his example. As an estate manager, Bibikov was a failure precisely because of his attitude to property: under his watch Tolstoy's purebred horses died of neglect.

When Sophia rejected Tolstoy's plan to live like peasants, he proposed turning their estate over to her. She rejected this, too. Since Tolstoy believed property was evil, she argued, why should he pass this evil thing to her? She had to raise their family and was still bearing children. Two years later, Tolstoy would give her power of attorney against her wishes and continue to live at Yasnaya. His play sheds light on the thinking behind his decision.

Nikolai Ivanovich.
Take over the estate, then I won't be responsible.
Marya Ivanona.
But you know I don't want to and what's more, I can't. I have to raise the children, nurse them, and bear them.[16]

Sophia would eventually manage the estate to free Tolstoy from his moral quandary and from the many obligations that came with ownership.

In June 1881, dressed in peasant shirt and bast sandals, Tolstoy walked to Optina Monastery[17] accompanied by his servant Sergei Arbuzov and a local teacher. "To be poor, to be a pauper, to be a beggar—that's what Christ taught. Without that no one can enter the Kingdom of God."[18] Taken for a simple pilgrim, he was assigned a humble room in the monastery hospice. "My pilgrimage was a great success," he wrote Turgenev. "I could count up some 5 years of my life which I would exchange for those 10 days."[19] He reported to Sophia that his impressions were new, important, and useful for his soul, and allowed him to experience the larger world.[20]

Her greater concern was his health: Tolstoy was walking on a highway with a knapsack and it was hot. With his headaches and blood rushes there was a risk of stroke, she reminded him.[21] Meanwhile at Yasnaya, baby Misha had a high fever and Sophia was attending to him.

The summer was particularly difficult for Sophia: the family was moving to Moscow before the school year. With another baby due in October, she was handling packing and other preparations. Tolstoy no longer objected to the move, but she was uncertain how he would take to city life. When he returned from Optina, Sophia went to Moscow to rent accommodations, uneasy about a task for which she had no experience.

Tolstoy estimated it would take her three days to check out twenty places and Sophia tried to meet the schedule. The city overwhelmed her with its heat, noise, and shaky cab rides on cobblestone streets; getting in and out of coaches was bothersome with her pregnancy. Most available houses and apartments were for sale only, she wrote him. There were huge houses for one hundred thousand rubles and small ones for thirty thousand. Apartments were expensive and not convenient for their large family and staff. She looked at houses offered at a discount and talked to shopkeepers to find out why this was the case.

Nonetheless, two days later she rented Prince Volkonsky's house on Denezhny Lane for 1,550 silver rubles annually, a reasonable price.[22] She liked it because of a large, isolated study overlooking the garden. "It was precisely this splendid study that later made Lev Nikolaevich despair because it was too spacious and too luxurious."[23]

In July and August, Sophia returned to renovate the house according to Tolstoy's instructions. He wrote from Samara, where he was inspecting the farm; he felt guilty that she was working so hard, given her condition. Yet he sent specific instructions on how to redo the wood floors: they had to be lifted, treated with lime to destroy the damp, and insulated with sheep wool. Tolstoy spent many hours sitting at his desk, immobile, and cold floors bothered him.

From his letters Sophia sensed that he was rested; it was the opposite with her, torn as she was between two houses, tired, and stressed. Employing some of his philosophy, she wrote Tolstoy, "I know that one needn't be in a hurry, that one needs to be serene, that all material things are futile, and so forth. I'm not looking for work but it finds me, and in the end, I'm always busy with something essential."[24]

Tolstoy drank twelve cupfuls of *kumis* a day and hunted on the prairie; his appetite and sleep were soon restored. He cheerfully described the farm, the crops, and the harvest with three hundred reapers. The horses made him happy and he wanted to ship several to Yasnaya; he was delighted to see the colts, strong despite the drought. At this time, he made a note in his diary, referring to his lifestyle in Samara: "Idleness. Shame."[25] He was experiencing conflicting emotions toward his property: he continued to enjoy it, despite renouncing it. Sophia was aware of this complexity because he wrote her without inhibitions. As in the past, he estimated the profit from wheat sales, wondered whether they should plant next year, and asked Sophia's opinion.[26]

He also wrote Sophia that he had observed the family of their estate manager, Bibikov (the idealist landowner who gave up his property), and realized it was impossible to base one's life on ideals alone. In Bibikov's family he saw a reflection of his own. Refusing to accept lofty ideals, Bibikov's family pulled in reverse. The result was a compromise, disappointing for a reformer.[27] The experience taught him it was wrong to expect people to see things the way he did: Tolstoy admitted he was disabused "of the fallacious idea."

His attitude toward living in Moscow also changed, and "it's absurd to say—I came to believe in it." He realized how difficult it was for Sophia to work alone and wrote her with remorse:

I have wronged you greatly, my dear. I have wronged you uncon-
sciously and unwittingly, and perhaps that absolves me. My only excuse
is that in order to work under high tension as I have, and in order to
accomplish something, I had to forget everything else. And I confess
that I have forgotten you too often. In the name of God and our love,
take care of yourself! Postpone everything until my arrival. I will do
anything gladly and will do it well because I will try.[28]

In August, Sophia was divided between Yasnaya and Moscow, where she
had to deal with contractors and buy wallpaper, furniture, and other fixtures. It was not easy, knowing Tolstoy's simple tastes and yet his desire for
quality. Sophia ended up paying more than she had intended for a drawing room suite at a reputable store. After the shaky cab rides, with pain
in her belly, she consoled herself that it was all for their family, to make
everyone happy.[29]

Yasnaya, meanwhile, was teeming with family and guests, as the two
Tanyas, sister and daughter, staged theatricals. Amid this merriment, Sophia made final preparations for the move: corridors were crowded with
trunks, boxes of books, and bags of potatoes and apples. Some of their luggage and livestock, to be kept in a shed in Moscow, was dispatched separately.

Their move to Moscow, of which Sophia had long dreamt, was happening at a turbulent time. In March, the liberal Tsar Alexander II, who had
emancipated the serfs and promised a first constitution, had been assassinated by revolutionary terrorists. Tolstoy sent a letter to Alexander III,
seeking clemency for his father's assassins: "As wax before fire, every revolutionary struggle will melt away before the Tsar-man who fulfils the law
of Christ."[30] Although Sophia agreed with Tolstoy that "evil could be only
extinguished by good,"[31] she was against the letter, afraid it would anger
the government and cause the family trouble. When six revolutionaries,
including Sofia Perovskaya, daughter of the St. Petersburg governor-
general, were hanged, their executions helped recruit more extremists,
just as Tolstoy had warned.

Sophia's reaction to the assassination was personal: she was struck that
the tsar was killed at sixty-two and that "they wouldn't let him die, poor

man, in peace."[32] Unlike Tolstoy, she had no sympathy for revolutionaries and she could see nothing but anarchy in all this. Their Tula friends were saying that universities had become infested with revolutionary ideas, that the Petersburg university was "a den of thieves."[33] Son Seryozha was to study in Moscow and Sophia wished he would stay away from the mutineers.

In mid-September, the family boarded a spacious coach they nicknamed Noah's Ark, which took them and their possessions to the station. On the train there was a familiar fuss with the small children, warming up food and broth, and eating in their crowded compartment: "My head was clouded from exhaustion, and I felt nothing."[34]

The next morning, they were awakened in their new house by shouting street vendors, the clatter of carriages, and noise from their stable and cowshed. Tolstoy was downcast, the children complained, the staff, trying to cope with city life, was confused, "and it wasn't long before we sank into a mood of despondency and anxiety . . . The house was like a cardboard house, you could hear every sound, and there was no peace to be found in our bedroom or in Lyovochka's study. I was in despair and would spend all day in tension, trying to keep everyone quiet."[35]

Tolstoy was irritable and apparently forgot about his promise to help: "Lev Nikolaevich barely talked to me, making it clear that I was torturing him, poisoning his life, and I cried. Finally, he erupted with a stream of accusations, saying that if I loved him, I would have never chosen this huge room for his study, where each armchair worth 22 rubles would make a fortune for a muzhik, who could buy with it a horse or a cow."[36] (She could not help remembering that Tolstoy's black bear coat, bought with royalties from *Anna Karenina,* cost 450 rubles.)

Those first two weeks in the city were agonizing, as Tolstoy slipped into depression, "some kind of extreme apathy. He did not sleep or eat . . . and cried sometimes, which simply drove me insane."[37] In the final month of her pregnancy, Sophia felt crushed. But having to unpack and settle in, she put herself together and within a few weeks, family life was running somewhat smoothly.

Tolstoy soon rented two quieter rooms away from the house where he could work. He was writing a story, "What Men Live By," based on a legend he had heard from a peasant about an angel sent to earth. It was his first attempt at fiction since *Anna Karenina*. He gave this story to a children's magazine, which Sophia's brother Petya was copublishing. Turgenev also helped Petya get established and sent him his story "A Quail." In 1885, on a train to Moscow, Sophia met a merchant who told her that his children had read a wonderful story about a shoemaker and an angel. She recognized it as "What Men Live By" and said proudly that her husband wrote it.[38]

In the city, the family had scores of visitors coming to see Tolstoy. He was particularly impressed with Vasily Syutaev, a peasant and religious sectarian who, Sophia remembers, preached brotherhood and did not believe in protecting property: his house had no locks. Because his ideas were in accord with Tolstoy's, the family found this peasant remarkable. Tolstoy also enjoyed philosophical discussions with Nikolai Fedorov, who worked at the Rumyantsev library. (It was where Tolstoy conducted his research for *War and Peace* and where Sophia would place his archive.) Possessing an encyclopedic knowledge, Fedorov worked without pay and occupied a tiny cell crammed with books, a triumph of spirit over matter.

Tolstoy lived his separate life, full of intellectual pursuits and physical work. He befriended some day laborers and joined them in the Vorobyov Hills on the Moscow River banks, where they sawed wood. In mid-October, Sophia wrote her sister that this occupation seemed to benefit his health and cheer him up.[39]

Just before she gave birth, her small children became ill; Sophia was chopping fruit candy to help with their cough when a tall lady walked in. Nearsighted, Sophia did not recognize her mother. Lyubov Alexandrovna was much thinner and grayer, but still beautiful, with her regal bearing. She had arrived from Petersburg for a week and her visit was opportune because Tolstoy was perennially busy and Sophia needed comfort.

On October 31, Sophia bore another son, Alyosha. The doctor who examined her said she must have "infernal patience" to endure her nursing: she had deep cracks around her nipples and continued to suckle despite agonizing pain. As in the past, Tolstoy showed little sympathy. Tensions were building up as he reproached her for their life in the city because it was more luxurious. Sophia snapped under pressure. Four weeks after the birth, she suddenly became ill, developing "a terrible pain" in her stomach:

"I fell on the floor, screaming, and could not get up."[40] Tolstoy brought a medical expert, Professor Belin, whom Sophia described as "a complete idiot." He diagnosed bowel cancer, saying there was no hope. The family was in shock, until another doctor, Vasily Chirkov, suggested gallbladder colic.

That fall, despairing at the sight of city poverty, Tolstoy made several diary entries that revealed his state of mind. As a man of wealth, he felt morally responsible for social injustice. Determined to give up his property, he drafted a plan:

> Live at Yasnaya. Give the income from Samara to the poor people . . . Live all together: the men in one room, the women and girls in another. One room to be a library for intellectual purposes, and one a work room for general use. And since we are so spoiled, a separate room also for the sick . . . Sell or give away everything superfluous—the piano, furniture, carriages.[41]

In early 1882, Tolstoy participated in the city's census, inspecting several flophouses inhabited by vagrants and prostitutes. The sight of destitution and human misery was overwhelming: "Stench, stones, luxury, poverty. Dissipation. A collection of robbers who have plundered the people and conscripted soldiers and judges to guard their orgies while they feast."[42] He sympathized with the oppressed and criticized the rich. Even his family's ordinary life inspired his condemnation.

His impressions were employed in his treatise *What Then Must We Do?* When in February, Tolstoy retreated to their estate to write it, Sophia sensed his absence as a relief. From Yasnaya, he reported cheerfully that his nerves were stronger, he was calm, and he could not feel more at peace.[43] His work went well and he enjoyed his solitude; at Shrovetide (a festival to say good-bye to winter), a peasant from Yasnaya made him "delightful pancakes."

Sophia replied she was glad, while in fact she was bitter. She wrote him that her life with eight children was "a tangle of toil, haste, with lack of thought, time, health, and everything else that *men live by*."[44] (She was alluding to Tolstoy's recent fiction.) She wrote sarcastically that Tolstoy no longer could love his own children because he loved all of humanity.[45] His criticism of the family upset her: a lot had boiled in her heart. Writing him at the end of the day, tired, she thought of their small children, whom she would have to raise alone, since they no longer interested Tolstoy: "These little ones will be entirely mine, and I should not and will not have more. I don't need more suffering—if we live separate lives, let it be *completely* separate."[46] When Tolstoy wrote of his intention to return to Moscow, she protested:

> My dear Lyovochka, for the first time I wasn't happy to learn you're coming back . . . Tomorrow you'll be here, and again will begin to suffer, become bored, and blame me . . . Dear God! My soul is worn and aching from all this! . . . If you are well and occupied, why do you need to come back? . . . . My health is better. As for my spiritual needs, they're so deeply buried that I'm afraid to unearth them. And let it be so, for what would I do if these needs emerged? My spiritual and external lives are in conflict.[47]

Tolstoy came for a short stay, passionate after a separation. But as she remarked, "By then, I knew his passion would not last, while his despondency and coldness would return."[48]

While he was in Moscow, he again had hordes of visitors: his insatiable curiosity prevailed over his need to work. He would tell Sophia that he did not want to miss something of interest. And so, she found herself in the middle of an exciting life, describing it to her sister: "What a mass and variety of people are coming here! Men of letters, artists, *le grand monde,* nihilists, and I don't know who else I have not seen. After living in the country, this is making my head spin. Lyovochka is again calm, everything interests him but he retreats to the country to rest."[49]

Moscow was pulsating with cultural life in which Tolstoy was the center and Sophia a participant. Among people who visited their home was a famous portraitist, Nikolai Gay, a descendant of a nobleman who had immigrated to Russia during the French Revolution. Gay was "a genuine artist, sincere and passionate about his work, which he loved more than anything in the world."[50] He would paint Tolstoy, Sophia, and their daughters, becoming a family friend and a Tolstoyan. Sophia liked to hear Gay describe his paintings, which he did with such mastery that the actual works would occasionally disappoint her. With Kramskoy he was a founder of the Wanderers, a group of prominent avant-garde realist painters who wanted to bring art to the people. Gay shared Tolstoy's democratic ideas and his interest in Russian history and the Gospels. In 1889, Sophia saw Gay's *Christ in the Garden of Gethsemane* and admired it for its "solemn religious mood." The painting depicts Christ in the blue moonlight, praying as he looks to the sky, his disciples around him.

Sophia relished the company of her children's friends as well. Son Seryozha's university circle included Georgy Lvov, future head of the Provisional Government, and Savva Morozov, who would become a prominent industrialist and arts patron. A diligent student and musically gifted, Seryozha was also close to the sons of Count Vasily Olsufiev and frequented their home. Olsufiev, Tolstoy's old friend, was their neighbor in Moscow; his guests included university professors and scholars, whom Sophia also met. Daughter Tanya attended the School of Painting, Sculpture, and Architecture, and took instruction from Vasily Perov, Ilya Repin, and other distinguished artists who visited Tolstoy.

Sophia had dreamt of studying painting, but it was her daughter who got the opportunity. Tanya shared her love of art, music, and dancing. Sophia would accompany her to the house of Varvara Maslova, an aspiring artist. The Maslovs received painter Konstantin Makovsky and composers Tchaikovsky, Sergei Taneev, and Anton Arensky. With Tanya she attended Anton Rubinstein's piano performances.[51] Awed by his musical genius, Sophia later watched him conduct Beethoven's Ninth Symphony: "I forgot the entire world, my life, my children."[52]

Living in Moscow was also beneficial for the younger children. Their sons Ilya and Lev were enrolled at the private Polivanov gymnasium, which had a strong humanities program. This school would produce a generation of brilliant intellectuals and artistic elite, including poets and writers Valery Bryusov, Maksimilian Voloshin, Andrei Bely, and painter Alexander Golovin, who would work for Diaghilev's opera and ballet with designer Léon Bakst. The boys could have benefited from instruction by university professors and academicians brought in to teach senior grades. But they did not: unlike Seryozha, these boys had the reputation of being "talented but bone lazy."[53] Although Sophia tutored them daily, she could not infuse them with her energy and sense of purpose.

Holiday time in the city was demanding: daughter Tanya had to be chaperoned, while the younger children wanted to see the circus and a puppet show. Sophia tried to satisfy them all and wrote her sister that the children were tearing her apart, "selfish as usual."[54] And there were also social obligations. Many people, curious to meet Tolstoy's wife, came to see her. Society ladies were taken aback by her unpolished speech and straightforwardness: "They looked at me with bewilderment, surprised with my youthful appearance and naive candor . . . I had to *learn to live.*"[55] Countess Praskovia Uvarova (née Shcherbatova), whom Tolstoy had courted as a bachelor, was among the first to visit. Sophia would later remark that these women envied her marriage to a celebrity, unaware of what it entailed: "And what good was my life with this celebrity? Work, work, and work."[56]

Tolstoy wrote from Yasnaya, asking her to buy a white purebred stallion for 350 rubles and instructing her to get several if she negotiated a better price. In addition, he specified what she should pay for shipping the horses to Yasnaya. He had forgotten to leave her enough cash for these purchases (Tolstoy still managed their finances) and she did not want to point this out. She bought several stallions, paying in bonds, and made clear to Tolstoy that this assignment came on top of everything else: "I taught Masha, nursed Alyosha, negotiated the price with the horses' salesmen . . . Are you happy with me?"[57] Although Tolstoy apologized for loading her with these additional duties, he would make more requests.

It was not the extra work that annoyed Sophia: she found her husband's contradictions unfathomable. He recently criticized her for their family's supposedly "luxurious" lifestyle and demanded they give up their property. And yet, he wanted her to make expensive purchases: "He was so inconsistent that no one in the world could understand what he wanted. You may write one thing but fail to follow it in life. Particularly surprising was this purchase of expensive horses juxtaposed with his extreme denial of property and money."[58] But since Tolstoy was happier when occupied with his hobbies, Sophia suggested he should have a stud farm at Yasnaya, "to have it like a *toy.*"[59] She was concerned that Tolstoy's depression had returned and he was suffering from "terrible fatigue" and sadness.[60] Sophia analyzed the situation, writing Tolstoy:

I am beginning to think that if a happy man suddenly begins to see *only* terrible things and shuts his eyes to everything good, he must be ill. You need to take treatment. I'm saying this from the heart because it's clear to me. I'm terribly sorry for you; I wish you could reflect on my words and your condition without annoyance; you might then find a way out. You've had this hopelessness before, long ago; then you used to say it was "from lack of faith" that you wanted to hang yourself. And now what? Now that you've got faith, why are you unhappy again? Haven't you known before that there are hungry, sick, miserable, and wicked people? Look around: there are also healthy, happy, and kind people. I hope God helps you, what can I do? . . . I can only love and comfort you, but you don't need this anymore. What do you need? I wish I knew.[61]

Tolstoy responded that he needed her love: "And there's nothing that can revive me as your letters have revived me . . . I need my solitude and your love and nothing else can give me greater joy in life."[62] He was determined to criticize her less in Moscow: "I wouldn't be lying if I were to say I was nervously ill."[63] In March, when he wrote that he had an idea for a fictional work, Sophia felt it offered new hope:

I was seized with joy when I read you wanted to write in the *poetic genre* again. It was as if you felt what I've been longing for. That's where salvation and joy are to be found, that's where you and I will unite again, what will comfort you and will illuminate our lives. This work is genuine, you're made for it, and outside this sphere there is no peace for your soul. I know you can't force yourself but I hope God helps you to retain this spark and grow it. I'm thrilled by the idea.[64]

From his letters, where Tolstoy vividly described a spring day at Yasnaya, Sophia felt living there invigorated him. He had saddled a horse and brought a gun but did not fire a shot, just "listened to the thrushes, the grouse, the mice on the dry leaves, the dogs barking beyond the forest, the gunshots near and far . . . The moon rose on the right from behind the clouds; I waited till the stars were visible and rode home."[65] It was the world of nature and poetry they both loved, the world captured magically in his fiction.

During that day, which Tolstoy poetically related to her, Sophia carried out his requests. He had asked her to help a needy student, so she visited the Dyakovs and other wealthy friends, reading his letter to them and soliciting donations. Also, his proofs of *A Confession* had arrived from the journal *Russian Thought* and she dispatched them to Yasnaya. (The work was later banned by censors.)

This came on top of problems at home. Their English governess was ill and had to be taken to the hospital. Lev had a fever and was given quinine; delirious, he was sleepwalking. Meantime, Ilya refused to study for his exams, played dice (*babki*),[66] and went drinking with some house painters. Sophia found him and dragged him home; he resisted and was rude. She wrote Tolstoy: "I told him that it was my duty to protect him and that . . . he could even beat me, if he liked, but I will continue to care for him till my last breath."[67] Tolstoy responded with some analysis: "I'm sure they are behaving badly, and you're cross . . . It's safer to behave badly towards a good mother than a bad one, and for that reason they behave badly more often."[68] It was then that Sophia began to recognize the negative sides to city life.

In May, she described recent developments to her sister. Tolstoy had arrived and called Moscow "a large latrine and a contaminated bunk." He compelled her to agree and to make "a resolution never to return to live here." Then, with a change of heart, "he suddenly rushed about the streets and crescents to look for a house or an apartment for us. So, you go figure; the wisest philosopher could not!"[69] Tolstoy bought a house in the outskirts, away from their circle of friends, in the working-class neighborhood of Khamovniki. He liked the isolated location, its large garden, and the forested park surrounding the house. The property belonged to a civil servant, Ivan Arnautov, to whom Tolstoy paid twenty-seven thousand rubles, finalizing the deal in July.

Inspection revealed the attics were rotten, but Tolstoy was determined to remodel the house with an architect. Arriving in Moscow to supervise renovations at the end of May, he let Sophia go to Yasnaya. They switched roles: while Tolstoy attended to practical affairs in the city, Sophia was reading philosophy at Yasnaya with Urusov. She enjoyed "the eloquence, luster, and plasticity of Seneca" and "composed wisdom" of Marcus Aurelius, whose *Spiritual Teachings* she read in Urusov's translation.

Tolstoy was now buying furniture and fixtures for the new house: "Having renounced property and money, Lev Nikolaevich bought many things, carefully selecting the pieces . . . He bought screens of redwood, chairs for the living room, mirrors with bronze, various little tables, etc."[70] This was the infamous redwood furniture for which Sophia was later criticized and, yet, she remembers that he enjoyed buying it. He also purchased a new carriage, contrary to his recent plan "to give away everything superfluous—the piano, furniture, carriages."

That summer, Tolstoy lived in an unfitted wing of the house with their two older boys. They played Robinson Crusoe, Sophia would say, trying to be resourceful and provide for themselves. Once, needing a grater to shred horseradish, Tolstoy, instead of buying one, took a piece of metal from the roof and punctured holes in it with a nail. The grater would cost five kopecks, Sophia pointed out, struggling to understand his economy. It was not easy to understand: she had recently watched Tolstoy shove a twelve-thousand-ruble banknote in his pocket with indifference.[71]

Later that summer, when Tolstoy joined the family, they all played Postbox, a literary game he invented. On weekdays, the Tolstoys, Kuzminskys, and their guests wrote literary pieces and deposited them in a postbox set up in the hall upstairs. These contributions had to be anonymous. On weekends, when the contents were read aloud, writers would be identified by their style. (Sophia contributed poetry, in French and Russian.) It would not take long to recognize Tolstoy. In a satirical piece, "Medical Bulletin on Inmates of the Yasnaya Polyana Lunatic Asylum," he portrayed Sophia, himself, and the family. Tolstoy was aware of his tendency to go to extremes for the sake of an ideal. He described himself as "Patient No. 1," suffering from a mania to reform the world.

> *No. 1.* (Lev Nikolaevich) . . . The crux of his madness is that the patient considers it possible to change people's lives by words. General symptoms: dissatisfaction with the existing order of things, condemnation of everyone except himself, an irritable garrulity irrespective of his audience, frequent transitions from fury and exasperation to an unnatu-

ral, lachrymose sentimentality . . . Treatment: complete indifference of those surrounding the patient to what he says; occupations of the kind that will consume all the patient's energy.

No. 2. (Sophia Andreevna) Belongs to the harmless category, but has to be shut up at times . . . The madness is expressed in the patient's belief that everyone demands everything of her and that she cannot manage to get everything done . . . Treatment: strenuous work. Regime: isolation from frivolous and worldly people.[72]

That summer the family lived through a calamity. On June 30, one of the worst thunderstorms on record struck Tula province, causing a major train derailment near the village of Kukuevka. Seven passenger cars fell into a vast hole when the steep rail embankment was destroyed by runoff. They were buried under mud and water. Fifteen hundred people excavated for two weeks to recover the bodies. The official report, which appeared only a month later, announced forty-two dead and many more injured. To learn more about the tragedy, the Tolstoys drove to a nearby station, where they heard rumors of several hundred dead. (Such news could not be reported in the newspapers.) They watched a train slowly pass by: soldiers, sent to dig out the corpses, stood on a flatcar, singing to their drums. Tolstoy would refer to the tragedy in *What I Believe:* Kukuevka became a metaphor for disaster for long after.

Occupied with this event, Tolstoy dismissed their children's illnesses. When Ilya caught typhus, Sophia fed him thin soups and administered treatment. Tolstoy did not help look after their son. She told him that he cared little about their own children; Tolstoy stormed off and slept in his study. The quarrel continued the following day when "he shouted at the top of his voice that his dearest wish was to leave his family."[73] She suffered through an anxious night. Hurt and confused, she wrote in her diary that her wish was to die: "I long to take my life." As far as she was concerned she had done nothing to deserve his words. For this reason, his threat to leave home affected her all the more: "I shall carry the memory of that heartfelt, heart-rending cry of his to my grave."[74]

Telling Sophia of his wish to go away, it turned out, was unrelated to immediate events at home. That year, in a letter to a correspondent, Tolstoy referred to the Gospels and his determination to serve God: "And if a man leaves his home, his father and mother, his brothers, wife and children, he will find 100 times more homes and fathers here in this world and eternal life as well."[75] It was in this mood that he expressed his wish to leave. In her diary, pondering his beliefs, Sophia observed: "He is filled with Christian notions of self-perfection, and I envy him."[76]

She was the first to ask forgiveness, which moved Tolstoy; the children saw them hug and cry together in his study: "Now they are so kind and tender to each other; they have not been like that for a long time."[77] From the time Tolstoy's spiritual crisis began, their teenage children had heard him berate Sophia. And they also began to attack her over trifles. Daughter Tanya noted in her diary: "Lev and I set about criticizing Mamma. Lev shouted at her terribly and howled."[78] Tolstoy's criticism was proving contagious and made Sophia a ready target; from then on, she was on the defensive.

When in October, the family returned to Moscow, their new house was still being renovated. They were crammed downstairs until Christmas while carpenters finished their work. In the meantime, the children had a round of intestinal flu and Sophia barely left home. The windows of their Moscow house overlooked the park and it felt as though she was still at Yasnaya, especially since her domestic routine was unchanged. "I still sew . . . it's a very isolated life, and I look at the trees."[79]

Daughter Tanya began to take instruction from the painter Illarion Pryanishnikov:[80] the lessons took place at the house of Sergei Nikolaevich, Tolstoy's brother. Sophia also attended and Tolstoy came to observe. They used plaster sculptures of antiquity as models, drawing Antinous, whose masculine beauty Sophia admired. The lessons lasted long enough for her to make several sketches while learning anatomy and proportions.

Tolstoy was also studying: he took Hebrew lessons and read the Talmud with Solomon Minor, Moscow's first rabbi. He asked the rabbi whether Jews observed the principle of nonresistance to violence (turning the other cheek). Minor returned the question, asking whether Christians observed it. Tolstoy knew they did not and would describe the episode in *What I Believe.*[81]

Tolstoy's study of Hebrew was remarkable during the reign of Alexander III when anti-Semitism became government policy. Persecution of Jews and other minorities was on the rise and was soon to become one of

Tolstoy's major causes. The rabbi's visits to their Gentile family were likely without precedent. Sophia, although unable to match Tolstoy's religious tolerance, welcomed the rabbi to her home. She described him as "a very respectable, clever, and pleasant Jew,"[82] a remark revealing contemporary prejudice. But Sophia's attitude would begin to change, later enabling her to intercede with the government on behalf of a Jewish woman.

In Moscow, Tolstoy's depression returned: that winter, he noted in his journal that he was suffering from "terrible mental agonies."[83] His despair is apparent in his long letter to journalist Mikhail Engelhardt, with whom he discussed the teachings of Christ and the principle of nonresistance. Admitting his own inconsistency and failure to live by what he preached, Tolstoy entreated his young correspondent: "Teach me how to escape from the snares of temptation which have encompassed me, help me and I will fulfill them . . . If I lose my way and stagger—help me, support me in the real path."[84] The letter remained unsent. Sophia preserved it, noting on the envelope that Tolstoy wrote it to a complete stranger, a man he had never met.[85]

Tolstoy's letter reveals he was ardent in his desire to practice his beliefs. He needed a follower, more consistent than himself, to keep him steady on his chosen path. And it was not long before he found this dogmatic follower in Vladimir Chertkov, a man who would become Sophia's adversary. Tolstoy's passion for the ideal led him to divide people into allies and foes. He remarked that he was "too irritable and too insistent" at an early stage of his conversion and Sophia could not follow him: "At that time I presented my new understanding of life in such an unpleasant and unacceptable form that she felt a natural revulsion. Now I feel that she will never be able to attain the truth in the way that I have. The fault for closing the door to her is mine."[86]

The next several years were more demanding for Sophia. Tolstoy pressed her to accept his doctrine and threatened divorce. But the more he pressed, the more she resisted. In her view, the sacrifices she had to make were "impossible" and "undefined."[87] "I am expected to renounce everything, all my property, all my beliefs, the education and well-being of my children—things which not only I, a fairly determined woman, but thousands of others who *believe* in these precepts, are incapable of doing."[88]

Chapter Eight

Separate Lives

THE ARRIVAL OF 1883 was celebrated in a close family circle with champagne. Sophia cheerfully wrote sister Tanya: "Lyovochka is in such good spirits, just lovely! God willing, this lasts."[1] She wanted to enjoy this happy interlude to the full. In early January, she escorted daughter Tanya, now eighteen, to a ball at the house of the city mayor, Prince Alexander Shcherbatov.[2] The social elite gathered at his house, including the Moscow governor-general, Prince Vladimir Dolgorukov.

This was Sophia's first major ball, and for it she had a black velvet dress tailored for 250 silver rubles and put on "extremely rare and expensive" muslins, originally worn by Tolstoy's mother. Although thirty-nine, Sophia had little social experience and was patronized by older women, including a lady-in-waiting, Ekaterina Ermolova. Standing in a crowd of "veterans" but feeling like a debutante, Sophia enjoyed her own and her daughter's success. An acquaintance, Mikhail Sukhotin, who would later become her son-in-law, told Sophia she was "amazingly" beautiful: "That's who must be invited to dance."[3] Tanya, in a white tulle dress, had the cotillion with the orchestra's conductor, her face showing "so much happiness and triumph that all of the veterans and I could not help smiling."[4] The ball was "terribly jolly"; they made hordes of acquaintances, and stayed for supper, returning at six in the morning.

During that winter, Sophia went to several other balls, concerts, plays, and exhibitions with Tanya. After years in the country both were eager to go everywhere, see everything, and amuse themselves. Sophia attended lectures and literary evenings at the Polivanov gymnasium, where her boys were enrolled. The majority of students came from families of scientists, university professors, and statesmen, a milieu strikingly different from the aristocracy she met at the balls: "Everything was so new and jolly."

While she relished social life, she also knew Tolstoy disapproved of it and felt guilty for loving what he had renounced. "But I was *unable* to stop. I simply couldn't."[5] Although she enjoyed this entertainment only briefly, her love of balls would be criticized by Tolstoy's religious follow-ers. They would fault her for failing to understand her husband. But her need to amuse herself when Tolstoy's mood was darkening was natural: such activities provided escape.

Watchful of Tolstoy's moods, Sophia wrote in her diary, "Lyovochka is calmer and more cheerful; he does sometimes get in a rage and blame me for everything, but it doesn't last so long now, and doesn't happen so often."[6] To appease him, she was particularly dutiful after a night out: "I was busy all day: I instructed Andryusha and Masha in Russian and also in French and German. I did a lot of sewing, ran the household, and would not waste a minute of my time."[7]

Their Moscow house was now cozy and the family loved it. After classes, the children played in the garden and made icehouses, which they illuminated with candle ends, just as she had in childhood. They all skated at the Patriarch's Ponds, downtown, along with their friends, and Sophia masterfully glided on the ice, surrounded by her children.

Tolstoy was absorbed in writing *What I Believe,* in which he presented his religious doctrine. He was emerging as the founder of a new religion, prepared to teach people how to live. Sophia understood his teaching in terms of moral perfection and self-sacrifice. She wrote to Tolstoy about this work as she read it: "Of course, one cannot argue with the need for people to perfect themselves and one must remind people *how* to do this, and show the ways. But still, I must say that it's *difficult* to give up all of those toys in life that one enjoys playing with."[8] (This was a veiled refer-ence to Tolstoy's expensive hobbies.)

Sophia knew that Tolstoy's nonfiction could not be published in Russia: he was arguing that the entire establishment, its social order, as well as the peace and security of his own family, were based on law that Christ had rejected. At first upset with his moral writings, she now found them "very interesting" and even took pride in his religious work: "But he must do it, it's God's will; and they may even serve His great purpose."⁹ She reported to her sister that Tolstoy wrote "articles on Christianity" and "we are on friendly terms."¹⁰ His criticism of privilege and city life was "painful" to her "but I know he cannot do otherwise."

> He is a pioneer, he walks ahead of the crowd, and points out the way that people must take. And I belong with *the crowd* . . . I move with it and I see the light of a lantern carried by such pioneers as Lyovochka. Of course, I recognize it as a *light,* yet, I cannot move faster: the crowd, my milieu, and my habits are holding me back.¹¹

In the spring, when a fire destroyed twenty-two buildings in the village of Yasnaya Polyana, Tolstoy was quick to organize relief. He wrote to Sophia that people urgently needed seed for planting and asked her to get in touch with his brother Sergei Nikolaevich: he wanted to buy his oat seed for the fire victims. Two weeks later, Tolstoy made additional requests: he needed Sophia's help with his publishing and estate matters. And a week later, he put her in charge of all his business.

Sophia was not present on May 21, at a law office in Tula, when Tolstoy gave her power of attorney. He addressed the document, "To her excellency, kind madam, and dear wife Sophia Andreevna. I entrust you to manage all my affairs."¹² His playful style suggests he was relieved to sign his property away. The same day, Tolstoy hurriedly left for their Samara estate without stopping in Moscow to say good-bye to Sophia.

When she received the power of attorney document, she cried: "I felt that although Lev Nikolaevich frequently told me of his love, in reality he loved me little, having shifted to my shoulders the responsibility for the family, the management of the estate, the house, his books, etc."¹³ Her role as estate manager, given that Tolstoy believed property and money were evil, made her vulnerable to his criticism.

From Samara, Tolstoy wrote to apologize for leaving in such haste. His letters were affectionate and nostalgic. He needed Sophia as much as his work: these two kept him alive. He promised on his return to be "nearer" to her than before.[14] Sophia refused to believe this as she grappled with new responsibilities. She asked him to explain how it was possible to be "nearer" under the circumstances. It would be good to bring back their past, when they were together in all their beliefs; but family life did not satisfy him. "Sometimes, I think that your great tenderness comes from the reasons I dislike."[15] She was getting used to the idea of a "new happiness," which involved "freedom for both . . . Then there are no reproaches, no quarrels, but, of course, neither is the bond intimate, which pulls at one's heartstrings . . ."[16] Tolstoy replied with a passionate letter: he loved her as strongly as before, while she was destroying his love.[17]

In Samara, Tolstoy was liquidating their farm, selling livestock and other assets, and renting out the land. At first, seeing that his property was neglected in winter and that some colts died, he was annoyed. But he overcame this, forgave the manager, and they cried together. Giving up property felt unburdening, he wrote Sophia. He said he was as relieved as he had been years ago, when fire at Yasnaya destroyed the greenhouses with their peach trees.[18] (However, Sophia remembered how he was crushed when the bittersweet smell of burning peach blossoms filled the air. The trees were planted by his grandfather.)

Tolstoy estimated that proceeds from the Samara sales, ten thousand rubles, would pay off their mortgage in Moscow. He also decided to ship forty-five horses to Yasnaya, the best and "most interesting breeds." Sophia welcomed this decision, no matter how inconsistent it was with his new beliefs, because he needed his *toys*. Perhaps she was relieved to discover that a part of Tolstoy hadn't changed: she recognized the man she used to know and love, with all his human weaknesses.

Meantime, she learned that Bibikov, their Samara estate manager, sheltered twenty people at their farm, several of them charged with antigovernment activities. Police had established surveillance over the place. Troubled that the rebels lived there, she wrote Tolstoy that these people were "alien and repulsive to me."[19] She feared they wanted to "possess" Tolstoy morally.[20] He replied to reassure: he disagreed with the revolutionaries on a major point, their use of violence, which he believed "morally wrong."[21]

Although Tolstoy was aware the authorities were watching him, he still met with the religious sectarians, the Molokans. A report about the meeting was promptly sent to the Samara governor, which Tolstoy casually mentioned to Sophia: "Let them report."[22] She was annoyed, replying that this would cause "trouble and grief" for the family.[23]

While Tolstoy was in Samara, sister Tanya visited Yasnaya. Sophia described their life, which had not changed: cricket in the evenings; going for rides, walks, and swims; chatting and singing; teaching Greek, Russian, German, and French. "Perhaps you are reading this and thinking to yourself, 'They are still busy with nonsense . . .' It's hard for me, Lyovochka, to know that you disapprove of me and my entire life and believe it not serious enough."[24] She was living the life they used to share and love, and which he described in *Anna Karenina*. In the past it was ideal; now he called it "idleness." This life, which seemed so "natural, even very good and happy to us," now depressed him. "For me," Sophia wrote, "it's all illuminated with the beauty of summer and nature, with my love and my duty toward the children; the joy of reading (I'm reading Shakespeare), and much more. It's sad that none of this can satisfy you any longer, very sad."[25]

Sophia read Turgenev's story "The Clock" to her children, nephews, and nieces, and danced with them on the veranda. "I don't feel guilty that I'm not doing some invented work . . . I'm happy to have a moment of leisure."[26] In the meantime, the small children had whooping cough and she tended to them. She also had patients to look after and attended a peasant woman with typhus. "I have so many patients, Lyovochka . . . I have become a real doctor."[27]

She was also copying *A Confession,* soon to be published in Geneva. Quoting from this melancholy work in her letters, she joked about it to Tolstoy, perhaps hoping to drive away his despondent mood: "Don't torment yourself, Lyovochka, that you don't work. Live, drink, eat, and enjoy pleasure, as Solomon says in your *Confession,* which I am copying in French without a letup."[28]

Before his return she wrote, "I have no other desires but that you keep drinking the *kumis* and that it calms you, that you'd return agreeable, healthy, and young, young in spirit, as before; we would then thank God for the happiness . . . and wish nothing and invent nothing."[29] This happiness was not to be: in less than a year, Tolstoy attacked her in his diary for failing to practice his religious doctrine.

However, his exuberant mood would return. Back at Yasnaya, Tolstoy joined the family in their activities and evening discussions. On Sophia's name day, he ambushed her and Prince Urusov on their walk, hiding in the hollow of a tree and howling like a wolf. Urusov presented Sophia with a saltshaker of Saxony porcelain, "shaped like a charming girl . . . with bright blue eyes. 'I'd like to have a girl like that,' I said, laughing, and thanked Prince Urusov for the gift."[30] She would remember this when she bore Sasha, a charming girl with blue eyes, the next year.

When the family returned to Moscow, Tolstoy remained in the country to complete his treatise. After a restful summer, Sophia was overwhelmed with responsibilities: the children's schooling, managing property, and Tolstoy's business affairs. The printers were publishing *What I Believe* as a separate edition. She read proofs and dispatched them to Tolstoy for final review. As well, she offered her critique: the intensity of his feeling had disappeared from this polished version. (In 1885, when this work appeared in Paris, she was happy with its success, writing Tolstoy that he had followers in France. He was pleased with her letter.)

Tolstoy was hoping that Russian censors would pass a limited edition of his treatise and so contracted printers to produce fifty copies, to be sold at an exorbitant twenty-five rubles.[31] Only the rich could buy it, but, after all, this was the audience at which he aimed his criticism. The work was banned: the head of the Moscow Civil Censorship Committee wrote that it "undermines the foundations of social and governmental institutions and wholly destroys the teachings of the Church." In February 1884, the police seized most copies from the printers. But unlike other banned literature, *What I Believe* was not burned by the censors. Instead, it was distributed to government officials who preserved it in their private libraries; as a result, copies survive to this day. Tolstoy was pleased that his book was read by top officials and that his message reached the government. (Illegal copies of the work also began to circulate. The ban only boosted its popularity.)

In the fall of 1883, Tolstoy refused to accept jury duty, since it contradicted his new principle—not to swear an oath. As a nobleman he could send a letter exempting himself and pay a fine, but he chose to appear in person. Arriving at the district court, after hearings began, he announced publicly that being a juror was against his religious beliefs. Sophia pointed out that a peaceful written resignation would not have contradicted his principles, whereas his public statement angered some, in violation of his nonresistance doctrine. Although determined to be humble, he remained a proud man. Sophia wrote: "It excited you—to state it publicly and take a risk."[32] The authorities could have put him on trial, she wrote; if imprisoned or exiled, his family would suffer as well. But Tolstoy welcomed suffering for his religious beliefs.

Tolstoy was working at Yasnaya; in Moscow Sophia handled the family's practical life. Her days were taken with buying firewood, fixing mattresses, repairing wells, cleaning closets, paying bills, and shopping. She helped the boys with their essays and corresponded with the Samara manager, to try to make sense of his entangled transactions. She also had to oversee the shipment of those forty-five horses to Yasnaya. She had eight children and one husband to look after, she wrote Tolstoy, and "to clothe, to feed, and to teach them takes so much time."[33] It surprised her that while she used to love the city, she now yearned for tranquillity.

When painters Illarion Pryanishnikov and Vladimir Makovsky, Konstantin's brother, visited, she listened to their conversation and, again, experienced a "mad longing" to study art. But because her responsibilities had increased, she had to postpone this dream. And there was more uncertainty in her life—fear of a new pregnancy—of which she wrote Tolstoy.

At Yasnaya, Tolstoy enjoyed his solitude and wrote that "only eating alone is dull."[34] Sophia finished his sentence, "and living alone is much better . . . I know my duty is not to upset you. You might be finally having a good working day—and I am upsetting you."[35] By now, she was certain of her pregnancy. As she wrote her sister, she felt like "screaming of despair and rage."[36]

Told the news, Tolstoy wrote he was glad they would have a child; Sophia's unhappiness came from her *révolte*. It would be easier for her and people around her if she assumed a more accepting attitude: "Why can't you surrender?"[37] Sophia thought his position was morally superior and felt crushed: "If *I* were bad before, now I am loathsome! And if *you* were good, you have become so much better!"[38] Her pregnancy explained her abnormal state, Tolstoy replied: "I know, I've heard, that it's terribly oppressive for the soul."[39]

Meanwhile, Sophia attempted to induce a miscarriage: she took scalding baths and jumped from a dresser. To a nanny who tried to talk her out of this, she said that Tolstoy considered leaving her and their children. When her attempts failed, she approached a midwife in Tula, asking for an abortion. The midwife, afraid of exposure, refused: she would perform an abortion for someone else, but not for Countess Tolstoy.

In December, Sophia had a nervous collapse and remained prostrate for two weeks, refusing to eat, wash, or talk. Doctors gave her quinine and caffeine, which made her feel worse. Tolstoy, summoned to Moscow, walked around with a "tense and miserable expression,"[40] irritable even with daughter Tanya, whom he called "the worst of all his children."[41] Only weeks later, realizing her family needed her, Sophia summoned her strength and returned to the whirlpool of life.

She attended a series of balls and theatricals in the New Year with Tanya. Balls were her "tavern" where she could forget herself, she wrote her sister. Learning that Sophia was pregnant, one of her acquaintances quipped that she was taking out two daughters at once.

Tolstoy wrote how sorry he felt for Sophia and Tanya for attending balls; he described his life at Yasnaya and an orphaned peasant boy who visited him. Sophia sensed his letter was meant to contrast "the poverty of the people and the absurd splendor of balls."[42] She begged him to be less critical: "I don't enjoy life, I don't value it. It's clear to me now that I will never attain moral perfection. And I cannot enjoy material pleasures because of the sensible and severe critic beside me, who makes me despair."[43]

In 1884, Tolstoy took lessons from a shoemaker to learn to stitch boots and made the first pair for their servant Agafya Mikhailovna. Sophia learned more details from Sergei Nikolaevich, who visited his brother at Yasnaya. Disheveled, in dirty stockings and a peasant blouse, Tolstoy was bent over a workbench, making shoes for the servant while a school-teacher read *Lives of the Saints*. Sophia was fuming as she related this to sister Tanya: "Such buffoonery and indifference to his own family is so disgusting to me that I will even stop writing him. Having sired a heap of children, he can neither find joy in his own family nor do any work for them . . . It's so hard for me now to handle everything at once, the large family, the grown-up boys, and my pregnancy, that I'm eagerly looking forward to getting sick or to getting run over by a horse, just to have some rest and escape this life."[44]

She later wrote Tolstoy of her regret that his "intellectual powers are wasted on chopping wood, heating samovars, and stitching boots, all of which is good as a diversion, but not a vocation."[45] Learning that he was mixing dough and baking bread, she sighed, quoting a proverb: "Let a child amuse himself as long as he doesn't cry."[46]

Around the world, news that Tolstoy was making shoes created a sensation. Particularly memorable to Sophia was a newspaper's comment that Tolstoy had put aside his pen to help improve the quality of shoes and clothing. Little did his fans realize that this was more than just an eccentric hobby. In his nonfiction Tolstoy depicted the poor and their way of life as righteous and their menial work as virtuous. He was also reinventing himself as a holy man.

During the spring, Tolstoy spent several months in the city, which became a trial for him and the family: he was depressed, suffered insomnia, and was unable to write.[47] Sophia wrote in March: "Lyovochka has become very unhappy recently; his eyes look severely and critically, and he is silent. I am not asking what troubles him and what he is thinking about; when I encouraged his openness in the past, he would break out into loud, desperate cries, disapproving of my way of life. But now, I can't take it anymore, I'm not strong and healthy myself and, so, I'm silent as well."[48] They lived like strangers, she added, on good terms but lacking openness.

Tolstoy's new routine was austere. He would get up early, before everyone else, and tidy his room. Then he spent hours studying: he was then interested in Chinese philosophers and writers. Evenings were spent on shoemaking lessons. His diary reflects this monotony: "Read about Confucius . . . After dinner I went round to the cobbler's. How bright and morally refined it is in his dirty, dark corner." He idealized the poor and criticized his family, which in contrast appeared idle, leading a life of luxury: "Tried to talk to my wife after dinner. Impossible . . . The one thorn, and a painful one."[49]

Family and friends observed Tolstoy making shoes: the small workroom was always full of people. Tolstoy learned to drive tacks into the sole, proud of his progress. Sophia remained skeptical: "Today, Lyovochka made a galosh and brought it to show, saying, '*C'est délicieux!*' But the galosh is badly stitched and the style is ugly."[50] Friends ordered his boots as souvenirs. Fet paid six rubles for a pair, showing them off along with a

Tolstoy in 1898, in the yard of their Moscow house in Khamovniki.
Photo by Sophia Tolstoy.

certificate he composed himself: these boots were made by the author of
War and Peace on January 15, 1885. Tolstoy was annoyed with Fet and his
epicurean attitude to life and referred to him in his diary as "a sick man."[51]

Fet visited Sophia that winter, sitting beside her and drinking tea from
a samovar, while she sewed. He continued to dedicate his poems to her and
would joke that there was nothing else he needed in Moscow but a pleasant
hostess and a samovar. In a letter to Strakhov, Fet described the changes in
the Tolstoy household. He was deeply sorry for Tolstoy, that "most kind
and noble man and first-rate talent" who had become badly divided in his
heart. "The head of the family, the father of numerous children, renounces
material life . . . I am asking you, what other contemporary woman could
bear what the countess had to? . . . None!"[52]

Although Tolstoy resolved to avoid getting angry, he continued to disapprove of everything the family lived by: "I can't sympathize with them.
All their joys, the examination, social successes, music, furniture, shopping—I consider them all a misfortune and an evil for them."[53] Daughter

Tanya annoyed him because of her enjoyment of life: "The terrible thing is that their cheerfulness, especially Tanya's—a cheerfulness which isn't the consequence of work (they don't do any) but of malice—is an unwarrantable cheerfulness."[54] He criticized their eldest son, who would later participate in his causes: "Seryozha is impossibly obtuse. The same castrated mind that his mother has. If you two should ever read this, forgive me; it hurts me terribly."[55] Sophia impugned his criticism of the family in a letter to him: "It's sad that you love *your* own children so little; if they were peasant children, it would be a different matter."[56] A while later, she would tell him that physical blows were less hurtful than his reproaches.

Tolstoy, whose fictional characters were complex, now perceived the world in black and white, noting in his diary: "All wise men and saintly people in the world are on my side."[57] He needed dedicated followers to spread his ideas. In October 1883, he met Chertkov, who expressed keen interest in his religion. Tolstoy, then fifty-five, soon addressed his twenty-nine-year old disciple as "my dear, close friend."[58] The relationship would prove injurious to his marriage.

Sophia's first impression of the young man was favorable and she wrote Tolstoy that she liked Chertkov "very much."[59] She described him as "tall, handsome, manly, and a true aristocrat."[60] Her impression would change, however, as Chertkov's influence on Tolstoy increased. In January 1884, sensing that Tolstoy idealized his follower, she wrote: "Will you continue to shut your eyes *deliberately,* as not to see anything but good in some people? That's blindness!"[61] She feared Chertkov would further alienate Tolstoy from his family, which, in fact, happened.

Chertkov was the only surviving son of very rich parents. His family in Petersburg had close connections to court: his father was an adjutant-general to Alexander II. Chertkov's religiosity was likely inspired by his mother, Elizaveta Ivanovna. She was a follower of Lord Radstock, an English Christian evangelist who created a stir among the Russian aristocracy in the mid-1870s. Chertkov had a typical career as an officer in the Guards and enjoyed "all three classic vices—wine, cards, and women . . . without restraint."[62] Then came his awakening: he began to preach the Gospels while still in the army. Upon leaving the military in his twenties, he settled on his family estate in southern Russia. There he engaged in charitable work, organized a trade school, a village store, and a bank for peasants. At the time he met Tolstoy, Chertkov believed preaching the Gospels was his "main mission" in life.[63]

In his letters to Chertkov, Tolstoy began to describe his life at home as martyrdom. Only months into their relationship, Tolstoy trusted his disciple to know his private life, writing to him: "I suffer because my wife does not share my convictions."[64] That same year, Tolstoy allowed Chertkov to read and copy his diaries, a privilege reserved in the past for Sophia. When learning about this, she observed that Tolstoy now wrote his diary with the disciple in mind. Chertkov would later skillfully use these critical entries to vilify Sophia and portray Tolstoy as a saint. But Tolstoy's words have to be interpreted in a broader sense. He and Sophia had a greater understanding than what he implied. While she did not share some of his principles, she understood him as a man and artist.

On her side, there was no lack of understanding and support, even when Tolstoy criticized her and the family. That summer, she read and corrected the German translation of *What I Believe*. Her reading list for the year included books of interest to Tolstoy: Rousseau, poems by Saadi, and Chinese writers. When he praised *Essays* by the French Renaissance writer Michel de Montaigne, she asked Tolstoy to bring the book to Moscow. Sophia would make detailed notes about the books Tolstoy had read. From her notes we know he kept Montaigne's *Essays* on his desk and re-read them the year he died. Montaigne was also an influence in 1884, when Tolstoy began his novella *The Death of Ivan Ilyich*. A year later, when Sophia became his publisher, Tolstoy gave this novella to her as a gift on her name day.

In the summer of 1884, Tolstoy's mood became more extreme. In June, just before Sophia gave birth to daughter Sasha, she mentioned their losses in Samara. The expensive stallions Tolstoy had bought had been neglected and were sold at a loss. Her remark angered Tolstoy because he did not want to be reminded of his past. He described the incident in his diary: "Went for a bathe. Came back cheerful . . . and suddenly there began some absurd reproaches on my wife's part about the horses which I don't need and which I only want to get rid of. I said nothing, but I was terribly depressed."[65] Sophia watched him pack his knapsack and leave. She caught up to him in the alley and asked where he was going. " 'I don't know, somewhere, maybe to America, forever. I can't stand living at home any longer,' he replied with tears in his voice."[66] She told him her labor pangs had begun and begged him to stay, but he only quickened his steps. When he returned the same night, Sophia made it to his study: "Forgive me. I'm in labor, perhaps I'll die." He saw her to her room, still angry, as his diary reveals. That ghastly June night when she gave birth to Sasha would be forever etched in her memory.

Baby Sasha was a gorgeous girl with black hair and blue eyes. A child of conflict, she would rebel against her mother. When she was born, Sophia refused to nurse her: rejected by her husband, she "could not feel anything at all for the baby." A wet nurse was engaged. In a letter to Chertkov, Tolstoy called Sophia's refusal to nurse her own child "the most inhumane ... and unchristian act."[67] Because of his attitude she could not nurse even if she wanted to: "It would do nothing but harm for the baby ... I was nervous and constantly on the verge of tears, fearing Lev Nikolaevich's disapproval."[68]

A month later, Tolstoy made another scene when she refused to have intercourse. He packed his knapsack again, an event he described in his diary: "During the night I got ready to go away, packed up my things and went to wake her up. I don't know what was the matter with me—bitterness, lust, moral exhaustion—but I suffered terribly. She got up, and I told her everything, told her that she had ceased to be a wife. A helpmate for her husband? She hasn't helped me for a long time, but only hinders me. A mother to the children? She doesn't want to be. A nurse? She doesn't want to be. A companion of my nights? She makes a bait and a plaything even out of that. I was terribly depressed."[69]

Sophia had several hysterical fits that summer. She told Tolstoy in a letter that her hysteria humiliated her: "It's my most shameful memory, although I'm not responsible for my condition."[70] Tolstoy saw her refusal to have sex as malice. In the fall, when he learned she had suffered inflammation after the last birth, he wrote her compassionate and guilt-laden letters.

However, back in July, he had looked at her from his position as a holy man, noting in his diary: "She's beginning to tempt me carnally ... But cohabitation with a woman alien in spirit—i.e. with her—is terribly vile."[71] He blamed her for both tempting him and rejecting him. As a result, he was so severe that "we were afraid to talk to him. Everyone was silent and felt depressed ... Never before had Lyovochka's mood been so *extreme* and never before was it *so* difficult to find the point where we could meet by yielding to each other."[72] That same month, Sophia wrote her mother, begging her to visit.

Tolstoy's mood possibly reflected a recent change in his lifestyle. In 1884, he attempted to give up smoking, wine, meat, and tea all at once. As he was a heavy smoker till then, quitting this habit alone was hard. He gave up hunting and, as well, cards, merely sitting beside the players and watching. Another change in his routine was getting up at six to do physical labor. And he no longer traveled to Samara, which used to relax him. In addition, he wrestled with desire, viewing physical love as sinful.

Sophia's mother arrived at the end of July. She listened to both sides. As Tolstoy's childhood friend, she knew how to manage him: within days peace was restored. He noted in his diary: "Sonya and I were reconciled. How glad I was. Actually if *she* were to take it upon herself to be good, she would be very good."[73] On Sophia's birthday, the family played Postbox, their literary game. She contributed a sentimental poem, "The Angel," in which the relationship of a couple is disrupted by the devil's meddling and restored by the touch of an angel's wing.

But in October, when Sophia returned to Moscow, she was again a physical and emotional wreck: "Every expression of feeling agitates me excessively, I fear emotions, and I only try to run things smoothly, without tipping the balance, and keep busy. I was instructed to stay at home and rest, avoid movement, going out, and excitement."[74] Suffering from vaginal bleeding, severe pain, and fever, she saw a gynecologist. When she reported the result of the examination to Tolstoy, he destroyed the letter: "I tore it up [the letter] and will keep tearing [them] up." He became "repulsive" to himself, writing her, "It's me, brutal and selfish animal."[75] Sophia was quick to reassure him: "It's not your fault, we both are to blame, and, besides, this may have been caused by some injury during birth."[76] When she was diagnosed with inflammation of the uterus and took regular painful treatment, Tolstoy was troubled with her condition and suggested that she ask her doctor about birth control.[77] She responded she had no moral strength to confront the doctor with "the questions you imply . . . I trembled from embarrassment and pain."[78] To her sister, she wrote that the inflammation would likely leave her infertile, but this was not to be.

In the fall and winter, the couple lived mostly apart, which helped reconcile their differences. Tolstoy wrote "good, caring, and affectionate" letters and she appreciated his sympathy. His peace of mind was even more important to her. At Yasnaya, Tolstoy resumed his old routine, taking leisurely walks and playing the piano "with great enjoyment."[79] From his letters, she understood that he "must be in a splendid mood." It was the mood she knew and loved, which had inspired his fiction. She wrote to help fan that spark of inspiration: "Your enjoyment of music, nature, your desire to write—that's where you're *genuine,* the very man you want to destroy in you, that splendid, sweet, kind, and poetic man, whom everyone so loves in you. But you won't destroy him, no matter how you try." She made a resolution as to what her role beside him should be, and announced in the same letter, "I'm determined to *fulfill my duty* toward you as a writer and a man who needs his freedom above all; so, I'm not asking anything at all from you. And I am guided by the same sense of duty toward the children."[80]

Tolstoy was writing *The Death of Ivan Ilyich.* In December, when in Moscow, he read a piece to the family, Sophia thought it "a bit gloomy but very good."[81] The novella depicts his hero's spiritual transformation while he is dying from cancer. The hero's alienation from his family was familiar to Sophia, who had lived through Tolstoy's conversion and estrangement.

That same fall, while still undergoing treatment, Sophia investigated how to start her own publishing business: she visited printing shops and paper manufacturers. Tolstoy's contract with the Salaev Brothers, who had published his collected works, was to expire the following year, 1885. According to her memoir, Tolstoy himself proposed that she publish a new edition of the works. "He gave me no money at all . . . but suggested that I publish it myself."[82] She had no experience and was frightened by the complexities of all business and publishing affairs.

When in 1885 Chertkov asked Tolstoy about her publishing, he replied that he had given Sophia power of attorney, enabling her to manage their property and publish his works. After explaining this delicate matter, Tolstoy added, "Now forget about it."[83] But the disciple would not forget.

To start publishing, Sophia had to borrow ten thousand rubles from her mother and fifteen thousand from a friend, a landowner, Alexander Stakhovich. As she explained to sister Tanya, the business could be profit-

able, "but everything is terribly entangled, and I have so many new responsibilities that I simply despair sometimes and think, 'No way, I can't
handle this!'"[84] She had decided to undertake this venture because the
family needed money. Since moving to Moscow, expenses increased, while
income from both estates dwindled. Yasnaya now produced negligible income and there was another bad year in Samara.

Sophia enumerated the household finances to Tolstoy: there were three
thousand rubles in their account, enough for three months in Moscow.
Basic expenses—city taxes, household needs, groceries, school fees, staff
salaries—came to 910 rubles per month.[85] (This did not include entertainment because there was none that winter.)

Tolstoy replied that happiness did not depend on money or education.
In terms of moral well-being, it was more important for each family member to cut back on expenses. But if they needed money, it could be found
("unfortunately," he added). One could begin selling forest and horses; in
addition, there was income from the sale of his works.[86]

At this time he was excited by his new idea for managing Yasnaya
himself. Tolstoy shared this plan with Sophia in his letter of October 23.
He wrote her that he wanted to run Yasnaya in accordance with his principles of "justice, peace, and, if possible, kindness." His intention was to
prove that the rich could voluntarily and gradually give up their property.
Previously, he wanted to ignore property altogether, afraid that his contradiction would be pointed out. "Now, I think I've grown out of this."
Sophia replied that it was only fair, since he was living on the estate much
of the year, for him to manage it on his own, and that she was willing to
help.[87] But Tolstoy's idea was soon abandoned: "I knew that his dreams
and projects would remain in his head, while practical solutions would
be left up to a steward, to me, and to providence."[88] Tolstoy remained de-
tached from the management of the estate but expected Sophia to run it
according to his Christian principles. This would, for example, involve
managing the estate without defending her right to property, a contradiction she was unable to resolve. She would be violating his principles if she
were to report thefts, enforce payments of debts, or even refuse a peasant's
request.

Tolstoy did not have a uniform idea to divest himself of property. His
play *And the Light Shineth in Darkness* captures some of his inconsistencies

on the issue. His hero drafts several plans: give up the property altogether, leave a plot for himself and his family, or transfer everything to his wife. Like Tolstoy, his hero expects his wife's endorsement and support.

As Sophia later remarked, Tolstoy put her at the center of all his fantasies. Indeed, he continued to use her as a model even in his nonfiction. At the end of the year, she read part of his treatise *What Then Must We Do?* The work conveyed his impressions of city poverty. Sophia, copying it, was offended by his criticism of their family's lifestyle and insisted that Tolstoy exclude remarks concerning their sons. He apologized and changed some passages, making them less personal. But even with his revisions, she saw his finger pointed at her in a passage criticizing upper-class women who viewed their pregnancies as a misfortune.

When Tolstoy's treatise was published (censors allowed only excerpts to appear), readers' opinions were split. Some were confused by the ambiguity of his style. His attacks on science and pronouncements about women's roles appeared archaic and were even mocked. Tolstoy also discussed God-given responsibilities of the sexes. Men were meant to perform physical and intellectual work; their role seemed to end there. He discussed women's destiny with pathos. A woman-mother was to give birth herself, nurse, cook, sew, wash, teach, and morally instruct her children. His treatise ended with an appeal to women-mothers: the future of the world and its salvation is in your hands. But along with this prominent mission, Tolstoy entrusted women with all other responsibilities, as in his own family. In early 1885, when he was completing the treatise, Sophia expressed hope to her sister that Tolstoy would relax and not produce any more works of this sort.[89]

While Sophia was starting her publishing venture, Tolstoy and Chertkov launched Intermediary Press. Their objective was to produce edifying literature the poor could afford. Intermediary published Tolstoy's moralistic stories and other writers of social significance, including Chekhov and Dickens.

When Intermediary employees visited Yasnaya, Sophia received them in "good grace."[90] She sympathized with their idea of producing books for mass audiences but as a publisher was wary that Tolstoy would give his new work to them. To Tolstoy, her publishing was unimportant because it was only meant to raise money for the family. Not until later would it become apparent that both their ventures were necessary. Aside from printing an authenticated version of his works, she fought to lift the publication bans on his nonfiction and *The Kreutzer Sonata*.

As publishing had to be fit in among her other duties, it was unwelcome at first. Turning the annex of their Moscow residence into her office and warehouse, she stacked unsold volumes, neglecting even to insure them. But gradually, she began to invest her heart in this activity, discovering an opportunity to explore her talents and work independently.

Chapter Nine

The Money Brought Me No Joy

I N FEBRUARY 1885, Sophia traveled to Petersburg to complete the publishing research she began in Moscow. A new twelve-volume edition of Tolstoy's collected works was to come out at the end of the year and she was handling all stages of production, from ordering paper to proofreading, as well as sales. She had one week to master knowledge that was mostly foreign to her.

Tolstoy's editor, Strakhov, had suggested that Sophia meet Anna Dostoevsky, the writer's widow. Anna had been producing her husband's works for years. As a young stenographer before her marriage, she helped Fyodor Dostoevsky meet a critical deadline. Becoming indispensable to him from then on, she took his dictation and nursed him through epileptic attacks and a gambling addiction. Dostoevsky called her his "guardian angel." Anna thought the same of Sophia, following their first meeting: "I was convinced that she was the veritable guardian angel of her husband's genius."[1]

She would describe Sophia enthusiastically: "The countess made a very favorable impression on me. It was with genuine pleasure that I confided to her all the 'secrets' of my publishing work, gave her samples of subscription books and announcements I had distributed, cautioned her against certain mistakes I had made, and so forth."[2] A shrewd businesswoman, Anna shared her methods of dealing with booksellers and advertising.

Instead of buying expensive newspaper announcements, she distributed printed notices. Sophia would adopt these practices, writing Tolstoy that Anna Dostoevsky "herself publishes her husband's books and in two years made a net profit of sixty-seven thousand. She gave me useful advice, surprising me that she gives a discount of only 5 percent on the retail price to booksellers."[3] Anna published not only for profit, as she had admitted, "but mainly because I had found myself an interesting business."

In addition to publishing practices, there was much that Sophia had to learn on her own. Tolstoy's nonfiction was banned, unlike Dostoevsky's works, and she had to fight with censors to lift the ban. And this was not all. Whereas Dostoevsky had wholeheartedly approved of Anna's publishing activity, Sophia would meet with hindrance from Tolstoy.

Her publishing would conflict with Tolstoy's intention to renounce his copyright. One example of his changing views on copyright was with *The Death of Ivan Ilyich*. That year, Tolstoy gave her the novella to publish exclusively in the collected works. "I was extremely pleased and grateful to Lev Nikolaevich but later he . . . gave the story to the public domain, along with other works written after 1881"[4] (the date of his spiritual conversion).

At the start, Tolstoy took interest in publishing: while she was in Petersburg, he proofread the last volume containing his nonfiction, *A Confession, What I Believe,* and *What Then Must We Do?* But later that same year he began to refer to it as *her* business, thus distancing himself from the moneymaking operation.

In Petersburg, Sophia's schedule was packed: she was combining business with family affairs. Her mother and many cousins lived there. She stayed with sister Tanya, now also living in Petersburg, arriving when her ten-year-old son, Misha, was diagnosed with typhoid. Despite this commotion, Sophia interviewed paper salesmen and printers at the house. When she received production estimates she discovered costs were higher in Petersburg.

As soon as Sophia returned to Moscow, Tolstoy arranged to leave for the Crimea with Prince Urusov, who had been diagnosed with emphysema. Wrapped in a woolen plaid, coughing and wheezing, Prince Urusov came to say good-bye to Sophia. Previously, she had bought him an expensive respirator to use during the cold season, and he kissed the hands of his "benefactress." They spent an evening together, discussing only "abstract subjects, Lev Nikolaevich's teaching, and our reading of philosophy."[5] But there was more than conversation to the evening. For Prince Urusov, the Tolstoy family had replaced his own: he was godfather to several of their children and Sophia "always felt happy and relaxed" with him.[6] Now Sophia's friend was dying: in the summer, she would see him for the last time.

From the Crimea, Tolstoy described exotic flora—vines, olive and almond trees—and "the deep blue sea." The two visited Sebastopol, where Tolstoy was stationed three decades earlier during the Crimean War. Driving through the battlefields, Tolstoy found a cannonball—perhaps one he had fired himself—and gave it to Prince Urusov as a keepsake. For Sophia, who read *Sebastopol Sketches* in her girlhood, his letters evoked the days when she dreamt of joining Tolstoy at the front. Describing to her his walks in the mountains and by the shore, he wrote: "It was a moonlit night, cypresses covered the slopes like black columns, fountains gurgled everywhere and down below—the 'incessant sound' of the blue sea."[7] Sophia had never seen the mountains or the sea and yearned to travel. She had to stay in Moscow to look after their family and her publishing. "I am writing to you, to the distant world of beauty, poetry, and warmth, from my cold, practical world of material cares and haste."[8] Tolstoy had renounced the material world as futile; therefore, everything she lived by, her cares for the family, the children's upbringing and education, her efforts to earn money, were of no interest to him. But someone had to support the family, look after their small children, and endure their difficult teenage boys, who were gambling and demanding money to cover their losses. (Tolstoy, admitting he was no better at that age, had, of course, withdrawn from their upbringing.)

To speed up publication of the collected works, Sophia engaged two printing shops. She was swamped with proofs, writing sister Tanya, "To save eight hundred rubles of a proofreader's fee, I boldly decided to undertake this work myself, and now I'm harnessed for five months ahead."[9] For a missed deadline she would pay a big fine, but in more than two decades' publishing this never happened.

Despite the pressure, she enjoyed rereading Tolstoy's prose: his novel *Childhood* moved her to tears again. She read it with the same emotion as at fourteen, even forgetting to correct the typos. Tolstoy's artistic talent was pure gold, she wrote him, and so unlike his recent nonfiction. She disliked his current didactic style, and told him that if everything extraneous were scrubbed away, the gold would shine again.

At midnight, putting aside the proofs, she rushed to fetch daughter Tanya at a costume party, finding herself, after hours of proofreading and solitude, in a cheerful crowd, dancing, singing, and playing charades. Back home, she proofread until three in the morning. Next day, there were more proofs and Tolstoy's correspondence—a flood of letters with requests "for vacancy, money, advice, to read their work, etc."[10] To relax, she worked on a literary translation for herself alone, finding it "jolly and interesting." There was little time for leisurely reading but she picked a book by French philosopher Elme Marie Caro, *Le pessimisme au XIXe siè-cle,* and could not tear herself away.

In April, back from the Crimea, Tolstoy stayed in Moscow with the family. But city life soon depressed him and he wrote in his diary to disapprove: "Today. Thought about my unhappy family: my wife, sons and daughters who live side by side with me . . . If only they themselves could understand that their idle life, supported by the work of other people, can only have one justification: that of using their leisure in order to come to their senses, to think. But they deliberately fill their leisure with frivolous activities."[11] However, there was no leisure or frivolity for Sophia: she was "horribly busy" proofreading, supervising homework, sewing, and looking after son Ilya, who had a bad fever. She wrote sister Tanya that she moved from one chore to another, working all day without respite. Her labors appeared futile to Tolstoy because they supported a family life that clashed with his ideal, one that could not be found in a manor house but "in a peasant hut among working people."[12]

In the summer, when the entire family assembled at Yasnaya, Sophia would emerge from her room looking for volunteers: Tolstoy's original text had to be read aloud while she checked the proofs. In the evenings, she would read the proofs alone for a second time. Daughter Tanya, son Seryozha, and Nikolai Gay Jr. (the artist's son) would usually assist her. But getting help was difficult: the family, reflecting Tolstoy's attitude, did not take her publishing seriously, "as if it's a caprice or a fancy of mine."[13]

Tolstoy was haymaking with the peasants, an activity that soon involved the family and guests. Accepting Tolstoy's scheme of things, the masters worked for the peasants. Daughter Tanya recalled, "As soon as the sun had dried the dew, my sister and I shouldered our rakes and set out with the other women for the hayfields, where the men, including my two brothers Ilya and Lev, had been scything since four in the morning." The women raked the swaths, spread them to dry, and later stacked the hay into heaps. "It was not for the master we were working though, but for the peasants, who as payment for harvesting the hay received half of every field they cut."[14] The following year, wearing a peasant *panyova* (a colorful woolen skirt) with an apron, Sophia joined the family, replacing a village woman who was unwell. She worked with too much enthusiasm, over-exerted herself, and was soon diagnosed with bladder inflammation. She took this as a lesson: "I realized . . . the absurdity of our meddling as nobles in peasant life and work, to which we were unaccustomed."[15]

When in August, their teenage sons Lev and Ilya had to retake their gymnasium exams, Sophia supervised their preparation in Moscow. Lev suffered from a nervous disorder and was in a "difficult" mood. Ilya re-fused to study and "talked of nothing but hunting and dogs." Just before Sophia's birthday, Ilya failed his exam. In tears, she asked the principal to allow a retake. She related this to Tolstoy, knowing he could not sympa-thize because he had renounced ambition for their children.

On September 23, the Tolstoys' wedding anniversary, the fam-ily learned of Prince Urusov's death. A few months earlier, Sophia had seen him for the last time: he had asked her to visit and she traveled to his brother's estate near Bryansk, an ancient town southwest of Tula, with daughters Tanya and Masha. In the guest room, Sophia "found a splen-did bouquet of roses on a bed table, a plate of peaches and plums from the greenhouse, a bottle of gorgeous Parisian perfume, 'Portugal,' and a note, 'the final gift from a devoted friend.'" She was further moved when he thanked her "for everything I gave him in life." His death left a "ter-rible void" in her heart. In her memoir, she wrote: "I could only love and admire such men who had a spark of religious faith and a spark of talent from God."[16] She drew on Prince Urusov and Fet, another longtime ad-mirer, to create the faultless hero in her novella *Who's to Blame?*

That year, Sophia had her portrait taken at a reputable studio. She was forty-one and beginning her vocation as a publisher. Her eyes, which Tol-stoy describes in *Anna Karenina* as "truthful," glow with devotion and new resolve. When she sent this photograph to Fet, he replied with a verse:

"And here's a portrait. It's similar and different." Over the years, Fet gave her newly published volumes of his poems, inscribing them, "To my ideal Countess Sophia Andreevna Tolstoy from her old bard." She treasured this relationship and read Fet's poems to Alexandrine when the old courtier visited Yasnaya in the 1880s. "I realized that love plays a prominent role in a woman's life . . . no matter whether she is young or old."[17]

Sophia in 1885 when she became Tolstoy's publisher.

Before going to Moscow for the winter, Sophia put the estate and garden in order. Every year, they planted more forest, thousands of spruce and oak trees, and expanded their orchard, mostly apple trees but also pears, cherries, and plums. Boxes of fragrant Antonovka late-fall apples (a variety popular in Russia and described by Bunin in his famous story) were shipped to Moscow. After days of planting, packing, tutoring children, and proofreading, Sophia wrote sister Tanya that she was numb with fatigue.

In Moscow, she looked into her publishing affairs, again read proofs, checked printing expenditures, and directed the printers to bind the volumes. Chertkov and Paul Biryukov (later Tolstoy's biographer but at this time an employee of Intermediary) arrived with a letter from Tolstoy. In it he advised Sophia to discuss subscription to the collected works with Ivan Sytin, a prominent publisher who handled printing for Intermediary.[18] Later, Tolstoy drafted subscription terms advantageous to the public, with which she complied.

Tolstoy stayed to work at Yasnaya and the couple corresponded daily. He was finishing *The Death of Ivan Ilyich* in the vaulted room downstairs where he had worked on *War and Peace*. For Sophia, his return to fiction was a joy: "May God help you."[19] The story would appear in the final volume of the collected works, along with his other yet-unpublished masterpiece, "Kholstomer: The Story of a Horse."

Having dismissed the servants, Tolstoy performed their duties himself: starting stoves and hauling barrels of water from the well. "The water is clean, the horse is good . . . the work is agreeable; in a word, I had rarely experienced such enjoyment."[20] Sophia found it hard to accept that while Tolstoy could perform the duties of their servants, he could not help her at home. It was for the sake of his intellectual work, "which I value more than anything else," that she made sacrifices. And what was the point of dismissing the servants at Yasnaya? Why send away the peasant who wanted to work till the end of the month and dismiss the cook, happy to continue working for the pension he was paid?[21]

In the meantime, Sophia alone was raising the family and looking after business. Proofreading gave her eyestrain, she complained, and their sons only asked for money. With all this she simply wanted Tolstoy's sympathy: "Love me, don't criticize me, and support me, if you can."[22] He replied in a moralizing letter: "I would like to help you, but you know yourself that I can't do so . . . All those things—or at least the majority of them—which disturb you, namely: the children's schooling, their progress, money matters, book matters even—all those things seem to me unnecessary and superfluous."[23] In her memoir, she would comment, "Certainly, it was much easier to live like this, with his new principles, rather than raise difficult sons, publish new editions, run the household, and do other work . . . In our family, Lev Nikolaevich lived by personal choice; as for me, I only lived by necessity, while yearning for a spiritual and serene life."[24]

Subscriptions to the collected works began to pour in, while the fate of the twelfth volume with Tolstoy's controversial nonfiction was not yet known. Sophia traveled to Petersburg in November to meet with Evgeny Feoktistov, who had a high position in the censorship hierarchy. Over a decade as head of the Department of Press Affairs, Feoktistov shut down fifteen liberal newspapers and magazines. His duty was to protect the public from the dangers of information and freedom of speech. Tolstoy, due to his immense talent and popularity, created a major problem for the department, since his nonfiction was directed against the Church and the state. It was Sophia's first encounter with the censors and she was determined to "invest every effort" to clear the volume.

Petersburg was gloomy and cold this time of year, its palaces obscured by fog. From the station, Sophia hurried to Feoktistov's house before he left for his office. She knew him personally from her youth. Feoktistov bore an official mien: lifting the ban on Tolstoy's nonfiction was impossible. Sophia still asked him to read the volume. The situation had been exacerbated by the recent confiscation of Tolstoy's articles from several revolutionaries arrested in Kiev. For the censor this confirmed Tolstoy's nonfiction had a corrupting influence. Sophia's position was that publishing it in the collected works was less harmful than a ban, which only encouraged illicit circulation.

Soon after, she received a "nasty official" reply from Feoktistov: Tolstoy's nonfiction addressed issues of faith and therefore the decision was up to religious censors. The only official who could resolve the matter was Konstantin Pobedonostsev, ober-procurator of the Holy Synod, the highest functionary in the Russian Orthodox Church. Sophia needed Feoktistov's help to arrange an appointment, but he was avoiding her. She resolved to sit in his foyer until her request was satisfied.

Just before her critical meeting at the Holy Synod, she received a letter from Tolstoy, asking her to intercede on behalf of his follower Alexei Zalyubovsky. The young man had been arrested and exiled to a penal battalion for refusing military duty. The case had to be brought to the attention of the minister of war or the chief of general staff, which Tolstoy asked her to undertake: "I ask you very, very much."[25] Sophia's heart sank when she read this letter. She was petitioning government officials to lift the publication ban on Tolstoy's nonfiction. Now she had to plead on behalf of a follower, arrested for reading these works and modeling his life on them. This made her role dubious, she pointed out to Tolstoy: "Now of your business, dear Lyovochka; it's very unpleasant and painful to me but I will act on your behalf with more energy than I would for myself."[26]

Anna Dostoevsky promised help through some old connections to the chief of general staff. In addition, Ekaterina Shostak, Sophia's second cousin and director of the Nikolaevsky Institute for Noble Girls, became involved. Shostak's institute was patronized by the empress. Inviting Sophia to a recital, she introduced her to important people, one of whom knew the chief of general staff. Sophia was now enjoying her role, writing Tolstoy, "I'm respected here, and I feel very important and calm."[27]

When she finally secured a meeting, her conversation with the chief was successful. Sophia reported to Tolstoy that *his* business would be positively resolved, while *her* publishing affairs "would likely not be." The case of Tolstoy's follower was reviewed and two years later he was granted full exemption from military service. She would later again petition on behalf of other young followers, seeking pardon for their offenses and visiting them at detention houses.

On November 26, Sophia spoke with Pobedonostsev. He knew her father and had met Sophia in childhood when he was adviser to Alexander II.

Pobedonostsev met me at the door and led me to his huge dark office, inviting me to sit down in an enormous leather armchair. He stood in front of me, a tall wiry figure, with a serious and unkind expression on his smoothly shaven face. After hearing my requests and arguments regarding the banned articles, he began to pace quickly from one corner of his office to another, explaining the impossibility of publishing Tolstoy's religious works ... Among other things, Pobedonostsev said, as he stopped in front of me, looking straight into my eyes:

"I have to tell you, that I feel very sorry for you; I used to know you as a child; I loved and esteemed your father and I believe it's a great misfortune to be the wife of such a man."

"Oh, that's news to me," I replied. "Not only do I consider myself happy, but I know that everyone envies my marriage to this talented and intelligent man."

"I have to tell you," Pobedonostsev continued, "that I cannot recognize your husband's intellect. Intelligence is harmony and your husband is made of extremes and edges."

"Perhaps," I replied. "But according to Schopenhauer the human mind is only a lantern lighting man's path, while a genius is a sun which illuminates the world." [She had read Schopenhauer in German, but paraphrased in Russian.][28]

Pobedonostsev did not respond to this. Later in Moscow, Sophia received his official reply: the volume with Tolstoy's nonfiction was banned irrevocably. In a defiant letter to the ober-procurator she mentioned that the *Orthodox Review* recently published Tolstoy's *A Confession* for a limited audience, yet religious censorship did not allow her to publish it in the collected works: "It turns out that . . . the banned, harmful essays can appear under the wing of the Orthodox magazine and religious censorship." She argued that the interest in Tolstoy's writings was immense and the public would find ways to read them; the ban was an unfair decision and Russia's shame. Her letter ended with the Schopenhauer quotation and an appeal: "Let's be merciful or at least fair to a Russian genius."[29]

The rest of the collected works was ready for shipment when the censorship decision arrived. Sophia had to replace Tolstoy's nonfiction with his recent prose, reprint the twelfth volume, and dispatch it separately. Meanwhile, she was receiving about thirty requests a day from subscribers, more than expected. Working long hours in her publishing office, Sophia was unaware of an approaching storm.

Tolstoy, living in Moscow for the winter, suffered from the incongruity of his position: Sophia was about to make a large profit from his works, in which he had renounced money and property. In an unsent letter to his disciple Chertkov, he accused her of compromising his teachings by selling his books: "I would go downstairs and meet a customer who would look at me as though I were a fraud, writing against property and then, under my wife's name, squeezing as much money as possible out of people for my writings."[30] (The twelve-volume edition she produced cost eighteen rubles. In comparison, Tolstoy recently had wanted to sell a limited printing of one treatise, *What I Believe,* at twenty-five rubles.)

But while Tolstoy agonized over the conflict between his ideals and their family's practical life, Sophia's position was no easier. He had given her power of attorney and suggested that she publish his works. She knew that by striving to support their family, she violated his principles. As she wrote her sister, "Our entire life is in conflict with Lyovochka's convictions and to concur with them . . . in our daily life is impossible . . . It's painful to me that I have inadvertently become the means to all of this. These persistent demands of life, from which Lyovochka ran away, have besieged me with greater force."[31]

Years later, she would read a long letter that Tolstoy had written her at this time but did not send. In it, he accused her of deliberately opposing him: "I renounced my property, began to give what people asked of me, renounced ambition for myself and for the children . . . You pulled in the reverse, the opposite direction: sending the children to grammar schools, bringing out your daughter, making friends in society . . . It was all going on in a field of activity I regarded as evil."[32] When she read this, Sophia was appalled. The letter, which Tolstoy hid from her, was meant for posterity. She preserved it and merely noted in the margin: "A letter from Lev Nikolaevich to his wife, neither given nor sent to her." Among other things, he accused her of failing to understand what he had written in his religious works, which she struggled to push through censorship.

Shortly before Christmas, Tolstoy walked into her publishing office while she was working. Sophia described what happened next in a dramatic letter to sister Tanya, prefacing it with the remark that, luckily, there was no real grief in their family, only an *invented* one.

As it happened so many times before, Lyovochka became extremely gloomy and nervous. One day, I am sitting and writing; he walks in, I look up—his face is dreadful. Until then, we lived splendidly, *not a single* unpleasant word was exchanged between us, just nothing at all. "I've come to say that I want to divorce you, I can't live like this, I am leaving for Paris, or America." You know, Tanya, if the house had collapsed on top of me I couldn't have been more surprised. I asked him, "What happened?" "Nothing. But you can only go on loading things onto a cart for so long. When the horse can't pull it anymore, the cart stops." What exactly it is I've been loading onto the cart is unknown. But then the shouting, the reproaches, and insults began to pour . . . And when he said: "Wherever you are the air is poisoned,"

I went for a trunk and began packing. I wanted to get away and stay with you for a while. But the children ran in, sobbing . . . He pleaded: "Stay!" So I stayed; but he suddenly began to sob hysterically . . . imagine—Lyovochka—is all trembling and shaking of sobs. I felt a rush of pity for him; the four children, Tanya, Ilya, Lyova, and Masha, were all weeping and wailing. I went into a fit: not a word, not a tear . . . But the anguish, the grief, the pain, the nervous distress, the feeling of rejection, all this still remains in me. You know, I drive myself insane by often asking: so, what's wrong, what have I done now? I never left the house; I worked peacefully on the edition until three o'clock in the morning.[33]

Daughter Tanya, then twenty-one, remembered that "terrible winter night." The children sat in the hall, listening to their parents argue upstairs. "The pitch of their voices never fell, and you could gauge the intensity of their emotions . . . Neither of them would budge an inch. Both were defending something more important to them than their lives: she, the well-being of her children . . . he, his very soul."[34] In the morning it was decided that Tolstoy, in Tanya's company, should spend Christmas at the Olsufievs, their old friends who owned a large estate thirty-five miles outside Moscow. Sophia was glad Lyovochka would rest in the country "in the care of a good family."[35]

A small sleigh was prepared. Sophia parted "almost affably" with Tolstoy, loading her husband and daughter with coats, rugs, and food for the road. Anxious after a sleepless night, "her big dark eyes shining with pent-up emotion,"[36] she advised them of what to do if caught in a blizzard. By evening, she received Tanya's letter describing their journey as fun: she and Tolstoy drove in turns and the sleigh upset several times.

The Olsufievs' estate was far more luxurious than Yasnaya, and although the family had close ties to court and was known for its entertainment and good food, they escaped Tolstoy's criticism. He regained his peace of mind, writing that his nerves were much stronger there. His despair and depression gone, he was sleeping perfectly, and promised Sophia that he would "not be upsetting and tormenting you again, as I have of *late.*"[37]

Sophia wrote her daughter that she was "sincerely glad that you and

Papa are well and that he is resting . . . But why is he not bellowing at the Olsufievs? . . . Don't they live even more luxuriously?" From Tanya she learned that Tolstoy played cards with their hosts and enjoyed a masquerade. She wrote back that she had never felt so lonesome over the holidays, which she spent working on the edition. "My nerves are terribly upset; I am choking with tears and spasms every minute . . . Fear of madness is so great that I cannot overcome it. Such personalities as mine, which cannot be broken by physical strain, break down mentally."[38] Stress brought back a litany of problems: tremor, neuralgia, headache, and insomnia. "We have no guests, and there's no *Christmas tree and no merriment.* I don't dare *entertain* or invite anyone to see me so pitiful . . . I'm sitting at the desk with my envelopes."[39]

To stop subscription to the collected works was impossible: "Once the machine is set in motion, the wheels are turning." Besides, as she wrote Tolstoy, work was a cure from mental anguish: "As for my work on the edition, I can tell you this: I escape in this hard labor till I'm bemused; this is my *tavern,* where I forget all problems of my family life . . . One needs to escape from all these scenes, reproaches, and sufferings."[40]

She felt that Tolstoy's ideal of loving humanity had destroyed their family happiness. How was it possible that his principles of goodness and truth, when he practiced them, produced nothing but *malice* and *discord? "Discord* not between some thieves but between peaceful and *loving* people? . . . How painful and sad!"[41] Chertkov had quarreled with his mother. Another follower took the property from his own family and gave it away, inflicting suffering on his own wife and children. This proved that Tolstoy's *new* path was dark and uncertain (by dark she meant fanatical). She pleaded to return to their "*old* and *established*" path, their old happiness, everything they used to share and love.

After working into the night, she would sleep in, finding the small children, Sasha, Alyosha, and Misha, waiting for her. They would lie quietly on their bellies by her door, peeping through the gap underneath it to see whether she was up, so they could run in and hug her. "It's a great joy to be so loved, at least by the little ones." They needed her and loved her "without questions and doubts."[42]

Returning to Moscow after the holidays, Tolstoy "touchingly" made peace with her, "on a condition never to bring up the past." Sophia promised to forget but could not let go of her pain. To sister Tanya, she wrote, "I have never been so unfairly and cruelly insulted as this time."[43] There were two paths for her: divorce—"leave this house . . . leave all this cruelty, all these excessive demands on me"—or change nothing and "carry on as before."[44] She decided to keep the family together, for the children's sake, and support them with publishing proceeds, even though she was criticized for it.

Once, while she was working on the edition, Alyosha, four, walked in, stopped by her desk, and looked at her with his large, gray eyes. He asked if she could sit with him and she refused, saying there was lots of work. "It's always work, work, you never come to sit with me." When in mid-January 1886, he died of quinsy (a severe case of tonsillitis), those words painfully reverberated in her heart. "Why couldn't his father, instead of stitching boots, making flatbread, fetching water, and chopping wood, share his wife's duties, allowing her to take some time for her motherhood?"[45]

On the day Alyosha became ill Sophia was at a publishing meeting. Upon her return, a nanny told her that he had caught a cold while outside in the wind. Sophia spent the night in the nursery. When Alyosha developed a "barking cough" and began to suffocate from croup, she made footbaths, compresses, vapors, and chest rubs. In the morning, she sent for Filatov, the celebrated pediatrician, who found the boy's tonsils swollen but said it was nothing serious. Yet Alyosha was getting worse. Tolstoy and daughter Masha sat beside him when he became delirious. He died thirty-six hours later.

In her memoir, Sophia would write that there was nothing "as painful and dreadful as a mother's grief at the loss of her child. I remember standing beside the little coffin, holding my hand over Alyosha's stiffened and cold little forehead, when Lev Nikolaevich walked in. He stroked my hair and said, 'That's how you will age—from grief.'"

With son Ilya, Sophia visited several cemeteries to find a resting place for Alyosha. At the old Novodevichy Cemetery, lots sold for the steep price of 250 silver rubles, and the idea of "bargaining for land" was repugnant to her. Sophia's brother Petya, head of the Moscow regional police, suggested a cemetery recently opened in Pokrovskoe, where Sophia was born and spent her childhood. She drove there, visiting the place for the first time since her marriage. The cemetery was on a hill, overlooking the River

Khimka and the groves around her family's former dacha. She wrote sister Tanya: "Do you remember our 'Switzerland' in Pokrovskoe? . . . The place where you got lost when we went mushrooming . . . all those places that seemed so wonderfully poetic and beautiful in childhood . . . Tanya, if I die in Moscow or vicinity, that's where I want to be buried. It's such a fine place, simple, and good, the land is pristine, godly, its nature so beautiful."[46] She went to the Pokrovskoe Church to order the service, meeting the priest and local peasants who remembered being treated by her father. They came to the funeral and carried the coffin up the hill.

Tolstoy could not attend because he was suffering from an infection. And he could not share Sophia's grief, writing Chertkov of his feeling of spiritual elation; a child's death no longer seemed cruel and inexplicable.[47]

In February, Nikolai Gay, who had painted a portrait of Tolstoy in his Moscow study, decided to make one of Sophia. He depicted her as an aristocrat but was dissatisfied with the result; he felt she must be painted as a mother. A month after her son's death, Sophia was posing in a black fur cape with two-year-old Sasha in her arms. Her face was lifeless; while holding Sasha, she wished it was a portrait with Alyosha.[48]

As usual, Sophia coped with grief by keeping busy: "When I'm not posing, I'm copying, writing business letters, teaching the little ones . . . and doing various house chores; we also have swarms of people visiting."[49] Aside from Gay, who was staying in their house with his son, there were Tolstoy's disciples, Chertkov and Biryukov. Sophia liked Biryukov, a graduate of the naval academy: his presence was almost imperceptible. Chertkov, however, bickered with her; when she asked him when he was leaving for Petersburg, he replied that he was in no hurry. Sophia was surprised, knowing that he had a fiancée, Galya Dieterich, in Petersburg.

Nikolai Gay Jr., also a Tolstoyan, was now Sophia's publishing assistant: she needed help with bookkeeping and shipping. When the twelfth volume with Tolstoy's new prose was reprinted and proofread, it had to go through censors again. Sophia was afraid they would cut some passages from *The Death of Ivan Ilyich* or refuse to pass the volume altogether. "But I believe that they won't dare: this would mean a scandal across Russia!"[50] The volume appeared in spring with Tolstoy's splendid photograph, which he had taken at Sophia's request.

The new edition sold out quickly; Sophia followed up with a cheap edition in small print. Strakhov, who visited Yasnaya that summer, provided editorial advice and helped proofread it; to thank him, Sophia knitted him a woolen blanket. Tolstoy wished to reduce the price on the second edition even more and told Strakhov that it "should cost only 8 rubles . . . He wanted to avoid making a profit completely but there would be a profit of 25–30 thousand. This year, the estates produced only 1.5 thousand [rubles]."[51] Sophia suggested donating part of their publishing profit. As she wrote Tolstoy, she could generate money to feed a multitude of hungry people.

Her letter was in response to one Tolstoy had written en route to Yasnaya (he was traveling on foot). Despairing over the poverty he witnessed, he wrote: "On the roads, in the pub, in church and round the houses everyone is talking about the same thing—need. You ask: what can we do, how can we help? We can help by giving seeds and bread to those who ask for it, but it's not really help, it's a drop in the ocean, and besides, this help is self-defeating. If I can give to one or 3, why not to 20, or 1,000 or a million? Obviously I can't give to all, even by giving everything away."[52] She disagreed with his idea that charity was unimportant in the grand scheme of things: helping a few people would make a difference and it was even better to feed a million.

Tolstoy walked from Moscow to Yasnaya with Nikolai Gay Jr. and Mikhail Stakhovich, a family friend. When they began this journey, Sophia drove them in a landau to the Kiev highway, beyond the city gate. She watched them go with knapsacks, dressed as simple pilgrims. It took them six days to walk 130 miles to Yasnaya; on the way, they slept in peasant huts, living mostly on bread and tea. Tolstoy proved stronger than his young companions.

In the summer of 1886, describing life at Yasnaya, Sophia wrote, "Everyone here is haymaking, my husband, our sons, and the guests; the girls, myself, and other womenfolk do the raking . . . It's jolly but tiring."[53] But in July, Tolstoy injured his leg while carting hay for a peasant widow and developed an infection. Because he refused medical help, Sophia nursed him with home remedies. When he developed a high temperature, she no longer could wait for permission to bring a doctor.

She took an overnight train, arriving in Moscow in early morning. First, she drove to Iverskaya Chapel by Red Square to pray for her husband's recovery. (The ancient Iverskaya icon was believed to work miracles. The royal family stopped in this chapel before a coronation and merchants before concluding a deal.) That same day, she returned to Yasnaya with Dr. Chirkov, a celebrity. Tolstoy refused to be examined but submitted when Chirkov said he had left many patients waiting. He told Sophia that if they had not acted urgently, Tolstoy would have died from blood poisoning. (Their old friend Dmitry Dyakov died from blood poisoning in 1891, after injuring his leg.) When Tolstoy's wound was disinfected his temperature dropped, but recovery took a long time. For two months she was his nursemaid "and what I had to do was so natural, so simple . . . The harder the work, the happier I was." But once Tolstoy began to recover, "he has given me to understand that he no longer needs me."[54]

Again there were tensions: Tolstoy lectured her in front of the family "about the evils of money and property." And again, he criticized her for selling his books, expecting her to make "impossible, undefined sacrifices" for the sake of his ideal. She lost her temper, arguing that while she sold twelve volumes for eight rubles, he had sold his one novel, *War and Peace,* for ten.[55] However, her argument had no support from the family: the children, particularly the daughters, criticized her for opposing their father. The girls had recently come closer to Tolstoy in understanding his philosophy and began to share his view that property was sinful. But while Tolstoy and the children criticized her for making money, they also pressed her for cash. "Lev Nikolaevich . . . constantly comes up to me with that air of indifference, malevolence, and even hatred, and demands that I give him more money to give to all his minions and paupers."[56] Seen as a moneylender, she was despised and felt bitter.

In late fall, Sophia received a telegram that her mother was dying in the Crimea. She set out at once. At forty-two, it was the first time she traveled through the mountains, to the Black Sea; despite the sadness of the occasion, she was looking forward to it. From the train, she took a landau to Yalta, along a picturesque mountain road: "On the way, swift rivers and springs, with colorfully dressed Tartar women fetching water in their tall pitchers; the radiant sky, dark blue, unlike ours; I liked it all, all. I have never been abroad, I have never traveled."

When the landau broke down, passengers had to wait at a station. Sophia took a stroll down the highway and heard a monotonous sound.

Curious, she went closer to focus and then, "I shrieked at the top of my lungs, 'The Sea!' I have never seen the sea before, and the magnificent spectacle of the large body of water, with its noise, its eternal movement of waves back and forth—amazed and excited me terribly . . . The rising tide and the receding tide signify the infinity and the eternal movement of life."[57]

In Yalta, Lyubov Alexandrovna and Sophia's three brothers, Sasha, Petya, and Vyacheslav, lived in a waterfront hotel. Tolstoy's sister, Maria Nikolaevna, also came to bid farewell to her childhood friend. Lyubov Alexandrovna lay on a chaise longue on a balcony with a view of the sea; she was dying of pneumonia. One evening, wearing a handsome lace kerchief and sitting up for what she called a "ball," she asked her children to light candles and serve tea. For Sophia, it was a sad and blissful time, an escape from the complexities of her marriage into a cordial family relationship. Her mother was buried in Yalta in November. Years later, Sophia would revisit the Crimea on account of Tolstoy's illness.

That same year, Tolstoy wrote a new play, *The Realm of Darkness,* and Sophia was copying it enthusiastically. It was a psychological drama from peasant life. "It is very good. The characters are wonderfully portrayed and the plot is full and interesting." Tolstoy depicted his peasant characters with uncompromising complexity and candor, showing their dark sides, the brutality of the very people he idealized. Sophia was moved to tears by the power of the play and was humbled by his artistic talent: "I must be careful and considerate with him, and save him for his work, which is so dear to my heart."[58]

United through their work and the success of the play, the couple enjoyed "a peaceful and happy winter."[59] *The Realm of Darkness* circulated in manuscript and Sophia gave readings in Moscow, inviting acquaintances. She reproduced the play with Tolstoy's intonations, which she remembered from his "superb reading." To Tolstoy, working at Yasnaya, she wrote that the play made a "powerful impression" on her listeners, who praised the originality of the plot and language. Lev Polivanov, the gymnasium director who was present, said that the play would become one of the biggest events in Russian literature. She wrote Tolstoy, "I knew this from the first act, which I was copying with such zeal at Yasnaya Polyana."[60]

The play was also read at her sister's home in Petersburg, before important officials, and at court, to the royal family. "Everyone is shouting about it, everyone is delighted."[61] Alexander III liked the play and allowed the imperial theaters to produce it. Rehearsals had just begun when, on instructions of the Holy Synod, the play was banned. Censor Feoktistov communicated to Sophia that a theater production was unthinkable. The play depicted adultery and murder, and characters spoke a language "impossible in its cynicism . . . I believe that nothing of the kind was ever staged in the world."[62] (The premiere was in Paris the following year, while in Russia, it was staged only in 1895 by Petersburg's Alexandrinsky Theatre.) Sophia wanted to continue fighting but Tolstoy discouraged her.

When in February 1887, the inexpensive edition of Tolstoy's collected works was released, Sophia noted that she had "completely lost interest in it. The money brought me no joy—I never thought it would."[63] In two years, she made sixty-four thousand rubles, becoming almost as successful as Anna Dostoevsky. But this led only to more conflict and put her under fire. The harder she worked as a publisher and estate manager, the more Tolstoy disapproved of her.

Chapter Ten

The Martyr and the Martyress

I N MARCH 1887, Sophia copied Tolstoy's treatise *On Life*.[1] She admired it because "it had lots of idealism,"[2] and, as she wrote her sister, because it was a purely philosophical work. Unlike his other nonfiction, it was free from partiality and censure. Tolstoy discussed the meaning and purpose of life, as expressed by philosophers from antiquity to modern times. He also explored an idea that had long interested him—whether life can escape destruction by death. Upon completing this work he concluded that death did not exist.

Sophia soon began to translate it into French, admitting it was difficult without a good philosophical vocabulary: "There are some expressions, which even our philosophers, like Grot, doubt how to translate."[3] She had consulted the idealist philosopher Nikolai Grot, whom Tolstoy had engaged to prepare his treatise for publication. To expand her knowledge of the subject, she attended Grot's lectures at Moscow University. The following year, she completed her translation and shortly after, it appeared in Paris.

Although *On Life* was her favorite among Tolstoy's philosophical works, certain ideas struck her as "unjust." She disagreed with the message that "one should have to renounce one's personal life in the name of universal love." The idea seemed to justify neglecting one's own family: "I believe that there are obligations which are ordained by God, that no one has the right to deny them, and that these obligations actually promote, rather than hinder, the spiritual life."[4] While Tolstoy told her that her life was not spiritual enough, she argued that it belonged to her husband and children and that it was just as spiritual as his abstract renunciation. Looking after one's family was a godly responsibility, she believed.

Unlike Tolstoy's followers who took his religious views as absolute, Sophia doubted his doctrine was workable. By then, she had met with many Tolstoyans, who stayed with them in Moscow and at Yasnaya. The family dubbed them the "dark ones" because of their gloomy, bearded looks and obscure backgrounds. They modeled their lives on Tolstoy's nonfiction, and on his ideas, which they wanted to implement blindly. They denounced money, property, and careers; most of them lived at others' expense. As Tolstoy worked his entire life, it was hard for Sophia to understand what he had in common with these people.

Among these young followers was Isaak Feinerman, who came to live in Yasnaya Polyana village. He gave his money and property to the poor, leaving his pregnant wife and child without means. Sophia was outraged that Tolstoy had befriended this man and allowed him into their house. She commented on Feinerman in her diary: "However fanatical his beliefs may be, and however beautifully he may express them, the fact of the matter is that he has left his family to eat at others' expense, and that is grotesque."[5]

As much as Sophia disliked the man, she was supportive of his family, encouraging his wife, Esfir, to take training as a midwife. As she was Jewish, Esfir was not allowed to stay in Moscow, not even for the three days of exams. In 1887, when the police deported her, Esfir wrote Sophia about her desperate situation. Sophia met the chief of Moscow police, asking that Esfir be allowed to stay. "He brusquely refused; then I got angry and told him, 'Don't you think that I could hide this woman in Moscow?' And so, I did hide her and she passed her exams."[6]

When, like many Tolstoyans, Feinerman was exiled, Tolstoy continued to correspond with him, praising him for suffering for his beliefs. Sophia worried that people indicted for antigovernment activities frequented their home and that Tolstoy corresponded with those under police surveillance. From some letters, which she read, Sophia discovered that even revolutionaries now considered him *"their own."* She found it appalling and wrote Tolstoy, who was at Yasnaya: "Isn't it idiotic not to understand that everything you preach is in direct opposition to terrorism."[7] It was frustrating to Sophia that people who read his works failed to understand that Tolstoy disagreed with revolutionaries on one fundamental issue—their violent methods. But this confusion was unavoidable because Tolstoy rejected their social order as unjust and sympathized with ideals of equality. His banned nonfiction was popular among revolutionaries and was confiscated during their arrests. The government believed that he advocated primitive socialism.

In early March, five terrorists conspired to kill Alexander III. This was six years after his father was assassinated. Tolstoy had foreseen such a rise in revolutionary violence; when Sophia communicated this news, he heard it "in despondent silence."[8] He knew the government would execute the conspirators and this would only strengthen revolutionary ranks.[9]

Persecution of Tolstoyans also intensified: arrests and exiles were ongoing. One follower was apprehended for distributing copies of Tolstoy's banned article "Nikolai the Stick," which told of brutal punishments in the army under the tsar Nicholas I. Tolstoy confronted the chief of the Moscow constabulary, arguing that he was the author of the article and they should arrest him. The chief replied that Tolstoy's fame was too enormous for their prisons to contain it. While Tolstoy was spared, Sophia wondered how all this would affect their family.

She asked Tolstoy why he corresponded with people of "most frightful reputation."[10] Some followers, like Nikolai Ozmidov, made a living copying and selling Tolstoy's banned works. Sophia wondered what such people had in common with Tolstoy. Ozmidov had a dairy shop in Moscow, which went out of business and was auctioned off; he then supported himself by helping circulate Tolstoy's nonfiction. When Sophia asked why he corresponded with Ozmidov, "a scoundrel," Tolstoy calmly replied, "Well, if he is a scoundrel, I am more use to him than I am to others."[11] In fact, as a spiritual leader, he forgave his followers' shortcomings. It struck Sophia that while Tolstoy applied exacting standards to their family, he was liberal with his spiritual children. He now wrote impersonally to Sophia and warmly to his followers.

Sophia was not alone in her dislike of Tolstoyans. Bunin, who became influenced by Tolstoy's ideas as a young man and briefly joined an agricultural commune, would write that "with some exceptions, the Tolstoyans . . . were an absolutely unbearable lot."[12] Aylmer Maude, also a Tolstoyan at one time, admitted that there were many fanatical and disagreeable people in their movement.

Sophia was suspicious of Anatoly Butkevich, twice arrested for antigovernment activities. When he first visited their home, she left him waiting downstairs; on his second visit, she invited him for tea. Silent, with "a fixed expression on his face," wearing blue-tinted spectacles, he looked impenetrable and did not inspire her trust: "There is no way of knowing what he believes in." Yet, he called himself a Tolstoyan. "What unattractive types Lev Nikolaevich's followers are! There is not one among them who is normal."[13] Thronging around Tolstoy, they took his time, something Sophia and the family would not dare.

Her judgment of people came from practical life: her publishing business, managing finances, supervising house staff, and raising children. It was a "blunt and matter-of-fact" attitude, unlike Tolstoy's. Despite the superb knowledge of human nature revealed in his fiction, Tolstoy could be wrong about individuals. Idealistic, he often trusted people who would deceive him. Sophia wrote: "You imagine people and turn them into *types*. You ignore people's shortcomings, eliminate things that don't suit you, and you idealize and poeticize them. But in real life it's different, and I meet people in life."[14]

She felt Tolstoy idealized his disciple Chertkov. The disciple's letters, which she read before dispatching them to Tolstoy, were filled with flattery and cunning. He asked Tolstoy to send him various drafts of his work, concealing that he was developing an archive. Instead, he wrote deviously that reading the drafts allowed him to feel spiritually close to Tolstoy. Chertkov also asked that Tolstoy send him work to copy: he had a group of people, "close in spirit," who would handle it quickly. Sensing "lies and rancor," Sophia decided that Tolstoy should distance himself from his disciple: "He must end this relationship with Chertkov . . . we must get as far away as possible."[15] But instead, Tolstoy distanced himself further from his family.

Their family was now split into factions. Daughter Masha, sixteen, was Tolstoy's favorite and first among her siblings to express interest in his teaching. In February, Sophia invited some family members for a dance to celebrate Masha's birthday. Masha complained to Tolstoy, knowing his disapproval of entertainment, that she was against having a party. Tanya argued that her sister was insincere: it was impossible not to love dancing at her age. Sophia was upset with this ideological division, writing to her sister: "My poor children are utterly confused morally and don't know which way to go . . . The older children are left on their own to find their way in life."[16] In fact, Tolstoy's teaching did not provide guidance for practical life.

When the eldest, Seryozha, graduated from university, he sought his father's formal advice about his career. Tolstoy, who had taught him math in childhood and hired teachers to prepare him for university, replied, "Take a broom and sweep streets."[17] Sophia would tell this story to show just how impractical Tolstoy's advice was. Since he had renounced ambition for himself and the children, he believed the meanest occupation was the best.

Because of the ongoing disagreements over their upbringing, Sophia lost all authority with their older children: "I feel I am a total zero, everyone is against me, and everything I used to believe good, fair, and useful is now being destroyed."[18] Toward the small children she felt nothing but pity and, for this reason, was spoiling them. "I have an old woman's anxiety for them and an old woman's tenderness for them."[19]

In April, she worked long hours in her office, balancing books and writing numerous business letters to subscribers, tasks neglected by her publishing assistant. Nikolai Gay Jr. was at Yasnaya with Tolstoy, so she handled this "boring and difficult" work. Because Gay wanted to join a Tolstoyan agricultural commune, Sophia had to find a new assistant. (A student, Osip Gerasimov, whom she hired, would remember her warmly: later, as deputy minister of public education, he would recall his first job with Sophia.)

She was also launching a new edition of Tolstoy's works. To produce it quickly, Sophia used three printing shops and was flooded with proofs. She had approached several proofreaders but first had to test them; meantime, she proofread alone. In the mornings, there was also banking, tutoring Misha, and running chores; to relax, she would attend Grot's lectures. Tolstoy wrote that she could find "a whole regiment" of proofreaders if she advertised; it was bad for the soul to be perennially overworked.[20] Sophia replied that working around the clock was like drinking and was her way of escape.[21]

She spent Easter proofreading; at midnight, when the bells began to toll across Moscow, she got up and listened to their rumble, imagining a festive crowd chanting "Christ has risen." For the first time, she was not in church for Easter, and "it was very sad," she wrote Tolstoy, that neither he nor their three older boys were at home.[22] Some of their children now refused to go to church; she also attended less frequently.

At Easter, reading the Gospels alone, she wrote Tolstoy that she understood why he was "all immersed" in them and that such faith required a great spiritual effort. Referring to the Gospels, she added that one needs to enter the *narrow* gate and take the *narrow* path, most demanding and difficult. "We, sinners, take the *wide* path, and it's hard to switch."[23]

She asked Tolstoy who was copying for him at Yasnaya. In their blissful past, when his manuscript traveled to her desk, he was interested in her opinions; she alone shared his life and work. "You write and I, copying, grasp your thoughts, follow them, and live your life, with love."[24] Now, many helped in his work. Their family life and their Yasnaya house were also shared with followers whom Sophia found tedious. "This is the price we must pay for Lyovochka's fame and the originality of his ideas."[25]

In the summer, Yasnaya was full of life, activity, and teeming with people: aside from family, there was a stream of visitors. The place now attracted fans from around the world. A German professor of archaeology, interested in Tolstoy's ideas, came with his family. George Kennan, an American explorer and writer, had published an article discussing Tolstoy's idea of nonresistance; it sparked much interest.

Old friends were also visiting: Tolstoy's editor, Strakhov, gave Sophia publishing advice. Portraitist Repin came to paint Tolstoy, who was occupied with several projects at the time, revising his *On Life* and doing agricultural work. Repin made a portrait of him with an open book on his lap. The artist also followed him to sketch what would become the famous *Portrait of Leo Tolstoy as a Plowman on a Field*. Sophia liked the painting but objected when she learned it was going to be lithographed to sell prints. Tolstoy was plowing a field for a peasant widow and if his charity work was publicized, people could get the impression he posed for the picture. Her objections were ignored and the picture was published widely.

Tolstoy asked their guests to help copy *On Life* and take dictation, dividing them into groups. His copyists included philosopher Grot and Alexandrine, who visited in July. She was paired with the public prosecutor Sasha Kuzminsky, sister Tanya's husband. They took Tolstoy's dictation in his study, while other groups copied in the drawing room. Later, Tolstoy gave a reading for all, lasting several hours. Sophia also contributed: she wanted to publish the book as a separate volume. At her suggestion, it was divided into short chapters to make it more readable. (But in the end, it was banned and confiscated in Russia.)

Family and guests spent several evenings with actor Vasily Andreev-Burlak, a masterful storyteller. Listening to him until two in the morning, Tolstoy laughed without restraint, causing Sophia to fear for his heart. The actor also told a story of a man he had met on a train, a wife murderer. Tolstoy would allude to this story in his novella *The Kreutzer Sonata*.

That summer, Yuly Lyasota, a talented young violinist, played in Yasnaya. Enjoying himself "immensely," Tolstoy accompanied on the piano as they performed sonatas by Mozart, Weber, and Haydn. He had a distinct piano style, which never failed to move Sophia: "He always plays with such extraordinary feeling and such perfect phrasing."[26] During another musical evening in their Moscow house, Lyasota and their son Seryozha played Beethoven's "Kreutzer" Sonata. Never again would she hear it performed with such passion as on that night, when Tolstoy told her it expressed every conceivable human emotion. Afterward, Tolstoy proposed that the guests collaborate, each developing the theme in his own genre. Someone would play Beethoven's sonata while Andreev-Burlak would tell the story of the wife murderer, torn by jealousy, and Repin would draw an illustration. *The Kreutzer Sonata,* which Tolstoy began to write that fall, was inspired by this performance; it told of human passions and of the cruelest of them all, the sex urge.

For Sophia, the summer marked an interlude of happiness and love: "There is a bunch of roses . . . on my table, we are just sitting down to a splendid dinner, the storm has passed and it is mild and calm outside, and my dear children are with me . . . sweet gentle Lyovochka will soon be back—this is my life and I revel and thank God for it."[27] In the absence of his followers who had vacated the estate to make room for guests, Tolstoy was an artist and "a sweet, happy family man."[28] One day son Seryozha was playing a waltz on the piano when Tolstoy, to the delight of their children, asked Sophia to dance.

That summer, Sophia resumed photography, a hobby she had enjoyed at sixteen. She bought a large-format Kodak camera, which captured images on glass plates. These she developed in a dark attic room, a labor-consuming process she had to master. She fixed and washed the prints, sticking them to a window to dry. Among her first pictures was a family portrait on the steps of their Yasnaya house. Their eight children are sitting and standing; Tolstoy—in the middle—hugs Sasha, the youngest. Sophia, in a white dress, is behind him.

The family in 1887. Sitting, from left: Sergei, Lev, Tolstoy with daughter Sasha, Sophia, Ilya, Mikhail. Standing from left: Maria, Andrei, Tatyana.
Photo by Sophia Tolstoy.

At forty-three, Sophia was pregnant with their thirteenth child, the couple's last. In August, physically and emotionally drained, she noted that their family life had become more complicated. With every pregnancy came a valid fear of dying in labor; each time, she would rush to complete unfinished projects. The most important was sorting Tolstoy's archive to deposit for safekeeping. It included his priceless drafts of *War and Peace, Anna Karenina,* and other literary works; she also wanted to file his diaries, letters, and portraits. She had been arranging his archive over the years and in early September deposited it in the Rumyantsev Museum.

The couple's twenty-fifth wedding anniversary was on September 23. Sophia's brother Sasha gave them a silver goblet. Her brother Stepan, recently married, arrived with his wife, Maria Shvartsman. Stepan had transcended religious and class lines: Maria was Jewish, although baptized as Christian Orthodox to marry him. She was also a provincial actress and single mother. "Quiet, meek, and quite a stranger to us all, she then enjoyed my brother's great affection."[29] Although the marriage was short-lived, Sophia continued to correspond with Maria. In 1892, when during a widespread famine Sophia organized relief, Maria enlisted as a volunteer. She died of typhus in a remote village, helping set up canteens.

The Tolstoy wedding anniversary was celebrated modestly: family and friends sat for dinner. When Dyakov, their old friend, proposed a toast to their happy marriage, Tolstoy muttered, "It could have been better." Hurt by his remark, Sophia wrote years later, "These words exemplified my husband's impossible demands, which I, despite my best efforts and hard work, could never satisfy."[30]

When in October, Sophia and the children went to Moscow, the two older daughters, Tanya and Masha, stayed with Tolstoy at Yasnaya. They were beginning to assist him and copy for him, as their mother had. In Moscow, Sophia carried on with her publishing. In the daytime, she kept busy and was able to ignore her fatigue and neuralgia. But in the evening, the chronic pain defeated her: she wrote sister Tanya that she spent nights sitting up.

Her pregnancy was overdue and she suffered from painful complications, which kept her in her room. After Tolstoy arrived in Moscow, the house was teeming with new people coming to see him. Sophia joined the

Family and guests at Yasnaya Polyana, 1888. Sophia is at the far left, and Tolstoy in the middle.

company when he had interesting visitors, such as a French philosopher and a professor from Prague.

Son Ilya, their first child to marry, had a wedding on February 28, 1888. Unwell and embarrassed about her appearance, Sophia did not go to the church. Tolstoy, rejecting ritual, also stayed home. Ilya and his bride were both young and "untested by life,"[31] which made Sophia skeptical. But the young folk looked forward to the occasion. Daughter Tanya escorted her brother to the church, noting in her diary, "We felt such delight, happiness and triumph about the event to be. It was a marvelous morning, brilliant and frosty."[32] The bride was from an artistic milieu: her father was the head of the School of Painting, Sculpture, and Architecture, where Tanya had studied.

A month after the wedding, Sophia gave birth. This last birth was the most trying of all. "For two hours I screamed wildly. Never before did the suffering drive me so insane. Lyovochka and the nanny wept—they stayed with me the entire time . . . A quarter to nine, a boy was born. Lyovochka took him in his arms and kissed him, a miracle unseen before! He is happy it's a boy and treats him with special care and protectiveness . . . But to me, he looks like one and the same baby, the extension of the previous, not a new face."[33] It was indeed the first time that Tolstoy kissed their baby. He usually avoided young children: "I cannot hold a little bird in my hands without trembling inwardly, and I am just as afraid to hold a young baby."[34]

The lastborn was christened Ivan, or Vanechka, as they called him at home. The letter *i* was needed to complete Tolstoy's acronym "silami," which means "by strength." The boys' names, in order, were Sergei, Ilya, Lev, Andrei, Mikhail, and Ivan. The girls' names, Tatyana, Maria, and Alexandra, formed the acronym "tma," "darkness." Ivan completed the sentence: "We conquer darkness by strength."[35]

The child of an elderly father and a robust but nervous mother, Ivan "was sickly, skinny, and so delicate, that it inspires pity to look at him."[36] The entire family, including the children, insisted that Sophia suckle the boy. But she could not stand the pain and now nervousness and tension added to the ordeal.

A fortnight later, Tolstoy packed his knapsack and left for Yasnaya on foot, accompanied by Gay junior. Although upset that he left so soon, Sophia wrote that she hoped his pilgrimage would shake him up and inspire some fiction. She also told of nursing the baby, how she endured "infernal pain" and prayed for patience. Tanya, who watched her mother breastfeed, would remember: "I still see her, a child cradled in her arms, head thrown back, teeth clenched in her determination to conceal that pain."[37] From Yasnaya, Tolstoy advised her not to despair but to "find meaning and goodness in your sufferings."[38] In his work *On Life,* he had added a chapter about the meaning and benefit of physical suffering.

In April, when *On Life* was banned and six hundred copies confiscated, Sophia was left with the printers' bills.[39] A new mother once again, she now had to face this publishing crisis. Around this time, she spoke with their son Lev, who asked, "Are you happy, Mama?" It took her a while to reply: "Yes, I consider myself happy." He continued: "So, why do you look like a martyress?"[40] She could say nothing.

By then, she knew that in his diary, Tolstoy had described his family life as martyrdom: "Lord, help me. If this is my cross, so be it; let it weigh me down and crush me."[41] Yet, he was free to live in Yasnaya, tilling the land and surrounded by followers. He could lead this life of spiritual improvement because she relieved him of responsibility. While Tolstoy lived as he wished, she was "harnessed into a complex life—the family and publishing affairs."[42]

Chapter Eleven

Who's to Blame?

I N 1888, TOLSTOY resumed writing *The Kreutzer Sonata,* the story of "how a man killed his wife." Sophia copied the novella and was familiar with all its variants; however, for the first time she could not sympathize with her husband's fiction. In the novella Tolstoy repudiates sexual love as sinful, even in marriage. It was his most controversial work and would generate a flood of response.

Tolstoy, who had idealized family happiness in *Anna Karenina,* now preached that happy marriages did not exist. In *The Kreutzer Sonata,* he again drew from his betrothal and marriage, but his goal was to show the disastrous consequences of sexual love. His new ideal was absolute chastity, although he admitted it would mean the annihilation of humankind.

Readers were struck by *The Kreutzer Sonata* and its Afterword, in which Tolstoy defends his ideas. Bunin remembers that many found it unfathomable that "a man who had fathered thirteen children could rise up against conjugal love and even against the continuation of the human race itself. They said that *The Kreutzer Sonata* could best be explained by the fact that Tolstoy was old and that he 'hated his wife.'"[1]

Such was the power of this work that readers would model their lives on it, making vows of celibacy, and some even castrated themselves. Others, realizing that Tolstoy was not celibate, joked that should he have another child, it would be the real "Afterword." A reporter from the British newspaper the *Pall Mall Gazette* was skeptical when he heard Tolstoy condemn sex. After visiting Yasnaya Polyana, the reporter commented it was a good thing that Tolstoy, the idealist, had a sensible wife who shielded him from "too abruptly attempting to realize his dreams." If he had been celibate and free to implement his theories, the world would not have known Tolstoy the writer. "He has been saved by the sound common sense of the estimable lady, who is the mother of his children, and the head, and heart, and soul of his household."[2] Sophia preserved the newspaper clipping, grateful for a voice in her defense.

Strakhov, whose judgment Tolstoy trusted, was among the few who could point out his flaws. When this openness was encouraged, Strakhov wrote that Tolstoy lived "by the sentiment of the day." He could "throw out" extreme and paradoxical pronouncements and passionately reject the very things he used to defend. "Personally, I criticize you for your forgetfulness, that you forget the former life of your soul."[3] Sophia believed this observation was "very true."[4] Tolstoy's weakness was also his strength, since renouncing the past allowed for perennial renewal. But for the family, adjusting to his sudden transformations was enormously difficult.

Life went on as before, but with nine children it was even more taxing. Sophia wrote her sister: "Vanechka's birth and nursing was the last drop which filled the vessel of my life to the brim . . . Now it's time to publish the edition, and so I move from one task to another, like a machine."[5] Sister Tanya, who also had recently given birth, managed to write a book of children's stories, which Sophia was helping to market in Moscow bookstores. Unlike her sister, she only had time for necessities: "I don't spend a minute for myself, in three nights I had an hour and a half of sleep with the baby; yet, I do love those whom God had sent me to love, and I do not philosophize."[6]

In May, she packed to go to the country with the children. Tolstoy was living in Yasnaya with his followers and she anticipated the "devastation" and dirt they brought to the house. Overworked and annoyed, she wrote Tolstoy, asking him to send good horses and a comfortable carriage to the station. Her request of comfort was against his principles but she did not care: "I'm old, my nerves are upset, I have no time for *ideas*."[7]

That summer, Tolstoy, his follower Biryukov, daughter Masha, and Nikolai Gay (the artist) built a hut for a peasant widow. Sophia came to watch their construction: "I remember how they cut the straw, pounded clay, sprinkled it with water, mixed it together, and tossed the mixture onto the walls with spades. Lev Nikolaevich came home dirty, covered with mud." Gay was proud that he was learning to build stoves; upon hearing this, Sophia replied: "It would be better if you painted and Lev Nikolaevich wrote a novel. Why, such great artists and pottering about in mud!"[8] She told Tolstoy that he could take as much money as he needed and hire help. But he ignored her suggestion because his goal was self-perfection and manual labor the means.

Describing family life during that summer and fall, Sophia wrote matter-of-factly to her sister, "Of Lyovochka I can say that he, thank God, is in good health, hauls water from the garden well, chops wood, and stitches his leather boots."[9] She believed this work therapeutic, helping Tolstoy overcome his continuing depression.[10]

In late fall, Sophia launched a low-cost edition of Tolstoy's works. This was the fourth issue and a reprint, except for the final volume, which would include Tolstoy's latest work. An unpublished portrait of Tolstoy as a young man was a novelty she was proudly offering readers. But in December, the photographer engaged to reproduce this portrait for publication distributed extra copies, despite her protest. She could not take legal action without Tolstoy's consent and his views on property were well known. Moreover, Tolstoy told her he could not sympathize with her over the edition and criticized her for making a profit.[11]

Yet, her only interest was supporting their family: "You are always carefully avoiding the question of family responsibilities; if I did not have these responsibilities . . . I would dedicate myself to serving the public good . . . and help the underprivileged classes as best I could. But I cannot, for the benefit of strangers, let my children, given to me by God, grow up uneducated scoundrels."[12]

In the winter, Tolstoy applied to teach in an evening school for factory workers. (His application was rejected by the authorities.) When Sophia asked why he refused to teach his own children, Tolstoy lost his temper and shouted at her.[13] Compared with his cause—educating the illiterate and impoverished majority—Tolstoy felt their family needs appeared petty.

Life in Moscow was always more complicated for Sophia. On top of the children's schooling and nursing Vanechka, she ran the large household. She had to generate cash, balance books, and pay bills. And she continued to clothe the children herself. At ten months, Vanechka became ill and, according to doctors, was showing symptoms of tuberculosis. Sophia lost sleep and looked pathetic, which only inspired Tolstoy's criticism: "Sonya loves her children with such a morbid passion because they are the one real thing in her life."[14] She was offended by this dismissive remark. He discounted her efforts to educate and raise their children, believing that her motherhood was merely guided by animal instincts. Perhaps he expected spiritual sacrifice: "He wanted some religious feats from me."[15]

During Vanechka's illness Tolstoy's routine was unchanged. Thinking that the boy would die, he noted that he experienced "a strange feeling of pity for the child, of reverential awe in the presence of this soul, this germ of a most pure soul in a tiny, weak body. His soul has only just been dipped in the flesh."[16] Upon reading this entry, Sophia was struck by Tolstoy's lack of compassion, apparent from the beauty of his metaphor.

In March 1889, Tolstoy traveled to a friend's estate. In his absence, the couple's differences were less perceptible and what they shared became more important. As in the old days, he reported to Sophia about his health and his work. She was pleased that he was resting and working in peace: "My heart is always with you, despite our disagreements; deep inside, I know how dear you are to me and how greatly I value and love you."[17] When Tolstoy sent a loving letter, she replied that it uplifted her morally: "If you criticized me less, did not ignore me, and loved me more, how much better I would be!"[18] But their unity did not last: Tolstoy was writing *The Kreutzer Sonata.*

The novella's theme was marital jealousy, a passion that had tormented Tolstoy for years. During the blissful days of *War and Peace* he had dismissed a guest named Pisarev, suspecting him of getting too cozy with Sophia. The young man had merely helped her serve cups of tea. At the time, Tolstoy wrote a skit, *The Nihilist,* which the family staged in Yasnaya. He depicted himself as the jealous husband who evicts the nihilist; Sophia played the husband with "great success."[19] Later, Tolstoy laughed off his jealousy in *Anna Karenina:* Levin expels his guest, suspecting that Kitty enjoys his company. But in *The Kreutzer Sonata* the wife's relationship with a guest musician ends in her murder. In early versions of this novella Tolstoy depicted his heroine as downright unfaithful, but Sophia pleaded to make her innocent, like Desdemona. Tolstoy gradually altered the "guilty" verdict: in the final draft, his heroine's adultery is merely implied.

Sophia believed Tolstoy invested features of his raging jealousy in his hero. Her opinion was widely shared by family and friends, including Fet, who remarked that in *The Kreutzer Sonata* Tolstoy was analyzing his own jealousy.[20] Tolstoy deliberately recycled autobiographical episodes of his betrothal, familiar to readers of *Anna Karenina*. What added to the shock was that now Tolstoy's hero and his mouthpiece in the novella was a wife murderer.

When the novella was later read in the Kuzminsky apartment, Strakhov observed its effect on sister Tanya. She was so restless and emotional that her reaction was almost as interesting as the story itself.[21] For people who knew the Tolstoy family closely, the novella made for painful reading. Tolstoy barely altered sensitive episodes. Sophia recognized herself at thirty-six, when doctors taught her methods of contraception, and was reminded of the effect it had on Tolstoy.

> The means employed by those scoundrel-doctors evidently began to bear fruit; she became physically stouter and handsomer, like the late beauty of summer's end. She felt this and paid more attention to her appearance. She developed a provocative kind of beauty which made people restless. She was in the full vigor of a well-fed and excited woman of thirty who is not bearing children. Her appearance disturbed people. When she passed men she attracted their notice.[22]

Commenting on the passage, Sophia wrote, "But it was not yet my *ultimate* beauty. I was healthy, strong, and youthful for a long time, because I needed energy for my life's work."[23] Such detail did not make it into the novella, the focus of which is sexual love. Tolstoy's hero, Pozdnyshev, compares his wife, neither pregnant nor nursing, with "a fresh, well-fed, harnessed horse" whose bit has been removed.

Sophia had heard Tolstoy's diatribes against women and read some crude remarks in his diary. Once, after returning from a walk in the city, Tolstoy told her that he was disgusted by the central department store. It sold women's clothes designed to stir men's sensuality; the place was "worse than a syphilitic hospital."[24] In the novella, Tolstoy develops the idea into a social theory, saying that millions "perish at hard labor in factories merely to satisfy woman's caprice. Women . . . keep nine-tenths of mankind in bondage to heavy labor." His hero goes on to say that a lady dressed for a ball is a "dangerous and illicit" object and he is tempted to call the police to get it "removed and put away."[25] For Sophia, the sentiment was familiar, since Tolstoy objected to her attending balls. But never before was he so extreme in his denunciation of women. In 1889, congratulating son Ilya on the birth of his daughter Anna (his and Sophia's first grandchild), Tolstoy remarked, "I now look on all girls and women with pity and contempt."[26] Such was his mood when he wrote *The Kreutzer Sonata.*

Throughout this work Tolstoy argues that marriage is not a Christian ideal but an obstacle: "The prophets have said that all mankind should be united together in love . . . what is it that hinders the attainment of this aim? The passions hinder it . . . If the passions are destroyed, including the strongest of them—physical love—the prophesy will be fulfilled, mankind will be brought into unity."[27] Tolstoy admitted that his ideal of absolute chastity was unattainable, yet he refused to set a more realistic goal for mankind or for himself.

In marriage, his refusal to compromise his ideal led to painful disappointment. Sophia was copying *The Kreutzer Sonata,* in which he described physical love as "swinish passion." But while renouncing sex as sinful, he continued to make love to her. Sophia knew that despite his renunciation of sex, it remained extremely important to him. She was caught in these contradictions and felt that Tolstoy was unconcerned with her experiences.

Tolstoy now viewed her as a source of temptation and when he succumbed, he hated her for the passion she inspired. After insisting they should have sex, he would denounce it in his diary as sinful: "It was so disgusting, I felt I'd committed a crime."[28] He considered her an accomplice, an idea he would also project in his novella. For Sophia this presented a dilemma: "If I refused to be that accomplice of his, he would be only more unkind and restless."[29] His abstract idea of spiritual love was destroying their genuine bond. It was better, she told him, not to have high moral principles, expecting "some sort of perfection," but to have a sense of right and wrong. Tolstoy argued it was important to strive for an ideal.[30]

"He wrote *The Kreutzer Sonata,* rejected sexual love, while in his diary in August 1889, noted: 'Thought: what if there should be another child? How ashamed I should be, especially before the children. They will reckon up when it was, and will read what I'm writing.'" For Sophia, his perennial struggle and dissatisfaction with himself were difficult: "Lev Nikolaevich treated himself severely, as one can see from his diaries. He aspired for perfection and analyzed every stir of his soul."[31] And he did not spare Sophia his merciless analysis, since she was closest to him; he applied the same unattainable standards to her as to himself. She believed that his idealism made him intolerant: "I see that your Christianity has made you hate your family and me, but I don't understand why."[32] Tolstoy employed her remark in his autobiographical play *And the Light Shineth in Darkness.*

Sophia herself read *The Kreutzer Sonata* to their children. The reading and the discussion that followed took place in September, just before their wedding anniversary. The novella described marriage as "nothing but copulation." Present during that reading, Tolstoy recorded daughter Tanya's remark that the heroine's crime (flirting with a guest musician) was small compared with her punishment. Tanya, twenty-five and unmarried, admitted in her diary that the novella made her feel "lost, unhappy and lonely."[33] She had dreamt about marriage in the past but did not dare anymore. Yet, remaining single was also not her ideal.

Soon after their anniversary, Sophia told Tolstoy she felt alone in the family and wanted to throw herself under a passing train. She had loved him very much, "only nothing came of it."[34] Although his novella deeply offended her, she was soon promoting his work. In October, she reported to Tolstoy from Moscow that the novella made a "huge" impression on their friends at a reading she attended. She dispatched the manuscript to her sister in Petersburg, where Anatoly Koni, the lawyer and statesman, read it to a large gathering.

Sophia lived that winter with Tolstoy and the small children in the country. The Yasnaya house was in need of repair and she had stoves rebuilt and walls whitewashed. Daughter Tanya was in Europe, where Sophia had dreamt of going. From Rome, Tanya asked to send her 350 rubles. To Sophia's surprise, Tolstoy supported Tanya's request and even reminded her about it.

Seryozha was an official of a local council, or *zemstvo;* Ilya was married and lived separately. Lev was a university student in Moscow. Daughter Masha, entirely dedicated to Tolstoy and his causes, assisted in his work and received his followers. Sophia was concerned about Masha's future, since her prospects of marriage were bleak: "Her mind, heart, and life have been mixed up."[35] Masha spoke of her desire to join an agricultural commune with Tolstoy's follower Biryukov, who had earlier proposed to her. As he was penniless, Sophia ignored the proposal.

Describing their routine to sister Tanya, Sophia wrote that she spent nights with Vanechka, who was recovering from the croup. She tutored Andryusha and Misha in music, geography, and divine law. After dinner she played with the small children, then sewed and copied. In the evenings, the family gathered in the living room: Tolstoy played chess with a visitor, while the children played pickup sticks or did woodworking. Occasionally, they read aloud.[36]

That fall, Sophia expanded the garden by several hundred fruit trees and supervised the planting of 6,800 spruce and 5,300 oak. Trying to establish a plantation in poor soil, on a hill (a location chosen by Tolstoy), she consulted a German-educated forester. After a decade, when the forest covered the entire hill, it became the family's favorite place to gather mushrooms. Tolstoy took his regular morning walks in the new plantation, which he called "the Spruces." During the difficult last years of their marriage, Sophia came here with her grief, sawing deadwood and weeping alone.

Her planting was put on hold when she traveled to Moscow on publishing business. There she also attended Fet's birthday, celebrated with pomp because it was the year of his golden literary jubilee. Fet was so glad she came that he wanted to kneel in front of her, which Sophia did not allow. The table was magnificent; as a guest of honor she was seated between Dyakov and Fet.

Before Christmas, daughter Tanya returned from abroad and decided to stage Tolstoy's unfinished comedy *The Fruits of Enlightenment*. While Tanya was in Tula selecting a cast from among her friends and rehearsing the play, Sophia had carpenters build a stage. A local architect designed the set. Sophia looked forward to having family, friends, and neighbors over, but on Christmas Eve, Vanechka developed a high fever and she was torn between treatment and lodging the guests. There was such a mass

of people that beds were arranged even on the stage. During the performance Tolstoy "laughed infectiously" but later, analyzing his feelings in
his diary, wrote, "But I'm ashamed the whole time, ashamed at this foolish
expense in the midst of poverty."[37] Upon reading this, Sophia remarked
that it was impossible to know when he was displeased.

In January 1890, Sophia sent a volume with *The Kreutzer Sonata* to the
censors. The ober-procurator of the Holy Synod, Pobedonostsev, told the
main censor, Feoktistov, that the novella was a powerful work and he did
not think it should be banned in the name of morality. (This would be only
hypocritical: the novella called for higher morality than sanctioned by the
Church.) But in spring, Feoktistov informed Sophia that the novella was
banned.

By then, *The Kreutzer Sonata* was circulating in numerous handwritten
copies. Strakhov wrote Tolstoy that instead of saying "How are you?" people would ask, "Have you read *The Kreutzer Sonata?*"[38] Chekhov sent his
copy of the novella to Modest Tchaikovsky, the composer's brother. Everyone wanted to read the work, which discussed sexuality and relations
between the sexes with unprecedented openness. Sister Tanya reported to
Sophia that it was also read at court. Opinion in the royal family was divided: Alexander III liked the work, while the empress was shocked.

Entire households read the novella and people said there was not a single housemaid who had not read it. Because everyone assumed Tolstoy
drew on his own marriage, many began to see Sophia as a victim. Tolstoy's brother Sergei Nikolaevich even expressed his condolences. Sophia
learned that the tsar, upon reading the novella, had remarked he was sorry
for Tolstoy's poor wife. All this made Sophia more determined to publish
the work: "I wanted to show that I wasn't a victim at all."[39] She would appeal to the highest court in the country to lift the ban.

Tolstoy had already moved on to other projects: he started writing *Resurrection,* his last major novel, and a novella about a monk, *Father Sergius,*
his short masterpiece. Their two daughters were copying for him; Masha,
nineteen, was also allowed to read and copy extracts from his diaries. (At
this time, Tolstoy began to hide them from Sophia.)

He wrote in his diary, "I often said to myself: if not for my wife and
children I would have lived a saintly life."[40] Sophia, who continued to read
his diary despite his prohibition, knew how far her husband was from his

monastic ideal, remarking, "One should not be an animal, but nor should one preach virtues one doesn't have."[41]

At forty-six, she still lived in fear of pregnancy. When it was confirmed she was in fact pregnant, Tolstoy admitted his shame to his diary. In addition, Sophia developed inflammation of the womb, a chronic condition for her. She underwent treatment: leeches were applied to her womb, a procedure so painful it induced a miscarriage. When she told Tolstoy, he was just as relieved as she was. "We told none of this to the children, since we both were ashamed."[42] It was her sixteenth pregnancy, and her last.

That summer, she worked with Tolstoy's biographer and German translator, Rafael Levenfeld, reading his manuscript and checking information from diaries, letters, and other documents. Learning from her sister that Strakhov also planned to write about Tolstoy, Sophia replied, "I am very happy . . . Does he need materials? I would gladly . . . find everything he needs."[43] She dreamt of collaboration and investing energy in creative pursuits.

But in December, she had to deal with a crisis on the estate. A Yasnaya warden caught several peasants felling trees in the family's birch plantation. When the village policeman was called, Sophia asked Tolstoy whether charges should be laid; after pondering awhile, he replied that the peasants "should be given a good fright and then forgiven."[44] However, once the matter was in police hands, criminal charges were laid without an option of pardon. Tolstoy, furious that the peasants received a six-week jail sentence, forgot his indecision and blamed Sophia, "so once again it was all my fault." She protested to authorities but the sentence could not be revoked.[45]

The incident was publicized because several Tolstoy followers, including Biryukov, were at Yasnaya and witnessed events. At night, pacing the drawing room, Tolstoy repeated his demand to give their land to the peasants and said he would otherwise leave home. The conversation would make it into Biryukov's biography. In the eyes of the disciples, Sophia violated Tolstoy's nonresistance doctrine. But it was unclear how to implement it and what exactly she should do in practical situations.

Sophia felt that Tolstoy "had absolutely . . . no desire to understand *my* side."[46] The thieving peasants were punished in her name and when their families came to complain, Tolstoy sent Sophia to placate them. "Being expected to manage the estate and the household 'in a *Christian spirit*' is like being gripped in a vice, with no possible escape."[47]

She was continuously under pressure as Tolstoy's publisher. Despite the ban, she included *The Kreutzer Sonata* in the final volume of the collected works, hoping censors would allow it in a limited edition of three thousand copies. In February 1891, the volume containing the novella was seized by police. Sophia was soon informed that volume thirteen was irrevocably banned. She decided to appeal to Alexander III. "In my mind I keep composing speeches and letters to the Tsar, imagining what will happen and thinking endlessly about what I should say."[48] She first wrote to family and friends in Petersburg with connections to court. Elena Sheremetyeva (née Stroganova), the tsar's cousin, persuaded him to receive Sophia.

Her idea to meet the tsar on his behalf annoyed Tolstoy. He told her to stop "fussing" about the volume, particularly since he planned to renounce the copyright on *The Kreutzer Sonata*. Tolstoy allowed her to produce it in the collected works, although he also wrote to Strakhov that he did not want to make money on it. It was the first time he spelled out his intention to give up the copyright: "This morning I told Sonya with difficulty and trepidation that I would announce that everyone would have the right to print my writings. I saw she was distressed."[49] If she loved him, he added, she would herself publish a statement surrendering the copyright on his new work. Sophia argued this would deprive the family of income. When she cooled off, she told Tolstoy that he could publish the statement himself and that material considerations were petty compared to the pain of their estrangement. They cried together and made peace.

Sophia, however, was not giving up her struggle to lift the ban on *The Kreutzer Sonata*. As a publisher, she had obligations to readers—and had already promised the novella would be included in the collected works. The books were shipped with a printed slip: "Due to circumstances beyond the Publisher's control, Volume 13 cannot be released."[50]

Arriving in Petersburg at the end of March, Sophia wrote to the tsar to formally request an appointment. Before sending the letter she discussed it with Strakhov, who suggested revisions.

The meeting was delayed by the death of the grand duchess Olga Fyodorovna. Sophia watched the funeral procession from Tanya's Petersburg apartment, which faced Nevsky Prospekt. The mourning royal family halted all court activity for nine days and Sophia spent two anxious weeks before obtaining the invitation. Meanwhile, to prepare her case for the tsar, she met Feoktistov of the censorship committee. She asked him why the final volume was banned. He read the orders of the Holy Synod and the police department that prohibited the nonfictional works *On Life* and *What Then Must Be Done?* Sophia's strategy was to display indignation: those two works had already been published in abridged form. Feoktistov was taken aback because he did not know this; he promised to review the matter. Knowing of Sophia's upcoming meeting with the tsar, he quickly passed the volume for publication and delivered it in person to Tanya's apartment.

On the evening of April 12 an invitation came from the palace: the appointment was scheduled for the following morning. Sophia felt "enormous relief": her thoughts were already at Yasnaya with Vanechka, who now had become ill with chicken pox. She cleared up unfinished business, paid bills, and packed her trunk so that she could leave immediately after meeting the tsar.

The next day, in a black mourning dress, she drove to the Anichkov Palace. There was a minor complication in the antechamber: the doorkeeper had no instructions to receive Countess Tolstoy. The tsar's footman was summoned, impressive in his red and gold uniform and large, three-cornered hat. He said he had such instructions and ran up the staircase to report her arrival; Sophia excitedly followed. It was only afterward that she realized she was running—and with her asthma, she was unable to draw a breath. "The first thought that came into my head was that this business was not worth dying for. I imagined the footman coming back to summon me to the tsar and finding my lifeless body . . . Then I remembered that the thing to do when a horse has been driven too hard is to lead it about quietly for a while until it recovers. So I got up from the sofa and took a few paces around the room. That did not make it any better though, so I discreetly loosened my stays and sat down again, massaging my chest and thinking about the children."[51] By the time she was called, she had recovered her breath and composure.

The Kreutzer Sonata had been banned on the personal order of Alexander III. He followed in the steps of his grandfather, Nicholas I, a personal censor of Alexander Pushkin. The relationship between the emperor and the most talented poet of his day was legendary and invited imitation: Alexander III aspired to patronize Tolstoy. Sophia knew from the tsar's cousin, who helped her arrange the appointment, that the tsar expected her to ask him to be Tolstoy's personal censor. In fact, Alexander III was acting as such, having banned *The Kreutzer Sonata;* now, he alone could permit its publication.

The government was upset with Tolstoy's religious and social writing and was hoping he would return to fiction. So Sophia began her interview by saying Tolstoy had an idea for "something rather similar to *War and Peace*." Tolstoy indeed had started a new major novel, *Resurrection*. The tsar responded, "Ah, how good that would be! What a very great writer he is!"

Once she had the tsar's ear, she complained of the growing government prejudice against Tolstoy. His recent works were banned; Tolstoy was disturbed by the presence of secret police in Yasnaya: spies reported on his meetings with followers. The tsar admitted he was aware of it. He asked Sophia about Tolstoy's relationship with his young converts, particularly with Chertkov, whose family he knew. Sophia was unprepared to discuss the topic. After a moment of hesitation, she told the tsar about Tolstoy and Chertkov's publishing venture, which produced edifying literature for the poor. But her main point was to distinguish between Tolstoy and revolutionaries. Tolstoy's ideas of nonresistance and universal love were helping to convert rebels: he managed to turn around many who were previously on a "sinful political path."

Because Tolstoy's return to fiction was an attractive idea to the tsar, she kept bringing it up. Lifting the ban on *The Kreutzer Sonata* would be "a gracious attitude" to the writer "and, who knows, it may even encourage his work." The tsar asked whether Sophia would allow her children to read the novella. She replied that although the work "has unfortunately taken a rather extreme form," the central message was that an ideal was always unattainable. Since the perceived ideal was total chastity, "people can be pure only in marriage." (The novella suggested the opposite, that celibacy was always "better and nobler" than marriage.) Tolstoy's unfathomable message now sounded sensible to the tsar. "Could your husband not alter it a little?" the tsar asked. Tolstoy did not make changes to his completed works, Sophia replied, "and, besides, he says that he has grown to hate this story." (Tolstoy indeed came to hate the novella. Once he completed a work, he wanted to move on.)

The tsar allowed publication of the novella in her limited subscription. Sophia asked that he personally censor Tolstoy's collected works, to which the tsar replied she could send them directly for his perusal.

Her account of the audience was eagerly awaited by family and friends who gathered at Tanya's apartment. She was congratulated on her success. Later, Alexandrine told Sophia she made "an *excellent* impression" at court. But at Yasnaya, the reception was cold: Tolstoy chided her. They could not keep promises she had made. (This was likely in regard to sending works to the tsar.) He and the tsar had managed to ignore each other until now and this arrangement suited him best. Tolstoy was upset that Sophia had complained his manuscripts were "stolen" and copied without his consent. But it was true: his article "Nikolai the Stick" was copied without his knowledge and proofs of *The Kreutzer Sonata,* which circulated in handwritten copies, had been smuggled from the printing shop. Tolstoy was interested to learn what Alexander III was like—and Sophia described him, adding that the tsar was rather shy and had "a pleasant melodious voice." This soft voice and manner strangely reminded her of Tolstoy's disciple Chertkov.

Summarizing their conversation, Sophia wrote to her sister that Tolstoy wanted her to believe that permission to publish *The Kreutzer Sonata* in the thirteenth volume was unimportant. "All this is said just to oppose me, and so I don't believe any of it, for how is it possible not to rejoice at such a brilliant completion of the affair? And how can one be indifferent to the Russian public left without Volume 13 and my losses?"[52]

She recalled her Petersburg trip with pride: "I cannot help secretly exulting in my success in overcoming all the obstacles, that I managed to obtain an interview with the Tsar, and that I, a woman, have achieved something that nobody else could have done! It was undoubtedly my own personal influence that played a major part in this business."[53]

In May, Sophia corresponded with censors about the novella: the tsar had given her only verbal permission to publish it. Once this became official, she printed three thousand copies of volume thirteen. The books were sold out the following month. In July, she was allowed to produce an additional twenty thousand.

At the height of her publishing success, Tolstoy wrote Sophia in Moscow that he wanted to make volumes twelve and thirteen public property. He asked her to publish an announcement in the newspapers that he was renouncing copyright. A draft of his statement was attached with the option to publish it over his name or her own. But an announcement at this time would hinder sales. Moreover, permission to publish his censored works was given to her exclusively and for limited subscription. It was "wicked" to release them to the public. This would violate the agreement with the tsar.

However, none of this concerned Tolstoy: he remarked in his diary that every ruble "obtained from books is shame and suffering to me." But Sophia could not surrender her responsibilities: "I spend all the money from his books on *his* children."[54]

Within days of their conversation, Tolstoy told her he was sending his copyright statement to several newspapers. Sophia was outraged: "I felt how terribly unfair he was being to his family, and I realized too for the first time that this protest of his was merely another way of publicizing his dissatisfaction with his wife and family." She accused Tolstoy "of being vain and greedy for fame." He shouted back that she "only wanted the money, and that he'd never met such a stupid, greedy woman . . . It ended with him shouting 'Get out! Get out!'"[55]

In desperation, she signed Tolstoy's statement, then wrote a suicide note and ran out of the house, determined to kill herself. The idea that she should end her life in the manner of Anna Karenina had become a fixation. For the second time in two years she intended to jump under a moving train. Luckily, Sasha Kuzminsky, sister Tanya's husband, walking in the woods, spotted the deranged Sophia. She later remarked that crossing paths with Kuzminsky had saved her life: God did not want her to commit this sin.

In September, while in Moscow, Sophia received the final text of Tolstoy's copyright statement, which he asked her to publish in the newspapers the *Russian Gazette* and *New Times*. It announced that his works, written after 1881, were in the public domain: anyone in Russia and abroad could now publish them free of royalty. He had renounced copyright on the two final volumes of his collected works, which included his censored nonfiction and *The Kreutzer Sonata*. In addition, he released his novella *Ivan Ilyich,* which he gave to Sophia as a present when she became publisher. "What a coincidence," Sophia wrote him, "the novella *Ivan Ilyich* was given . . . to me and taken away from me on the same day, September 17. It hurts."[56] September 17 was her name day. Now, her present was Tolstoy's statement. He asked that she send it to the newspapers "with a good feeling," since it was a good deed. Tolstoy was trying to convert her. Sophia agreed to send the statement: it was published two days later. But in her heart, she never believed that renouncing copyright was the right thing to do. At the end of her life, she remarked it was "unfair" to deprive their large family of income. "I knew that rich publishers, like Sytin, would profit from my husband's work . . . And it seemed to me that for God, in whom I believed, it did not matter whether it was I who sold Tolstoy's works or it was Sytin and Suvorin."[57]

The family at Yasnaya Polyana, 1892. From left: Mikhail, Tolstoy, Lev, Andrei, Tatyana, Sophia, and Maria. In front, Vanechka and Sasha.

After Tolstoy renounced his copyright, the censored novella appeared in a separate edition. The tsar said Sophia had deceived his trust. But *The Kreutzer Sonata* was brought out by underground publishers, which was not her fault. Sophia was still not forgiven at court in 1911: the empress refused her an audience.

In the Tolstoy family, the copyright drama would move into the background within a month. A widespread famine in Russia was now at the center and everything else forgotten. Tolstoy and the children soon left to organize relief in several provinces, and Sophia urgently sent them nine hundred rubles and warm clothes for their winter journey. It was the beginning of a large operation that united the family and the entire country.

Yet, the story of *The Kreutzer Sonata* did not end there: Sophia wrote a counternovella, *Who's to Blame?* She worked on it during the "long and solitary winter evenings" of 1892–93, in Moscow. Her goal was to describe a young woman and her idealization of love, as opposed to male materialism. She wrote in her diary: "A woman wants *marriage* and a man wants *lechery,* and the two can never be reconciled. No marriage can be happy if the husband has led a debauched life."[58] The work's subtitle, "A woman's novella," captured the genre.

Sophia leads an indirect dialogue with Tolstoy to remind him of certain experiences in their marriage which he had left out. Her heroine, Anna, is eighteen when she accepts a proposal from Prince Prozorsky, a middle-aged bachelor. Learning about his sexual past is a shock to the virgin: "Anna, who has not even considered that at thirty-five the prince would have loved someone . . . felt like crying." (Sophia had made such an abrupt discovery during her betrothal, from Tolstoy's bachelor diaries, which he had given to her.)

On the wedding night, Prince Prozorsky makes love to Anna while they are driving to their country estate. It is depicted as a rape. When Anna becomes a mother, she slaves with her body in turns for husband and children. In the margin of her manuscript, Sophia quotes from *The Kreutzer Sonata* about the enslavement of women, if only to strengthen this point: "The woman must be her husband's mistress even while she's pregnant or nursing." Her heroine is not an accomplice of her husband's sin: she merely yields to his demands, while yearning for an unattainable spiritual life.

She challenges *The Kreutzer Sonata* on the issue of motherly love, which Tolstoy calls an animal feeling. Sophia argues that it is one of the highest manifestations of the human spirit. Since it is a counternovella, all major events parallel *The Kreutzer Sonata,* including Anna's illness, followed by her doctor's advice on contraception. But unlike Tolstoy, Sophia sympathizes with the idea.

Her story does not introduce an alternative sexual morality. As in Tolstoy's work, physical love is seen as destructive and sinful. In *The Kreutzer Sonata* the murder of a wife is a crime of passion, and the use of a dagger—piercing garment and flesh—symbolizes a sexual act.[59] Tolstoy's hero stabs his wife near the piano where she sits with her violinist friend: his jealousy is inflamed by the sound of music, "that most exquisite voluptuousness of the senses."

In Sophia's novella the weapon and the place of murder are also meaningful: Anna is a victim of Prozorsky's paranoiac jealousy. Suspecting his wife of infidelity, Prozorsky throws a marble paperweight, which hits Anna on the temple and kills her. Sophia may have been recalling *War and Peace,* which depicts a similar episode. In Tolstoy's novel, Hélène narrowly escapes being killed during a quarrel with Pierre when he throws a piece of marble at her. Or Sophia may have drawn this episode from real life: a marble paperweight found today on Tolstoy's desk is chipped, as if it had been thrown with a mighty hand.

Sophia's characters remain one-dimensional, which she likely sensed, having remarked in her memoir: "Inexperienced as a writer I poorly accomplished my task, although I wrote with much zeal, drawing my novella over the background of *The Kreutzer Sonata* by Lev Nikolaevich." Responding to Tolstoy's text was an impossible task: his artistry was overpowering.

Sophia had circulated her manuscript among friends and family. Daughter Tanya stated the family's opinion in front of Sophia and guests: "So long as we are alive, nothing that Mother writes will be published."[60] Son Lev, who would also respond to *The Kreutzer Sonata* with a novella, *Chopin's Prelude,* did not want Sophia's published. He wrote her a pompous letter: "As father's wife, as our mother, who fulfilled her mission the best possible way . . . you deserve high praise. But if you were to ruin that standing of yours with an outpouring of your groundless frustration, in a badly written novella, you will depart from your important destiny as wife and mother . . . and you will lose your path."[61] Sophia was undeterred by this pressure. As Tolstoy's wife, she faced many disadvantages, including this significant one: her life had been portrayed by the ingenious writer. That her work would only appear posthumously did not discourage her either. It was published only a century later.

Chapter Twelve

The Brotherhood of People

I N 1891, NEWSPAPERS were filled with reports of looming famine. In June, half the Russian provinces were devastated by scorching heat, and massive crop failure was predicted. The situation was exacerbated by Russia's grain export. Peasants were still forced to pay taxes, although tax collectors knew they had nothing left. The government received false reports from agricultural officials who, living in cities, were remote from the hardship. When an exodus from the villages began, the crisis could not be concealed. Hundreds of thousands would die of hunger and disease in two dreadful years, 1891 and 1892.

To save the millions of starving people, huge quantities of grain had to be shipped directly to affected areas. When the government awoke to the need, a special relief committee was organized, chaired by the heir to the throne, the future Nicholas II. But its efforts were ineffective because no assessment of the problem had been made, railways were inadequate, and there was no distribution system.

During this critical time, the intelligentsia took the initiative, discussing how to prevent famine. Hundreds of volunteers would travel to stricken areas, making assessments and distributing aid. Among them were the famous writers Tolstoy, Chekhov, and Vladimir Korolenko, who also reported on the situation in the newspapers. It was from their reports that the country—and the government—learned about the crisis.

At the start of this campaign, the writer Nikolai Leskov wrote Tolstoy to ask what should be done. Tolstoy replied: "I think the most effective remedy against the famine is to write something which might touch the hearts of the rich."[1] Without informing him, the newspaper *New Times* published extracts from his private response to Leskov, under the title "L. N. Tolstoy and the Famine." Tolstoy spent a sleepless night, worrying that the letter, meant to remain private, was unedited and clumsy.

But once it was published, he felt pressure to act. The next morning, he told Sophia of his plan to organize canteens for the hungry. He was leaving immediately to publicize the campaign and wanted Sophia to donate money from publishing. She could not help but remind him that this request came on the day his copyright statement appeared in the press. Earlier that summer, when Tolstoy spoke of preventing famine, she had pledged two thousand rubles for the starving. "I wanted to choose one district and give every starving family there so many *poods*[2] of flour, bread or potatoes per month."[3] This had not stopped Tolstoy from renouncing the copyright. Now she had to find the money from her straitened publishing income: "What is one to make of him!"[4]

Meanwhile, sons Seryozha and Ilya became involved with the local Red Cross. Son Lev left to organize relief in Samara. Tolstoy, his daughters, and his niece Vera Kuzminsky spent September and October inspecting villages in the afflicted areas between Tula and Ryazan. They decided to spend the winter at the estate of Tolstoy's friend Ivan Raevsky, near the village of Begichevka, one of the worst afflicted. Raevsky was an official of the local council, himself involved in the relief effort. His estate, located one hundred miles southeast of Yasnaya, became the headquarters for Tolstoy's operation. (Raevsky would die of influenza, which he contracted while organizing soup kitchens.)

Sophia realized the dangers of living "in the middle of nowhere," away from the railroad, without medical help, and surrounded by want and epidemics.[5] She knew of dysentery, cholera, typhus, and smallpox in the region and worried about Tolstoy and their daughters. Tolstoy was sixty-three and had chronic intestinal problems, so typhus could kill him. A flu epidemic was an additional worry. Their four small children in Moscow had contracted the virus.

Raevsky had organized several canteens for the starving and Tolstoy adopted his method. After his death, Tolstoy and the girls remained at his estate, opening more canteens. From their letters, Sophia realized that the money she had sent was but a drop in the ocean: the need was far greater than had been anticipated. At the end of October, Tolstoy wrote an article, "A Terrible Question," which he asked Sophia to proofread and offer to the *Russian Gazette*. This national newspaper, with a circulation of over twenty thousand, had correspondents across Russia, in Europe, and in America. It had high standards and was dubbed a "professors" newspaper, since academics participated in preparing editorials. Contributors included Tolstoy, Chekhov, Korolenko, and other liberal writers. Public initiative was given special attention and good coverage.

Tolstoy's article posed a question: was there enough bread in Russia to feed the hungry? When it appeared on November 6, the newspaper was reprimanded by the minister of internal affairs for publishing the disquieting piece. But Tolstoy's article only urged the government to act. Suspecting he was right, it issued an order to estimate the country's wheat stocks. Sophia reported this to Tolstoy, having learned the news herself from her brother-in-law in Petersburg.

Even before this article was published, Sophia had made an appeal for donations. She wrote it on a sleepless night on November 1. The next day, she showed it to Strakhov, who offered a few suggestions and remarked that it was written from the heart.

> My entire family has left to help the needy. My husband, Count Lev Nikolaevich Tolstoy, and our two daughters are in the Dankovsky district setting up canteens . . . Two older sons are working for the Red Cross, helping people in the Chernsky district; a third son has left for the Samara province to open soup kitchens.
>
> Having to stay in Moscow with our four young children, I can only help by supporting my family materially. But the need is so immense! On their own, people are powerless to satisfy such great demand. Meantime, each day you spend in a warm house, each piece you swallow, are living reproaches that at this moment someone is dying of hunger. We all, living here in luxury, cannot bear the sight of even the slightest pain inflicted on our own children; so, how can we bear the sight of exhausted mothers, whose children are dying of cold and hunger, or of old people with nothing to eat?

That's what my family has seen. Here's what my daughter is writing from the Dankovsky district about the canteens, which the local nobility has set up there with their own funds: "I visited two canteens: in one, arranged in a tiny chicken coop, a widow is cooking for twenty-five people. When I entered, many children were sitting at the table, eating cabbage soup in a very orderly fashion . . . A few old women were lining up, waiting their turn. I talked to one of them, and she began saying how they live and broke into sobs . . . They are only alive because of this canteen, at home they have *nothing* at all . . . Here they eat twice a day and with the firewood it costs about . . . 1 ruble 30 kopecks per month to feed one person."

This means thirteen rubles will save one person and see him to the next harvest . . . If each of us will feed one, two, ten, a hundred people—as many as we can, our consciences will be eased. God willing, we will never have to live through another such year! And so, I want to ask all of you who can and are willing to help, to support my family's undertaking. Your donations will go directly to feed the children and old people in the canteens, which my husband and children are organizing. [The mailing address of their Moscow residence and the locations of Tolstoy and their sons were provided.]

On November 3, her letter appeared in the *Russian Gazette* and that same day, people began to bring donations. The response was overwhelming: within the first twenty-four hours, Sophia received fifteen hundred rubles. Her appeal was reprinted by newspapers across Russia and in the West. She found herself in the middle of a huge undertaking, with donations coming from Russia, Europe, and the United States. Such was the trust people had in Tolstoy and his family. Some thirty thousand rubles were eventually sent directly to her. According to her estimate, in two years the Tolstoy family collected two hundred thousand rubles and, most important, the aid was distributed directly to the starving.

At the height of the campaign Sophia received one hundred donations a day. She felt responsible for every ruble. Meeting everyone who came to her door, she was moved by people's compassion. They were from all walks of life—teachers, aristocrats, and merchants; young girls, children, and old people also brought their savings. Sophia registered every donation, replied to each letter, and sent receipts. When sending funds to Tolstoy and the children, she demanded they account for the money and keep accurate records of how aid was distributed. They would need to publish reports and every detail mattered. "I am receiving donations all day," she wrote Tolstoy, "how to distribute them depends on you."[6] When Tolstoy read her published appeal for donations, he wrote, "Your letter is very good." He felt, however, that she praised her family too much.[7]

To make the best use of the public money, Sophia asked Tolstoy what exactly was needed and in what quantities. Meeting shopkeepers and merchants, she told them their produce would go to the hungry. They responded with good prices on rye, corn, barley, peas, and flour, which she bought by carloads. Describing the mood of the day, Sophia remarked, "We all had but one thing in our mind: to help the starving people."[8] In just one month Tolstoy and his several volunteers opened twenty-eight canteens, feeding more than a thousand people. The operation continued to grow.

In November and December, Sophia dispatched carloads of grain and vegetables. Because scurvy was widespread in the villages, Tolstoy asked her to send sauerkraut and onions, both major sources of vitamin C. Sophia found a farmer who could deliver these in huge quantities. When she mentioned it was for Tolstoy's canteens and read extracts from his letters, they began to talk like old friends. She was given the best-quality produce at bargain prices. The sauerkraut was a great success, Tolstoy wrote; all of her donations were very much needed. He also praised her for the cloth she had sent.

Savva Morozov, the prominent industrialist, donated 3,500 feet of fabric, and Sophia mobilized her domestic staff to sew clothes. Rail transport was free with a special Red Cross permit, which she obtained. When volunteers began to come forward, she employed some, including Nikolai Gay Jr. She also selected volunteers for Tolstoy: she herself interviewed them and gave reference letters to the most promising.

The cause had united them, and for the first time in years Tolstoy wrote her from the heart. Sophia sensed his "genuine closeness and compassion," which she badly needed. She tended to their small children who had the flu, while struggling with her asthma and neuralgia. When Tolstoy suggested that the daughters should return to help her, Sophia declined.

Their undertaking was "wonderful and useful" and she was glad the girls were well occupied.[9]

Tolstoy sent drafts of fiction and nonfiction: "I am sending you an article about the canteens . . . Read it, revise, and copy it."[10] This article related his experience establishing canteens. Tolstoy wrote it in one day, after Sophia had proposed the topic. When she read his letters to other volunteers, they wanted to know more about his canteens, since it was an efficient system; now he shared his practical knowledge.

Tolstoy's article was published in December and Chekhov read it with interest. As he was also involved in distributing aid, he found Tolstoy's advice invaluable, remarking that it would be best to publish such an article in the *Government Herald,* the official organ of the Ministry of Internal Affairs. But Tolstoy's articles were censored because they exposed social ills. His piece about the canteens was not carried by a major newspaper. In fact, the Department for Press Affairs already forbade all national newspapers from publishing articles by Tolstoy. Because of reader demand, the article on canteens was issued as a separate brochure. Tolstoy's method of distributing aid was finally employed across the country, with more canteens opening each day.

But Tolstoy also had doubts about his role in organizing famine relief. Some of his followers disapproved of his involvement, pointing out that distributing aid contradicted his idea that money was evil. In November, at the height of the campaign, Tolstoy wrote apologetically to one of his followers that he had been "dragged into this work of feeding the starving." It was "abominable" to distribute the money of the rich but once involved, it was impossible for him to stand aside. "My wife wrote a letter asking for donations, and without my noticing it I've become a distributor of other people's vomit."[11] While some disciples, like Biryukov, participated in the relief, others took a cautious stand. During the famine his disciple Chertkov lived at his mother's estate in the Voronezh province, copying Tolstoy's work *The Kingdom of God Is Within Us.* His correspondence with Tolstoy reveals that he was more concerned about abstract religious ideas than the issue that was consuming the nation.

Yet it was during this disaster that the principle of universal love could actually be tested. It was a rare moment in history when the entire nation, people of all classes, came together, united by their compassion. Sophia witnessed this while receiving donations from across the country. She wrote her sister that work on the famine was beneficial for Tolstoy, since he was surrounded by "ordinary people," not his fanatical followers.[12]

During the famine she and Tolstoy had no disagreements on the copyright issue: he himself instructed her to accept the royalties for his article "A Terrible Question," published by the *Russian Gazette*: "If they offer any money for it, take it—the more the better—for our kitchens."[13] Sophia accepted the royalties and sent him the money. (Daughter Tanya noted in her diary that her father was inconsistent.) Taking the initiative, Sophia demanded royalties from the Imperial Theatre in Petersburg, which staged his play *The Fruits of Enlightenment*. The director refused, although she wrote that the money would go to the victims of famine. Her request was granted when she addressed the minister of the Imperial Court. Royalties of 2,200 rubles went to the relief, which she registered in her financial report.

Tolstoy and the daughters returned to Moscow in early December and spent ten days at home. He noted in his diary: "Joy. Relations with Sonya have never been so cordial. I thank Thee, Father. This is what I asked for."[14] They spent Christmas separately. Staying in Moscow with the small children, Sophia canceled festivities, finding them inappropriate during the famine. She made no visits and did not receive anyone, except family: upstairs rooms remained unlit. Since there was an epidemic of smallpox in Moscow, staying at home was also practical. She vaccinated herself and the children, except sickly Vanechka.

During a rare outing, she saw a charity bazaar outside the Bolshoi where aristocrats with their lackeys arrived in carriages. Trinkets, dolls, and champagne were sold by aristocrats and merchants to benefit famine victims. But the displays of luxury seemed incongruous at such a time, Sophia wrote Tolstoy: "The booths—some like seashells emerging from marine foam (champagne), or a Chinese umbrella . . . or a flower pavilion—so odd that it's meant for the needy, huddling for warmth on a stove."[15]

Tolstoy and the girls returned for a monthlong stay at the end of December—and this time, Sophia decided to change places with Tanya.

On January 23, 1892, she traveled to Begichevka with Tolstoy and Masha, while Tanya stayed in Moscow with the children.

Tolstoy looked beyond the immediate task of distributing aid. Since his ultimate purpose was to reform mankind, what he had accomplished seemed insignificant. He was becoming dissatisfied with relief work. He had dreamt of seeing the "brotherhood of people," the rich renouncing their privileges and sharing their wealth. But what he saw was far from this: distribution of aid provoked "greediness . . . begging, envy, deceit." And he was "in the middle of it."[16]

Sophia's goal was only to feed the hungry, so she had no doubts about her role. She joined Tolstoy to inspect the canteens in several villages to see for herself what they were accomplishing. They took a train from Tula, finishing their journey in a sleigh: "The weather was ghastly; it was raining and thawing, a heavy grey sky bore down on us and a fierce wind howled . . . Masha was sick the entire journey and I worried that Lyovochka would catch cold in the wind."

When they arrived at the Raevsky estate and settled in, Sophia audited the books, then toured the canteens with Tolstoy. One hundred were now open and were feeding thousands of people. In one hut, forty-eight people were fed. "They were all in rags, wretched and thin-faced. They came in, crossed themselves and sat down quietly." The majority were old people, children, and new mothers, the most vulnerable. They were given two dishes for lunch and supper: cabbage soup with rye bread, followed by potatoes or other vegetables or porridge.

The hardest part was deciding "which people are the neediest, who should go to the canteens, who should get the firewood and clothes that have been donated." Sophia and Tolstoy talked to the village elder and the families to determine who was worst off. They also drove out in a small sleigh to inspect mills and distribution centers. The route was hazardous and their sleigh overturned on the drifts. "We got back at dusk. On one side the red sun was setting, and on the other the moon was rising. We drove along the steppes, following the course of the Don. It is a flat, bleak place, but there are several old and new estates picturesquely scattered along the banks of the river."

A village tailor she hired made coats from cloth donated to her in Moscow. She helped sew and cut; they made twenty-three coats. When she distributed the coats to the orphaned boys, dressed in rags, their delight was indescribable: "They were *warm and new*—some of them have never in their whole lives had such a thing."[17]

It was Sophia's first time witnessing such want; in Yasnaya and nearby villages peasants were much better off. Here she saw people spending the winter in uncovered huts because straw from the roofs was burned as fuel. "In a hut, completely uncovered, there were six children, half frozen. Cold, hunger, dampness, but the children, to my surprise, were perfectly healthy and even cheerful." The Tolstoys immediately bought straw for the roofs.[18]

On February 3, Sophia returned to Moscow. While driving the thirty kilometers to the train station, she was caught in "a horrible blizzard, one of those that occur no more than twice each winter. But I was happy to have seen all the difficult work that my children and Lev Nikolaevich were doing." By the end of her stay, she had an impression that Tolstoy was tired of material concerns and was beginning "to withdraw into his habitual world of abstract ideas."[19] But even earlier, he had written in his diary that despite being active, he felt "empty in the sense of spiritual life. I've written nothing in my notebook except the names of peasants asking to use the soup kitchens, etc."[20]

In Moscow, Sophia faced a public relations crisis. When Tolstoy's article "On the Famine" (one in a series) was banned in November, he asked Sophia to send it to Emil Dillon, a correspondent for the *Daily Telegraph* in London. (He had translated *The Kreutzer Sonata* into English.) "Let them publish it," Tolstoy instructed her, adding that the Russian newspapers would later reprint it.[21] Dillon translated and serialized it, beginning in January 1892, in the form of Tolstoy's letters to England, entitled "Why Are the Russian Peasants Starving?"

A conservative daily newspaper in Russia accused Tolstoy of advocating the overthrow of the entire social order and spreading socialist propaganda.[22] (It was one in a series of attacks on Tolstoy by the reactionary press.) The newspaper quoted from Tolstoy's article in the *Daily Telegraph*. The subversive phrase "people will rise" did not appear in the original. This phrase, suggesting revolution, was introduced when portions of the article were translated back into Russian. The matter caused a government uproar. But Tolstoy had not called for revolution; to the contrary, he wanted to avoid it.

When Sophia returned to Moscow, the very first letter she received was from sister Tanya, telling her that the cabinet had held an urgent meeting to discuss whether Tolstoy should be exiled abroad. The tsar was against this extreme measure, saying he did not want Tolstoy to be seen as a martyr. However, he was offended by Tolstoy's exposé and allegedly remarked that he had been betrayed to the English. Sister Tanya urged Sophia to act.

Sophia was appalled that the government believed Tolstoy had sided with revolutionaries. "Only in Europe they understand Lyovochka properly," she wrote her sister. "There they will not take him for a revolutionary, they understand he is preaching the opposite."[23] The attack on Tolstoy was made during the famine, when he worked beyond his strength to provide relief: "Never before had he been so meek. Never before had he been so useful directly to the state, since it was at his initiative that canteens were opened across Russia and all of society began helping people in league with the government."[24]

There were rumors in Moscow that Tolstoy would be put under house arrest at Yasnaya or exiled either abroad or to Solovki, a notorious monastery on an island in the northern White Sea. Sophia reacted by sending a flurry of letters to friends with connections to court. She sent a letter of protest to the *Government Herald* but it remained unpublished. Then she wrote the minister of internal affairs to refute allegations by the conservative newspaper.

Tolstoy also received her anxious letters: "You will ruin all of us with your provocative articles. Where's your *love and nonresistance*? With 9 children, you have no right to jeopardize their safety and mine."[25] She begged him to explain the situation by writing a denial. Alexandrine, who had met with the tsar, said he would be placated by Tolstoy's denial.

This opinion was confirmed by the Grand Duke Sergei Alexandrovich, the tsar's brother and Moscow's governor-general, whom Sophia met on February 10. Her message was that associating Tolstoy's name with revolutionaries only bolstered their cause. It was in the government's interest to resolve the matter. The grand duke suggested Tolstoy publish a letter in the *Government Herald:* "Just a few words from the count, and the emperor and everyone else will be immediately calmed."[26] (In 1905, the grand duke was assassinated near the Kremlin by revolutionary terrorists. Like his father, Alexander II, he was killed by a bomb.)

Sophia had to delicately maneuver between the irritated government and the stubborn Tolstoy, who was reluctant to write a denial: he blamed the government for establishing the censorship that caused the problem. On February 12, he sent a letter, explaining that his idea was misinterpreted through the double translation. The *Government Herald* refused to publish it, arguing that they had not started the polemic. But Sophia managed to publish Tolstoy's letter: she duplicated one hundred copies, which she dispatched to the government and periodicals across the country. At the end, she wrote Tolstoy: "Tanya said to someone in Moscow, 'I am *tired* of being a daughter of a famous father.' And how I am tired of being the wife of a famous man!"[27]

In February, Sophia wrote sister Tanya: she felt her family "had gone to war" and could not help worrying about them every moment.[28] Son Lev and later daughter Tanya were brought to Moscow with dysentery and she supervised their treatment. But in April, in addition to banking, checking financial reports, and other business, she sat for a portrait. Tolstoy had engaged a talented student of Repin, Valentin Serov, to make her oil painting. Serov depicted her relaxing in an armchair, wearing a fur cape—an atypical pose.

Tolstoy remained in Begichevka until midsummer, opening more shelters and canteens. His major concern was getting a new crop planted: he distributed seed and horses to villages. From February to July, his correspondence with Sophia concerned only this most important issue: the relief effort. He sent regular requests for thousands of rubles and carloads of grain, vegetables, and firewood. Sophia allowed his operation to run smoothly, sending the donations to satisfy his demands and keeping track of transactions. It was an arduous task, since she also sent relief to other volunteers. Son Lev had opened 150 canteens in Samara and she dispatched carloads of food and goods to him. And she helped the artist Nikolai Gay and his son, who dispensed relief near Petersburg, to purchase carloads of grain and firewood.

She also helped with regular financial reports, to which she and Tolstoy attributed great importance: the public gave generously because it knew how the money was spent. Reading one of the reports, Tolstoy remarked:

"Everything is very good."[29] In addition, she edited and proofread Lev's financial reports from Samara.

Sophia helped Tolstoy to complete reports because he was bored with accounting. One of these became a bestseller: Sophia wrote him that the public bought up five thousand copies of the *Russian Gazette,* containing this report, and more had to be printed. It included the moving story of Tolstoy's encounter with famine survivors, a man and his teenage son, who spent winter in a distant village without aid.

In April and May, Sophia received several indirect requests from Chertkov to send aid to Voronezh province. It was addressed to Tolstoy: "Please, Lev Nikolaevich, when you'll be writing your wife, ask her to send more sauerkraut, beets, and pickled vegetables to us."[30] The disciple reported that his province was just hit by famine and peasants were dying of scurvy. Almost a year into the famine, Chertkov toured villages around his estate and discovered that scurvy was a problem: "The disease can be quickly helped by improving the quality of food."[31] But unlike others making requests (e.g., son Lev ordering two carloads of peas and six carloads of rye), Chertkov did not specify the amount to be sent. He did not mention onions, widely used in Russia to prevent scurvy. Still, Sophia dispatched a carload of vegetables to Voronezh province.

In early May, Chertkov thanked her for sending the relief. But this was not why he wrote: the disciple was admonishing Sophia for her remark that Tolstoy was "a tired and nervous old man." Upon receiving one of Chertkov's letters, addressed to Tolstoy, she had asked the disciple not to load him with requests. (Chertkov was perennially asking Tolstoy for favors.) Sophia's words provoked Chertkov's tedious reply. His ambiguous sentences ran to a half page: "I do not see a nervous old man in Lev Nikolaevich; to the contrary, what I am used to seeing—and I daily receive the factual confirmation of it—is someone younger and spiritually more resilient . . . than people surrounding him."

In addition, the disciple described Sophia's relationship with Tolstoy and instructed her on how to understand him. Infuriated by his letter, she replied mockingly, "As you are naively writing, he is more intelligent than all of us! How is it possible even to make such a comparison? We are ordinary people, extremely narrow-minded, while he is a phenomenon of the century. And if I cared for him for thirty years, I don't have to now learn from you or anyone else how to do this." To Chertkov's suggestion that she had been sent to Tolstoy as a cross to bear, Sophia replied that only God could judge a man and wife. She concluded, "I have nothing more to tell you except to wish you more kindness and simplicity, and less meddling in other people's lives."[32] The disciple made copies of his and her letters and sent them to Tolstoy with his comments.

During the famine, Sophia had put aside her publishing business to work with Tolstoy. Meanwhile, Chertkov was settling personal scores and collecting Tolstoy's manuscripts, to benefit himself alone. In June, he asked Tolstoy to send him reader response to *The Kreutzer Sonata,* correspondence that would supplement his archive. His letters to Tolstoy were sprinkled with petty attacks on Sophia. Following the allegations by the conservative newspaper, to which Tolstoy wrote a denial, Chertkov inquired whether Sophia had published it against his will. As Tolstoy's future biographer, he wanted to "establish the truth."[33] Chertkov was copying Tolstoy's work *The Kingdom of God Is Within Us* while scheming against his wife. Evidently he was not absorbing the book's message.

Strakhov, who knew Sophia closely for two decades, would later write Tolstoy, "I have learned (but I admit, not at once) to respect Sophia Andreevna deeply. She possesses enormous energy . . . devoting it all to others; few are capable of living such a life, perhaps only women and rarely men. I have always . . . felt the deepest link between you and her, a bond as close as it can possibly be, stronger than that between a child and his mother and father, the merging of two people, as in the Gospels."[34] But while Strakhov's view remained confidential, Chertkov's would penetrate many biographies.

In July, people from neighboring villages came to Sophia with intestinal infections. There were cases of dysentery around Yasnaya and rumors of cholera. Relating this to Tolstoy, Sophia tried to persuade him to return from Begichevka. She asked him to spare himself for intellectual and artistic work; he was not a young man, and she had no strength to face another such difficult year. Their family had shown a good example and now it was others' turn to take up the cause.

With Biryukov replacing him in Begichevka, Tolstoy came in July to Yasnaya to carry on writing *The Kingdom of God Is Within Us.* But his stay was short, since another crop failure was expected and the need remained desperate. That summer and fall, Tolstoy and his daughters returned to the affected regions, where they continued to provide relief until the good harvest of 1893. Tolstoy's participation helped attract world attention to the problem: Western newspapers, such as the *Times* of London, sent correspondents to report on the famine. The Quakers sent donations from England; corn and flour arrived on steamships from America. A committee for famine relief, created in the West, asked Tolstoy to act as intermediary for distributing money and aid. Replying to a member of this committee, London publisher Fisher Unwin, Tolstoy wrote, "It is a great joy to me to see that the brotherhood of people is not an empty word, but a fact."[35]

In the fall of 1892, Tolstoy expressed surprise that Russian society was growing indifferent to the famine, while need remained. As Sophia had observed, the collective initiative to provide aid had given way to general feelings of "helplessness and submission to the disaster."[36] Her pool of donations had dried up. In November 1892, she sent Tolstoy eight hundred rubles—royalties from his play and the published article. She was still helping with financial reports. But on the whole, she was returning to her habitual life and family responsibilities.

Chapter Thirteen

I Long to Be Alone with My Family

IN JULY 1892, after Tolstoy returned to Yasnaya from Begichevka, the family assembled to discuss division of property. A year earlier, Tolstoy had suggested dividing the estate among the family members, and he himself allocated their portions. Vanechka, the youngest, and Sophia were given Yasnaya because Tolstoy would live there and she had to be with him.

At first, Sophia welcomed Tolstoy's decision, since it was time for their grown-up sons to be independent. Yet, such division usually takes place when people prepare for death. So, as she wrote her sister, it was depressing and odd: "There is something sad and improper about the way this division affects the father. Well, it's not my business. I didn't plan it."[1]

The division of property would create problems because it contradicted Tolstoy's belief that land must belong to the peasants. His disciple Chertkov was quick to point this out. In addition, the older children began to dispute their shares, which upset Tolstoy. Yet the idea was his; Sophia simply handled the practical side, obtaining documents and dealing with notaries. She tried to maintain family peace, which was not easy, since the older sons were "grabbing for the biggest bits."[2] She also had to protect the interests of the four small children and assume guardianship over them.

An unpleasant incident took place when Masha, the most idealistic among their children, refused to accept her share. Her selflessness did not inspire imitation; to the contrary, it led to further friction because Masha exposed her siblings' greed. The others said that she was playing a "mean trick."[3] Tolstoy took this personally because Masha alone did what he hoped the rest would do. He complained to Chertkov about his children's conduct, but asked that it remain confidential. Tolstoy even instructed him to destroy his letter but the disciple preserved it.

Sophia knew that Masha's decision was impractical and predicted that she would later ask for her share. (This, in fact, happened upon her marriage in 1897, when she requested and received her inheritance.) Meanwhile, Sophia had to do additional paperwork to ensure that her daughter was not left penniless. "What a laborious, tiresome, complicated business this is, both in principle and in practice."[4] It took her two years to settle everything.

In September, Sophia visited Sergei and Ilya at their estates in Tula province. Ilya, the father of two, mismanaged his estate and was perennially in debt. The grandchildren were a joy and her relationship with Ilya was good, despite friction over money. Her third son, Lev, had left university without graduating: he suffered from a nervous disorder. His erratic character resembled his father's, but without Tolstoy's genius. Sophia supported Lev's literary attempts and sent his story "Montecristo" to a magazine that published it. She also allowed him to use her diary when he needed certain material.

For another winter, Sophia lived separately in Moscow with the small children. Tolstoy, needing solitude and peace, remained at Yasnaya with the older daughters. Upon receiving a kind letter from him, Sophia replied at once: "I felt your heart in it . . . and my life became illuminated once again."[5]

She had to live in Moscow because teenage Andryusha and Misha attended school. Their lack of diligence upset her and she tutored them daily. When Misha practiced violin, she accompanied on the piano. During such recitals Vanechka, four, and Sasha, eight, danced in the drawing room with their dolls. Sophia's heart went out to Vanechka, not her healthy daughter. The boy was unusually delicate as though "not made for this world."[6]

The older daughters continued to accompany Tolstoy on tours to the famine-stricken Begichevka. An acquaintance told Sophia she saw an exhausted Tolstoy walking through deep snow to inspect canteens. The daughters were consumed with his causes and writing, their lives becoming "an appendage" of his. Tanya, twenty-eight, and Masha, twenty-one, were still unmarried. Their devotion and sacrifice to Tolstoy replicated Sophia's. Aside from copying, they taught peasant children in Yasnaya, as Sophia had; they lived isolated lives, which suited Tolstoy. She believed children should make their own choices and wrote Tolstoy that as parents they must be unselfish. They should encourage their daughters to experience life themselves and to discover their needs. "Will they ever have *their own* personal lives? . . . Years go by, youth passes."[7]

In November, Sophia visited Fet and his wife, Maria Petrovna. Fet had been unwell for two months: he'd developed bronchitis and a heart condition after a flu. Inhaling artificial oxygen helped little. He told Sophia that he was not afraid of death but hated suffering. Rereading *War and Peace* in his final days, he said he now knew why the dying Prince Bolkonsky was cold with Natasha: "Now I understand how surprisingly accurate this is. When a man is dying, his love is dying as well."[8] He admired *The Death of Ivan Ilyich,* where Tolstoy depicts the agonizing loneliness of a man dying of cancer, his fear of death, and, in the end, his acceptance of it, his liberation and escape into eternity and light. If Tolstoy were to come now, Fet told her, he would bow to the ground before him for having known and described this sense of loneliness. Tolstoy was then reading Fet's translation of *Faust* and sent him a bow through Sophia.

Fet's last book, *Reminiscences,* was about to be published: he was reading the galley proofs. The book described his first meeting with Sophia when she was eighteen and his vision of the young countess, running at Tolstoy's summons, in her white dress, a cluster of barn keys dangling from her belt.

Fet died on November 21, shortly before turning seventy-two. Sophia attended his funeral at the university parish church. According to his wishes, Fet was dressed in his official uniform as gentleman of the chamber. (He had recently obtained imperial permission to resume his noble status and his father's name, Shenshin.)[9] The gold-embroidered military uniform looked strange on the poet. Sophia placed a rose on his chest, as he had asked to be done in a poem: "Give this rose to a poet."[10] There was a blizzard when she arrived at the railway station; from there the coffin was taken to the cemetery. Fet was buried in the Shenshin family vault at the ancestral estate. Sophia had lost a close friend of many years and a poet whose artistic mastery she admired. She described his funeral in a prose poem, later published with her collection in 1904.

Fet's widow visited Sophia in the winter of 1893. His collected works were being prepared for publication and Sophia advised her to include Fet's photographs at different ages. Sophia was herself producing a new illustrated edition of Tolstoy's collected works. When she had launched this edition in November 1892, Sophia sought Strakhov's advice. In the past, she had compromised quality because she was focused on publishing *The Kreutzer Sonata* and other censored work. Now that she had the censors' permission, she could aspire to higher standards. She needed an experienced editor and no one was better than Strakhov, to whom Tolstoy had entrusted *Anna Karenina*.

Sophia had been performing the tasks of editing and proofreading without formal training. For example, she did not know the protocols for captions under photographs or for designing content to make it more accessible. All of this was simple for Strakhov. She also sent him illustrations she wanted to include, asking for his blessing. Her plan was to open each volume with a photograph representing Tolstoy in the relevant period of his life. "You can't imagine how your help is dear to me. With your guidance I feel everything will be well."[11] This edition was the first attempt to publish Tolstoy's collected works and to document his life. Sophia included photographs and daguerreotypes of Tolstoy, along with portraits by Kramskoy, Repin, and Gay and photographs of Yasnaya and their house in Moscow.

Strakhov advised her on how to juxtapose Tolstoy's fiction and nonfiction. In the past, Sophia could not think about presentation. *The Kreutzer Sonata* had been placed at the very end of the final volume to make it easier to remove if it was banned. Now she considered what was best for the reader.

Sophia was determined to handle the proofreading of the entire thirteen volumes by herself. Strakhov found this unreasonable and advised her to hire an assistant and spare her eyes. Despite being very nearsighted (eyestrain constantly bothered her), she insisted it was impossible to find a good proofreader in Moscow. She could trust the final reading to Strakhov only. Before sending him a batch of proofs, she would read them twice. Daily, she invested seven hours in this work, often finishing at four in the morning. Her proofreading saved the family twelve rubles a day. But the sum hardly mattered: she was paying five rubles *an hour* to Misha's violin teacher.

Proofreading Tolstoy's novels brought back memories of the happiest years of her marriage. She wrote Tolstoy that she was again "living in the world of *War and Peace*." She continued to discover new horizons, being "surprised, enchanted, and puzzled" by the novel. "How silly I was when you wrote *War and Peace,* and how ingenious you were!"[12] The Bolkonsky family (modeled on Tolstoy's) now interested her more than the Rostovs (modeled on hers). She looked forward to working on *Anna Karenina*.

Strakhov shared her admiration for Tolstoy's artistry. An authority in French as well as Russian, he corrected some grammar in the French opening of *War and Peace*. This proved Sophia's point: it was impossible to *hire* an assistant for such work. She wrote Strakhov that assistants are sent to one by fate: "God has sent me a selfless, hardworking, and ingeniously clever assistant in you."[13]

But despite this praise, Strakhov suspected that Sophia would reject his suggestions. He had worked with many ambitious people, publishers, and writers. (Aside from collaborating with Tolstoy, he had worked for Dostoevsky and coedited his journal *Vremya*.) When, in September, Sophia sent him the leather-bound volumes, Strakhov was in rapture: "A marvelous edition! I looked for misprints and could not find any. But more important, I am delighted that all of my labor has been accepted and it appears on these pages. I have to admit, I did not expect this. With your energy, I thought you couldn't help making it your own way."[14]

The new edition was Sophia's most important project that year. When Strakhov expressed his approval, she sent the volumes to prominent magazines, including the *Northern Herald,* published by Lyubov Gurevich, who was also an author and an acquaintance.

That fall, Sophia received the artist Leonid Pasternak (Boris Pasternak's father). He brought his illustrations to *War and Peace* and sought her opinion. Sophia hesitated to give it to him directly, realizing that Pasternak, in fact, wanted Tolstoy's opinion. She forwarded the illustrations to Tolstoy in Yasnaya with cautious praise. Educated in Europe, Pasternak called himself an Impressionist and was among the first Russian painters to do so. Tolstoy was interested in his style and later asked him to illustrate

Resurrection. "Pasternak's drawings are excellent,"[15] he wrote Sophia in 1898. She also welcomed Pasternak at Yasnaya, where he painted Tolstoy and the family.

Sophia wanted everyone to spend Christmas together and tried to persuade Tolstoy to come to Moscow. She told him how Vanechka, playing with an iron bust of his father, missed him. He found it in a corner of the drawing room, near the couch. "You should have seen his excitement and joy: he patted and stroked its head (what an imagination, he was oblivious to the cold iron). He walked around it and kissed it, forgetting we were watching."[16]

It was obvious that Sophia wanted Tolstoy to join them. He came in mid-November, but a month later, depressed by the city, unable to focus on his work, Tolstoy complained in his diary that he had been "dragged" to Moscow. He decried his family's life: "This luxury. This sale of books. This moral filth. This fuss and bother."[17] But shortly after, in a happier mood, he told a different story: "With Sonya relations are good. Thought yesterday, as I observed her attitude towards Andryusha and Misha: what a wonderful mother and wife she is in a certain sense. I suppose Fet is right that everyone gets the wife he needs."[18]

Fet and Strakhov were impressed with Sophia's ability to handle literary and business affairs with equal competence. She worked quickly and diligently. On one of his visits to Yasnaya, watching her work, Strakhov implored, "Please, don't hurry, Countess." Tolstoy, overhearing this, responded, "Yes, but she's been hurrying like that for thirty years!" Strakhov commented that living in such haste "must have been destined" for Sophia. She had been "hurrying" all her married life to keep pace.[19]

Sophia possessed the capacity and stamina for hard work, which women of her class could not match. She managed business affairs and was adept at housework, sewing, and cooking, and even wrote a cookbook. Noblewomen were not trained for such duties. When in Moscow on publishing business, she lived alone, without servants. Getting the house ready for a new school year was also something she did by herself. She wrote Tolstoy, "I clean dresses, coats, and shoes, tidy the rooms, repair things, do the laundry, make beds, and carry water."[20] Another letter described how she repaired broken closets and mended mattresses. A life of luxury, of which Tolstoy accused her in his diaries, was but a myth.

In 1894, Sophia was turning fifty. She was "a tired woman," as she described herself, having lived through many crises: sixteen pregnancies, miscarriages, the deaths of four children, and Tolstoy's difficult moods. She had more than her share of hard work, stress, and responsibilities. In the past, the idea of serving a genius and a great man gave her the necessary strength. But after his conversion, she lived in fear of criticism. This fear was wearing her out. Her head tremors when she was tired were noticeable. In addition to neuralgia, anxiety, and insomnia, she suffered mood swings, as menopause was approaching.

Small children gave her joy and provided escape. She now spent more time with them, reading, teaching, taking them to skate, to dance lessons, and to the theater. With Sasha and Vanechka she toured Novodevichy Convent to show them its medieval walls. This brought back memories of her childhood and the excursion her father had arranged to the ancient Kremlin towers.

Her unmarried daughters and son Lev were sources of worry. Lev's mental condition had deteriorated and Sophia sent him to Europe for treatment. From Paris, where he was undergoing therapy, his frantic letters revealed he was suicidal. Daughter Tanya was sent to France to watch over him. Afraid she might survive her son, Sophia wrote, "My heart is breaking with the strain; I live from one day to the next."[21]

In February, Sophia found a new task to consume her, translating a biography of St. Francis of Assisi by Paul Sabatier into Russian. The story of the medieval Italian saint who established a religious order, Friars Minor, had recently appeared in Paris. Tolstoy believed it would be "a wonderful" book for Intermediary to bring out. Having previously enjoyed translating Tolstoy's *On Life* into French, Sophia was happy to take on the project. Her translation of St. Francis's biography was published by Intermediary in 1895.[22]

Tolstoy was inspired by the example of St. Francis, who had renounced class privilege to idealize humility and Lady Poverty. St. Francis believed since his early days that he would be "adored by the whole world."[23] Sophia thought Tolstoy shared this aspiration. The biography gave an insight into the saint's conversion, suggesting similarities with Tolstoy. St. Francis was inspired by the Gospels to wander the land and preach, something Tolstoy had dreamt of. But unlike the medieval saint, he had a family.

In spring, Sophia received unwelcome news: Tolstoy's disciple Chertkov wanted to spend summer near Yasnaya. There had been serious friction between him and Sophia over Tolstoy's manuscripts, which Chertkov continued to collect. In the summer of 1893, Chertkov had given part of Tolstoy's archive and diaries for safekeeping to his friend General Trepov. As a Tolstoyan, Chertkov was under police surveillance and was afraid his home could be searched. Yet Sophia was furious that Tolstoy's archive was being kept clandestinely, and at the home of a military official. (Trepov, soon appointed chief of Moscow police, represented everything Tolstoy stood against. As chief and later governor-general, he would become known for his brutality.) Sophia realized that the disciple's influence over Tolstoy had grown. Later she commented, "This was the beginning of Chertkov's despotic, yet excessively reverential and loving relationship with Lev Nikolaevich."[24] The disciple's exclusive privilege to read and keep Tolstoy's private diaries was an intrusion into their marriage.

Despite her objection, Tolstoy supported Chertkov's decision to spend the summer near Yasnaya. The disciple rented a cottage within walking distance of the estate and moved in with his wife, Galya,[25] and son, Dima. Daughter Tanya found Chertkov's proximity frightening, explaining in her diary, "He will try to meddle in Papa's work and our way of life, and almost by force will require us to follow his advice and instructions."[26] Chertkov had recently attempted to turn Tanya against her mother. In February, he wrote Tanya a letter proposing she give up her inheritance and "fine clothes." He also advised her on how to denounce her mother. First, she had to spend time with Sophia, drawing closer to her, to win her trust. When the "maximum of mutual softening" was reached, Tanya should condemn Sophia for opposing Tolstoy's doctrine.

However, Tanya felt it was "wrong to condemn and expose one another."[27] She was beginning to doubt Chertkov's sincerity, discovering his double standards. Chertkov and Galya said it was wrong for Tolstoy's children to inherit property. Yet, their son, Dima, was well provided for. To Tanya's question as to whether Dima would be left with funds or without, Galya replied, "Of course, with."[28] In 1898, Chertkov would write Tanya from England begging a loan of ten thousand rubles, her inheritance money. Tolstoy got involved, informing Chertkov, through Galya, that son Lev agreed to lend the sum.[29] But, in fact, the money would be raised by Sophia. Commenting on Chertkov's pleas for money, she wrote in May: "The whole letter is unnatural—all the same old arguments about . . . money and the sin of possessing it, but the fact is that he is in debt all over the place . . . It's such utter *hypocrisy, that's* what I can't endure."[30] Indeed, Chertkov pressed Tolstoy's family to give up their property, while seeking their financial support.[31]

Sophia was open in her dislike of Tolstoy's followers who caused him embarrassment. The Tolstoyan agricultural colonies were notorious for various incidents, which led to their breakup. Such colonies had sprung up in the 1880s, but none lasted longer than a year: people who fled convention were a disagreeable lot. Their attempts to live and work together were doomed—quarrels were common, and since they rejected the law, there was no way of solving their disputes. They believed in the superiority of their moral principles but could not survive as a community. Commenting on what he perceived as a failure of their movement, Aylmer Maude would remark: "Again and again attempts have been made to cure social ills by persuading people to stand aside from the main stream of human life, and to save their souls by following an isolated course; but all paths of social improvement except the common highway trodden by the common man have proved to be blind alleys."[32] Like Maude, Sophia met many idle and inefficient "wanderers" among the Tolstoyans. She was appalled by scandals in the Tolstoy Colonies, which were widely known. In 1891, Nikolai Karonin, a populist writer, published "The Borskaya Colony," a story about intellectuals who founded a commune with the idea of helping peasants. Instead, they brought ruin: a peasant girl was raped and later committed suicide. The fact-based account appeared in the journal *Russian Thought* and produced a sensation, hurtful to Tolstoy's cause.

Some followers misinterpreted his teaching and Tolstoy himself considered them a burden. And yet, he did not give up his attempts to influence them. One of these young men, Pyotr Khokhlov, whom Tolstoy allowed to stay with the family, was mentally ill. (He later died in an asylum.) He harassed Tanya; her younger sister, Sasha, described it as her childhood nightmare: "Tanya runs through a dark corridor of our Moscow house, pursued by an unkempt madman."[33] Eventually, Sophia had to evict him and she wrote, "These are the people Lev Nikolaevich has brought into our intimate family circle—and it's I who have to send them packing. How strange that it should be these weak, foolish people, who for whatever morbid reason have strayed from the path of normal life, that throw themselves into Lev Nikolaevich's teachings."[34]

In April 1894, Sophia wrote her sister that Chertkov's presence in Yasnaya would draw other disciples and that her summer would be spoiled: "These Pharisees, cheats and hypocrites, one can expect nothing but harm from them." That summer, she saw little of Tolstoy, who spent a lot of time at the Chertkovs' nearby. In July, a crowd of followers arrived in Yasnaya, further alienating Sophia. She wrote Tanya: "When I am sad, I pick up an axe, saw, and garden scissors and escape to chop, saw, and cut dead branches. After several hours, I'm exhausted and this deadens my thoughts and feelings."[35]

In early August, she was swamped with problems on the farm. A wet summer had delayed the harvest. The new estate manager turned out to be a drunk and she had to take over from him. She hired farm laborers and then had to nag them to work. There were also renovations at Yasnaya: she had to oversee carpenters building an addition to the house.

Just before her fiftieth birthday, on August 22, Sophia went to Moscow with Andryusha, to enroll him in a lyceum, order his uniform, and find tutors. Tolstoy wrote that he missed her and felt sorry for her having to work hard. She came to Yasnaya for her birthday and shortly after returned to her busy routine.

In Moscow, she launched the new collected works and an edition of Tolstoy's *Primers*. She was swamped with proofs, reading them in a room with Andryusha and Misha to make sure they did their homework. Son Lev occupied a wing of their Moscow house, and getting along with him was difficult. Quiet, overwrought by his suffering, he would suddenly become hostile, shout at her, threaten to leave, and finally drive her to tears.

In September and October, Tolstoy lived at Yasnaya with the older daughters and the two small children, Vanechka and Sasha. Tanya, twenty years older, was like a mother to them. In the evenings, she and Masha would read them the family favorites—Defoe's *Robinson Crusoe* and Verne's *The Children of Capitan Grant*.

With the disciples gone, Tolstoy was the family man Sophia used to know. He wrote her that he loved her "very much"[36] and it was apparent that he enjoyed the children's stay. He reported on the house renovations:

the bricks had been delivered. When he mentioned that he had started a new fictional work, Sophia understood this was the story "about a master and his man."[37] Earlier, when Tolstoy had shared the idea with her, she sensed it would be his "real," artistic work. "How strange are these sparks of creativity," she wrote him. With advancing age, he wrote fiction sporadically. She treasured these interludes, likening them with rare sunbeams in late fall. "I cannot renounce my love of your *artistic* work and today I realized that's because I have experienced it with you, during my youth. And the daughters are now experiencing another side of your creativity, in their youth, and will love it more than anything else."[38] Perhaps her remarks were unpleasant, she added, as they would remind him of his past. Tolstoy replied it was not unpleasant to him: what she wrote about the daughters was true. And he recalled the period of artistic work as "enjoyable."[39]

In late October 1894, the country was shocked to learn that Alexander III had died. He was only forty-nine and his death from nephritis took many by surprise. Alexander III became the last Romanov to receive a timely burial at St. Peter and Paul Cathedral in Petersburg. From the Livadia Palace in the Crimea[40] his body was taken to the Kremlin in Moscow, where the principal funeral services took place; the burial was in Petersburg.

The tsar left a poor legacy: his policies had not kept pace with the country's industrial growth. He tried to impose one nationality, one language, and one religion, persecuting Jews and other minorities. To centralize power and suppress the opposition he undid his father's liberal reforms. But he brought Russia to the brink of revolution.

However, his funeral was unprecedented in scale and scope. According to contemporaries, never before was Russia "so occupied with funeral orations, articles, mourning, ceremony as on the death of that Emperor."[41] It was a show of confidence at a time when, in Tolstoy's words, the Russian monarchy was "drowning."

To ensure loyalty to his successor, Nicholas II, new protocols were introduced: children had to take an oath of allegiance. Sophia wrote Tolstoy that Misha had taken the oath, along with other pupils, and even female teachers at his gymnasium had to take it. "I cannot understand any of this!"[42] The oath was imposed on twelve-year-olds, which inspired Tolstoy's remark: "Do they really think they can bind children by it?" He went on to say that the autocracy could not be rescued by Orthodoxy: they would drown together.[43]

The tsar's sudden death generated gossip and Sophia related some of it to Tolstoy. People were saying that the tsar was poisoned by physicians. Among the doctors who tended to him and signed the death certificate was Zakharin, the Tolstoys' family physician. A mob broke the windows of his house in Moscow. There was also a rumor that Nicholas II wanted to abdicate. And there was speculation that Tolstoy had written a "manifesto" and read it somewhere in Moscow. Although Sophia knew this was untrue, she was afraid that Tolstoy might write something critical. She begged him not to contribute anything to foreign newspapers about the new reign. To her sister, she wrote that Alexander III was "honest, kind, and a man of peace." (He had granted her an audience.) The new tsar did not inspire her trust: she thought he was too young and "could fall under a bad influence."[44]

As Moscow prepared to receive the body of Alexander III, mourning flags hung from windows, black-and-white cloth adorned houses and shops, and funeral arches were erected at street corners and central squares. The university was closed for several days in fear of unrest, yet there were still student rallies in the city. Police patrolled the streets, especially near the Kremlin, where the main preparations were taking place. An immense catafalque was erected and a boardwalk built leading to the Cathedral of St. Michael the Archangel; the body would lie in state there.

Sophia did not reserve seats to watch the funeral cortege, but the small children, now in Moscow, begged her to see it. Anna Dostoevsky, who arrived in the city with daughter Lyuba, heard the Tolstoys needed seats. She could reserve them at the Historical Museum by Red Square, where her husband's archive was stored. On October 31, Anna arrived early. Cheerful and noisy, she said there was no time to spare: the funeral train was leaving for Petersburg at ten in the morning. She had seats at the windows overlooking Iverskaya Chapel, at the very entrance to Red Square.

Ironically, Dostoevsky was one of the main supporters of the regime and Tolstoy its main critic. But their families were interested only in the event. Sophia described to Tolstoy how the cortege appeared: the procession was comprised of sections of dignitaries and delegations. The coffin was covered with a golden pall, lined with ermine. When the cortege stopped by the chapel, the ancient Iverskaya icon, draped in black, was brought out. Clergy in white vestments, with burning candles and incense, stood by as Nicholas II knelt before the icon. The Prince of Wales and the Grand Duke Michael watched. Sophia had "a very good look" at the young tsar. He was in uniform, thin, his face "handsome and timid."

Afterward, Anna took Sophia and the children to the Historical Museum to show them Dostoevsky's archive. The writer's manuscripts, busts, portraits, and bookcases were kept in a bright, eight-cornered room. As Sophia wrote Tolstoy, Dostoevsky was given such a "jolly, clean, and neat little corner" and his widow kept adding more letters and papers.[45] Anna planned to open another museum and a parochial school in her husband's name.

In honor of the deceased tsar the poor were given a free dinner and alms of five kopecks at the monasteries. Sophia drove to the Novodevichy Convent, where a large crowd of women and children waited at the gate. They were admitted in parties of two hundred. Thinking Tolstoy would be interested, Sophia described the orderly dinner served by the nuns.

In spring 1896, during the coronation of Nicholas II, Sophia would see a different funeral procession in Moscow. As part of the coronation there was a feast on the Khodynka Meadow outside the city. A half million people arrived in the evening, but the place was not prepared for such a crowd and two thousand died in the crush. At dawn, Sophia saw a chain of covered carts laden with crushed bodies. Later, she told Tolstoy a story about a girl rescued on the meadow and he noted in his diary, "A wonderful story by Sonya about rescuing a girl on the Khodynka."[46] He made a draft of that story but did not complete it.

Before the New Year, Tolstoy was photographed at the Mey studio with a group of disciples, which included Chertkov and Biryukov. It was at Chertkov's request that Tolstoy posed for the picture. He tried to conceal it: Sophia had recently asked him to have their picture taken together and he refused. Learning that Tolstoy took his picture with the disciples, an offended Sophia went to the studio and obtained the negative plates. Later, she tried to scratch Tolstoy out with her diamond earring but failed and smashed the negatives.

When the disciples came to admonish her, Sophia was defiant: "Group photographs are taken of schools, picnics, institutions, etc., so I suppose that means that the Tolstoyans are an 'institution'! The public would seize on it, and they'd all want to buy pictures of 'Tolstoy with his pupils.'"[47] Tolstoy criticized her conduct in his diary on December 31: "As always, Sonya acted decisively, but thoughtlessly and badly."[48]

The year 1895 began with a quarrel and separation. Tolstoy, accompanied by Tanya, drove off to Count Olsufiev's estate. From there, he wrote cheerful letters and reproached Sophia for being unhappy. Ten days after the quarrel over the photograph, it still bothered her. She felt bad for having "acted rudely" and tried to explain that she was "provoked."[49] Tolstoy replied it was unfortunate that she kept talking about it. He was writing at the Olsufievs and taking walks; evenings, he joined the rest to play cards. Sophia remarked that he was able to relax there because he was "free of the critical gaze of his followers."[50] The Olsufiev estate had a telephone, which the Tolstoys did not have. Sophia's brief messages were read to Tolstoy on the phone from a post office.

In his absence, Sophia received a telegram that their Yasnaya house had been robbed. She traveled there to deal with formalities. Meanwhile, the children became sick with the flu and Lev had started electrical treatments, a therapy believed to help patients with various "nervous diseases."[51] He was soon hospitalized at a clinic near Moscow. But it was Vanechka's illness that tipped her balance. She was "dreadfully worried" when his temperature soared. Dr. Filatov said it was just the flu but she panicked: "Something has broken in me—I ache inside and cannot control myself."[52]

When Tolstoy returned to Moscow, Sophia helped him correct the proofs of his new story, "Master and Man." He did not let her have the story for the collected works, as he did not want her to profit from it. Instead, he gave it exclusively to Lyubov Gurevich at the *Northern Herald*.

At twenty-nine, Gurevich was a successful publisher who knew Tolstoy personally. Her popular magazine had a circulation of four thousand. In the past, it had published writers of the democratic camp. But since Gurevich bought the magazine in 1891, it published mostly symbolist poets and writers. It was a far cry from Intermediary, which produced moralistic stories and Tolstoy's new works. Sophia wondered why he gave the story to Gurevich: her magazine cost an exorbitant thirteen rubles. If

Tolstoy gave it to Intermediary, anyone could read it for twenty kopecks. Tolstoy would not explain to Sophia why he made this decision and why he would not contribute the story simultaneously to Intermediary and the collected works she produced.

This led to a quarrel. When Tolstoy declared he was leaving home forever, Sophia suspected he was in love with Gurevich. On a freezing winter night, she ran outside in her slippers and dressing gown, screaming, "Let them take me away and put me in prison or the mental hospital!" Tolstoy, also half dressed, ran after. He begged her to stop and dragged her home.

For several days Sophia remained in a state Tolstoy described as "close to madness and to suicide." She made several more attempts to flee but each time the children pursued her and brought her back. "She was suffering terribly," Tolstoy noted. "It was the devil of jealousy, insane, groundless jealousy."[53] (Two years later, in a letter to Sophia, Tolstoy admitted that he had been in love with Gurevich but that this feeling had only "lasted several days.")[54]

When peace was made, Tolstoy agreed to give the story simultaneously to Intermediary, the *Northern Herald,* and the collected works. He summoned doctors to examine Sophia. Gynecologist Vladimir Snegirev said she was going through menopause. Sophia refused to take the prescribed medications and returned to work: "I am correcting the proofs. I feel very humble to be involved in this great work, which often brings tears of joy to my eyes."[55]

The melodrama was over. But shortly after, the family was struck by genuine grief: Vanechka was diagnosed with scarlet fever. He died the following day, on February 23, 1895. Time stopped for Sophia: "I closed my life, my heart, my feelings, my joy."[56] Such sorrow she would experience again only with Tolstoy's death.

Later, as a widow, recalling her quarrel with Tolstoy, her breakdown, and suicidal threats, she would write, "With time I realized that the real cause of my utter despair . . . was my premonition of Vanechka's imminent death . . . I fell into exactly the same despairing state in the summer just before Lev Nikolaevich's death. Such times are beyond our powers of endurance. There are always plenty of opportunities for grief in our life. The question is whether we have the strength to survive them and control ourselves."[57]

Chapter Fourteen

A Song without Words

VANECHKA'S DEATH BROUGHT the family together and extinguished disagreements. Tolstoy wrote Alexandrine, "We have none of us felt as close to each other as we do now, and I have never felt either in Sonya or in myself such a need for love and such an aversion towards all disunity and evil."[1] Although he was pained by the loss, he philosophized that there was no death but "only a series of changes which happen to all of us." He wanted Sophia to share his religious attitude but she could not. For her, the pain from separation was physical.

She had invested all her love in her youngest son: Vanechka filled the void created by Tolstoy's estrangement. She would say that of all their children Vanechka looked most like his father, "with the same bright, penetrating eyes, the same earnest, searching mind." Tolstoy had also singled him out: "I had always thought that of all my sons Vanechka alone would carry on my good work on earth after I died."[2] Sophia had never seen Tolstoy so affected by loss, even though he described it in his diary as a "merciful" event, coming from God. "Lyovochka has grown bent and old; he wanders sadly about the house, his eyes bright with tears, and it's as though the last bright ray of sunshine of his old age has been extinguished."[3]

After the funeral, attended by many, Tolstoy and Sophia drove in a large sleigh to the Pokrovskoe cemetery, where son Alyosha was buried. "Lyovochka and I silently bore off our beloved youngest child, our one

Vanechka Tolstoy in 1894, shortly before he died.

bright hope." It was the area where Sophia was born and spent her summers and where Tolstoy visited her at the Behrs' dacha when she was a girl. "Lyovochka recalled how he used to drive along that road to our dacha in Pokrovskoe after he had first fallen in love with me. He wept and caressed me and spoke so tenderly, and his love meant so much to me."[4]

Tolstoy and their daughters were extraordinarily attentive to Sophia, as were friends and family. But she remained inconsolable, finding no peace as weeks and months went by. She spent hours beside Vanechka's portrait, which she had enlarged, and stood through long services in churches and cathedrals. Afterward, she would sit on the step with beggars and pilgrims, sometimes talking to a mother who had also lost her child. She tried to think that her suffering was necessary and that her soul, thus purified, would be united in eternity with Vanechka's pristine soul.

During these days Tolstoy observed how Sophia was transformed by grief. "The pain of separation immediately released her from all that was darkening her soul. It was as if doors had been thrown open and the divine essence of love which constitutes our soul had been uncovered. She astonished me during the first days by her amazing power of love."[5] He likened her suffering to childbirth: her soul had manifested new spiritual life. She continued to inspire him and in his diary he recorded an idea for a novel about a mother who "suffers over the loss of a child and can't be comforted."[6]

Sophia experienced hallucinations soon after her son's death and would wake up in terror, sensing the sticky smell of decay. It clung to everything in the house. "Then I would suddenly hear Vanechka's dear gentle voice."[7] In Moscow, she would see him sitting at his small desk. Being at Yasnaya was even more painful, since Vanechka was to inherit the place. Every tree she had planted there, every improvement she had made now reminded her of him.

At the end of April, she visited her sister Tanya, who now lived in Kiev. The trip helped divert her thoughts, as she described in her prose poem "In the Caves": "I had a great sorrow. I was desperate, I prayed, I traveled to churches and monasteries, and finally I came to Kiev. The beautiful city on the Dnieper, with its hills and orchards, with its ancient faith—I loved it."[8]

In Moscow, Sophia's despair and sense of void returned: "I feel I'm locked up here with my memories and my grief."[9] Nothing interested her. She wrote her sister that there was no sun, no nature, no flowers; household matters, farm problems, and even the children left her indifferent. Seryozha was to be married in July but she did not look forward to it.

One day in spring, as she lay on a couch in Moscow, the composer Sergei Taneev dropped in. They had met in the fall of the previous year when Sophia hosted a concert at home. After the funeral of Alexander III, public concerts and balls were canceled during the period of mourning, and musicians were glad to have work. She invited several professors from the Moscow Conservatory, including Taneev and Anton Arensky. They played Arensky's trio, Beethoven's sonatas, and a Schubert quartet. As she wrote her sister, any music connoisseur would have appreciated this concert.[10]

During the visit Sophia asked where Taneev planned to spend the summer. It turned out he did not have a place and was looking for a dacha to rent. At Yasnaya, the guest wing where sister Tanya and her family often stayed was now available. As nobody else in the family wanted it, she suggested Taneev could have it for free. When he accepted but insisted on paying, Sophia gave the money to charity.

Taneev's life was devoted to the world of the Moscow Conservatory, which he had entered at ten. A child prodigy, he studied composition under Tchaikovsky and piano under Nikolai Rubinstein. When Taneev was in his teens Tchaikovsky praised "the purity and power of his technique" and his ability to convey the idea of the performed piece. Taneev had arranged and performed Tchaikovsky's music, becoming the composer's close friend: after his death, he succeeded him as head of the Moscow Conservatory. In his turn, Taneev educated a new generation of musicians: Rachmaninov and Scriabin were among his students.

During a concert tour of France, the young Taneev had encountered Turgenev and Pauline Viardot. For Sophia, who had met both in childhood, this was an interesting connection. Although at the center of the Moscow music world, Taneev was an unassuming man. At thirty-eight, he still lived with his old nanny, Pelageya Vasilievna. Sophia would describe him as a "very private" man whom she could never fully know.[11] He looked ordinary until sitting at the piano, where he was transformed. "He had a distinctive style. Sometimes, he was a philosopher of music but occasionally played with a passion, unexpected of the man who was otherwise phlegmatic and utterly unemotional. He was ironic, loved jokes, good food, and looked extremely prosaic."[12]

In the summer, Taneev lived in his separate wing, joining the family in the evenings. He and Tolstoy played chess and agreed that if Taneev won, Tolstoy would read pages from his novel in progress, *Resurrection*. If Taneev lost, he had to play at Tolstoy's request. Listening to Taneev play, Sophia would forget her grief: the music numbed her pain and calmed her—and she wanted to prolong this blissful state. In the daytime, when Taneev practiced with his windows open, she sat outside, listening to Beethoven, Mozart, and Chopin. He was preparing for his evening recital; she looked forward to hearing these pieces again and being transported into another realm.

She would remark that music saved her from despair when nothing else could bring her back to life. Listening to Chopin's "Funeral March," she was able to think and dream on a different plane. In September, on her name day, Taneev came to play Beethoven's piano sonata, "The Tempest." Sophia described his performance in her novella "A Song without Words": "Pain of the loss, chaos of tormenting doubts . . . sufferings, temptations, and evil, all this was cleared away, like the sky is cleared after a thunderstorm."[13]

Taneev taught her to understand music as she had not before. She resumed playing the piano, trying to imitate his phrasing, and would practice up to five hours daily. At fifty-two, she began to take lessons from Miss Welsh, daughter Sasha's instructor, who had a private school in Moscow. "I live from one concert to another, I play and ask others to play for me," she wrote sister Tanya.[14] She purchased a season ticket to the Moscow Conservatory: "Intoxicated by music, having learned to understand it, I could no longer live without it."[15]

Music offered solace and she became addicted to the therapy. She found Taneev's interpretations particularly effective. It's now established that people can experience a sudden onset of musical interest as a result of trauma, which in Sophia's case came with the loss of her son. Fixating on a certain composer is also not uncommon.[16] But in her day, Sophia's obsession with Taneev's music—she attended his every concert—was seen as evidence of her attraction to the musician.

The children were embarrassed that she frequented Taneev's concerts. At the start, Tolstoy was more sympathetic than anyone in the family. Passionate love of music was not unknown to him and during *Anna Karenina* he would play the piano for hours. However, his tolerant attitude began to change: in the fall, Sophia read Tolstoy's diary, where he remarked that she had become "only more frivolous" after Vanechka's death. She was deeply hurt.

Soon after their son's death, when they became united in grief, she asked Tolstoy to destroy negative diary entries about her and the children. He promised to, since his criticism gave her "great anguish." It was even more painful knowing that Chertkov was reading the diaries and discussing them with Tolstoy. Some accusations—that Tolstoy's martyrdom was suffered at home—were familiar to Sophia from Chertkov's letters. Now Tolstoy called her "frivolous." The remark so upset her that although they were staying together, she chose to write him a letter:

Why do you always in your diaries, when you mention my name, treat me so spitefully? Why do you want future generations and our grand-children to know me as your *frivolous, evil* wife, who makes you un-happy? Perhaps it would add fame to you that you were *a martyr,* but how much it would damage me! If you'd scold me or even beat me for everything that, in your opinion, I did wrong it would be much easier for me to take, for this would pass. After Vanechka's death . . . you had promised to delete these angry words about me in your diaries. But you haven't done so . . . Are you really afraid that your posthumous glory would be diminished if you did not present me as your tormentor and yourself as martyr, bearing a cross personified by your wife? Forgive me for doing an evil thing and reading your diary . . . The temptation to peek into your soul was so great that I could not resist . . . When you and I are no more, others will interpret this *frivolousness* as they like and anyone will throw mud at your wife, for you have encouraged them with your words . . . I have always lived for you and your children and never behaved *frivolously* . . . and will die loyal to you, body and soul. I know that you have used the word *frivolous* in a religious sense, but who will understand this? . . . Please delete the spiteful words about me from your diaries. After all, this is only a *Christian* thing to do . . . Please spare my name.[17]

Upon reading her letter, Tolstoy remarked, "Never before have I felt so guilty and so full of emotion." Since his earlier journals with the most hurt-ful remarks were then kept by Chertkov, Tolstoy asked him to return the diaries, from which he deleted some forty lines critical of Sophia. Know-ing his diaries would be published, he made a note for his biographers: "*I repudiate those angry words which I wrote about her. These words were written at moments of exasperation. I now repeat this once more for the sake of every-body who should come across these diaries* . . . She was—and I can see now in what way—the wife I needed."[18] Sophia thanked him for the inner peace he gave her. If only this peace could last, she added. Her mistrust of Chert-kov was justified: by then, the disciple had made a copy of Tolstoy's diaries with the criticism of Sophia.

She had to return to her duties in Moscow—and Tolstoy watched as she left Yasnaya in a coach, looking sad and lonely. He wrote in his diary,

"I'm the only person she has to hold on to, and at the bottom of her heart she's afraid I don't love her, don't love her as much as I can, with all my heart, and that the reason for this is the difference in our views of life. And she thinks that I don't love her because she hasn't come to me. Don't think that. I love you still more, I quite understand you, and know you couldn't, couldn't come to me, and so are left alone. But you aren't alone. I'm with you, just as you are, I love you, love you to the very end with a love that could not be greater."[19]

He also wrote her that some clouds of disagreement could not diminish the light in the evening of their love: "the sunset will be bright and clear."[20] Sophia replied that his letter was a joy to her. The clouds darkening their love were not threatening, for their relationship remained sound. They both were looking to the end of their lives without fear, walking their different paths but "aspiring to the same goal—God."[21]

In October, Sophia was in Petersburg to attend two premieres—Tolstoy's play *The Power of Darkness* and Taneev's opera *Orestia*. From Petersburg, where she was with daughter Tanya, she wrote Tolstoy that his play was well received. *The Power of Darkness* was also staged in Moscow, and upon her return, she attended a performance.

The young Tolstoy had made friends with Nikolai Rubinstein and discussed with him an idea of organizing a music society in Moscow. Tolstoy's relationship with music later became complex, as is apparent from *What Is Art?* Becoming critical of modern opera, he did not attend even Tchaikovsky's *Eugene Onegin* after the composer had invited him. And although he attended a performance of Wagner's *Siegfried* at the Bolshoi, with Sophia and Taneev, he did not stay to the end.

In February 1896, Tolstoy wrote Sophia that he understood her interest in music and knew how one could be inspired by it. But learning that Taneev would spend another summer at Yasnaya, he made a jealous entry in his diary: the musician Taneev disgusted and annoyed him with his privileged position in their house. When Taneev arrived at Yasnaya, Tolstoy made scenes in front of their friends and visitors. According to Mikhail Stakhovich, a family friend, Tolstoy resembled the jealous Levin from *Anna Karenina* and Pozdnyshev from *The Kreutzer Sonata*. He succeeded in driving Taneev out.

The entire situation seemed to have been scripted in *The Kreutzer*

Sonata, written almost a decade earlier: Mrs. Pozdnyshev becomes attracted to a musician friend, provoking her husband's paranoic jealousy. Life was imitating art and society began to gossip about the musician living in the Tolstoys' house. Although Taneev had no women in his life, public opinion turned against Sophia—a married woman pursuing a much younger man.

Sophia soon received a letter from a concerned acquaintance, Leonila Annenkova, a lawyer's wife. She had visited Yasnaya in July and now advised Sophia that she must appreciate and love her uniquely talented husband and end her relationship with Taneev. Sophia replied that there was no need to convince her to love Tolstoy, with whom fate had bound her for thirty-four years; it was also unlikely that she could love him more than she already had. Further, it had been "persistently demanded" that she break her friendship with Taneev. But he had left Yasnaya a month before and would not likely return. "Our relationship was so pure, simple, and agreeable; yet, when I remember my husband's suffering, his blind jealousy, I feel frightened, bitter, ashamed, and I want to leave this life, to die, just to escape unfair accusations . . . It would be horrible to suspect me, for I'm past fifty-two! But I'm poorly expressing it: there are no *suspicions,* none are possible." There was only an egotistical demand, on Tolstoy's part, she explained, to be loved exclusively.[22]

Tolstoy most certainly was aware that Taneev, a man of Tchaikovsky's circle, was homosexual. Sophia knew, referring to his intimacy with students in her novella "A Song without Words," in which Taneev and his study are identifiable. Although Taneev no longer would spend summers at Yasnaya, he still came to play music and his attitude to Tolstoy remained reverential. The situation responsible for his departure was not reflected in his diaries. Sophia's friendship with him lasted a long time after, although with some strain, unavoidable under the circumstances. He visited over the years and was still writing to her in 1910, the year Tolstoy died.

Yasnaya received throngs of visitors in the summer of 1896. Tolstoy's guests included a young and talented pianist, Alexander Goldenweiser, who would frequent Yasnaya till the end of Tolstoy's life. Chertkov continued to visit, arriving with a retinue of six people, including his secretary.

In midsummer, the house was full, with twenty-two seated for dinner, overwhelming Tolstoy. Sophia accommodated his visitors and hosted receptions.

With the guests gone, Yasnaya returned to its routine: Tolstoy wrote in the mornings, played lawn tennis, and rode a bicycle. Sophia photographed him enjoying his new diversion. One of the pictures shows them together: she is nearby, looking fondly at him. Tolstoy at sixty-six became passionate about this pursuit and Sophia bought him a bicycle, which he rode for long distances, both in the city and the countryside.

In early October, Sophia still swam in the river, stopping when the temperature dropped below freezing: swimming in icy water calmed her nerves. She played piano three to four hours daily. The Taneev episode and Tolstoy's jealousy, like all their trials now, seemed to have brought the couple closer.

That fall, Tolstoy's letters to Sophia were extraordinarily kind. Sophia had told him that after Vanechka's death she had nothing to live for, words he remembered. Tolstoy, afraid of losing her, was alarmed by her emotional state and minor health problems. When a dentist discovered a growth on her gum, which left her indifferent, he was frightened. He wrote Chertkov that he only now realized how "dear and important" she was to him.[23] And he wrote in his diary, "I vividly imagined that she would die before me, and I became terribly afraid for myself."[24]

Music remained at the center of Sophia's life. She took lessons, attended concerts, and sight-read music. She had no illusion about her skill, writing her sister that her progress was extremely slow and that it was late for any accomplishment. "It's a kind of madness, but what can one expect from my distressed soul? I have still not recovered after Vanechka's death; I live from day to day . . . trying to kill time, amuse myself, find some escape and interest."[25]

The year the boy died, Sophia took her picture with Tolstoy. It was the thirty-third anniversary of their marriage. In the picture she is in a shapeless black dress, looking depressed and stooped like an old woman. A year later, at the height of her obsession with music, another picture shows her transformed: standing beside Taneev, she is more attractive than her daughters. She felt young; her energy and love of life were back: "My step is light, my body is fit—only my face has aged."[26] The improvement in her was impossible to ignore: she was alive again.

Sophia and Taneev (standing), 1896. In the front row, from left, daughters Maria, Tatyana, and pianist Konstantin Igumnov.

Describing Taneev's influence on her, Sophia wrote, "His presence had a tranquilizing effect on me . . . Sometimes, just meeting Sergei Ivanovich [Taneev], hearing his quiet, unemotional voice, would calm me immediately . . . It was a hypnosis; he was unaware of its healing effect on me. My state of mind was abnormal."[27] However, the idea that his music "hypnotized" her was suggested by Tolstoy, who had thus described her response.

In February 1897, Sophia attended Taneev's rehearsal and concert in Petersburg, which again provoked Tolstoy's jealousy. In fact, she had to be in Petersburg for publishing business, having recently launched a new edition of Tolstoy's collected works. She met the minister of internal affairs to discuss censorship. When she wrote Tolstoy about Taneev's concert, he responded impulsively: "It's terribly painful and humiliatingly shameful that a complete outsider, an unnecessary and quite uninteresting man, rules our life."[28] He later regretted reproaching her and causing her pain; Tolstoy himself was enjoying music at the Olsufievs' estate, where he was resting.

Later that month, Tolstoy and Sophia were both in Petersburg to see off several of his followers, banished for their involvement in the Doukhobor cause. Tolstoy supported these religious sectarians, who had been persecuted because of their pacifism and unorthodox beliefs. Chertkov and Biryukov, among the most active participants in the cause, had been exiled for publicizing their plight. Their sentences inspired an outpouring of sympathy: a stream of people came to bid farewell to the Tolstoy followers.

In letters to friends and family Sophia described their exile as "sudden and unjustifiable."[29] Tolstoy was happy with her reaction, writing Chertkov that she had forgiven him in her heart. But in fact, she would always put aside her personal feelings when Tolstoy's work and his interests were involved. (Unlike the others, dispatched to a remote corner in the Baltics, Chertkov was exiled to England, the place he himself chose. The special treatment was partly due to his family's connections at court.)

That winter, Sophia launched a new edition of the collected works, in fifteen volumes, and again handled the proofreading. She no longer could invest her heart in her publishing and simply maintained the business to support the family. Rushing to produce this edition because the previous one had sold out, she read proofs six to eight hours a day, until becoming "dizzy from work and insomnia."[30]

In mid-May, when Tolstoy was at Yasnaya, Sophia went to see him. When she left, Tolstoy wrote that her brief stay was "one of the strongest, most joyful impressions I have ever experienced: and that at the age of 69, from a woman of 53."[31] Sophia's answer did not reflect his mood. The rise and fall of their relationship was like the tide. Now that there was a rise, she could not welcome it with the joy of old. She asked Tolstoy to cherish their relationship and to try not to spoil it with jealous thoughts and diary entries. She referred to his recent entry where he called her relationship with Taneev a "senile *flirtation* or even worse."[32] After reading it she told Tolstoy of her fear that people would later judge her from such pronouncements.

Although privately Tolstoy told her that her life had been "a pure and blameless one,"[33] in his diaries and letters he said otherwise. In one such letter Tolstoy complained that her relationship with Taneev caused him "terrible, unnecessary sufferings."[34] The letter was unsent but, as usual, preserved. He also made a bitter entry when learning that Taneev would visit for a few days in summer. Later, he cut out the page he had written on the spur of the moment, intending to burn it. But the page was not destroyed—it was preserved in the private archive of a disciple, Paul Boulanger. In 1938, the disciple's son sold the page to the State Literary Museum in Moscow. It was then published by another follower, Nikolai Gusev, and included in the Jubilee edition of Tolstoy's collected works.[35]

After Strakhov's death in 1896, Taneev was Sophia's only friend, and listening to music was her only interest. Tolstoy knew this but continued to press her to give up this pursuit. When he insisted she must extinguish her special feelings for Taneev and break relations with him, she replied that "both suggestions are utterly preposterous. One cannot simply *extinguish* the feelings one has for a person. As for *actions,* which *are* under one's control, I have done nothing I could be reproached with."[36] Tolstoy was also trying to reform her, writing in yet another letter that she must find a more important and worthwhile occupation, "certainly not playing the piano and listening to concerts."[37]

In the summer of 1897, Taneev made several short visits to Yasnaya, each time provoking Tolstoy's resentment. Sophia no longer could enjoy the visits because she dreaded scenes. But only a few months earlier, Tolstoy himself had invited Taneev to play in their house. At his request, Taneev and Goldenweiser performed Tchaikovsky's concertos on two pianos.

Having completed her proofreading in June, Sophia was back at her desk for another project: Tolstoy asked her to copy his nonfictional work *What Is Art?* She read it with interest, finding it paradoxical, provocative, and fascinating. But she also disliked its intolerant tone, particularly when it came to modern composers. Copying his revisions was painstaking. "I remember how I used to wait for my pages of *War and Peace* to copy . . . I used to write on in a state of feverish excitement, discovering new beauty in it . . . But now I am bored. I must work on something of my own, or else my soul will wither."[38] She had wanted to continue to serve Tolstoy "patiently and humbly" to the end of his life;[39] however, this role no longer satisfied her.

When she was dedicated to him in this way, Tolstoy seemed "calm and happy" and thanked her for copying and tidying his papers. She was also sewing for him and he was pleased when she made his skullcaps, linen shirts, and trousers. "Once again, he consumes my whole life. Does this make me happy? Alas, no. I do my duty towards him, there's some happiness in that, but at times I yearn for something different and have other desires."[40]

Sophia read biographies of famous people and musicians, including one given her by Taneev—Louis Nohl's *Life of Beethoven*. For this genius, creativity was at his center, and the lives of others mattered insofar as they helped enrich his work. It was all familiar to Sophia, whose life was auxiliary to Tolstoy's: "From me . . . he takes my labor, my copying for him, my concern for his spiritual well-being, my body . . . As for my spiritual life, it is of no concern or use to him . . . Yet the world bows before such men."[41] Reading allowed her to escape into the world of abstract thought, nurturing her independent interests in art, creativity, and philosophy.

In October, Sophia began "Song without Words," which explored her fascination with music and composition. It described Taneev's milieu, the masculine world of a musical conservatory and a subject people did not talk about, the clandestine relationships between teachers and pupils. "This evening I started on the first chapter of my story. I think it will be good. But whom can I ask for an opinion on it? I would like to write and publish it without telling a soul."[42] Having completed this novella in 1898, Sophia put it away as she had her previous one. Tolstoy never read her novellas.

Unlike *Who's to Blame?,* which drew from the marriage, "Song without Words" employed her own experiences. She was moved to write it after attending a concert of Józef Kazimierz Hofmann, a Polish-American composer and virtuoso pianist. After his performance, mesmerized fans "*kissed* his galoshes."[43] The spectacle offended Sophia, since she herself was a music fan but believed that worshipping a celebrity prevented fully appreciating his art. People imagine an artist's life to be thrilling, while in reality it is not. She had met many artists whose work she admired and who were unlike their creations: "A talented man puts all his understanding, all the sensitivity of his soul, into his work, while his attitude to real life is obtuse and indifferent."[44]

She knew that artists' lives were filled with monotonous routine and intense labor. Tolstoy endlessly revised his prose, striving for perfection, and rarely was satisfied with the result. Taneev, not nearly as talented, had told her that in order to play "for just a quarter of an hour" he had to practice for two months.[45] What interested Sophia about Taneev was not his life but the secret to his creativity, what gave him an idea for a musical piece and how composing differed from literary work. She had discovered a composer's world and was describing it in her novella.

"Song without Words" begins with a story of bereavement. Sasha, a young married woman, travels to the Crimea to see her dying mother. The monotonous noise of her train is transformed into a musical phrase and then a melody, "solemn, sad, and beautiful."[46] The musical hallucination comes during an intense emotional experience, as had happened with Sophia. The heroine's depression following her mother's death and her salvation through music also reflect Sophia's experiences. The author attempts to distance herself from her heroine: Sasha's husband and an only son are marginal to her life.

When a pianist at a neighboring dacha plays *Songs without Words* by Mendelssohn, Sasha's emotions are unlocked: she again feels the need to live and love. From that moment, her life becomes consumed with music and the musician. Carried away, she imagines inspiring him and serving his art. Like Taneev, the pianist composes a symphony. His name is Ivan Ilyich, like the hero in Tolstoy's novella *The Death of Ivan Ilyich*. Ivan enjoys Sasha's company because of her regard for his talent. She also gives him a flash of inspiration, which is described matter-of-factly. A vision of her in a white dress generates an idea, which the composer develops into a theme. He spends the night working more productively than ever; the result is a stunning melody.

In Ivan there is an attempt to create a multidimensional character. At the piano, he is a magician whose control over the keys is complete; when away from it, he is a person like any other. When he finishes playing, his energy and power are spent, his fire extinguished. He is utterly dedicated to his art: his time is divided among composing, performing, teaching, and writing a textbook.

The heroine is fascinated by these spheres of creativity and composing from which women are excluded. She visits Ivan's study, which in its description resembles Taneev's, with portraits of his mentors Tchaikovsky and Rubinstein. During a triumphant performance of Ivan's new symphony, Sasha dreams of marrying this famous man. But he is uninterested in her and other women. Meeting his young male student after the concert, he holds his hand longer than necessary.

Sasha is unaware of his homosexuality. When she becomes more demanding Ivan stops seeing her. The heroine escapes into madness: she drives herself to an asylum and asks to be admitted. She has failed to understand the creator's world: Ivan is grateful for the moments of inspiration and the few ideas she gave him, but otherwise he has no need for her. Upon completing his textbook he rewards himself with a trip abroad in the company of his favorite pupil, to enjoy what is described as "epicurean bliss."

The novella is crammed with factual scenes. Pictures of everyday Moscow life give a good sense of place and time. Although the heroine's visit to a military hospital is only loosely integrated in the novella, it is interesting on its own. A young conscript Sasha is trying to help is influenced by Tolstoy's pacifist ideas; he is in detention for refusing conscription. Sasha does not share his beliefs, arguing that it's naive to think that by renouncing military duty one can eliminate violence. The army will replace the pacifist with another man.

Such themes made Sophia's work unlike writings by other women of the day. The novella, however, was her last and it never saw the light of publication. To grow as a writer Sophia had to invest consistent effort, which was unfeasible. "I was wondering today why there were no women writers, artists or composers of genius. It's because all the passion and all the abilities of an energetic woman are consumed by her family ... When she has finished bearing and educating her children, her artistic needs awaken, but by then it's too late."[47]

Taneev would continue to give recitals at Yasnaya and Tolstoy, on his seventieth birthday, would praise his performance as "superb, quite the last word in music." In the late 1890s, Sophia remarked, "Lev Nikolaevich is no longer jealous."[48] (This may have been wishful thinking.) Her passion for music would subside as she explored her other talents. But she continued to say, "Music is the best occupation in the world."[49]

As 1897 was drawing to a close, Sophia and Tolstoy sat at the piano. She chose a duet arrangement of Schubert's "Tragic" Symphony, which Tolstoy was reluctant to play at the start. He told her "it was all a lot of nonsense and music was dead, but was soon playing with great abandon."[50] They met the New Year together, in harmony.

Chapter Fifteen

In Life's Whirlpool

D URING TANEEV'S VISIT in July 1897, Tolstoy made a sudden decision to flee, which Sophia would learn about later. He wrote two farewell letters: one was private, to her alone; the other "official." The latter, intended for posterity, describes his longstanding dream to dedicate his life to God. Like the Hindus who retire to the forests when they are old, he longed "for tranquillity and solitude." He sought accord between his life and beliefs.

In this same letter, Tolstoy outlined Sophia's contribution and their differences: "I remember with love and gratitude the long 35 years of our life together, especially the first half of that time . . . You gave to me and the world what you were able to give; you gave much maternal love and self-sacrifice, and it's impossible not to appreciate you for it. But in the later period of our life, during the last 15 years, we have drifted apart."[1] He did not, however, reproach her for not following him on his religious path.

In the end, Tolstoy changed his mind and stayed. He hid both letters in the upholstery of an armchair, where they remained for ten years. In 1907, he gave them to their son-in-law Nikolai Obolensky, asking that they be preserved. It was only after Tolstoy's death that Sophia received the letters. She quickly read the personal letter and destroyed it, keeping the "official." But even with these letters she never fully understood why Tolstoy had contemplated leaving at this time and why he decided to stay.

Tolstoy never stated his attitude to Sophia unambiguously. She herself did not know what his real feelings were, since in the diaries he criticized her, while in his letters he spoke of love. This is why Tolstoy wrote letters to posterity to explain their relationship. In one, he remarked that Sophia was the wife he needed: "She was the ideal wife in a pagan sense—in the sense of loyalty, domesticity, self-denial, love of family—pagan love—and she has the potential to become a Christian friend."[2] Despite such letters, Sophia was afraid that people would misinterpret their relationship. Even a perceptive man like Strakhov took years to understand that Sophia's differences with Tolstoy were external, that the bond between them was deep.

Their differences had to be emphasized to promote Tolstoy's image. He himself had given Sophia permission to publish his works. But he did not state this openly, so her publishing seemed at odds with his renunciation of money and copyright. He had given her power of attorney, requiring her to manage all his affairs and estate. Yet it appeared that she was holding on to the property he had renounced. Such apparent contradictions were blamed on Sophia. As she would say in her memoir, while the family lived together, she alone was criticized. "In the eyes of the world he can do no wrong for he is a great writer."[3]

In the families Sophia had known, including her birth family, fathers worked to support and educate their children. Tolstoy was indifferent to these concerns: his life was entirely consumed with his causes and his writing. Although Sophia assumed responsibility for their family, he still found it difficult to even *live* with them, occasionally saying it "would be murder" for him to be in Moscow. But he was free to choose and lived in the city when he was unwell, as in the winter of 1898.

In contrast, Sophia's life was becoming only more restricted. When in January she told Tolstoy she wanted to attend Wagnerian operas and Taneev's symphony in Petersburg, it provoked "an angry flood of criticisms." She was free to provide for her family but not free to enjoy herself. "And no one realizes that when I am alive, absorbed or transported by music, art, books or people, my husband becomes unhappy, anxious and angry." It was expected that she subordinate her emotional life to her husband and continue to serve him. But it has not been appreciated how her music experience transformed her.

Her interest in music was seen as a whim, although she had frequently said that it saved her from despair. Her urge to hear it was almost physiological: without it an "overwhelming sadness" returned, along with suicidal thoughts and hallucinations of smell. "It so permeated my entire being, and the bedroom, and all the air in the house, that I grabbed an orange, pressed it against my nose, and fled. It was so horrible that I wept."[4] She told Tolstoy she feared for her sanity.

Tolstoy, who had found salvation from his despair in religion, had told Sophia that it was as impossible for him to return to his old ways as it was for a goose to go back into its egg. Sophia, however, was expected to return to her old routine after losing her son, which she could not.

Her obsession with music was seen at home as something morally wrong. Tolstoy called it an addiction, nagging her to admit it was bad and to give it up.[5] She felt he simply wanted her to make another sacrifice for him. Everyone in the family was on Tolstoy's side, refusing to recognize her need for occasional rest and diversion. Even sister Tanya, who was closest to her, said she must give up both her love of music and her relationship with Taneev because of the distress to Tolstoy. No one realized, however, what mental suffering it would cause Sophia to forgo them.

Women's emancipation was sister Tanya's favorite topic and during her visits she would bring it up. She liked to show off her progressive views and engage Tolstoy in the discussions. Sophia knew he was against emancipation and there was no point arguing. As well, Sophia held the view that it was not freedom that women needed, but their husbands' help. Now, when their conversation turned to equal rights, Sophia was listening. What Tolstoy said touched her in the raw: "No matter what work a woman did—teaching, medicine, art—she had only one real purpose in life . . . sexual love." But that means, Sophia exploded, that "whatsoever she might strive to achieve, all her strivings would merely crumble to ashes . . . I admonished him for his perpetually cynical attitude to women, which had made me suffer so." Her independent interests in classical philosophy, art, music, and literature were not taken seriously. Because of Tolstoy's attitude toward women, she had failed to earn his trust. "He resents every independent move I make . . . every hour spent at the piano . . . Yes, it is difficult to live under any sort of despotism, but jealous despotism is frightful!"

After several months' pleading with Tolstoy to let her go to Petersburg, she traveled there in March. But Taneev's symphony was "atrociously" performed and tickets for Wagner's *Tristan and Isolde* were sold out. She ended up reading proofs she had brought and running Tolstoy's errands: he had asked her to take an article to Gurevich at the *Northern Herald*.

Because Tolstoy did not want Sophia to profit, he gave his new work to other publishers. Many approached him personally and he found it difficult to refuse them. When he completed *On Art* he wanted to send it to the *Journal of Philosophy and Psychology*. Sophia reasoned that to read it in the *Journal* the public would have to buy a two-year subscription. Readers would benefit if he gave it to her to publish in the collected works. She was incessantly arguing that while Tolstoy let other publishers profit from his work, he did not allow this for his own family.

During this conversation, in the presence of sculptor Ilya Ginzburg, who had recently made Tolstoy's and Sophia's statuettes, Tolstoy shouted, "I shan't give it to you!" Sophia was humiliated and feared that people would conclude she fought for money. Later, alone, he said he could *forbid* her to sell his works. She replied that they were certainly *his* works, *his* property, but the money went to support *his* children. "I also said that it was with this money that I paid for his saddle-horse, his asparagus, his fruit, his charity work, his bicycles, and so forth, and that I spend less on myself than on anyone else." (In the end, he did give her *On Art:* it was simultaneously published in the collected works and by Intermediary.) Later that spring, when Tolstoy was in Yasnaya organizing a local famine relief effort, he asked her to donate money from her publishing. As a perennial supporter of his charities and causes, Sophia needed little persuasion.

The family was growing: now there were grandchildren. Yet the children still expected Sophia to support them financially. None of them, except the eldest, Sergei, were trained to work and provide for themselves. Daughter Masha had recently married Nikolai Obolensky, who was penniless. Both Sophia and Tolstoy were displeased with the match. As Tolstoy remarked, "I was sorry for her, as one is sorry for a thoroughbred horse that is made to cart water."[6]

Sophia in 1900 with her grandchildren Sonechka (in her arms) and Lyova.
Photo by Sophia Tolstoy.

Son Lev, who had married Dora Westerlund, daughter of a Swedish physician, decided to sell the Moscow house. After the division of property, the Moscow residence, which had cost fifty-eight thousand rubles, belonged to him. When Lev suddenly arranged to sell it through a broker, without consulting Sophia, the family was stunned. Tolstoy said it would be "a shame" to sell the house and asked her to buy it from Lev. She did not have the money because she was producing a new edition and owed printers. And she could not take on more stress: "Any sort of trouble or change terrifies me at present." But she did raise the money by selling investments.

Her days were filled with such humdrum affairs, of no interest to her. "I am *tired* of this never-ending battle, and all the hours of hard work I devote to the house, the children's education, business affairs, publishing, managing the children's estates, looking after my husband, keeping the family peace." She continued to work, despite apathy, insomnia, and nervous troubles, remarking in her diary that none of this was visible to outsiders. Her soul had become "fragile" and she was easily upset. There were also problems with the younger sons' behavior. She wrote Tolstoy that her work did not give satisfaction and she was like a hard-driven horse. In her diary, she admitted that she was terrified of herself, of her despair and suicidal thoughts. From this point on, she reasoned, there were two paths: one to spiritual perfection, the other to weakness and deterioration. "And I feel that I am now taking this last path, and it frightens and saddens me." She confided her fear of spiritual decline to Tolstoy, along with her desire not to give up; she was praying that God would give her the strength of wisdom.

She played the piano for relief: "Even when I play myself it suddenly makes everything clear, fills me with peaceful joy, and enables me to see all life's worries in a new light, calmly and lucidly." An unexpected visit by Taneev was a welcome distraction: he wanted to play a new piece he had just composed. He also played a piece from his new symphony: "We sat chatting quietly, and read an article of music criticism. One always has such a peaceful, sincere, interesting time with him. We get on so well—it is a great shame that L. N.'s jealousy weighs so heavily on this pure, simple friendship." Taneev came to seek her opinion on his new work, just as Tolstoy would have done in the past.

Later that year, she hosted a musical evening with Taneev and Elizaveta Lavrovskaya, a singer and professor at the Moscow Conservatory. All the while, Tolstoy received many artists, including painter Repin, composer Rimsky-Korsakov, and a young opera singer, Feodor Shalyapin, just beginning to conquer the stage. Sophia described him as "a blond giant, good-natured, and remarkably talented in every respect, in singing, drawing, storytelling."[7]

Tolstoy's presence in Moscow drew other visitors—many of them complete strangers. Beyond being a great writer he was a sage, a teacher of life, and people wanted his view on every subject. Sophia overheard one visitor ask his opinion on the Second Coming of Christ. Peasants, schoolteachers, foreign correspondents, and factory workers all came to see the writer Lev Tolstoy. Possessing a "boundless curiosity," he met with everyone. "I should go mad if I had to live like Lev Nikolaevich," Sophia reflected. "He writes all morning and wears himself out mentally, and all evening he talks non-stop, or rather preaches, as his listeners generally come for advice or instruction."

Daily, Sophia would welcome people who had not come to visit her, but wanted to meet Tolstoy. While producing the latest edition of his collected works, she noted in her diary, "Proofs, solitude, sadness." Tolstoy was now "constantly besieged by people," his fame distancing the two.

On his seventieth birthday, August 28, Yasnaya was teeming with visitors who came to congratulate him. Forty people were seated for dinner outdoors. Drinking to Tolstoy's health was improper since he preached total abstinence. When a toast to Sophia was proposed and everyone cheered, she was shocked by the unanimous "show of affection." Because Tolstoy never praised her openly, she was agitated and her heart pounded.

During *War and Peace,* a visitor to Yasnaya had called Sophia "a nurse-maid" of her husband's talent. Now she was also a nursemaid of his physical health. Tolstoy had serious intestinal trouble and it was she who ran his baths, looked after his diet, made compresses, and massaged his stomach with camphor oil. He required almond milk in his tea and Sophia provided it.

Not many people appreciated that Tolstoy could only write at Yasnaya. Sophia made it possible by managing the estate, supporting their family, and shielding him from material cares. He wanted the freedom to think and write in solitude and she gave it to him. That spring, he wrote to Sophia, upon his return from a ride in a budding forest, how splendid he felt, physically and spiritually. Tolstoy was at the time completing *Resurrection* and a novella, *Father Sergius.* He also had started on his masterpiece *Hadji Murat.* For his disciples his need to write fiction was irrelevant: Tolstoy was made to feel it was almost a vice and was embarrassed by it. He did not write any important fiction while Chertkov was still in Russia.

Tolstoy's fame was now nearing its zenith: he would receive ovations at train stations and other public places. His moral authority inspired awe even among famous people. Director Konstantin Stanislavsky, who would create his own acting system with an international reputation, was intimidated when at thirty he met Tolstoy socially. He was at a loss for words when asked about the subject he knew best—a play he was staging.

Unlike others, Sophia treated Tolstoy without reverence; she also could impart bitter truths to him. She would say that although he had renounced ambition, he came to love his fame. It surprised her that while Tolstoy preached humility, he posed for sculptors. In 1899, she photographed Tolstoy while he was posing for a bust by Pavel Trubetskoy. The picture also captures a follower, crouching on the floor and reading to amuse Tolstoy during the session.

Resurrection, which Tolstoy had recently completed, left Sophia disappointed. She thought it was a tendentious work and wrote Tolstoy about it: "I've always felt you *invented* it, as it did not come from the bottom of your heart and of your talent. You were *inventing,* not *living* it . . . I'd like you to rise higher, so that people reading it would feel they needed wings to reach you . . . so that your writing did not offend but improve people, so that your work and interest in it would last forever."[8]

Unlike his everlasting fiction, it had limited appeal, permeated as it was with defiance against the social order and the Orthodox Church. She found his mocking of Orthodox services and clergy offensive. In the past she had told him he must not think his religion was the only *true* one. When in the presence of his followers Tolstoy was "jeering and raging" against Church ritual, Sophia "loudly protested that *true* religion saw neither the priest's brocade cassock, nor Lev Nikolaevich's flannel shirt."

Soon after Vanechka's death, when Sophia needed something to hold on to and fill the void, she asked Tolstoy to let her copy *Resurrection.* She relates in her memoir that she approached Tolstoy "timidly," afraid he might refuse. Biryukov and daughter Tanya were already copying it and Tolstoy did not need her help. In addition, he remarked that Sophia's copying had "always caused trouble." She left his study in tears: "How could he forget the past?"[9] Later, when she read the novel, she thought that certain flaws could have been avoided if she had copied it. In the past, she had made suggestions that Tolstoy found useful.

In *Resurrection,* an aristocrat, Dmitry Nekhlyudov, seeks redemption for the sin he committed as a young man. Tolstoy was drawing from a story told by a lawyer friend, Anatoly Koni, as well as an event that took place in his own youth. As a young nobleman, Tolstoy had seduced his sister's chambermaid, and she was dismissed for their liaison; unable to find employment, she "ended up badly." His hero, Nekhlyudov, who has ruined a maid, Katyusha Maslova, later becomes transformed by his guilt. As a juror, he recognizes her in a prostitute being tried for theft and murder. In the draft Sophia read, Nekhlyudov atones for his sin by marrying the convicted prostitute and following her into exile. Sophia called this denouement improbable and "bitterly hypocritical."

Tolstoy later altered the ending and, on the morning of his seventieth birthday, told Sophia, "He doesn't marry her after all." She replied, "But of course he doesn't marry her! I always told you that if he did it would just be *hypocrisy*." Sophia reminded him of his own artistic principles, which he abandoned as a moralist. What he wanted to show in this novel could not happen in life.

Making an exception, Tolstoy requested royalties for *Resurrection* to help finance the Doukhobor migration to Canada. Sophia transferred ten thousand rubles paid by the Russian publisher to the Doukhobors' cause.[10] When in 1899 son Sergei accompanied the religious sectarians to Canada, Sophia was proud of his involvement. Despite this, she believed Tolstoy was inconsistent for collecting top royalties after he had renounced his copyright. And if it was possible to make exceptions for others, why not for his own family?

In January 1900, Sophia found a cause of her own, becoming a trustee in a Moscow orphanage for sixty children. Her fund-raising during the famine relief a decade earlier had not been forgotten. The orphanage depended on private donations and Sophia's involvement was important. "I was elected unanimously and thanked. I have no idea what needs to be done there, which makes it more exciting, although I am a bit afraid. I start tomorrow."[11]

After visiting this orphanage Sophia had misgivings. The orphaned peasant children she had helped previously had lost their parents to famine. The children in the Moscow orphanage were social outcasts, "picked off the streets and from the drinking houses, children carelessly born to . . . drunken women, children who are congenital idiots, children born with fits and defects." She faced a moral choice: why was it good and necessary "to save lives which offer absolutely no hope"? However, she decided with her heart and soon donated two thousand rubles to the orphanage. It was money that had emotional value to her because she had invested it for her beloved son. She called it "Vanechka's money." From this moment on, she became attached to the children and treated them as her own. She purchased a cow, knitted woolen hats, and bought toys. Once, when she arrived in the evening with boxes of oranges, the children, already in their nightclothes, ran to meet her: "The little ones all jumped into my arms, and hugged me and kissed me. That means the children *like* me, and that's the most precious thing for me."

The children were taught basic literacy and various trades, such as shoemaking, sewing, and cooking. At age thirteen, when they had to leave, employment was found for them. During board meetings Sophia argued against placing the girls as laundresses, the hardest and most miserably paid work. By fall, she was fully involved, collecting donations and organizing a benefit concert.

Sophia invited star musicians (Taneev was unable to come) and asked Tolstoy's permission to read one of his works. She asked for a fictional work and he gave her an unfinished story "Who's Right?" A socially critical piece, it was not suitable for the rich sponsors of the concert at Nobility Assembly Hall.[12] Since Tolstoy would not give her anything else, she had to obtain the censors' permission to read it.

But her problems were only beginning. The authorities feared that reading Tolstoy's social critique would draw a radical audience, so the Moscow police chief got into the picture. He asked her whether Sophia could help to pacify the crowd in the event of unrest. She dismissed this as preposterous. But the authorities sabotaged ticket sales: policemen in civilian clothes stood outside the concert hall, saying tickets were sold out. As a result, the low-cost seats were unsold and the concert was attended only by the rich.

While handling these duties Sophia had another serious impediment. In May 1900, the sight in her left eye became impaired due to a broken blood vessel. "I now have a permanent black circle in front of my left eye, a rheumatic pain and blurred sight . . . so all reading, writing, working and any sort of strain was forbidden." For six months she wore dark glasses and applied ointments to reduce inflammation, but treatment was ineffective and her impairment remained.

Although half blind, she continued to function, since everyone needed her. She handled the sale of the Samara estate the following month. When Tolstoy had divided the property among their family, he allocated this land to sons Andrei, Mikhail, and daughter Alexandra. Now they needed money and Sophia, as their guardian, could not refuse. She wrote Tolstoy that she sold the land for ten times the price he had paid twenty years earlier, proceeds higher than expected. So these three children would receive more than their siblings.

Her two younger sons wanted to stay in the military, where she had enlisted them. Now she looked after their promotion by meeting superior officers and paid her sons' allowances, tasks normally handled by fathers. In June, she visited son Mikhail at his regimental barracks in Moscow, a prized location she managed to get for him.

With her grandchildren, Sophia was reliving her motherhood. At Christmas, there was dreadful news from son Lev and his wife, Dora: they had lost their child. Although unwell, she set out for Yasnaya, where Lev and his family lived. "I arrived that evening and Dora threw herself into my arms, sobbing hysterically . . . But their grief was unspeakable! All the emotional agony I had endured with Vanechka's death surfaced from the depths of my soul, and I was suffering both for myself and my children."

A year earlier, in the fall of 1899, daughter Tanya married Mikhail Sukhotin, a widower with six children. She was thirty-five. When Tanya, in a simple gray dress and without a veil, came to see Tolstoy before the ceremony, he cried as if he were losing her forever. Like Tolstoy, Sophia had a sense of emptiness and loss with her eldest daughter's marriage: "It is not the empty cots that fill one with sadness, it's one's disappointment in those beloved children's characters and fates."

A year into this marriage and days after Lev and Dora lost their child, Tanya had a stillbirth. Upon learning of it, Sophia was "simply stunned." She drove out to Tanya's estate, Kochety, in Tula province. It was a day's journey by sleigh through a hazardous route. Tanya's hope of becoming a mother was dashed, but she put on a brave face. Her husband, Sukhotin, was traveling abroad and Tanya was alone with the stepchildren.

Soon after, daughter Masha also had a stillbirth. "To think that both babies were born dead! How unspeakably cruel! Children bring so many worries and so few joys!" Both daughters were unable to bear healthy children, a situation Sophia blamed on their vegetarian—practically vegan—diet. (It is, however, unknown what was responsible for a succession of stillbirths with both daughters. Tanya would eventually bear a healthy girl after treatment in Europe.) The only happy event that winter was Mikhail's wedding in January 1901. His bride, Lina Glebova, was from an aristocratic family. Sophia was preparing for her son's society wedding and tending to an unwell Tolstoy.

From domestic tasks she was abruptly called to public life. On February 24, 1901, Tolstoy was excommunicated from the Orthodox Church. When Sophia read the resolution in the newspapers, she reacted immediately: she expressed her outrage in an open letter to the Holy Synod and the Metropolitans. Two days later, her letter was published by the *Church Gazette* and later reprinted by newspapers across Russia and around the world. It was the first challenge by a woman to the heads of the Orthodox Church and still remains the only one known. Sophia wrote mockingly that the Synod's instructions were utterly incomprehensible to her, since "the religious life of a human soul is known to none but God, and mercifully it is not answerable to anyone." The Church "which I shall never renounce . . . was created by Christ to bless in God's name all the significant moments of life—births, weddings, deaths, human joys and griefs." Yet she knew even before the excommunication that priests had been secretly instructed by the Holy Synod to refuse a funeral service for Tolstoy. This refusal would only punish the people around him, the believers. She concluded that the decision of the Holy Synod would only inspire "great love and compassion for Lev Nikolaevich. We are already receiving expressions of this—and there will be no end to them—from all over the world."

Tolstoy read a draft of Sophia's retort to the Synod and smiled: "There have been so many books written on the subject that you couldn't even fit them into this house—and you want to teach them what to do with your letter."[13]

The excommunication decision had been published on Sunday and read by everyone. That same day support for Tolstoy began to pour in. He received baskets of flowers, telegrams, and letters from home and abroad. Hordes of people streamed through their house for several days, creating "a spirit of jubilation." Sophia believed the government could not have chosen a more unsuitable moment to attack him because of student disturbances in Kiev and Moscow. The mood in the streets was radical and the whole city—cabdrivers, shopkeepers, servants, workers, and students—spoke of Tolstoy's excommunication and laughed at the stupidity of the decision. They found it laughable because Tolstoy was more popular than the government.

Tolstoy received ovations when he went for walks. On Lubyanka Square, he met a large student march and was recognized instantly. They were protesting the government's draconian measure of sending student demonstrators to the army. Since he opposed the military draft, Tolstoy was their champion. The crowd cheered, "Hail to the great man! Hurrah!" Tolstoy escaped with the help of a mounted policeman. At the Wanderers' Exhibition, his portrait by Repin was garlanded with flowers and applauded; four hundred people signed a telegram, which was sent to Tolstoy from the exhibition. The portrait created so much commotion that it had to be removed.

Tolstoy's position as the foremost government critic commanded respect. The public mistrusted government institutions, of which the Synod was one. So excommunication only won him greater support. Sophia noticed a change in the public mood compared with a few years earlier, when student protestors were largely ignored or beaten by shopkeepers. Now everyone, including these shopkeepers, was saying that "the students are on the side of truth and the poor." While the authorities ignored the people, Tolstoy championed their causes.

As Tolstoy's publisher, Sophia had met the head of the Holy Synod over censorship. Pobedonostsev was now responsible for Tolstoy's excommunication. Her disdain for this official was deep; however, it did not affect her belief. To her, the Church was the place where millions of people brought their noble religious sentiments. "But I have no objections to the Church, with its ceremonies and its icons; I have lived amongst these things since I was a child, when my soul was first drawn to God, and I love attending mass and fasting." However, the children did not make this distinction.

On Palm Sunday, daughter Sasha, sixteen, suddenly refused to go to church, saying she had lost her faith. Sophia replied "that if she wanted to follow her father's path she must go the whole way, like him: he was extremely orthodox for many years . . . then he renounced the Church in the name of pure Christianity." Sasha was adamant—and Sophia went to mass alone.

Sophia's letter to the Holy Synod received public acclaim. Now that the moment of glory had passed, she faced her routine. As she remarked, "life goes on, remorseless, complicated and difficult as ever." In June, Tolstoy became dangerously ill: he had malaria and his pulse was that "of the death agony." Nursing him, Sophia dreaded losing the man whose life mattered to her more than her own. One morning, while she was putting a hot compress on his stomach, he gazed at her and said, "Thank you, Sonya. You mustn't imagine that I am not grateful to you or that I don't love you." She kissed his hands, saying that it was a pleasure to look after him and that she felt guilty she "could not make him completely happy" in the past. Events had separated them but nothing could alter "the powerful inner love that has bound us together all this time."

During his grave illness, they received an overwhelming number of telegrams and letters. Tolstoy said that the next time he starts to die, he must complete it in earnest, for it was indecent to trouble the public and newspaper correspondents. He surprised Sophia by telling her, with a sudden swell of energy, that life was beautiful.

To help Tolstoy recuperate, he and Sophia decided to go to the Crimea. Countess Sophia Panina offered him her luxurious estate in Gaspra by the Black Sea. Her mansion once belonged to Prince Golitsyn, minister of education for Alexander I. Tolstoy, the entire family, and some friends would spend almost a year there, beginning in early September. Having to care for Tolstoy, Sophia resigned as a trustee at the Moscow orphanage.

Tolstoy was weak and Sophia was concerned about the long train journey, so she arranged for a separate carriage to ensure his comfort and shield him from visitors. The news that the ailing Tolstoy was traveling south drew crowds to the stations. In Kharkov, several thousand people assembled on the platform, shouting, "Hail to the great writer!" Tolstoy came up to the window but was unable to speak: he was overcome with tears, excitement, and fatigue. Another crowd met them at the Sebastopol station.

As her husband's health deteriorated, Sophia felt she was entering a new stage in life: "I am haunted by the terrible feeling that everything is coming to an *end*. Something must *end*. L. N. and I have lived together for a whole era—thirty-nine years of our life . . . How will my life turn out? I can't predict anything." In Gaspra, she nursed Tolstoy for nine months, her husband becoming her baby. "I put my husband to bed every evening like a child. I bind his stomach with a compress of spirit of camphor mixed with water, I put out a glass of milk, a clock and a little bell, and I undress him and tuck him up; then I sit next door in the drawing-room reading the newspapers until he goes to sleep."

People who met Tolstoy at this time would say that while his body was failing, his mind blazed with ideas. Withdrawn into his world of thought, he resumed reading and dictating. A succession of doctors, including the personal physician to the Grand Duke Nikolai Mikhailovich, attended him. Meanwhile, Sophia administered baths, enemas, medications, massages, and a special diet. With help from the family she lifted him up, washed, changed him, and kept a night watch: "As long as I don't actually collapse, I love to look after him on my own." She had one goal in mind, "to nurse this beloved man back to life."

In late January 1902, Tolstoy developed pneumonia in both lungs and her diary reported his pulse, fever, and digestion. "My Lyovochka is dying . . . For others he is a celebrity, for me he is my whole existence. We have become part of one another's lives." Chekhov, who visited that winter and was himself a medical doctor, wrote his wife, Olga Knipper, that he feared Tolstoy would die before the letter reached her. The situation seemed so hopeless that the family even bought a burial plot in the Crimea. Tolstoy refused to give in to death and, observing him, Sophia wrote, "How frightful it all is: the painful struggle of a great soul in its passage to eternity and oneness with God, whom he has served—and all these base earthly cares here in the house."

It never stopped puzzling Sophia that she was the wife of such a famous man: "To think that the whole world loves, bows before this pathetic head which I hold in my hands and kiss." She also knew him as a "selfish invalid" who called her many times at night to adjust his pillow, cover up his legs, massage his back, or simply sit beside him and hold his hands. He was disturbed by the slightest rustle, and yet was upset if she would lie down on a sofa next door: "I can't call you if you do that." Finally, she protested in her diary: there was something about the genius that inspired everyone to toil for him; the doctors, attending him, even refused compensation. "Three doctors visit practically every day; nursing him is extremely hard work, there are a lot of us here, we all are tired and overworked . . . Lev Nikolaevich is first and foremost a writer and expounder of ideas; in reality and in his life he is a weak man, much weaker than us simple mortals."

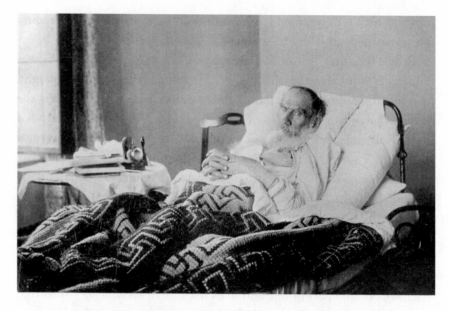

Tolstoy in 1902, during his illness in Gaspra, covered with a blanket
Sophia had knitted. Photo by Sophia Tolstoy.

Besides looking after the needs of her patient, Sophia ran the household
in Gaspra, where the family was gathered. Gorky, who visited, would remember her "sucked into the center of a whirlpool," while "astonishing
everyone by her ability to get everything done in time, to placate everyone,
to put a stop to the whinings of small-minded individuals at odds with
one another."[14] Two years earlier, when Gorky was in Yasnaya, Sophia had
photographed him and Tolstoy as they returned from a walk. Gorky was
overjoyed to receive this picture and wrote to thank her.

In Gaspra she resumed photography, studied Italian, and read; among
the books was Giuseppe Mazzini's *On Human Duty*. Tolstoy considered
it excellent and she was also impressed: "What marvelous ideas and
language—simple, concise, full of power and conviction." She read in five
European languages, discovering other cultures through such books as
Harold Fielding's *The Soul of a People*. Having never traveled, she was
interested to learn about Burma,[15] its traditions, and religion. Buddhism
fascinated Tolstoy and she now thought it was "much better . . . than our
Orthodoxy, and what a marvelous people these Burmese are." Her remark
may have been inspired by the memory of Tolstoy's excommunication, not

likely to happen among the Burmese. (Her interest in this culture would inspire her to translate Sydney Sprague's *A Year with the Bahais in India and Burma*.)[16]

When Tolstoy's pneumonia began to clear, Sophia was sitting beside him, exhausted, her eyes closed. Now that her main task was completed, her imagination stirred: "All sorts of dreams suddenly creep up on me, and plans for the most diverse, varied and improbable life." She had a sudden "passionate desire" to hear music, especially Taneev's music, "which has always had such a profound and powerful effect on me."

Shortly after, she alone traveled to Moscow to deal with business affairs and, as well, attend concerts and exhibitions. She had a musical evening, inviting her close friends, including Taneev. He played Schumann's sonatas and his own composition, "which gave me more pleasure than anything

Sophia, posing for Leonid Pasternak, 1901.
Photo by Sophia Tolstoy.

else." Soothed, she returned to Gaspra in May, only to find a new crisis. In her absence, Tolstoy became ill with typhoid. Again, she experienced the dread of losing him and sat with him during "terrible" nights.

Once, as she sat beside Tolstoy, she had a "sudden vivid memory of the distant past": she was walking from the skating rink (their frozen pond) at Yasnaya, carrying a baby while pulling a child in a sled. "And behind us and before us were happy, laughing, red-cheeked children, and life was so full and I loved them so passionately." She was reviewing her life. Two years later she began her memoir, which would become her most important work and take years to research.

It was time for wisdom, insights, and drawing a line: "I have served a *genius* for almost forty years. Hundreds of times I have felt my intellectual energy stir within me, and all sorts of desires—a longing for education, a love of music and the arts . . . And time and again I have crushed and smothered all these longings . . . Everyone asks: 'But why should a worthless woman like you need an intellectual or artistic life?' To this question I can only reply: 'I don't know, but eternally suppressing it to serve a genius is a great misfortune.'"

There were many things she still wanted to try, projects she had been putting off for years. To her surprise, nothing could extinguish her "desires and aspirations for something loftier, for a more spiritual, more significant life." In a while, she would take up painting, with the same passion she had applied to music.

At the end of June the family left for Yasnaya, where Tolstoy would now live indefinitely. He could no longer be in the city, since the doctors believed that serenity was essential to prolonging his life. Sophia, still torn between managing the estate and affairs in Moscow, was "back in life's whirlpool, with all its demands, griefs, worries and unresolvable questions which need to be resolved."

Chapter Sixteen

The Line Has Been Drawn

THE SUNSET OF their marriage promised to be peaceful. When alone, Sophia and Tolstoy were good friends. As Sophia wrote in her diary, "One simply has to close one's eyes to all the compromises, discrepancies, and contradictions, and see Lev Nikolaevich as a great writer, preacher and teacher." His life had to be arranged "exactly right," to allow him to carry out his mission, while her life had to be subordinated to his.[1]

In the fall of 1902, Tolstoy resumed *Hadji Murat,* the story of Russia's war with Muslim Chechnya. The work reminded Sophia of *War and Peace* with its epic character and artistic merit. It was written with a vigor that was surprising in a frail man. However, it would take Tolstoy another two years to complete this short novel.

Biographer Maude, who visited Yasnaya soon after the family returned from the Crimea, was "impressed by the atmosphere of love and respect that surrounded Tolstoy." Sophia was "most solicitous about her husband's health and comfort," having invited a doctor to stay with them permanently. Daughter Masha, who lived in a separate "wing" at Yasnaya with her husband, Obolensky, assisted Tolstoy with correspondence and copying. The Yasnaya mansion seemed shabby to Maude: the same "old fashioned, rather plain furniture, worn bare-board floors . . . and window-frames that needed repairing."[2]

Despite her advancing age, now manifested by failing sight and arthritis, Sophia still had "tremendous energy," daughter Sasha would remember. Although there was a gardener at Yasnaya, Sophia herself would clean the grounds, cut weeds, paint park benches and tables, and prune dead branches with her own set of tools. "She could not remain idle. For awhile she spent whole days learning to type. Also, in her late fifties, she developed a sudden interest in art."[3] In 1899, Sophia taught herself watercolor painting and copied illustrations for Tolstoy's "Kholstomer: The Story of a Horse." Because she had never taken instruction, everyone was surprised that her copies were successful.

In 1902, she copied portraits of Tolstoy's father, also in watercolors. Despite much effort, "the results were mediocre, but it was great fun and very interesting to teach myself *how* to do it." She also sculpted a medallion with profiles of Tolstoy and herself. It was her first attempt in this medium and there was no one to give advice. This made her only more determined to complete the project: "I occasionally sit up all night, as late as 5 a.m., straining my eyes."

Around this time, there was a fire at Yasnaya, Sasha recalled. In the evening, during tea, the family smelled smoke and inspected the samovar and stoves but could not find its source. Everyone went to bed except Sophia, who continued searching. Finally, she went to the attic, and when she opened the door, thick smoke came out. She alerted everyone and soon the household was mobilized, delivering water from the pond and up the stairs through a bucket brigade. The blaze was right above Tolstoy's bedroom and if Sophia had not found it, the ceiling above him would have collapsed overnight.

Such episodes did not make it into Tolstoy's "official" biography, but something else did. That fall, there was friction with daughter Masha over Tolstoy's copyright. Tolstoy did not yet have a formal will, but in 1895 made several requests in his diary concerning his literary property. He had previously given up copyright on his works written after 1881. But he did not renounce copyright on all his writings because Sophia's labor went into producing *War and Peace* and *Anna Karenina*. Now it was revealed that Masha had secretly asked Tolstoy to sign a diary entry that expressed his posthumous wishes. This was done when Tolstoy had malaria and was not expected to survive. In that entry he asked that his heirs put his work in the public domain: "But I only ask this, and I don't will it."[4] Masha attempted to give more weight to this request by copying the entry and getting her father to sign it. Learning this, Sophia demanded that the paper be given to her. Notwithstanding the paper's legal status, Sophia was protesting the secrecy and scheming behind the arrangement. She told Tolstoy—openly—that she would not fulfill his wish. To make all his works public property after his death would deprive the family of income and line the pockets of rich publishers.

The episode would be included by Chertkov and his associates in their biographies of Tolstoy. Although in England at the time, Chertkov was never far away and requested that Masha and Obolensky send him copies of Tolstoy's correspondence and report on occurrences at home. Masha was upset by Chertkov's interference in her father's life and work and eventually distanced herself from the disciple. But in 1902, still under his influence, she opposed her mother. It turned out that Masha and Obolensky intended to publicize the paper. She got Tolstoy to sign it to support their claim that Sophia had sold his works against his will. When Obolensky was shouting about this, Sophia realized just how much was happening behind her back. The incident demonstrated that trust among family members had been lost. Of course, the family was supported with her publishing proceeds, which made this latest criticism absurd.

Sophia spent 1903 almost uninterruptedly in the country, except for a few trips to Moscow on business. She was publishing a new edition of *War and Peace* and reprinting Tolstoy's fifteen thousand copies of collected works, the largest circulation ever. Despite hiring a proofreader, she handled the final reading of several volumes herself. In the end, she developed eye inflammation, requiring her to consult a specialist.

Publishing income not only supported the family, it was essential for the ailing Tolstoy, who continued to live at the estate and needed doctors and a special diet. With children and grandchildren dependent on her, Sophia was constantly under pressure. Son Ilya, heavily in debt, his wife expecting a sixth child, sought her help. Sophia refused to lend more, as she explained to her sister: "I'd like to help them all, but what right do I have? I am only managing property of the Tolstoy family, I don't own it. If I were to help Ilya, it would be at the expense of my other children."[5]

In January, when Tolstoy had the flu and an irregular pulse, she resumed her night vigils beside him. Kerosene lamps were lit in many rooms; the family and one of the doctors took turns with her. When Tolstoy was in pain and could not sleep, he was given a morphine injection. By March, he felt stronger and they went for a sleigh ride through the woods. In the evening, Sophia put him to bed and tucked him in, as always, and he stroked her cheek with "fatherly love." Their roles had become confused, but she still rejoiced at any expression of his love and tenderness.

That same month, she wrote sister Tanya of her different tasks: in addition to proofreading and running the household, she supervised farm construction and preparations for planting. Yasnaya in March was beautiful and she took drives along the frozen river, enjoying the spring weather, the glistening landscape, and the reflection of the sun from the ice.

In the summer, the place was besieged by visitors: "Not even to mention the children and grandchildren, it's pleasant and natural to have them, but the relatives, the strangers, the foreigners, and all kinds of people crowd at Yasnaya Polyana all the time."[6] She did not invite anybody and yet there was no end to guests and fuss with lodging and feeding them. Tolstoy's seventy-fifth birthday drew another diverse crowd of visitors and family.

That summer, addressing his guests with a boyish grin, Tolstoy cursed doctors and medicine. Sophia kept quiet until he remarked that according to Rousseau, "doctors were in league with women." She then reminded Tolstoy that doctors in the Crimea had worked "selflessly, intelligently, and disinterestedly to restore his health." Annoyed that he put her in the same league with doctors, she wrote in her diary, "My husband blames me for everything: his works are sold against his will, Yasnaya Polyana is kept and managed against his will, the servants serve against his will, the doctors are summoned against his will . . . There is no end to it . . . And meanwhile I work like a slave for everyone and my life is simply not my own."

Now recovered, Tolstoy wrote at regular hours, went for rides, and played cards in the evenings with visitors; he looked cheerful but "has become more stooped."[7] Daughter Sasha also assisted him, copying his manuscripts on a Remington typewriter. For Sophia, there was harvest to oversee and more improvements on the farm: seventeen thousand trees were planted that fall. "We live monotonously and quietly at Yasnaya and time is slipping away terribly fast, which happens when there are no events."[8]

In September, during a spell of summery weather, she enjoyed the "extraordinarily beautiful days and nights." The alleys in the park where she took strolls were illuminated by red sunsets; she saw the world only vaguely now, through a blur, "the blue sky and the yellow, red and brown trees." She liked to capture this world with photographs, which allowed a clearer look, and took a picture of herself in the alley, leaning on a white umbrella. She photographed Yasnaya in winter, the mesmerizing forest in snow she otherwise could not see; her pictures captured every detail.

At Christmas, the house was again crammed; daughter Tanya's family alone, with the stepchildren, consisted of eight people. Sister Tanya also visited but now no one would describe her and Sophia as a team: after forty years and different lives, they were emotionally disconnected. The holidays were tiring and "there was simply no time to rejoice."

In January 1904, Sophia traveled to Moscow with her nineteen-year-old daughter Sasha. She had to deal with Sasha's finances and give her a taste of cultural life. She took her to Goldenweiser's and Taneev's concerts, Chekhov's *The Cherry Orchard,* which gave Sophia "immense pleasure," and a symphony concert with Shalyapin, "the most intelligent, talented singer I have ever heard in my life." Sophia would see his magnificent performance in Mussorgsky's *Boris Godunov* just before he helped to stage it in Milan.

But her main business was Tolstoy's archive in the Rumyantsev Museum. The building was now under repair and, to her dismay, she was told to find another place. She was annoyed: "What sort of rubbish could be more important than Tolstoy's manuscripts and the diaries for his whole life?" Remembering that Anna Dostoevsky kept her husband's archive at the Historical Museum by Red Square, she went there. The eighty-year-old curator became euphoric when he heard about Tolstoy's manuscripts: "Can we take them? But of course we can, bring them immediately! Oh, what a joy! My dear lady, this is history, you know!" Everyone in the museum was overjoyed and treated her with the "esteem due me as Lev Nikolaevich's representative." They showed her two rooms in the tower, which were directly opposite Dostoevsky's. Sophia drew a floor plan and sent it to Tolstoy, who approved it. In addition to his manuscripts, she was asked for his collected works, busts, portraits, letters, and personal items. Her diary also interested the curator: the life of Alexander III was being chronicled and her audience with the tsar was part of his history.

Transporting Tolstoy's archive to the new location, more than a mile, took a complete day for Sophia and museum staff. Because Sophia wanted to make sure nothing was lost or stolen, several policemen guarded the entrance as soldiers loaded boxes onto coaches. When the archive was safely in the Historical Museum she and the staff took inventory. She then decided to store all of Tolstoy's papers and things there, to save them "from the mindless plundering of his children and grandchildren."

The most difficult task was cataloging Tolstoy's vast correspondence, work she continued both with the museum librarians and on her own. To her sister, she wrote that sorting out Tolstoy's letters and manuscripts would be enough to consume "several human lives."[9]

The museum gave her a sun-filled study in the tower. As she worked there in solitude, time flew, so she was surprised when a librarian told her it was three o'clock and the place was closing. The following month she would begin to write her memoir. The idea had been suggested by her father, upon her marriage. If she described her life with Tolstoy accurately, said Behrs, there would be much interest. Working with the biographical material in the museum was a starting point. Her chronicle would begin with her childhood in the Kremlin, a stone's throw from this tower. She was still full of energy: after a day in the archive, she went home and sight-read Arensky's opera.

At the end of January 1904, Russia plunged into war with Japan. Tolstoy watched the events closely. He wrote to condemn the war and world governments for unleashing violence. His article "Bethink Yourselves," which he sent to Chertkov in England, would later appear in the *Times*. The war stirred the entire country, "from the Tsar to the lowest trooper."[10] The prevailing mood was patriotic, especially when Russia suffered losses. Sophia, back at Yasnaya, wrote her sister about how it affected their tranquil countryside: "Everyone is excited. Yesterday, Lyovochka, without telling us or his doctor, rode to Tula for the telegrams. Dinner is not served on time: the staff is reading the telegrams and newspapers in the kitchen; today, more people went to Tula to learn about the war."[11]

War was tragedy, she wrote her sister in March: both sides, the Russians and the Japanese, will "mourn their dead, hurt, suffer, and die."[12] Their countryside was also stirred by the war: in villages horses were drafted and conscription began. In May, en route from Moscow to Yasnaya, Sophia saw draftees at the station, crowds of women weeping and wailing, while someone shouted "Hurrah!"

When son Andrei, twenty-six, volunteered for the front, her attitude to war was tested. To be sent into the army Andrei needed her permission. But granting it would upset Tolstoy: "I suffered and struggled with myself for a long time before I finally decided to petition." Her decision was made when Andrei told her that he could enlist without her help, although it would be more difficult.

Sophia invited Andrei's wife and children to live at Yasnaya. In August, she saw her son off: he enlisted as a senior cavalry orderly. His regiment was departing to Manchuria from Tambov, then a large city southeast of Moscow. Sophia was at once proud and saddened by his departure. She blessed him at the station, where a dense crowd of relatives and friends also waited: "I kissed Andryusha, made the sign of the cross over him and could look at no one else." She sensed the emptiness "only mothers will know" and felt "connected with everyone grieving over the fate of their children, husbands, brothers and loved ones." After six months Andrei was discharged with a nervous disorder.

Many times in her life Sophia had experienced a need "to look ahead, to be active . . . and seek new experiences." Having mastered watercolor technique, she now taught herself to paint in oils. This pursuit distracted her from thinking about the war. "Recently, I became fascinated with painting and worked to exhaustion; I was driven by my curiosity, how do they paint in oils? And so I began to copy Repin's portrait of Lyovochka, the one that is in my bedroom. Today I finished it and hung it to dry; I still have to work on details. Painting is terribly jolly but difficult; during this time I could do nothing else and Lyovochka feared for my sanity."[13] The portrait she was copying was of the aged Tolstoy at his desk, reading a booklet.

She photographed herself at work: brush in hand, she stands near the portraits hung by the window, smiling. In May, after copying another portrait, she wrote her sister that painting in oils helped her to better appreciate art. With no training, she produced successful copies, demonstrating artistic giftedness and remarkable persistence. "Of course . . . it's late now, no point in learning, there's no future."[14] She copied other portraits before attempting, the following year, Kramskoy's famous painting of Tolstoy. While copying this portrait she relived the time he worked on *Anna Karenina.*

Sophia copying Repin's portrait of Tolstoy, 1904.
Photo by Sophia Tolstoy.

That year, *Journal for All* published her collection of prose poems, reflecting on life, death, mother's grief, faith, and nature. She submitted nine poems under the pen name "A Tired Woman." On her personal copy she signed her full name: "Countess Sophia Tolstaia, wife of Lev Nikolaevich." She later would read these poems to the family and guests at Yasnaya.

In December, the family was joined by Tolstoy's disciple Biryukov, who had returned from exile. During his stay, while Biryukov worked on his authorized biography, Tolstoy skimmed through his diaries and letters to Sophia. "His whole life seemed to flash before him," she remarked. Biryukov told her that Tolstoy confided to him "he could not dream of any greater family happiness," that Sophia had given him everything, and "he could never love anyone so much."

It was even more precious to hear this from Tolstoy: "He suddenly burst into tears, caressed me and started telling me how much he loved me and how happy he had been with me all his life. Then I began to cry too; I told him that if I was not very happy sometimes it was my own fault, and I asked him to forgive me." She had long yearned for such a moment of "deep and serious recognition of our closeness."

A while later the family learned "dreadful news from Petersburg." On January 9, 1905, the Imperial Guard fired at demonstrating workers outside the Winter Palace; hundreds were slaughtered. The workers were petitioning the government for such reforms as an eight-hour workday. It was a peaceful march, led by a priest, and there were children in the crowd. In response to this massacre, named Bloody Sunday, a half million workers went on strike. A wave of political terrorism, peasant unrest, and mutinies swept through the empire from 1905 to 1907.

In the fall, the country became paralyzed: newspapers did not publish and bakeries, railways, and factories stopped. Yasnaya inhabitants felt the impact when rail workers walked off a train, leaving 110 passengers at the station nearest the estate. Travelers were fed and slept in their carriages and in the station house. Sophia wrote in her diary that they were anticipating "the strike to finish and the trains to move." There was also tension in the house because daughter Tanya was near the end of her confinement. In November, after many stillbirths, she bore a daughter, Tanechka.

That year, turning sixty-one, Sophia noted in her journal, "I simply don't feel old." She worked simultaneously on several projects. Her most important one was her memoir: she made good progress and read chapters to the family. There were also her oils: she painted the flora at Yasnaya, landscapes, the guest wing, and her self-portrait. She made pencil drawings of herself and daughter Sasha. However, these pursuits had to be squeezed between chores: "I want to do so many different things, but haven't the time or leisure."

She spent several days cataloging the Yasnaya library: she wanted to deposit the books Tolstoy had received as presents in the Historical Museum. She copied her letters to Tolstoy, so the museum would have duplicates. In the summer, she traveled to Moscow to launch another edition of his collected works. She spent several days in the tedious business of ordering paper and paying bills. She was unwell when she launched the new edition: pains in her uterus occasionally kept her in bed. Gynecologist Snegirev had recently examined her at Yasnaya during such an attack. She took her illness calmly and told Tolstoy, before the doctor's visit, that her condition was not likely to improve. When feeling better, she played the piano and painted, doing "a little bit of everything." A constant stream of visitors to Yasnaya was distracting. "It's quite impossible to write my memoirs, work on my oil painting, play the piano or do anything—one's whole life is held up by this crowd of useless people." She was referring to visitors, correspondents interviewing Tolstoy, and Chertkov's friends frequenting their home.

Among regulars was pianist Goldenweiser, whose company Tolstoy enjoyed. Dr. Dushan Makovitsky, follower and friend, now lived with the family, attending to Tolstoy and chronicling Yasnaya events. In December, returning from Moscow, Sophia observed, "It is very crowded—too crowded. There were 18 for dinner."

Days after her return from Moscow she read about riots: "There have been barricades and shooting . . . The post and railways are on strike." The country was in chaos: "They are robbing the banks and looting the landowners, the soldiers and sailors are mutinying, there is no government." At Yasnaya, they were reading books on the French Revolution, since Tolstoy compared it with the present situation.

The relationship between peasants and landowners grew tense. Even at Yasnaya, where peasants were always helped and treated well, there were conflicts. Peasants grazed cattle on Yasnaya meadows, stole trees, and refused to work. Sophia was overwhelmed by problems she could no longer solve: "The Yasnaya Polyana estate is deteriorating and is increasingly unprofitable; I cannot do it and hate it." In the summer of 1906, to raise money, she leased their apple orchard for five thousand rubles. Sophia maintained the estate for the family and Tolstoy, who would not be moved.

That summer, Chertkov was at Yasnaya, visiting from England. The Manifesto of 1905, signed by Nicholas II, granted political amnesty and abolished censorship. Chertkov would be allowed to return to live in Russia in March 1906, but would choose to stay in England for two more years. Meantime, Chertkov was looking for a place to build in the vicinity of Yasnaya.

While Chertkov was there, an unfortunate incident took place: the bailiff arrested several peasants cutting oaks on the estate. The peasants petitioned Tolstoy to defend them and Sophia was summoned, since she was responsible for the estate. What transpired entered several diaries. Chertkov, some other disciples, daughter Sasha, and son Lev beseeched Sophia to pardon the peasants, who stood nearby. With all this pressure on her, Sophia resisted. The incident was painful and embarrassing to Tolstoy, who had retreated to his second-floor balcony. He intimated to daughter Sasha that he was tempted to leave home, an intimation that soon spread throughout the household.

Chertkov and other disciples criticized Sophia for hiring armed guards, which contradicted Tolstoy's teaching of nonviolence. Her refusal to release the peasants further established her guilt. During his stay at Yasnaya, Chertkov did not help matters, publicly attacking her and escalating tensions. He seemed to have an appetite for antagonizing people and forcing them to choose sides.

Sophia believed it was her duty to defend Yasnaya from plunder and destruction. It was not only the residence she protected: the place would soon be a national museum. She wanted to preserve it intact, particularly knowing that some trees on the estate Tolstoy himself had planted. With few exceptions, she did not pardon peasants who cut timber in their forest. And she did not dismiss the guards, despite Tolstoy's request.

The political climate had changed, and in a few years, many estates would be robbed and set afire. The relationship between peasants and landowners was no longer idyllic and even Tolstoy, despite his generosity, was not exempt. The following year, he told Goldenweiser that he sensed the peasant hostility was directed at him personally.[15] As long as Tolstoy remained at Yasnaya, Sophia tried to ensure his safety.

While all this was happening, she was seriously ill. One month after the incident, she was "overcome by excruciating pains" from peritonitis. It was related to a fibroid tumor in her uterus and, possibly, a pelvic abscess. On August 22, her sixty-second birthday, gynecologist Snegirev, summoned to Yasnaya, decided she urgently needed surgery to remove the tumor. Tolstoy was against the surgery, but when it was explained that Sophia would die, he dropped his objection.

Preparations began: instruments and medications were urgently ordered from Tula. Snegirev would later publish a paper describing what was then a rare procedure: laparotomy (it involves an incision through the abdominal wall). He was nervous, having to perform the surgery outside a clinic and on the wife of a celebrity.

Before the surgery, Sophia confessed, took communion, and bid her farewells. "My love for L. N. and the children overwhelmed me with its power." As custom required, she asked everyone to forgive her, family and servants alike. Tolstoy, crying when he left her bedroom, noted in his diary that she was "touchingly sensible, truthful and good." On September 2, the day of her surgery, he went by himself into the woods, leaving instructions to let him know the outcome by ringing the bell. His distress and dread of losing her surprised even the family. When the bell rang once, he knew that Sophia had made it.

Sophia was still unconscious from the chloroform when Tolstoy came to see her. He wrote in his diary, "They operated today. They say it's been successful. But it was very hard for her."[16] The tumor in Sophia's uterus was the size of a child's head, the surgeon told Sasha, and, besides, it ruptured while being removed. Sophia suffered "endless pain" and was given morphine injections to assuage it.

Four weeks later, she was able to walk with a cane. At the end of October, she resumed her activities: she practiced the piano, painted landscapes, sewed, and played with her granddaughter Tanechka. She was planning to participate in a charity concert in Tula where she would read an excerpt from Tolstoy's work. But in November, there was another family crisis: daughter Masha came down with pneumonia and developed pleurisy within a week. Tolstoy was at her bedside when she died on November 27 at thirty-five. Sophia wrote to sister Tanya: "Did I survive to bury my children?"[17] It was windy and cold on the day of the funeral, when she followed Masha's coffin to the Yasnaya Polyana stone gate. "I cannot believe Masha is gone."

Sophia drowned her depression in work: soon after, she was typing letters on a Remington. In the New Year, she worked energetically on her memoir and traveled to Moscow for research at the Historical Museum. By the end of 1907 she completed four parts of her sizable memoir, "My Life," comprising hundreds of pages. She would later add several more parts, but this represented the core of her chronicle.

In February of that year, she had read her memoir to Tolstoy and he had encouraged her work. She read him another portion in March: "Lev Nikolaevich . . . praised my writing, which pleases me." Family and friends also approved of it. However, her memoir would be denied publication. Sophia's work was confined to the archive for eight decades and used by a handful of chroniclers of Tolstoy's life. Her memoir perpetuated her fate—to contribute anonymously.

Sophia wrote it while attending to many domestic and estate matters. "I started writing, and intended to write all day, but everyone kept disturbing me." She was called when another theft of timber was discovered and more peasants petitioned her for a pardon. While revising the memoir, she had to oversee planting and roof repairs.

In May, there was a scare when Tolstoy became ill with bronchitis. Learning from his personal doctor, Makovitsky, that he was running a high temperature, Sophia almost fainted at first but quickly took "strenuous measures" to bring it down. Again she was nursing Tolstoy to recovery and sitting nights with him. The following month, Tolstoy was well enough to swim in the river and go for rides.

In the summer, Yasnaya was crowded with tourists wanting "to take a look at Tolstoy." From Tula, 850 schoolchildren with teachers arrived to tour the estate. They spent a day swimming, singing, dancing, and drinking tea; Sophia took their photographs. Two weeks later, there was another excursion of schoolchildren. Delegations of teachers, peasants, and workers wanted simply to shake Tolstoy's hand. Several visitors were from America. Chertkov and other disciples were regulars: that summer, he rented a cottage within walking distance of Yasnaya.

Estate affairs had become entangled and chaotic, reflecting the general mood in the country. Sophia had to resolve labor disputes: "The haymakers . . . wouldn't go out to mow, and refused to let anyone else go. I had to settle the whole thing myself—the bailiff is quite useless." Adjusting to the new times, she sold two hundred acres for a negligible ninety rubles to the Yasnaya peasants. However, such concessions would not appease them.

The Yasnaya experience reflected a peasant mutiny that swept the country that year. Their orchard was raided at night; crops were collected and carted away. Honey was stolen from hives. Burglars broke into the guest wing and stole property. Twenty peasants with clubs ambushed the bailiff, threatening to kill him. Peasants continued to raid the woods: 133 oaks were stolen and sold in Tula. In September 1907, Sophia wrote a friend, Leonila Annenkova, "Living in Russia, especially in the country, has become impossible."[18] That same month, there was a shooting in the woods, an incident Sophia reported to the governor. She asked for armed guards, realizing she would be in trouble with Tolstoy. The authorities sent seven guards, a police officer, and a sergeant; they searched the village, looking for firearms, and made arrests. They also began to check the passports of all Tolstoy's visitors.

Sophia and Tolstoy during their wedding anniversary in 1907.
Photo by Sophia Tolstoy.

Just before their forty-fifth wedding anniversary, Sophia had "distressing conversations" with Tolstoy, who was critical of the police presence. Despite armed patrols, more timber was stolen, which resulted in more arrests: "Unpleasant news about the theft of yet more of our oaks, and an unpleasant conversation with Lev Nikolaevich about the guards." Two armed Cossacks sleeping in their house could not but upset the man who had repudiated the state, army, and police. "Relations with L. N. are cool: he is angry about the guards and the harsh treatment meted out for the theft of the trees." And since their arguments were overheard by his disciples, ever-present at Yasnaya, Sophia's behavior was seen as malicious.

During these prerevolutionary years, managing an estate was a daunting task in itself. Trying to manage it on "Christian principles" was impossible. They lived in days of unprecedented hostility: beginning in 1905, hundreds of police, priests, and officials were killed by revolutionary terrorists. By the end of 1907, during the peak of violence, nearly 4,500 state officials were killed or injured in terrorist attacks. On May 19 of that year, Sophia's youngest brother, Vyacheslav, a chief engineer working on the construction of Galernaya Harbor in Petersburg, was killed by extremists. Reading an account of his murder in the *Russian Gazette,* she was "petrified with horror and grief."[19] In the fall, Tolstoy received a telegram with a death threat from an extreme right-wing organization. (He had previously received such threats from ultranationalists after his excommunication.) All this could not but alarm Sophia.

In Tolstoy's view, the shooting incident and the thefts on their estate were trifles. He wrote in his diary that most horrible were not the robberies and murders but the feelings that caused peasants to commit these crimes. Sophia did not share his philosophical attitude and had no time to ponder global issues. With her children, grandchildren, and Tolstoy living at Yasnaya, she was concerned only with their safety.

At seventy-nine, Tolstoy felt "a considerable weakening of everything, especially memory."[20] Sophia was frightened when he forgot the name of his new secretary, Nikolai Gusev, who had lived at Yasnaya for some time. He was hired on Chertkov's recommendation and while working for Tolstoy was arrested for distributing his banned nonfiction. Tolstoy forgot this entire episode and asked Sophia, "Who is Gusev? Why is he in jail?" She remembered this young man, whom she'd questioned on his arrival and who'd told her he had never read Tolstoy's fiction. To Sophia, Gusev was typical of other disciples who knew Tolstoy only as their religious leader and not as a writer of genius. Gusev returned to Yasnaya after his release and continued to work as Tolstoy's secretary.

In the remaining years of Tolstoy's life, the disciples practically moved into Yasnaya, driving away other visitors who did not belong to their circle. Sophia sensed her trials were not over and remarked, in a letter to her sister, that she feared "more losses and more blows" from fate.[21]

But in 1907, she was still able to enjoy life, attending concerts and exhibitions in Moscow. In December, she painted portraits, played music, and printed photographs. At Christmas, Yasnaya was a cheerful place because the young folk wanted to have a party; Sophia also danced—with daughter Sasha.

Chapter Seventeen

In the Name of Universal Love

IN MARCH 1908, Tolstoy fainted in his study. Sophia was in the library, on the same floor, when his secretary, Gusev, called for help. She ran in to find Tolstoy unconscious. He was lifted to a divan and Sophia rubbed his head and hands with cologne and ammonia. When Tolstoy regained consciousness, he did not remember his fall or any events of that day; he had apparently suffered the first of several strokes. According to daughter Sasha, "he spoke, but he had forgotten everything; he did not know his name or where he was."[1] Unperturbed by the event, he later joked about it: "I had a fainting fit. And it made me feel very good. But the people round about me made a *fuss* over it."[2] He was referring to Sophia summoning doctors. She was alarmed, writing her sister that "for awhile, his memory was completely gone."[3]

When Tolstoy fainted again the following month, his memory loss lasted longer and Sophia felt he had become more aloof. He did not recognize his son Misha, and when daughter Tanya returned from a long journey in Switzerland, he met her with indifference. Yet he was able to resume his routine, riding almost daily, although now accompanied.

Nearing eighty, Tolstoy was entering his "last stage," Sophia judged. "His body seems to live a separate life, and his spirit exists on an altogether higher plane, independent of his body and indifferent to the earthly life."[4] She was trying to nurture and prolong his life, while sensing he was "in a hurry to do as much work as he can."[5]

During these final years Tolstoy's followers still wanted him to flee his ancestral estate to live in accordance with his principles: he received letters urging him to leave Yasnaya. In January, his disciple Evgeny Popov (Chertkov's associate from Intermediary) expressed his dismay that Tolstoy continued to live on the estate in contradiction of his ideal of poverty. Tolstoy replied meekly and explained it was impossible for him to leave home without inflicting pain on his wife.[6] A complete stranger wrote a letter, demanding, "Why are you not a pauper? And what prevented you from becoming one but instead drove you to live in conditions which exclude poverty and even the slightest need?" Tolstoy replied that he failed to live in accordance with his ideal because he was weak and that he had repented his weakness before God.[7]

Yet Tolstoy continued to dream of fleeing home and even wrote in his diary that it would be "such a desirable and joyous thing to go away and be a beggar, thanking and loving everyone."[8] But his flight had to be decided only in his heart. With many people urging him to flee, he contemplated whether he should take such a step: "The main thing: would I do it for myself, if I fled?"[9]

His disciples constantly pointed out that despite his renunciation of property, Tolstoy simply transferred his estates to his wife and children. The Yasnaya peasants petitioning for pardons refused to believe that Tolstoy was not the master; they said he was hiding behind his wife. Their words touched him in the raw. "They can't accept the fact that I'm not the master—especially since I live here."[10] For his disciples, who wanted to see him as priestly, blaming his contradictions on Sophia became necessary.

The people she accommodated and fed—Tolstoy's secretary, his personal doctor, Dushan Makovitsky, and his disciples—all criticized her in their diaries. Goldenweiser expressed a popular view when he wrote that Tolstoy's "greatest feat in life" was his patience with Sophia,[11] an idea Chertkov promoted for many years.

In the summer of 1908, Chertkov returned from England. During a previous visit to Russia he bought land from the Tolstoys' daughter Sasha, a few miles away from Yasnaya, in Telyatinki. There Chertkov built a two-story mansion, along with workshops, stables, a bathhouse, and sheds. His expensive construction came as a surprise to many, including his friend Goldenweiser, who discussed the subject with Tolstoy. Uninterested in earthly matters, Tolstoy only observed that while Chertkov was trying to settle in his neighborhood, he himself would be soon moving to a very distant neighborhood.[12]

By winter, Chertkov's place housed a colony of thirty-two Tolstoyans who were not only fed but received a salary of fifteen rubles a month from him. His secretaries and various assistants also lived there. Describing this in her diary, Sophia wrote that the colonists, including Chertkov's son, Dima, and his several friends, who were village lads, received a salary for doing nothing; they were "the envy of all the others" in the neighborhood.[13] His house was also the center for Chertkov's proselytizing activities among peasants. Coming to listen to him preach the evils of money, Sophia was annoyed with Chertkov's hypocrisy: he was a rich man.

Chertkov's properties in Russia and in England were far more luxurious than the Tolstoys'. His Tolstoyism was a facade: although in his house, servants and masters dined together, they received different menus, reflecting their status. Chertkov claimed he had no servants but would get Tolstoyans to work for free. His close friendship with Tolstoy protected him from criticism. By then, he had many critics, having quarreled with every major Tolstoyan he had worked with. Although highly unpopular, he was the sole leader of their movement. Years of correspondence with Tolstoy and Chertkov's ability to manipulate others secured for him exclusive privileges. It was in response to his pressure that Tolstoy turned over to him all negotiations with foreign publishers and gave him the right to publish his first editions. This became possible because Chertkov convinced Tolstoy that his publishing firm was morally superior to everyone else's. Tolstoy's biographer Maude, who along with many others disapproved of Chertkov, was unable to voice his opinions until much later.

Living in the same neighborhood, Chertkov now visited daily and Sophia remarked with annoyance that the disciple "practically moved in with us and almost never leaves Lev Nikolaevich alone."[14] Chertkov was photographing Tolstoy, making close-up portraits of him while he wrote in his study, and documenting his activities on the estate. When Chertkov invited an Englishman, Thomas Tapsell, to be his assistant photographer, Tolstoy confided to daughter Sasha that he was not pleased "but I cannot refuse Chertkov anything."[15] Sophia pointed out that it was against

Tolstoy's principles to have an exclusive relationship: "While preaching 'universal love,' he has created for himself this 'person closest to him'—in other words his *idol*."[16]

On August 28, Tolstoy's eightieth birthday, Yasnaya was flooded with uninvited visitors, photographers, and journalists. Every major newspaper and journal ran articles on Tolstoy: Sophia collected seventy-five. In addition, there were two thousand telegrams from home and abroad, and gifts. As usual, the table was set outside for Tolstoy's birthday. Suffering from phlebitis, he was in a wheelchair, his swollen leg outstretched.

Sophia's life was now consumed with her "constant effort looking after Lev Nikolaevich, whose health is becoming visibly weaker."[17] She made little progress with her memoir, and it was with effort that she completed her account of 1891, the year she worked alongside Tolstoy on famine relief. It was difficult to focus on the past while absorbed with the present. She wrote her sister of problems with the house and the estate requiring her absolute attention. "It's *necessary* to pump water from the basement . . . Building a dam in the lower pond is also *necessary*."[18]

At the end of her marriage, Sophia was simply trying to justify her "superfluous" existence. Her copying was not necessary because Tolstoy had plenty of scribblers. He also had photographers, secretaries, biographers, and a personal doctor. Deep in her heart, Sophia knew that her labors were no longer *necessary* and usually not welcome.

When Tolstoy handed her a draft of his fiction to copy, she wrote, "Today I resumed my old work."[19] Having found several rough drafts of his masterpiece *Hadji Murat,* she copied them to escape depressive thoughts and to relish his fiction: "It's so good! I simply couldn't tear myself away from it."[20] She deposited these drafts and copies along with letters in the growing collection of Tolstoy's manuscripts in the museum.

Excluded from the circle of Tolstoy's disciples, Sophia was alienated at home and felt desperately alone: "They are all against me, and I work for them all."[21] In 1908, Sophia suffered from lack of balance and fluctuating moods: "I am easily frightened . . . and I am afraid of everything."[22] The main cause of her anxiety was the intrusion of many people who separated her from Tolstoy.

Those who surrounded the great man during his final years were only bathing in his fame. Among them was writer Pyotr Sergeenko. He was the acquaintance who had given Tolstoy his first automobile ride and had brought a gramophone to Yasnaya. Tall and stooped, Sergeenko was eloquently described by Chekhov as "a funeral hearse stood on end."[23] Sergeenko and his son, Alexei, would become involved in the conspiracy around Tolstoy's secret will.

With many people in the drawing room and Tolstoy listening, Sergeenko senior provoked Sophia to speak her mind on the sensitive issue of copyright. For an anthology Sergeenko was producing, he wanted a portion from Tolstoy's early fiction and nagged Sophia to give permission. Tolstoy had renounced copyright on works after 1881 and anyone could publish them, but Sergeenko was trying to infringe on Sophia's right to the earlier fictional works. She refused, saying she could hire a lawyer to defend her right as publisher. Disciples were taking notes and the incident made its way into their diaries. Sophia knew they would say nothing good about her: "They are all out to attack me, condemn me and bring all sorts of malicious evidence against me."[24] Ironically, the collected works she produced were the cheapest and most satisfying to readers, as Maude observes.[25]

Tolstoy's doctor, Makovitsky, was also part of the inner circle, taking diligent notes on other occasions. When Tolstoy objected to his scribbling, Makovitsky learned to write with his hand in his pocket, where he kept small pencils and paper. His *Yasnaya Polyana Notes* would yield four sizable volumes.

Sophia had made many attempts to reconcile with the disciples, and when the government intensified persecution of the Tolstoyans, she interceded on their behalf. In the spring of 1909, the police deported Chertkov from Tula province for his proselytizing activities. Since he was persecuted as a Tolstoyan, Sophia wrote to protest. In her letter in the *Russian Gazette* of March 11, she described Chertkov's expulsion as an unlawful act, since it was made "without establishing his guilt and taking the matter to court." Recounting that several policemen entered Chertkov's home to read him the order, she wrote, "Clearly, Chertkov is being accused for his proximity to Tolstoy and disseminating his ideas. What ideas are these? That one must not kill, that one ought to love everybody, that any violent revolution should be prevented, etc. To be sure, hurtful ideas, aren't they?" Her letter was reprinted by other newspapers. Chertkov ignored her gesture of goodwill and, shortly thereafter, conspired against her.

Back in 1904, while still in England, Chertkov sent Tolstoy a questionnaire, to determine whom he wanted to appoint as his literary heir. It was the beginning of Chertkov's struggle to become the executor of Tolstoy's will. Tolstoy believed his legacy should belong to all and that everyone should have the right to publish his works. With his fame, it was enough to state this in his diary. In 1908, he dictated to his secretary, Gusev, "I would be glad if my heirs would make all my writings public property."[26] But it was important to him that his heirs carry out his intentions freely and willingly, that strife not be created among them over the right to his work.

Because Tolstoy did not recognize government institutions, he did not want a formal will. To persuade him to make one, Chertkov had to malign Sophia and the children. He claimed the family could not be trusted to carry out Tolstoy's intentions. And he persuaded Tolstoy it was in the interests of their cause to make such a will, and to keep it a secret from the family and the rest. Once Tolstoy consented, the fate of his legacy, which belonged to all, was in the hands of a small group of disciples. Chertkov masterminded the plot and chose who would participate.

Goldenweiser, who was drawn into the conspiracy, was on friendly terms with Sophia. They had known each other for years: Sophia updated him about Tolstoy's state of health. That summer, Sophia heard him play Chopin and Schumann at Yasnaya: "lovely."[27]

Another important participant was daughter Sasha, twenty-five. Tolstoy was the center of her universe, while her relationship with Sophia was difficult. She was too young to have witnessed her parents' blissful time when Tolstoy wrote his novels and needed Sophia's assistance. After Masha's death she became closest to Tolstoy among her siblings, making her indispensable to Chertkov. Later, becoming disillusioned with him, she described Chertkov as despotic and found his views incompatible with Tolstoy's teaching. But in 1909, she became Chertkov's ally in a struggle against her mother.

Sophia knew that Chertkov was angling for Tolstoy's copyright and, with typical impulsiveness, spoke her mind in front of others. In July, she approached Tolstoy, asking him to formally grant her copyright to his works. "He refused—emphatically, sharply, and unpleasantly. I flew into a passion, but then the result was so painful that we made it up. L. N. was both materially and morally right to refuse. But how hard it is for a person to renounce property, despite what he preaches!"[28] Her anxiety only aggravated matters: she annoyed Tolstoy, who was being pressed by Chertkov to make a legal will. Tolstoy then consulted a lawyer friend staying at Yasnaya about writing a formal testament.

In early September, Tolstoy traveled to see Chertkov at his uncle's luxurious estate, Krekshino, where he lived after his expulsion. Tolstoy's secret testament would be signed there. Sophia had a premonition, commenting in her diary, "A sad farewell and departure."[29] Although the purpose of this trip was to deal with a covert matter, Tolstoy's journey was a very public event: his departure from Yasnaya was filmed by the French cinematographic firm Pathé. When Tolstoy boarded the third-class railway coach with his retinue, which included his servant, daughter Sasha, Goldenweiser, Dr. Makovitsky, and Chertkov's son, Dima, he was instantly recognized. So many people were trying to see him that Makovitsky was afraid there would be a crush. At the Moscow station, men took off their hats to Tolstoy and everyone was silent. Newspapers reported his arrival and his state of health. Sophia read an alarming report that he was unwell and sent a telegram to Krekshino. Tolstoy replied he was in good health, and that she could join them.

Several days later, when Sophia arrived in Krekshino, she was surprised by the warm welcome. "It was all very friendly, gracious and comfortable."[30] But according to Goldenweiser and daughter Sasha, she was dreadfully nervous throughout her stay. At the time, Chertkov told Tolstoy that his children's intentions were to appropriate the works, which he put in the public domain. Tolstoy remarked in his diary, "I simply can't believe it."[31]

The testament was drafted soon after, on September 18. Tolstoy proclaimed all his works public property and gave editorial executorship to Chertkov. Sasha copied the document and it was signed by Tolstoy, Goldenweiser, Sergeenko junior, and Alexander Kalachev, a vagabond. Chertkov managed to keep the whole affair secret from Sophia, although she was in the same house. Later that day, Tolstoy left for Moscow with Sophia and daughter Sasha.

Chertkov had announced in a newspaper the date of Tolstoy's return to

Moscow, which drew a "rapturous" crowd of five thousand to cheer him. They crammed the station square, hung from posts, and stood on railcars to see him. As the crowd squeezed in, Sophia noticed panic in Tolstoy's eyes. The stream of people swept them to their Tula train. Aboard, a pale Tolstoy, jaw trembling, bowed at the window. He was drained, and as he lay down, he fainted.

Back at Yasnaya, he fainted again, and his speech was slurred. Sophia wrote her sister that she was afraid to overlook some serious condition and "fail to react immediately. And mainly, I am afraid that he can die without me."[32] Tolstoy's memory became hazy, he complained of "ill health . . . and lack of mental activity."[33] He resumed his walks but tired quickly.

Soon after, Chertkov, after consulting his Moscow attorney about the will, learned it was invalid. It was not legal to give the rights of literary works to everyone; an heir must be designated. Learning that Chertkov wanted the attorney to redraft the will, Tolstoy complained in his diary, "The conversation . . . was painful on account of Chertkov's demands, because it's necessary to have dealings with the government."[34]

Daughter Sasha helped persuade Tolstoy to sign the new draft. She told her father what Chertkov had been telling him all along: her siblings were "greedy" and wanted to profit from his writings after his death. Coming from Sasha, at the time when his death seemed near, Tolstoy was convinced: "My death is what they wish for. Yes, yes, yes."[35] He would sign it, even though dealing with the government was against his principles.

As Dr. Makovitsky had remarked on October 26, the will, to be signed at home, was "a secret known to few." Tolstoy signed it on November 1, noting in his diary it was "quite boring."[36] Despite being drafted by Chertkov's attorney, the new will was still claimed to be invalid. Tolstoy had designated daughter Sasha as the heiress, with the understanding she would pass his works to the public domain. But Chertkov claimed that provisions in the event of Sasha's death had not been made. Perhaps his claim made it easier to justify further redactions. When Tolstoy signed the final version in the summer of 1910, the disciple was named executor. (This latter appointment was stipulated in a separate memorandum, drawn up by Chertkov himself, which Tolstoy signed.) All this satisfied Chertkov's ambition and established his authority over Tolstoy's legacy, which belonged to everyone. To the world, Chertkov would say he had to carry out Tolstoy's wishes. However, he would inspire more strife and division in the family during this final year of Tolstoy's life.

Sophia went to Moscow in December to launch what would be her last edition of Tolstoy's collected works. Shortly after her arrival, she received a telegram from Yasnaya: Tolstoy had a high temperature. She spent an anxious night, without undressing, waiting for the first train to Yasnaya. In the morning, a telegram revealed that Tolstoy was better. Nonetheless, she rushed to Yasnaya with a doctor. Tolstoy was annoyed: "Sophia Andreevna arrived. It's very unpleasant. I simply can't put up with it patiently."[37]

Yasnaya was crammed with children and grandchildren who came for the holidays. Sophia, "exhausted and cheerful," made presents, prepared a puppet show, and helped to sew costumes for a masquerade. Tolstoy, as usual, criticized his family's merriment and "insane luxury."[38] Just before Christmas, Sophia's collection of children's stories, *Skeleton Dolls,* was published. She had designed illustrations for it and included two stories— one about her son Vanechka, a "real" incident from his life; the other by Vanechka himself: he had dictated the story "The Saved Dachshund" to her.

In January 1910, Valentin Bulgakov, Tolstoy's new secretary, arrived at Yasnaya. A young philosophy student, he was recommended by Chertkov to replace the exiled Gusev. Promoting him to this post, Chertkov "warned" Bulgakov that "Tolstoy's wife, both in her character and her views, would be thoroughly unsympathetic, not to say hostile." Bulgakov was surprised because his first impression of Sophia, two years earlier, had been favorable: "I liked the direct look of her sparkling brown eyes; I liked her simplicity, affability, and intelligence . . . And, naturally, I could feel only the greatest respect for her as Tolstoy's wife."[39]

That winter was uneventful, allowing Sophia to resume her memoir and catalog the Yasnaya library. Makovitsky described her labors: "Sophia Andreevna, coughing and complaining that the work was difficult, tidied up the journals, registered the books received in the recent months in a catalog, put them away in book cabinets, and gave instructions about preserving newspapers. She works very quickly and thoroughly."[40] Aside from this, there was her usual sewing: she made a "Tolstoyan" flannel blouse for Bulgakov and clothing for the orphaned village children. Tolstoy had asked her to look after several orphans, two brothers and a sister. She later arranged for them to live in a Moscow orphanage and placed them in special schools to learn crafts and agriculture.

In March and April, Sophia traveled to Moscow on publishing business and to research her memoir. She attended Rachmaninov's concerts, where he performed his compositions: his music was "hard to understand at first, but interesting."[41] She visited son Misha's family and her "darling grandchildren" and met Taneev. At a lecture of the Tolstoy Society she received her first recognition. When her assistance to Tolstoy was cited, the audience—scholars, artists, and literati—gave her an ovation. Their understanding of her role differed from that of Tolstoy's disciples.

Returning to Yasnaya before Easter, she proofread the new edition, balanced accounts, and looked after house repairs. In May, when she complained to Tolstoy of overwork, he retorted, "Who is forcing you to do all this? Drop everything and go elsewhere . . . Anywhere . . . to Paris."[42] The remark produced a violent reaction: Sophia broke into sobs and rushed outside. She ran onto the highway, "gasping with agitation and exhaustion," and lay in a ditch, remaining there until a cart was sent to fetch her.[43]

That month, Tolstoy was cold to her, while continuing to receive letters from Chertkov and meeting him. She felt she was "no longer necessary to him. The Chertkovs have priority now."[44] Although Sophia did not know about the secret will (she would not discover it until mid-October), she sensed Tolstoy was hiding something. When Tolstoy traveled to their daughter Tanya's estate, Kochety, Sophia, who had not been invited to join him, went separately. She found Tolstoy, his retinue, and Chertkov. Her presence was unwanted and she returned to Yasnaya alone.

During that summer, when Tolstoy again visited Chertkov, now at his rented cottage near Moscow, Sophia was in a state of near-madness. She now suspected a homosexual relationship between them. On June 22, she wrote in her diary, "I am disgusted by his senile affection toward Chertkov . . . I want to die and I am afraid of suicide . . . My heart, head, soul—everything hurts . . . Love is lost, ruined."[45] (This entry and others like it were never published for fear of compromising Tolstoy.) Her tangled handwriting reveals her despair.

Tolstoy's relationship with Chertkov did have the appearance of a love affair, with covert meetings and intimate correspondence. Sophia felt Tolstoy was subordinated to Chertkov's will, and was even afraid of him. In turn, he protected Chertkov from criticism, a privilege Sophia did not enjoy. As if to confirm her suspicion, Tolstoy told her, "Chertkov is the person who is closest to me."[46] When Sophia tried to discuss the matter openly, Tolstoy "flew into a terrible rage such as I have not seen for a long, long time."[47] Watching them sit close on a couch, Sophia was heartbroken, jealous, and bitter. At the end of her long marriage to a genius, she was not only tired, she was nervously ill and could not control her emotions. At the mere mention of Chertkov, she sobbed and trembled.

In late June, Sophia learned that Tolstoy had given his latest diaries (covering the past ten years) to Chertkov. What made it more hurtful was that they contained entries disapproving of her. She demanded Tolstoy recover the diaries, but he refused.

By then, Chertkov had returned to his mansion near Yasnaya, which was possible because of his mother's influence in court: she was a friend of the Dowager Empress Maria Fyodorovna. On July 1, Sophia wrote to Chertkov, asking him to return the diaries: "If you have any feelings for me and for Lev Nikolaevich's peace of mind . . . then I beg you, with an aching heart and a readiness to love and appreciate you even more—give me Lev Nikolaevich's diaries!"[48] Chertkov did not have the moral right to keep them. Back in 1895, when making an informal will, Tolstoy specified that everything in the diaries about his married life that might give pain to anyone should be destroyed. Now Chertkov struggled to preserve the negative entries and threatened Sophia that he'd use them against her.

Arriving at Yasnaya, Chertkov conferred with Tolstoy and Sasha behind closed doors to decide "what we should do about the diaries."[49] That same day, Chertkov shouted at Sophia, "I shall use the diaries to unmask you! If I really wanted to I could really *drag you and your family through the mud!*"[50] Being bullied in her own house by Tolstoy's disciple, Sophia wrote, "How insulting that my husband did not even stand up for me when Chertkov was so rude to me. How he fears him! How he has subjugated himself to him! The shame and the pity of it!"[51] Sophia sensed Chertkov "has taken complete control of him."[52]

The dispute over the diaries lasted another two weeks. On July 12,

Sophia, "weeping and trembling," asked Bulgakov to approach Chertkov and persuade him to return the diaries and restore peace at home. Bulgakov felt "deep compassion" for her and, besides, also wanted the feud to end.

The meeting took place at Chertkov's house, in the presence of his indispensable assistant Sergeenko junior. Fixing his large, restless eyes on Bulgakov, Chertkov asked him whether he and Sophia knew where the diaries were kept. "And with these words, to my utter amazement, Vladimir Grigorievich [Chertkov] made a hideous grimace and stuck out his tongue at me."[53] When Bulgakov said he did not know, Chertkov was relieved and ended the conversation. By showing compassion for Sophia, Bulgakov had lost Chertkov's trust.

It was only when Sophia threatened to commit suicide that Tolstoy commissioned daughter Sasha to fetch the diaries. But before they were returned, Chertkov and his assistants hastily copied compromising passages about Sophia. The diaries were later deposited by daughter Tanya in a state bank in Tula.

On July 22, Tolstoy signed another redaction of the will. In "absolute secrecy," the conspirators met in a forest, near the village of Grumont, where, sitting on a stump, Tolstoy signed the document. His witnesses were Goldenweiser and Sergeenko junior. Another witness, Anatoly Radynsky, was simply a member of Chertkov's household and was unaware of what he was signing.

Bulgakov was impressed by Sophia's intuition: when the conspirators returned for tea, she acted "as if something awful and irreparable had just happened." The table was set outside, the samovar was boiling, and there was a bowl of fresh raspberries. No one touched his tea: "Everyone was strained and dejected." They all sat "as if serving a prison sentence."[54] Days later, Tolstoy wrote in "The Diary for Myself Alone": "Chertkov has involved me in a struggle, and this struggle is both very depressing and very repugnant to me."[55]

In early August, his biographer and disciple Biryukov, having learned about the secret will, told Tolstoy it would have been better to gather his family and announce his wishes openly. This would be more in accord with the spirit of Tolstoy's teaching. Immediately after, Tolstoy wrote to

Chertkov, "It was bad that I acted secretly, assuming bad things about my heirs and, most important, I undoubtedly acted badly in making use of the institutions of the government I renounce in drawing up the will properly."[56] Chertkov in a long letter reminded Tolstoy of the circumstances necessitating the will and of his family's "mercenary intentions." Tolstoy replied to Chertkov, expressing his "sorrow and repentance for having caused you pain by my letter."[57] The exchange demonstrated Chertkov's control over Tolstoy.

With Chertkov's dominance, their "bright, honest family atmosphere" had been destroyed. Sophia wrote, "Everything is so sly, secretive and dishonest these days."[58] Conspiracy was alien to her and to Tolstoy: throughout their marriage they hid nothing from each other. Chertkov, on the other hand, seemed to thrive on secrecy and conflict.

In July, Sophia was examined by several doctors. Professor of neurology Grigory Rossolimo and physician Dmitri Nikitin were summoned to Yasnaya with Tolstoy's consent. Rossolimo, who specialized in child personality and behavioral disorders, diagnosed her with "paranoiac and hysterical states, with a predominance of the former."[59] The diagnosis became known to all and was used to harass Sophia. Goldenweiser alleges Rossolimo told Sasha her mother was "feebleminded."[60] Sasha treated her mother viciously and even spat at her during her attacks of hysteria and anxiety. Following this attempt to pronounce her mad, Sophia wrote in her diary that she had the support of her sons: "My sons have been splendid, and have united to defend me."[61]

Tolstoy was upset with Sasha's ill feelings toward her mother. He believed Sophia was nervously ill and "one cannot help feeling compassion for her."[62] To Chertkov he wrote, almost pleading him to have mercy on Sophia, "I know this seems strange to you, but I'm very often terribly sorry for her. When you think what it's like for her alone at nights, more than half of which she spends awake with the vague, but painful awareness that she isn't loved and is a burden to everyone except the children, you can't help being sorry for her."[63]

Tolstoy's last year has been described by many biographers. Yet something seems to have escaped their notice: it was as tragic for Sophia as it was for Tolstoy. Nearing eighty-two, Tolstoy had months to live. He had endured several strokes, was frail after many illnesses, and wanted peace. Sophia, almost sixty-six, was nervously ill and exhausted. Betrayed by her daughter, insulted at home, she was also alienated from Tolstoy, to whom she had dedicated her life and whom she deeply loved. During these final months together they both were suffering.

That summer, a desperate Sophia rolled in hysterics, made suicidal threats, and tore up Chertkov's picture. After Tolstoy's death she would torment herself with these memories and regret having lost control. However, that same summer she attempted to leave home and wrote Tolstoy in her farewell letter that he had exchanged her for Chertkov.[64] At the station, she met her son Andrei, who prevailed on her to go back.

At Yasnaya, there was a warm reunion with Tolstoy, who thanked her for staying. "He entered my room with tears in his eyes . . . And he embraced me and kissed me, clasping me to his thin chest, and I cried too and told him I loved him just as passionately and intensely as when I was a girl . . . But the moment I broached the subject of his conspiracy with Chertkov, he closed up and would not talk about it, although he did not deny that they had conspired together . . . He has been so strange lately . . . he takes fright at the mere mention of Chertkov's name."[65]

On September 23, their forty-eighth wedding anniversary, Sophia, in a white dress, went for a walk in the park. When Bulgakov offered his congratulations, she said, "On what? . . . It's such a sad . . ." And she covered her face and wept.[66] On the previous night, she wrote in her diary that never before had her relationship with Tolstoy been so distant. Tolstoy reluctantly agreed to have their picture taken but assumed an adamant pose. In that picture, Sophia is holding on to Tolstoy's arm; he looks ahead morosely.

But even this sullen attitude could not protect Tolstoy from the criticism of his disciple and daughter Sasha, who believed he should not have posed for the photograph with Sophia. Chertkov expressed his disappointment in a long letter. In his "Diary for Myself Alone," Tolstoy wrote, "A letter from Chertkov with accusations. They are tearing me to pieces. I sometimes think that I should go away from them all."[67]

Meantime, Tolstoy was about to suffer another stroke. On October 3, he returned from a ride and took a nap. Sophia found him sitting in bed and staring vacantly. She warned his doctor, "He will lose conscious-

The last wedding anniversary and the last picture of Tolstoy, September 23, 1910.

ness—I know it. His eyes are always like that before an attack." When she returned shortly after, Tolstoy was unconscious, his face distorted by convulsions.[68] Dr. Makovitsky and Sophia acted quickly. Pale, but in control, using her arsenal of home remedies, she applied icy compresses to his forehead, and hot water bottles and mustard plasters around his feet and legs, as well as prepared enemas. Tolstoy was twitching and quivering; during one powerful seizure he was thrown across the bed. Bulgakov and Biryukov could hardly hold him down.

When, late that night, Tolstoy regained consciousness, Sophia was sitting in his room, praying. "My whole being was overcome with remorse, pangs of guilt, prayer and the most desperate love for him—I would do anything for him . . . just so long as he lived and got better, so that I would not have to live with this gnawing guilt for all the anxieties which my own anxious state . . . have caused him."[69] The following day, Sophia made peace with daughter Sasha. Tolstoy not only recovered from the stroke but soon resumed his walks.

On October 12, Sophia found Tolstoy's "Diary for Myself Alone" and learned about his secret will. Devastated, she wrote in her diary: "I am hurt by Chertkov's evil *influence,* hurt by all their endless secrets, hurt that Lev N.'s 'will' is going to give rise to a lot of anger, arguments, judgments and newspaper gossip over the grave of an old man who enjoyed life to the full while he was alive but deprived his numerous direct descendants of everything after his death."[70] She found it painful that Tolstoy trusted Chertkov's "vile suggestion" of her mercenary intentions and that her entire life was not enough to demonstrate her selfless love.

She also wrote Tolstoy a letter, saying that the secret will would only serve an evil cause and generate strife and hatred. It would discount her life, which she gave to serve him. (Indeed, the secret will damaged Sophia's reputation and empowered Chertkov.) Tolstoy was upset by the "exaggerated tones" of her letter and, mainly, by her violation of the secrecy of his "Diary for Myself Alone." When Sophia came to see him, he told her to leave him in peace.

Since Tolstoy continued to meet Chertkov and correspond with him, Sophia lived in terror of a new plot. The couple's relationship had deteriorated: Tolstoy would taunt her, repeating that Chertkov was the person closest to him. Sophia initiated surveillance on Tolstoy's comings and goings, afraid that he would leave Yasnaya on the sly.

On October 25, she asked Tolstoy to let her read his exchange with Chertkov's wife, Galya. When Tolstoy refused, she saw "something ominous in his eyes" and had a premonition.[71] That same day, Tolstoy wrote in his "Diary for Myself Alone": "Suspicions, spying, and the sinful desire on my part that she should give me an excuse to go away."[72] Sophia had a sixth sense: the Chertkovs were discussing his flight and Galya even had a dream about it.

Tolstoy had contemplated leaving home many times but never with a destination in mind. On October 20, 1910, he wrote a peasant, Novikov, who lived in Tula province, asking to find a hut for him. Novikov's reply would come too late: the peasant strongly advised him to stay put. Novikov gave his commonsense advice without knowing of Tolstoy's strokes.

Chertkov and Sasha, who did know, encouraged Tolstoy to flee. Tolstoy's letter to Chertkov of October 26 suggests he had been discussing his flight with his disciple and his daughter.[73] "Sasha has told you about my plan, which I consider sometimes at moments of weakness . . . If I will embark on something, I will, of course, let you know. Perhaps, I will even need your help." It was agreed that Tolstoy would sign a telegram informing Chertkov of his escape with the assumed name Nikolaev. (Sasha would use a pseudonym, Frolova, in her clandestine correspondence.) It seems that even the date of his flight, October 28, had been decided. Tolstoy still believed these two numbers were providential for him.

And yet, describing the events that led to his flight in his diary, he held Sophia responsible. He tells of awaking the night before, hearing Sophia's footsteps in his study, seeing a crack of light under the door, and hearing rustling noises. Thinking that Sophia was searching his papers, "looking for something and probably reading," he became seized with feelings of "indignation and uncontrollable revulsion . . . I gasped for breath, counted my pulse: 97. I couldn't go on lying there, and suddenly I took the final decision to leave."[74]

Sophia's account is different: "His excuse for leaving was that I had been rummaging through his papers the previous night. I had gone into his study for a moment, but I did not touch one paper—indeed, there *weren't* any papers on his desk."[75] She stayed up late reading proofs and writing letters, then went downstairs to put the correspondence in the mailbag. On her return, she checked on Tolstoy, as usual, and, hearing he was awake, talked with him through the door. Certainly, there is no way to know which account is accurate, if either. Perhaps Sophia gave Tolstoy the excuse he wanted. But his account excludes his discussion of the flight with Chertkov and Sasha.

Before leaving Yasnaya, never to return, Tolstoy wrote a farewell letter. Although it was addressed to Sophia, it was meant for posterity: "My departure will distress you. I'm sorry about this, but do understand and believe that I couldn't do otherwise . . . I can't live any longer in these conditions of luxury in which I have been living, and I'm doing what old men of my age commonly do: leaving this worldly life in order to live the last days of my life in peace and solitude."[76] However, Tolstoy was to find neither peace nor solitude.

Newspapers reported his flight on October 30, describing it as a "heroic deed" and "a display of truth." Famous people were asked to comment on it daily; Bernard Shaw called it an "astounding example of non-resistance to evil," adding that *the evil* must have been truly impossible to bear." Biographer Maude was predicting that this final deed would elevate Tolstoy in his disciples' eyes to an "insurmountable height."[77] Tolstoy's flight was quickly becoming the stuff of legend.

Dr. Makovitsky began to chronicle events at 3:00 a.m. on October 28, when Tolstoy, nervous and trembling, woke him, told him of his decision, and directed the doctor to accompany him. It was cold and dark and on his way to the outhouse, Tolstoy bumped into some trees and fell over. He panicked that Sophia might wake up and prevent his leaving. Tolstoy had not the slightest idea where he was going but feared pursuit, so they were covering their tracks.

After taking a train to the next station, they rode horseback for about twelve miles on muddy roads. They had to cross a ravine and a frozen creek. Makovitsky made it with both horses and waited for Tolstoy. Holding on to trees, Tolstoy made it to the bottom; then, gasping for air, he crawled across the ice on his hands and knees. They took a morning train to Kozelsk, in Kaluga province. The fourth-class coach was packed with factory workers who were all smoking. The ride was painful for Makovitsky and for Tolstoy, with his heart condition and breathing problems. They were heading to the Optina Monastery near Kozelsk. From the station, Tolstoy sent a telegram to Chertkov, informing him of his flight and location, signing it "Nikolaev." The disciple replied the next morning: "I cannot express in words the joy I feel in hearing that you have gone away."[78]

For Sophia, Tolstoy's flight was devastating. She wanted to kill herself, but didn't succeed because she was closely watched. As she ran to the pond, she was pursued by daughter Sasha, Bulgakov, and others. The pond was deep and Sophia would have drowned had she jumped from the jetty into its middle. Because it had snowed the night before, the plank was slippery, and she fell, rolling into the icy water where it was only chest deep. Sasha pulled her out and summoned a psychiatrist.

Tolstoy learned of Sophia's suicide attempt from Sergeenko junior, who arrived in Optina on October 29 with mail from Chertkov. Sergeenko also told Tolstoy that the secret police had begun to search for him. The following day, Tolstoy was in the neighboring Shamardino convent, visiting his sister Maria Nikolaevna (she had become a nun late in life), when daughter Sasha arrived with letters from Sophia and family.

Sasha told Tolstoy that Sophia had discovered his location and was determined to pursue him with son Andrei. Tolstoy believed this and wrote bluntly to Sophia: "A meeting between us . . . is completely impossible."[79] He decided to leave Shamardino. On October 31, he woke up at four o'clock, anxiously talking about pursuit. He was already ill but wanted to leave immediately, fearing Sophia could take a morning train to Kozelsk.

But Sophia could not pursue Tolstoy for several reasons, the main one being she did not know where he was. On October 29, plagued by uncertainty, she wrote Tolstoy, "Where are you? Where? Are you well? Do not torment me, Lyovochka. I will serve you lovingly with my whole body and soul. Return to me. Return, for God's sake, for the sake of the love of God of which you speak to everyone."[80] On October 30, she wrote him, "I still have no news from you, dear Lyovochka, and my heart is torn." On November 1, after receiving his cold letter, she wrote to reassure him that it would be impossible for her to search for him: "I can barely move and also I do not want to force anything on you; do what you think is best." (After Tolstoy's departure Sophia had refused food and drink. She was constantly watched by nurses, who denied her movement.) She already had a premonition that they would "never see each other again."[81]

On October 31, Sophia tried to reconcile with Chertkov, asking Bulgakov to bring him to Yasnaya. Chertkov refused to make peace, astonishing Bulgakov with his "deep antipathy" to Sophia, "the more unpardonable in a man who considers himself a follower of Tolstoy." She tried again to reconcile, sending Dr. Grigory Berkenheim to Chertkov, but he again refused and sent a "hollow moralizing" letter.[82] The first to learn that Tolstoy was critically ill, Chertkov secretly left for Astapovo without informing Sophia and the family.

On November 2, Sophia received a telegram from a reporter for the *Russian Word,* saying that Tolstoy was in Astapovo and was dangerously ill. (Tolstoy, having developed a high temperature on October 31, left the train at this humble station.) When Sophia and the family finally arrived there, the place was besieged by correspondents. Tolstoy was dying of pneumonia in the stationmaster's hut and newspapers around the globe reported his temperature and pulse.

Sophia was photographed on the platform, peeking at her husband through a shuttered window. A reporter wrote, "It was the wife of great Lev Tolstoy, Countess Sophia Andreevna. They did not let her in to see the sick man."[83] Another reporter, who had met her before, was surprised by the change in her: she was an old woman, stooped, head shaking, with tears in her eyes.

Her infirmity emboldened the disciples. Makovitsky remarked that before her arrival, when they decided not to admit her to see Tolstoy, they "were still afraid of her." But when they saw her, their fear vanished: "She was not her former self; she was indecisive and timid."[84] Tolstoy was not told of Sophia's arrival; his opinion on whether he wanted to see her was not sought. A consensus was reached: meeting Sophia would devastate Tolstoy.

Inside the hut, aside from the stationmaster, Makovitsky, and other doctors who attended to Tolstoy were Chertkov, daughter Sasha, and Sergeenko junior. When Sophia came to the door, Sergeenko junior opened it and shut it in her face. Daughter Sasha also refused to admit her. Makovitsky noted: "Sophia Andreevna came to ask about L. N.'s health. She kept walking around the house and disturbing us."[85] To the disciples, her suffering was irrelevant.

> Round my husband was a crowd of strangers and outsiders, and I, his wife, who had lived with him for forty-eight years, was not admitted to see him. Doors were locked and, when I wanted to get a glimpse of my husband through the window, a curtain was drawn across it. Two nurses appointed to look after me held me firmly by the arms ... Meanwhile Leo Nikolaevich called our daughter Tanya and asked about me ... He said to her: "So many things are falling on Sonya. We managed things badly." No one told him that I had come, although I implored everyone to do this.[86]

Sophia was allowed to see Tolstoy on November 7, shortly before he died, when he was already in a coma. Even then, she could not approach his bedside but was directed to sit three steps away. Makovitsky and another man stood between her and Tolstoy, to prevent her from coming closer: "If L. N. would regain consciousness and she wanted to come near, we would block her way."[87] Sophia was allowed to come near Tolstoy only when he drew his last breath.

He was lying on his back, eyes closed, when she started saying farewell and begged him to forgive her. "I whispered tenderly to him, hoping that he could still hear me, that I was in Astapovo the entire time and that I loved him to the end . . . I can't remember what else I was saying but the two deep sighs, as though caused by an enormous effort, came in response to my words, and then there was silence."[88] She would wonder, as long as she lived, whether Tolstoy heard her.

Chertkov was calm during these difficult days. When Tolstoy died, he packed his suitcase and hurried to catch the train, accompanied by Sergeenko junior and daughter Sasha.[89] In Astapovo, about a thousand people came to bid farewell. Sophia "sat all day at the head of the bed."[90] Another crowd assembled when Tolstoy's coffin was put on the train. Chertkov tried to interfere with the funeral at Yasnaya, arguing, among other things, that the coffin should remain closed. The family protested because people came to bid farewell to Tolstoy and wanted to see him. Thousands attended the funeral, despite police restrictions. Tolstoy was buried in the Zakaz forest on his estate, in the place where, he believed in childhood, lay a magic green stick containing a secret to universal happiness.

Chapter Eighteen

And the Light Shineth in Darkness

IN WIDOWHOOD SOPHIA would become absorbed with her cause—preserving everything that concerned Tolstoy's life and work. This enabled her to summon her will and leave behind the ill feelings caused by outsiders' interference in her marriage. Once again, she would demonstrate her character and presence of mind.

Shortly after the funeral, "crushed with grief," Sophia came down with pneumonia. Later, accounting for the eighteen days when she was delirious, she wrote, "Ill." Her children and grandchildren were still at Yasnaya in November and sister Tanya, who had arrived for the funeral, stayed to look after her. In Chertkov's absence, Yasnaya was no longer torn by conflict, and daughter Sasha was now "affable." Dr. Makovitsky was back and Sophia wanted him to stay: he was her last link to Tolstoy.

As she gained strength, Sophia began to realize her loss; a sense of loneliness and "a dismal, frightening life ahead" overwhelmed her. It was "a little easier" during the day, when she was with people. During sleepless nights, alone with her thoughts, she was tormented with "unbearable depression, pangs of remorse . . . and painful feelings of pity for my late husband's sufferings."[1] Remembering her final year with Tolstoy, she now felt "unwittingly to blame for so much." Most painful was that she had not said farewell to Tolstoy nor made peace with him. She sensed that their separation was "eternal" and that her soul would never meet his.

The events in Astapovo shocked many. Anna Dostoevsky was among the first to express sympathy to Sophia and write of her outrage that strangers had separated her from Tolstoy in his final days. Anna had also shielded Dostoevsky from practical life and conducted his business affairs, for which she had earned a reputation as a moneymaker. She wrote that Tolstoy lived to eighty-two because of Sophia's efforts.

On November 9, the prominent lawyer and family friend Anatoly Koni expressed his deep gratitude to Sophia for having nursed Tolstoy's talent. A week later, she received a letter signed by twelve academicians of fine arts who recognized her contribution to Tolstoy and her importance to Russian culture. These letters were vital to her after the public humiliation she had been through. There were all sorts of rumors as to why Tolstoy fled home and why she was prevented from seeing him.

Sophia would read these letters to visitors at Yasnaya. She was not able to publish them because Chertkov soon started his defamation campaign in the press. Chertkov, his appointees, and his successors would now control everything written about Tolstoy in Russia and censor positive comments about Sophia. In fact, letters and articles in her support could not be published until the end of the twentieth century and then only in marginal periodicals.

She also received a letter from her gynecologist, Professor Snegirev, who had removed her fibroid tumor at Yasnaya. Snegirev recalled that Tolstoy's routine was timed to the minute to suit him and his work and it was Sophia who had arranged his life. Tolstoy "was indebted" to her for many things. And if he, a mere visitor, knew this simple fact, how could Tolstoy, with his genius, fail to perceive it? What drove Tolstoy to flee was inner conflict, the restlessness of the great tormented soul struggling to find peace before the end. Snegirev believed Tolstoy had sensed he was dying. After talking to another professor of medicine who had examined Tolstoy in Astapovo, Snegirev gave Sophia their hypothesis. Tolstoy's confusion, wanderings, and uncertainty of where he was going suggested he had a viral infection, which led to pneumonia.[2] Snegirev agreed with his colleague that Tolstoy was ill on the night he left home. (Snegirev's letter was also suppressed in the archives and only published in 1992 by a medical doctor.[3] Chertkov did not allow any challenge to his version of Tolstoy's flight, which put the blame on Sophia.) Snegirev was also bewildered that his positive remarks about Sophia were edited out of a 1909 anthology on

Tolstoy produced by his disciple Sergeenko. Snegirev's account of the surgery was left intact, but his comment that Tolstoy was indebted to Sophia was removed.

Professor Snegirev's letter forced Sophia to relive the difficult summer and fall of 1910 with Chertkov's meddling and the atmosphere of secrecy and hostility at Yasnaya. She told Snegirev of how Chertkov came to control the ailing Tolstoy and took away his drafts and diaries: "I spent my entire life reading, copying out and preserving everything my husband wrote . . . but at the end they were concealing and hiding everything from me." Although Chertkov claimed to be Tolstoy's "confessor," the very sight of this man drove Sophia to hysterics. For months she had lived in fear of Tolstoy leaving home: "Perennially expecting him to leave, I did not sleep nights, nervously awaiting him from the walks, peeking into his windows in the evening—is he around?" Now she had to live on to complete her major tasks: "It's necessary to sell Yasnaya to the state . . . It's also necessary to preserve the house, things, portraits, and Tolstoy's library."[4]

Explaining the true causes of Tolstoy's flight, Sophia would write a note to biographers: "The view that Lev Nikolaevich escaped to test his teaching is false. The most probable version is that he became ill, sensed intuitively he was dying, and fled to die . . . Accusations to his wife, his words about luxury, and his wish to stay alone, all this was false, invented."[5] (This note was also suppressed until 1992, when it appeared in a scholarly publication in Russia.) When she wrote this, Sophia was being harassed by various onlookers at Yasnaya who blamed her for Tolstoy's departure and death. In 1911, she had to publish a letter asking to be saved "from the curious and the judging."

On the fortieth day after his death, peasants came to pray for Tolstoy's soul. They decorated his grave with spruce branches and sang the ode to the dead, "Eternal Memory." Sophia was moved by their love for Tolstoy. "At that moment we were all experiencing the same thing together." Visiting the grave almost daily, she photographed it on Christmas Day, dazzled by the "beauty of nature and light of the sun."

Soon after Tolstoy's death, when Sophia was still in bed with pneumonia, Chertkov launched his first attack as executor of the will. On November 20, his attorney, Muravyov, sent a directive to the Historical Museum, where Tolstoy's original manuscripts and Sophia's own archive were kept,

Sophia at Tolstoy's grave in 1912. Photo by Sophia Tolstoy.

barring access to her. The lawyer ordered that the entire collection be kept in the museum temporarily, that no one be admitted to the safe, and that it remain sealed. Chertkov wanted to remove the original manuscripts from Tolstoy's brilliant literary period, which Sophia had copied and preserved. Since Tolstoy had approved of Sophia's decision to deposit his archive at the Historical Museum, there was no need to change the arrangement. What in fact Chertkov wanted was exclusive access to the manuscripts.

Sophia's goal all along was to prevent Tolstoy's papers from falling into private hands, which was why she deposited them with the public institution. She wrote the Museum Council to ask that the originals not be removed: they should be stored permanently in some state or scientific safe in Russia. She also sought access to the materials and her own archive, which she needed to complete her memoir. The museum, however, decided to seal the room until the matter was settled legally. This did not happen until 1914, when the Senate ruled in Sophia's favor. She had to wait another year to gain access to her materials and by then, at seventy-one, she had no energy for research and writing.

Tolstoy's daughter Sasha became involved in what her sister called "a shameful and unworthy struggle with her own mother."[6] Chertkov drew her into the battle over custody of the manuscripts and into his defamation campaign against Sophia. He needed Sasha, since he did not want to be seen as depriving the family of property and copyright. Later, he would squeeze her out.

On January 10, 1911, Chertkov and Sasha, using the issue of the copyright, tried to stop publication of the twenty-volume edition of Tolstoy's collected works, which Sophia had just produced. Failing to achieve any compromise with her daughter, Sophia remarked, "Sasha has threatened to damage my edition in every way possible—let her . . . How her late father would have grieved at her behavior."

The Kushneryov Printing Works received an injunction that said: "according to the terms of the will, the printing or publishing of the works of L. N. Tolstoy by any person besides Alexandra Tolstaia [Sasha's full name] is an infringement of her interests." The printers refused to comply, publishing their response in the January issue of the journal the *Russian Word*. Since it was Tolstoy's wife who had commissioned the printing, bought the paper, invested her labor in reading proofs, and deciphering the manuscripts, she owned the printing order.

Simultaneously, Chertkov launched a newspaper campaign against Sophia. In January, Sasha's open letter appeared together with Chertkov's in the *Russian Word*. She claimed that Tolstoy's wishes had been violated and insisted that his original manuscripts be handed over to her, since her father had designated her as heiress. Chertkov in his letter made spiteful remarks about Sophia and doubted that Tolstoy had given her his manuscripts.

He would wage this battle for years, giving interviews and circulating petitions in support of his cause. These petitions, published in newspapers, were signed by people who had grievances against Sophia. On February 12, 1912, such a petition appeared under the title "L. N. Tolstoy's Legacy," condemning Sophia's position in the dispute. Using daughter Sasha as his agent, Chertkov claimed the original manuscripts were needed to publish Tolstoy's collected works. Chertkov skillfully played his game, setting public opinion against Sophia: his petitions would generate reader response, enabling him to reply.

The newspaper campaign allowed him to keep his name in the public eye. He was perennially on the offensive, alleging that Sophia broke the conditions of the will and that he was fighting to establish the truth. Sophia commented in her diary: "The persecution continues. How will it all end!" The involvement of her daughter made it difficult for her to respond or to find support.

In 1912, deciding to explain matters to the public, daughter Tanya wrote an article describing Chertkov's role in her parents' marriage as detrimental. She revealed some of the motives behind the conflict over the manuscripts, instigated by Chertkov and Sasha. At the last moment, Tanya withdrew her letter, writing Sophia that she wanted to keep her hands "clean of all newspaper polemics."

In January 1911, Chertkov published his essay "The Last Days of Tolstoy," his account of the flight, in which he blamed Sophia for Tolstoy's departure. A year later, for the second anniversary of Tolstoy's death, he wrote an article, "The Blessing of Love. L. N. Tolstoy's Attitude to His Fellow-Men." In it he alleged that Tolstoy's illness at the end of his life was "the direct consequence of the shock he suffered from . . . the agonizingly painful conditions of his family life."

At the height of Chertkov's campaign in the newspapers, Sophia hurried to advertise and distribute the new edition. But in February, she faced a calamity: three volumes of Tolstoy's nonfiction were seized by police. The censors urged criminal proceedings against the publisher because Tolstoy's articles contained "blasphemy" and antigovernment content. "At worst they can throw me into the fortress and put me on trial," Sophia observed. This did not happen because old friends intervened to defend her. However, Sophia had to deal with the censors herself and find replacements for Tolstoy's banned articles.

Then there was the question of what should be done with Yasnaya. The estate included about 2,390 acres of farmland and forest, one-fourth belonging jointly to Sophia and the sons. Sophia's dream was to preserve the place intact—buildings, garden, forests, meadows, and arable land. However, the children did not have the means to maintain it: the sons were impoverished and had large families. In 1910, Sophia had twenty-five grandchildren.

In early 1911, she learned that sons Ilya, Andrei, and Mikhail had a plan to sell Yasnaya to rich American industrialists for 1.5 million rubles. She protested: "I find this most distasteful and sad and not at all to my liking. I should like to see Yasnaya Polyana in Russian hands, as public property." She also did not allow her son Andrei to contest the will.

On May 10, she wrote a letter to Nicholas II, asking that Yasnaya be bought by the state. It would be more profitable for the family to sell it by parcels to private owners; however, her duty and "most passionate wish" was to preserve it as a Russian cultural monument under state protection.

Soon after, the Council of Ministers decided to acquire Yasnaya for a half million rubles but the Duma refused to approve it. Sophia again wrote to the tsar, asking to "defend the cradle and the grave of a man who has glorified the name of Russia to the entire world . . . Do not let Yasnaya Polyana . . . be sold into private hands." The tsar replied that the government's purchase of Tolstoy's estate was impermissible. (The government and the Holy Synod doubted the need to glorify Tolstoy.) Despite this refusal, Sophia continued undaunted and two years later, she made provisions to establish the estate as a museum.

In November of 1911, she sold their Moscow house to the city Senate, requesting it be used as a library and museum. The proceeds, 125,000 rubles, were shared equally with six of her children. (By then, Sasha, who had inherited the copyright, was the wealthiest among her siblings.) Sophia made a detailed inventory of furniture, dishes, and other personal items before sending them to the Stupin warehouse. When the museum was established, her list allowed recovery of every piece. All were stored through the Great War, the Revolution, and the country's economic collapse, when robbery became widespread. In her careful cataloging, Sophia even described defects, making it simpler to identify the pieces later on. The infamous redwood furniture was damaged: varnish gone, chair seats ripped, mattresses torn, foyer couch missing a leg. With a large family and floods of visitors it could not be otherwise. Such was the "luxury" in the Tolstoy house.

She also made an inventory at Yasnaya, again describing every piece and telling its history. Her descriptions allowed researchers and visitors to understand Tolstoy's daily life. Some furniture and crystal came from his ancestors. The leather couch Tolstoy describes in *War and Peace* was the very one on which he and his siblings were born and on which Sophia gave birth to eight of their children. She described the round wooden table on which a morning tray of coffee was placed for Tolstoy and where he read newspapers and letters. On another table he played solitaire; the chair by his writing desk he had won in a Moscow lottery. Upon retiring for the night, he left his clothes on a spare couch for his servant, Ilya, to clean by morning. The first kerosene lamp in their house was Tolstoy's present to Sophia.[7]

She preserved the study the way Tolstoy left it in 1910. The candles on his desk were never lit after he extinguished them on that fateful night. The book he read that night was Dostoevsky's *The Brothers Karamazov* and it would remain opened on his desk. Sophia even kept the torch used by the Yasnaya peasant who rode in front of Tolstoy to light the road when he drove away.

Once full of life, the houses in Yasnaya and in Moscow stood empty as Sophia prepared them for sale, conducted inventories, and placed Tolstoy's things in storage. Her old life had come to an end: "It breaks my heart to destroy all my nests, which hold so many memories of a full and happy life."

Sophia copied Tolstoy's notebook of 1873, with his research notes for the unwritten historical novel about Peter the Great. Reading it again, she was just as fascinated as when Tolstoy had told her about his intentions. The notebook would speak to her and she despaired when the work was over: "I have finished copying L. N.'s notebook—to my great sorrow! Now I have nothing of his to work on!" She occasionally felt Tolstoy was still around, "as though he was just about to come in and I was going to tell him something."

Looking for work that could link her to him, she copied their diaries of 1910 and painfully relived that time. She wept for things that could not be put right but also felt that what had happened in the end "*could not* have been otherwise—it was foreordained." None of the things that had separated them mattered any longer: "My grief at losing Lev Nikolaevich is so . . . solemn and profound, that nothing else seems important."

In the summer of 1911, Sophia toured hundreds of visitors who came to Yasnaya to look at Tolstoy's grave and house. In June, there was an excursion of 125 people, and the next month two hundred peasant teachers. She talked to the visitors about Tolstoy and met "with a great deal of sympathy." On his birthday in August, three hundred people arrived, and on the first anniversary of his death, another five hundred. When alone, Sophia took flowers to the grave and fed the birds perched on it; she was happy when a flock would fly up and chirp cheerfully at her. She talked to her husband's soul, but "where is he? Tormenting, unanswerable question."

Tolstoy was always in her thoughts: "I live only for him and everything that concerns him." She painted copies of Ivan Pokhitonov's landscape, which depicted the Yasnaya hill where Tolstoy had played in childhood with his brothers, looking for the magic green stick. To keep the legend alive, Sophia gave copies of the painting to friends and told visitors to Yasnaya of Tolstoy's lifelong dream to discover the secret of universal happiness.

In 1911, Sophia published an album, *From the Life of Tolstoy: Photographs Exclusively by Countess S. A. Tolstaia.* It contained photographs of Tolstoy at Yasnaya and in Moscow, and a panorama of their life on the estate. She included some of her self-portraits: over the years she had photographed herself while painting, writing, and taking walks at Yasnaya. The album, expensive to produce, was limited to six hundred copies and was published by Messrs. Scherer, Nabholz & Co.

She also read and cataloged articles on Tolstoy and welcomed biographers who came to work at Yasnaya. Several were living there and using the library. She helped every biographer, supplying material and verifying information. Bulgakov was drafting his book about Tolstoy's final year. Biryukov came to request additional material for his biography. Semyon Vengerov, a literary historian and bibliographer, worked there on a grand scholarly edition of Tolstoy's works, supplementing it with commentaries, a brief biography, and illustrations. Later, Vengerov asked her to write a brief autobiography; it would appear in 1925, in Berlin, under the same cover as Anna Dostoevsky's in a volume called *The Two Wives.*

Tolstoy's former secretary, Gusev, was annotating Tolstoy's diaries at Yasnaya. Chertkov and Sasha were preparing the diaries for publication and Gusev's job was to verify information with Sophia. Gusev had just returned from a tour of Russia, lecturing about "the shattering" of Tolstoy's "illusion of family life." Sophia knew from the newspapers that he spoke about Tolstoy's flight and presented Chertkov's account of it. In 1912, she remarked in her diary, "Gusev came; he seems embarrassed to see me after his lecture."

Everyone was writing a memoir, including members of her own family, and wanted Sophia to contribute information. She allowed her son Ilya, sister Tanya, daughter Tanya, and others to use her letters and diaries. Son Sergei was writing a guide for Yasnaya tourists, to which she also contributed.

Sophia continued her memoir "My Life," aware that she needed material still locked in the museum. Her energy was declining: "How strange it is to feel the dying of the flame which burned within me all my life and kept me alive." She could only take her memoir to 1901, without her archive and the inspiration to continue. She prepared several extracts for publication from material she had written years ago. A chapter about her betrothal appeared in the journal *Russian Word* in time for her fiftieth wedding anniversary. It was published under the title "L. N. Tolstoy's Marriage." Reader response was warm: her piece was recognized for its ingenuity and was said to contain "the real Tolstoy, his soul."

In 1912, the wealthy publisher Sytin bought first rights to three volumes of Tolstoy's unpublished works from daughter Sasha. The money helped resolve the difficult question of how to dispose of Yasnaya. Sasha purchased two-thirds of the land from her brothers Ilya, Andrei, and Mikhail, and transferred it to the peasants to fulfill Tolstoy's wish. Sophia bought the remaining land from her sons to establish the museum.

As she would write in her autobiography, "I live in Yasnaya Polyana and preserve the house with the furnishings just as they were during Lev Nikolaevich's time, and care for his grave."[8] From the land distribution, she reserved 170 acres, which included house, grounds, orchard, and forest, which she and Tolstoy had planted "with so much love to improve our estate." In addition, she gave small parcels of land to the families of several of their servants.

In 1912, the tsar granted Sophia an annual state pension of ten thousand rubles. Her financial security created additional problems. Despite the land settlement, the younger sons continued to ask for money. In the past, she could refuse them, explaining that the money did not belong to her. But with the pension she did not have this excuse. In 1914, learning that several sons were gambling, she became infuriated, writing in her diary that Tolstoy was "a thousand times right to give his money to the peasants, rather than to his sons."

Sophia was now reading the Gospels every night, as Tolstoy used to. When son Sergei visited and played Chopin, Beethoven's sonatas, and a Weber sonata, it evoked earlier times. "As I listened to him play I vividly recalled Lev Nikolaevich, his eyes filled with tears and an expression of anguish on his face."

On trips to Moscow, she attended concerts of musicians she knew from the past, including Taneev; but his music no longer moved her. Nor was she interested in the new composers, artists, and writers making a sensation: "I am indifferent to everything, I died with my Lyovochka!"

The first two decades of the twentieth century would be celebrated in Russia as a time of cultural revival. The period was marked by exceptional creativity and new artistic movements, but Sophia was far away from this life. She did not attend exhibitions of the avant-garde artists, dismissing them as "decadent." She read French literature by Zola and Rousseau, which had interested Tolstoy. Time had stopped for Sophia with Tolstoy's flight: she had never recovered from the shock. Occasionally, she was surprised to find how her grief changed her, that she had lost her curiosity: "Where am I? Where is my love for the arts, nature, and people?"

Just before the New Year, 1913, Sophia began a project she found interesting. She was typing and annotating *Count L. N. Tolstoy's Letters to His Wife*. Although the originals were in the museum, she had copied them back in the 1880s. Beginning to prepare the letters for publication, she remarked, "That's a job I won't finish in a hurry. I shall relive the whole of my married life as I read them. It will be very hard at times." While copying, she could hear Tolstoy speak to her. "How much love there is in those letters! How could everything have changed so suddenly?" The letters told a true story of her marriage, she believed, and rereading them made her "agitated and happy." She hired an editor to revise the volume, which appeared in 1913. Sophia could not publish the entire collection, she explained in her introduction, because for some letters the time was not ripe. Her volume sold out within a year, requiring her to prepare a second edition. She worked on it for several more years, adding notes and biographical information about Tolstoy. The second edition also included his final letters to her from 1910. Preparing them was painful: Sophia felt that her "wound has not healed."

In the spring of 1913, Sophia traveled to the Crimea to join two Tanyas (her daughter and granddaughter) on their vacation. From the station, she took a motorcar for the first and, likely, last time in her life, arriving in Yalta "after various adventures with a burst tire." The Crimea was a journey into the past: Sophia visited her mother's grave, located "high on a hill with a view of the sea and mountains." She also visited Gaspra, memorable to her from Tolstoy's illness. It was with a pleasant feeling that she recalled the time she nursed her husband, when their family had assembled there and were united. The vacation was Sophia's last.

She was yet to live through events that would entirely change her country's destiny. The Great War, starting in 1914, would leave the Russian economy in shambles, prompting the tsar's abdication, two revolutions, and a long civil war. Millions would perish during fighting, famine, and epidemics. The world around Yasnaya was rapidly changing, but the Tolstoys' estate was frozen in time.

In July 1914, after reading the papers, Sophia remarked in her diary, "This ghastly war will lead to great misery in Russia." The draft in their village soon began and the prevailing mood was despondent: no one wanted to be torn from the land. The country was already starving, and knowing this, Sophia did not expect Russian victory. Her children, however, wanted to go to war. Sophia was appalled to learn that Mikhail had enlisted in the cavalry, an active regiment. Sasha had enrolled as a nurse and headed to the Turkish front. Lev also enlisted as a Red Cross representative.

At the end of July, Sasha came to say good-bye. She had not seen Sophia for some time and was surprised to find an aged and meek woman sitting in an armchair. " 'Why are you going to war?' my mother asked. 'That's needless. Your father was against the war, yet, you want to take part in it.'"[9] Sophia spoke impassively, "said little, mostly she drowsed, sitting in . . . the armchair where Father so loved to sit. Apparently nothing interested her. Her head shook more than formerly, she was all bent over, she seemed wizened, her large black eyes, which used to be so brilliant and snapping, were dull, she saw very badly."[10] Sophia was glad to have peace with her daughter: "Sasha was here . . . We tenderly said good-bye to one another."

As Sophia read accounts of the war, thinking of her children, her heart filled with "nagging anxieties." In October, she learned that one of her grandsons had been wounded and taken prisoner in Bohemia. "Dreadful sadness in my soul. Of my children I know nothing . . . A lot of talk, and it's all war, war, war." When Bulgakov, who continued to live at Yasnaya, wrote an appeal against the war, the police burst into their house and arrested him. Sophia, outraged, sent a letter of protest, published by several newspapers under the title "From Yasnaya Polyana."

That fall, Sophia traveled to Moscow to see Sasha, about to leave with her detachment for the Turkish front, and to pay the Stupin warehouse where furniture and Tolstoy's things were stored. The railways were congested with military cargo; tickets were hard to get, and trains crowded, making further travel unfeasible for her. When in the summer of 1915 she read about Taneev's death, she was "deeply shaken" but did not attend his funeral. She would only travel to Moscow now when it was absolutely necessary, to make final arrangements for Tolstoy's manuscripts.

The Yasnaya house came alive in the winter of 1914, when daughter Tanya, a recent widow, and Sophia's granddaughter moved in with her: "My granddaughter Tanechka is delightful, and Tanya is so close and dear to me." Her other children would visit and daughter Sasha would come during furloughs. Sophia would spend an evening listening to her, "full of experiences and stories" about the war.

When, in February 1916, son Andrei became dangerously ill in Petrograd,[11] Sophia traveled to see him, accompanied by Lev, who managed to get tickets. Andrei died of pleurisy days after their arrival. Her son's death and funeral seemed "almost immaterial": she had lost her ability to suffer deeply. That journey was her last; she was barely alive on her return to Yasnaya. "Life has become like a dream—I've lost my energy and interest in things." That year, sorting out Tolstoy's letters and those of her children, she discovered that she had outlived many of those she deeply loved: "I have recently had a sense of Lev Nik.'s presence, and there was a quiet, affectionate tenderness about his behavior to me. Where is he now? And where are all those who have left and whom I used to love?"

Newspapers reported bad news from the front and anarchy in the country. "I am engrossed in the newspapers. The war, the murder of Rasputin, the chaos in the government—it all fascinates and even disturbs me." The changes were sweeping and difficult to grasp. There were also changes at Yasnaya: many industrial workers and soldiers visited. As in the past, Sophia toured the groups through the house and to the grave. "People are always astonished at the simplicity of our life here."

In 1917, there was a spontaneous revolution in Russia, the forerunner to the Bolshevik Revolution later that year. It occurred in February, precipitated by acute food shortages and riots in Petrograd. Nicholas II abdicated in March with the country on the verge of collapse. A newly formed Provisional Government inherited a ruined economy and an unpopular war.

At Yasnaya, the revolutionary spirit manifested itself when workers from the nearby cast-iron foundry arrived with red flags and Tolstoy's portraits to pay respects to the house and widow. They sang and marched to the grave through deep snow to lay their wreaths; Sophia and the two Tanyas joined in. They stood "in the biting wind," listening to revolutionary speeches about freedom. Sophia responded with a short speech about Tolstoy's legacy and they all sang "Eternal Memory." Sophia reported in her diary, "An important day for Yasnaya Polyana."

From that day on, hundreds of industrial workers and soldiers came regularly to pay their respects. They marched through the Yasnaya alleys, singing "La Marseillaise," carrying wreaths with red ribbons and "magnificent red flags embroidered in gold and silver." Sophia thought this music was strange to hear in Russia. She saved the wreaths, piling them in a corner of Tolstoy's study. One of the officers told her that Yasnaya was "a sacred place" for the revolutionaries, just like Jerusalem for Christians or Mecca for Muslims. In June, two hundred soldiers came. "I showed a great many visitors around the house—about 70 . . . I am exhausted. It's quite beyond me now." A few days later, there were four hundred, marching to "La Marseillaise." "I showed L. N.'s rooms to more than 62 of them."

Throughout that year, peasants looted and destroyed landowners' estates across the country. Life became "frightening," even at Yasnaya. In October, around the time of the Bolshevik Revolution, Yasnaya inhabitants learned that mobs were coming to destroy their estate. The house was guarded by several militiamen, who would be powerless. Sophia and the two Tanyas were sitting on packed trunks, horses harnessed, ready to flee. "But suddenly news came—the Yasnaya Polyana peasants had met the mutineers with spades, scythes, pitchforks, and chased them away."[12]

Sasha returned from the front in December 1917 and, approaching

Yasnaya, could barely recognize the neighborhood: "Nearly every house in our district had been robbed and burned."[13] The old forest around Yasnaya was devastated by felling, but the buildings and grounds were unharmed.

Sophia was happy that Sasha "arrived at last" and that her two daughters and granddaughter were with her. Sister Tanya, also a widow now, recently came from Petrograd to stay for good. That winter the family gathered around the kerosene lamp to read *Eugene Onegin, War and Peace,* and Turgenev's prose poems. When Tolstoy's prose was read, Sophia again marveled at his artistry: "How good it is, and how profound." That year, she made a large crayon drawing of a burdock, the thistle Tolstoy describes in *Hadji Murat*.

Their isle of culture was surrounded by war. In 1918, just as the Bolsheviks concluded peace with the Central Powers, the country plunged into a bitter civil war. Sophia wrote in her diary, "Time flies, war continues, famine looms even closer." Provisions were running low, shops were empty, and there was "no bread or kerosene to be found." Sasha remembers this turbulent and hungry year: "What didn't we do in those days to get food? ... Gradually, even in the villages, potatoes disappeared."[14]

Yasnaya was put under special protection by the Bolshevik committee in Tula. Back in the fall of 1917, it had assigned soldiers to guard the estate and to preserve it intact. Sophia wrote in her diary, after a visit from the authorities, "It turns out that they are going to keep guard over everything, both the house and the books; they have spent the past three nights here already. This is most reassuring."

The Yasnaya inhabitants began to receive provisions from their district rationing committee. A telephone was installed in their house (Sophia's first), connecting Yasnaya with Tula and Moscow. Yasnaya was again becoming crowded. Nikolai Obolensky, Sophia's former son-in-law, came here with his family when their estate was burned and lived in a wing of the house. Bulgakov and Makovitsky were in the main house. New arrivals included Sergeenko senior and his son Mikhail: although uninvited, they settled in the main house, soon running it like masters.

By then, Sophia had handed over the management of Yasnaya to daughter Tanya. Withdrawn from all practical affairs, she cataloged the library, corresponded with biographers, and "worked on various manuscripts, papers, and other things concerning Lev Nik." She was annoyed when Sergeenko senior disrupted her work with conversations.

In 1918, the Yasnaya Polyana Society was organized in Tula, a new agency helping Soviet authorities to protect the estate. Its plans included constructing an asphalt highway to Yasnaya, building a library, and a peasant school. Sophia was skeptical: "Nothing will come out of it; it's an enormous enterprise." The society controlled Yasnaya until the summer of 1921, when it was nationalized by the new government. Sergeenko senior was elected chairman of the society and, as Sophia observed, he immediately became "infected with delusions of power." He occupied Tolstoy's library downstairs; his son sat in Tolstoy's armchair, "taking notes in the room where Lev Nik. used to write." It was only too memorable to Sophia that his other son, Alexei, had harassed her in Astapovo.

Sergeenko senior presented himself to the authorities as Tolstoy's friend. In Tolstoy's name, he requisitioned food, clothes, and other supplies from the government, but instead of distributing them to Yasnaya inhabitants, he kept them for himself. Sister Tanya ironically called him "the benefactor" because he would occasionally give them pieces of soap and chocolate as presents. His access to food and supplies made him "the sovereign of Yasnaya Polyana." He treated the three widows (Sophia, sister Tanya, and daughter Tanya) with impertinence, declining their requests: "Don't you know that your specific gravity is zero?"[15] Sophia wrote in her diary that he harassed her over Tolstoy's flight: "P. A. Sergeenko arrived and showered me with coarse, spiteful criticisms, blaming me for driving L. N. out of the house. What business is it of his? How *dare* anyone judge a man and wife?" He also lied to her that the authorities had discussed evicting her and her family and using Yasnaya as an orphanage. "I don't believe a word of it, but one feels constantly alarmed."

Sophia had good instincts about people, and had tried to chase away Sergeenko when Tolstoy was alive. Now he supervised the planning of the school in Yasnaya; but nothing was ever built and "the lumber disappeared." Years later, he would be involved in other scams. Eventually, the family and various Tolstoyan organizations publicly disclaimed their responsibility for Sergeenko's activities.[16]

In 1918, a colossal undertaking was launched to publish an edition of Tolstoy's works that would incorporate everything he had written. Son

Sergei and daughter Sasha, both keen to participate, were elected to the editorial board. In February, Sergei wrote to Sophia, "I plan to sort out manuscripts in the Rumyantsev Museum in the most energetic fashion. I shall keep a strict watch to make sure they don't take any of them away."[17] Sophia had moved Tolstoy's manuscripts and archive to this museum in 1915, after the dispute with Chertkov was resolved in her favor.

Now confident the manuscripts were in good hands, Sophia transferred the rights to them to her children, Sergei and Sasha, and gave them her keys to the boxes. She soon wrote in her diary that they were doing "an excellent job." Along with other board members, they worked in unheated rooms at the museum because, with the civil war, there was no fuel to heat the buildings; there was also no food for the museum staff and editorial board.

In the summer of 1918, Tikhon Polner, one of those preparing Tolstoy's complete edition, visited Sophia at Yasnaya. In his book *Lev Tolstoy and His Wife* he describes their meeting: "Calm and weary, she met me with dignity. She was then seventy-four. Tall, slightly stooped, very thin, she moved through the rooms like a shadow; it seemed that a gust of wind could take her away . . . Sophia Andreevna talked willingly but without a smile . . . With obvious pleasure, she read her memoir of the happy days in Yasnaya Polyana. She recited several poems dedicated to her by Fet. Of Chertkov she spoke without anger but with cold animosity. Her remarks about the last ten years of her life with her genius husband were not always kind. After falling silent for a moment, she would remark: 'Yes, I lived with Lev Nikolaevich for forty-eight years but I never really learned what kind of a man he was.'"[18]

In August 1919, Sophia wrote her farewell letter: "The circle of my life is closing, I am slowly dying, and to all those with whom I have lived, recently and in the past, I want to say farewell and forgive me. Farewell my dear children, whom I love so much, especially my daughter Tanya, whom I love more than anyone else on earth—I beg her to forgive me for all the pain I have caused her. Sasha too—forgive me for not giving you enough love, and thank you for your kindness to me in recent days."

Shortly after, she began to give away her things. "To my granddaughter I gave my gold watch and chain, which Lev Nik. gave me, and a large diamond brooch which was a present from him when we were engaged . . .

to my daughter I gave my mother's bracelet (gold) and a ring with two diamonds and a ruby, a present from Lev Nik. for all my help and labors when he was writing *Anna Karenina*." She had previously included daughter Sasha in her will.

On August 28, Tolstoy's birthday, she walked to the grave with a bouquet of wildflowers and sat there for a long time, "conversing silently" with him. Soon after, she wrote to her niece Varya Nagornova: "My life transits into eternity, where it began."[19] When pondering her life, she would see the contrast with Tolstoy's: "He *knew* how to win people's love. I never did."

By fall, Yasnaya was in danger of becoming a civil war battleground between the Reds and the Whites, as Denikin marched on Tula. "We're threatened with war and a battle near Yasnaya Polyana," Sophia wrote in October. The Red Army regiment was stationed in a nearby village: "They say the shells can kill us and destroy our house." In her last entry that month, already ill, Sophia wrote that it had been discussed how to defend Yasnaya. (The danger was averted when the Red Army won several decisive victories, stopping Denikin's advance.) Sophia's final letters were to Tolstoy's biographers. To one, she gave information about his early story "Polikushka." To another, she explained his attitude to the law.

She became ill in October: windows in her room had to be washed before the winter frames could be installed. Standing on the sill and cleaning them by herself, she was exposed to the cold wind, and soon after developed a "choking cough." Dr. Nikitin, who had treated Tolstoy during his illness in Astapovo, diagnosed her with pneumonia and later with emphysema. "She did not complain, did not moan, was very patient and gentle," Sasha remembers.[20] Sophia died on November 4, three days before the anniversary of Tolstoy's death, also from pneumonia, and was buried in the family cemetery, Kochaki, next to her children.

Sophia had remarked at fifty-seven, "Life is energy and struggle, constantly changing feelings, the ebb and flow of good and evil—life is life, there's no stopping it . . . Although when the time comes to stop it naturally, we must greet the end calmly and joyfully; then, contemplating God and submitting to His will, we shall be spiritually reunited with Him and physically reunited with Nature. And there can be nothing but good there."

Epilogue

I N 1922, CHERTKOV published *The Last Days of Tolstoy*. In the book's opening he wrote, "Now that Tolstoy's wife is dead, the chief obstacle to revealing the true causes of his [Tolstoy's] going away from Yasnaya Polyana is removed."[1] True to his promise to use Tolstoy's diaries against Sophia, Chertkov quoted the disparaging entries, which he had been collecting all along. He had read Tolstoy's diaries beginning in 1884, within months of their first meeting, and copied them. Tolstoy had trusted Chertkov with his intimate thoughts and expected confidentiality. But the disciple deceived his trust, behaving as if he owned Tolstoy, along with his works and teaching.

In *The Last Days of Tolstoy,* Chertkov compiled all the negative comments Tolstoy ever made about Sophia and added his biased interpretation. The theme is familiar: Tolstoy's martyrdom was suffered at home. He compares Sophia's treatment of her husband to "the tortures of the Inquisition, and exceeding them in their uninterrupted persistence and prolongation."[2] All her activities were "purposely calculated to wound, insult and revolt him [Tolstoy] . . . in his most sacred feelings." Chertkov blames Tolstoy's depression, or his "mental agony," on her cruel treatment: "No health could hold against such torments lasting over several months at a stretch." Sophia is portrayed as his tormentor and evil wife and Tolstoy as "a voluntary prisoner in his wife's house for . . . many years."[3] Since it was impossible to continue living with such a wife, Tolstoy had to escape.

When Maxim Gorky read Chertkov's book, he expected contemporary critics to destroy it: "I told myself that someone would surely be found to write to the papers that the direct and sole purpose of this concoction is to blacken the memory of the late Sophia Andreevna Tolstaia. But so far I have not come across a single review drawing attention to this honorable purpose. I now learn that yet another book is to come out, written with the same laudable intention of convincing the educated section of society that Lev Tolstoy's wife was his evil spirit."

Gorky wrote to clear Sophia's name and rebut the ludicrous accusations. He also felt that Tolstoy's legacy must be protected from his narrow-minded disciple. At the end of his life Tolstoy was surrounded by such acolytes who were but a cloud of flies, attracted by his fame and feeding on his great soul. Tolstoy was not only a creative giant but "the most complex individual," having renounced his own art as sinful. Sophia's role beside Tolstoy was at once difficult and responsible: she was the only woman in his life for almost fifty years and his active assistant. "She was his close, faithful, and I think, his only real friend."[4]

When he wrote this in 1924, Gorky was the most influential Soviet writer and public figure. Not only the city where he was born, but many trains, ships, parks, streets, libraries, and schools all across the country would be renamed after Gorky. And yet, even he could not curb Chertkov's evil tongue and stop the slander against Sophia. Upon her death, Chertkov's campaign was only beginning to gather strength. His account of the marriage would penetrate many biographies. Some ninety years later, Gorky's retort remains the only uncompromising voice in Sophia's support, and this is why it is quoted here.

Chertkov was immune to Gorky's criticism. He was well received by the Soviet government and had met with Lenin. Although he was an aristocrat with family connections to court, Chertkov did not have to emigrate after the Revolution. Moreover, he collaborated on government projects. The head of the Socialist state listened to Tolstoy's friend and publisher, Chertkov tells us, "with lively interest and sympathy."[5] Among other things, Chertkov discussed his plan to produce a Tolstoy edition incorporating everything he had ever written.

It was a project in which the Tolstoy family had participated since 1918, but now Chertkov wanted the leading role. The publishing plan was threatened, however, since the Soviet government was not interested in producing everything Tolstoy had written. His religious work could not be sanctioned by an atheist state. The government had a publishing monopoly, so the fact that Chertkov attained Lenin's support for the project is remarkable.

In 1924, upon Lenin's death, Chertkov met Stalin, who also endorsed his publishing plan. Soon after, Chertkov was appointed general editor and the government authorized the necessary sum, one million rubles. The project was to be overseen by the State Literary Publishing House. In the end, only fractions of this sum were paid, forcing Chertkov to repeatedly write to Stalin and members of his government, pleading for more money.

It was important to produce Tolstoy's ninety-volume edition, even with the limited circulation and subscription costing an unaffordable three hundred rubles. However, it was published by the state, contrary to Tolstoy's beliefs, and the contract was sanctioned by Stalin. Clearly, Tolstoy would not have approved of such arrangements.

Chertkov used his position as general editor to promote himself. In 1926, with much fanfare, he moved his sizable archive, containing Tolstoy's manuscripts and other material, to the L. N. Tolstoy State Museum at Prechistenka 11.[6] A government delegation was invited, red carpets were spread, and the press was there. When, shortly after, Sophia's part of the archive was moved to the same building, the press was not invited.

Chertkov would retain his position as general editor for life; before dying in 1936, he appointed his trusted assistant Nikolai Rodionov to replace him. Because publication stretched over three decades, Chertkov had to ensure his account of Tolstoy's flight was consistently presented. As Chertkov confided to Rodionov, he himself had edited material related to 1910, the year of Tolstoy's flight and death: "This year I reserved for myself because I don't want to give outsiders access to one of the most important periods of L. N.'s life; I will pass it on to you."[7] Rodionov's diary reveals that this most comprehensive edition of Tolstoy's work was infected with bias.

The ninety-volume edition (dubbed the Jubilee) became the major source for scholars about Tolstoy's life and marriage. A biographical article about Sophia describes her views as "hostile" to Tolstoy's. Her chronicle "My Life" was dismissed as "completely useless" to document Tolstoy's life and was described as not worth publishing. At the same time, the edition includes a flattering biographical article on Chertkov, emphasizing his ideological closeness to Tolstoy and his extensive contribution to him.

In 1920, when Chertkov met with Lenin, many intellectuals suspected of dissent had been exiled or purged. Among them was Tolstoy's daughter Sasha, arrested in March of that year and sentenced to three years in the GULAG.[8] Later, finding it impossible to work under the Soviets, she would emigrate, like her sister Tanya and Tolstoy's biographers Biryukov and Bulgakov. In the 1930s, the Tolstoyans were arrested in great numbers. The purges in the Tolstoyan agricultural colonies under Stalin led to their destruction. Chertkov, although a prominent Tolstoyan, had no problems adjusting to the new ideology. After his meeting with Lenin, he wrote, in the spirit of the day, that Tolstoy gave "his whole working time to intense spiritual labor in the interest of the working masses."[9]

Some other Tolstoyans also demonstrated their moral flexibility. Tolstoy's former secretary, Gusev, Chertkov's protégé, even made a spectacular career under the Soviets. Gusev received government awards under Stalin and was buried in the Novodevichy Cemetery in Moscow, an honor reserved for Soviet ministers and Party elite. It was with Gusev's help that Tolstoy's philosophy was purged of its major principle: nonresistance to violence. And a new image of Tolstoy as atheist and revolutionary champion was established.

Although Tolstoy's secretary for only two years, Gusev was appointed director of the L. N. Tolstoy State Museum in 1925. (He had succeeded Tolstoy's daughter Tanya after she emigrated.) Later he headed the Manuscript Department where the writer's archive and Sophia's papers were kept. As a professor at Moscow University during the height of Stalin's purges (1939–47), Gusev became a recognized authority on Tolstoy. His two-volume *Chronicle of L. N. Tolstoy's Life and Work* demeans Sophia, although it employs her letters and diaries. The biased accounts of Sophia in his chronicle would migrate into many other biographies. As the person in charge of the museum and archive, Gusev suppressed favorable information about Tolstoy's wife, along with publication of her memoir "My Life" and other prose.

In the early 1990s, after the fall of Communism, the L. N. Tolstoy State Museum staff attempted to publish Sophia's collected works. So far, they have succeeded in publishing only several extracts of "My Life" and one of her novellas.

Her memoir would have been published long ago had Sophia portrayed Tolstoy as a saint. But she spoke frankly about both his genius and his limitations. Some of her disclosures still will be hard for the public to accept. As Somerset Maugham wrote in *The Moon and Sixpence*, "The faculty for myth is innate in the human race." But Tolstoy's greatness will not be diminished if we unveil the truth and let Sophia's story escape the boundaries of the steel vault.

Notes

Prelude

1. Tikhon Polner, *Tolstoy and His Wife* (New York: Norton, 1945), 182.
2. Tolstoy's (LN) letter to Sophia (SA), June 20, 1867. Unless otherwise specified, translations of letters are by the author.
3. *The Diaries of Sophia Tolstoy,* trans. Cathy Porter (New York: Random House, 1985), 806.
4. Ibid., 417.
5. Ibid., 500.
6. Ibid., 470.
7. *Tolstoy's Letters*, ed. and trans. R. F. Christian (London: Anthlone Press, 1978), vol. 2, 562.
8. Ibid., 550.
9. *Tolstoy's Diaries* ed. and trans. R. F. Christian (London: Anthlone Press, 1985), vol. 2, 401.
10. Chertkov's letter to LN, October 28, 1910. In L. N. Tolstoy, *Complete Collected Works: Jubilee Edition,* ed. V. G. Chertkov (Moscow-Leningrad: Goslitizdat, 1928–58), vol. 58, 573. Referred to hereafter as *Jubilee Edition.*

Chapter One: Childhood

1. Tatyana Kuzminskaia, *Tolstoy as I Knew Him: My Life at Home and at Yasnaya Polyana,* trans. Nora Sigerist (New York: The Macmillan Company, 1948), 19.
2. Now Krasnodar.
3. Giacomo Quarenghi (1744–1817), Italian neoclassical architect and painter, best known in Russia as a builder during and after the reign of Catherine the Great.
4. Diminutive of Lyubov.
5. A Russified version of the name that appears on his birth and baptism certificate, Andreas Gustav.
6. Leonard Schapiro, *Turgenev: His Life and Times* (Oxford: Oxford University Press, 1978), 2.
7. Kuzminskaia, *Tolstoy as I Knew Him,* 5.
8. *Jubilee Edition,* vol. 47, 505.
9. The girl was brought up under the name of Varvara Nikolaevna Bogdanovich-Lutovinova.
10. Sophia Tolstoy, "My Life," part 1. The memoir is still unpublished and is quoted here for the first time. The manuscript is held at the L. N. Tolstoy State Museum in Moscow (GMT). Unless otherwise specified, all quotations in this chapter come from "My Life," parts 1 and 2.

11. Sophia Tolstoy, "Song without Words," GMT. The novella is still unpublished and is quoted here for the first time.
12. Kuzminskaia, *Tolstoy as I Knew Him,* 27.
13. Ibid., 5.
14. *The Diaries of Sophia Tolstoy,* 381.
15. Kuzminskaia, *Tolstoy as I Knew Him,* 34.
16. *The Diaries of Sophia Tolstoy,* 835.
17. Kuzminskaia, *Tolstoy as I Knew Him,* 43.
18. In 1841, Alexander II married Maria of Hessen-Darmstadt (Maria Alexandrovna).
19. Based on a fable by Aesop.
20. *The Diaries of Sophia Tolstoy,* 84.
21. Kuzminskaia, *Tolstoy as I Knew Him,* 44.
22. *Tolstoy's Diaries,* vol. 1, 164.
23. Kuzminskaia, *Tolstoy as I Knew Him,* 81–82.
24. Ibid., 61.
25. Leo Tolstoy, *Anna Karenina,* trans. Richard Pevear and Larissa Volokhonsky (New York: Penguin Books, 2002), 21.
26. *The Diaries of Sophia Tolstoy,* 830.
27. Ibid., 828–29.
28. Ibid., 832.
29. Ibid., 834–35.
30. SA letter to LN, August 28, 1862. In Sophia Tolstoy, *Letters to Tolstoy: 1862–1910* (Moscow-Leningrad: Academia, 1936), 45. Unless otherwise specified, translation is by the author.
31. *Tolstoy's Diaries,* vol. 1, 166.
32. *The Diaries of Sophia Tolstoy,* 838.
33. Ibid., 839.
34. Aldridge and Tolstoy first met in 1858.

Chapter Two: Family Happiness

1. *The Diaries of Sophia Tolstoy,* 840. The episode describing the wedding comes from *The Diaries*.
2. Leo Tolstoy, *Anna Karenina,* 445–46.
3. Sophia Tolstoy, "My Life," part 1.
4. *Tolstoy's Diaries,* vol. 1, 168.
5. Sophia Tolstoy, *Who's to Blame? Oktyabr',* no. 10, 1994.
6. *The Diaries of Sophia Tolstoy,* 3.
7. Leo Tolstoy, *War and Peace,* trans. Richard Pevear and Larissa Volokhonsky (New York: Alfred A. Knopf, 2007), 1149.
8. Kuzminskaia, *Tolstoy as I Knew Him,* 123. SA letter and LN's postscript come from Kuzminskaia's memoir.
9. Tolstoy's brother Sergei Nikolaevich.
10. *Tolstoy's Letters,* vol. 1, 169.
11. Ibid., 173.
12. The railroad was completed in November 1867.
13. *The Diaries of Sophia Tolstoy,* 8.
14. Ibid., 6.
15. *Tolstoy's Diaries,* vol. 1, 168.
16. SA letter to TA, November 11, 1862. Unless otherwise specified, translation is by the author.
17. *Tolstoy's Diaries,* vol. 1, 168.

18. Ibid.
19. Sophia Tolstoy, "My Life," part 2.
20. The painting is in the L. N. Tolstoy State Museum in Moscow.
21. *The Diaries of Sophia Tolstoy,* 9. This episode and SA's dream come from *The Diaries*.
22. *Tolstoy's Letters,* vol. 1, 177–79.
23. Kuzminskaia, *Tolstoy as I Knew Him,* 136.
24. Sophia Tolstoy, "My Life," part 2.
25. Ibid.
26. *Tolstoy's Diaries,* vol. 1, 174.
27. Ibid., 174–75.
28. *The Diaries of Sophia Tolstoy,* 11.
29. *Tolstoy's Diaries,* vol. 1, 175.
30. *The Diaries of Sophia Tolstoy,* 10–13.
31. Ibid., 14.
32. Kuzminskaia, *Tolstoy as I Knew Him,* 139.
33. *Tolstoy's Diaries,* vol. 1, 169.
34. *The Diaries of Sophia Tolstoy,* 14–15.
35. Kuzminskaia, *Tolstoy as I Knew Him,* 144.
36. *Tolstoy's Diaries,* vol. 1, 176.
37. *The Diaries of Sophia Tolstoy,* 14.
38. *Tolstoy's Diaries,* vol. 1, 176.
39. Ibid., 178.
40. Sophia Tolstoy, "My Life," part 2.
41. *Tolstoy's Letters,* vol. 1, 180.
42. SA letter to TA, February 13, 1863.
43. Kuzminskaia, *Tolstoy as I Knew Him,* 171.
44. Sophia Tolstoy, "My Life," part 2.
45. A. A. Fet, *Moi vospominaniya* (Munich: Wilhelm Fink Verlag, 1971), 425–26.
46. Sophia Tolstoy, "My Life," part 2.
47. Sophia Tolstoy, "The Autobiography" in *The Two Wives: Tolstoy and Dostoevsky* (Berlin: Izclatelstvo, Pisatelei, 1925), 24. Translation is by the author.
48. Maria Petrovna Fet came from a distinguished family. Sophia would meet one of her brothers, the renowned clinician Sergei Botkin.
49. *The Diaries of Sophia Tolstoy,* 21.
50. *Tolstoy's Diaries,* vol. 1, 177.
51. SA letter to TA, May 6, 1863.
52. SA letter to TA, May 12, 1863.
53. *Tolstoy's Diaries,* vol. 1, 179.
54. Leo Tolstoy, *War and Peace,* 324.
55. Ibid., 1157.
56. Mastitis is inflammation of the breast usually caused by infection.
57. Kuzminskaia, *Tolstoy as I Knew Him,* 211.
58. *The Diaries of Sophia Tolstoy,* 22. This episode and LN's note come from *The Diaries*.
59. Kuzminskaia, *Tolstoy as I Knew Him,* 196.
60. Likely the war in the North Caucasus in which he had participated as a young man.
61. *The Diaries of Sophia Tolstoy,* 24–25.

Chapter Three: Natasha

1. Kuzminskaia, *Tolstoy as I Knew Him,* 233.
2. Sophia Tolstoy, "My Life," part 1.
3. Sophia Tolstoy, "The Autobiography," 17.

4. *Tolstoy's Letters,* vol. 1, 76.
5. *The Diaries of Sophia Tolstoy,* 17.
6. SA letter to Semyon Vengerov, May 5, 1914.
7. Sophia Tolstoy, "The Autobiography," 15–16.
8. *The Diaries of Sophia Tolstoy,* 27.
9. Kuzminskaia, *Tolstoy as I Knew Him,* 211.
10. Ibid., 255.
11. Behrs letter to SA, January 1864.
12. Sophia Tolstoy, "My Life," part 2.
13. SA letter to LN, December 7, 1864.
14. LN letter to SA, December 11, 1864.
15. Sophia Tolstoy, "My Life," part 2.
16. SA letter to LN, December 7, 1864.
17. Sophia Tolstoy, "My Life," part 2.
18. *Tolstoy's Letters,* vol. 1, 182.
19. *The Diaries of Sophia Tolstoy,* 41.
20. LN letter to Alexandrine, July 5, 1865.
21. SA letter to LN, November 25, 1864.
22. SA letter to LN, August 10, 1864.
23. LN letter to SA, August 9, 1864.
24. SA letter to LN, April 23, 1864.
25. LN letter to SA, April 23–24, 1864.
26. SA letter to LN, November 12, 1866.
27. LN letter to TA, October 25–26, 1864.
28. Diminutive of Sophia.
29. SA letter to LN, December 9, 1864.
30. SA letter to LN, November 30, 1864.
31. SA letter to LN, November 26, 1864.
32. SA letter to LN, November 25, 1864.
33. Ibid.
34. *Tolstoy's Letters,* vol. 1, 187.
35. SA letter to LN, November 22, 1864.
36. *Tolstoy's Letters,* vol. 1, 187.
37. A printer's page in the *Russian Herald* contained thirty-four thousand characters.
38. SA letter to LN, December 3, 1864.
39. Kuzminskaia, *Tolstoy as I Knew Him,* 288.
40. SA letter to LN, December 5, 1864.
41. LN letter to SA, December 4, 1864.
42. LN letter to SA, December 6, 1864.
43. Ibid.
44. *Tolstoy's Letters,* vol. 1, 190.
45. Sophia Tolstoy, "The Autobiography," 18.
46. SA letter to LN, November 30, 1864.
47. SA letter to LN, December 5, 1864.
48. An old oak grove on the Yasnaya Polyana estate.
49. SA letter to LN, December 9, 1864.
50. Leo Tolstoy, *War and Peace,* 664.
51. Ibid., 475.
52. *Tolstoy's Letters,* vol. 1, 190.
53. LN letter to SA, December 10, 1864.
54. Sophia Tolstoy, "My Life," part 2.
55. Tatyana Tolstoy, *Tolstoy Remembered,* trans. from the French by Derek Coltman (New York: McGraw-Hill, 1977), 38–39.

56. *Tolstoy's Letters,* vol. 1, 192.
57. SA letter to LN, July 29, 1865.
58. SA letter to LN, July 31, 1865.
59. Ibid.
60. LN letter to Alexandrine, February 4, 1866.
61. Sophia Tolstoy, "My Life," part 2.
62. *The Diaries of Sophia Tolstoy,* 41–42.
63. LN letter to SA, November 14, 1866.
64. SA letter to LN, November 14, 1866.
65. *The Diaries of Sophia Tolstoy,* 42.
66. Sophia Tolstoy, "My Life," part 2.
67. Nikolai Gusev, *Chronicle of L. N. Tolstoy's Life and Work* (Moscow: State Literary House, 1958), vol. 1, 346.
68. Kuzminskaia, *Tolstoy as I Knew Him,* 448.
69. *The Diaries of Sophia Tolstoy,* 42–43.
70. Ibid., 42.
71. Sophia Tolstoy, "The Autobiography," 15.
72. *Tolstoy's Letters,* vol. 1, 216.
73. Leo Tolstoy, *War and Peace,* 1116.
74. Kuzminskaia, *Tolstoy as I Knew Him,* 397.
75. Sophia Tolstoy, "My Life," part 2.
76. SA letter to TA, July 27, 1866.
77. *Tolstoy's Letters,* vol. 1, 220.
78. Leo Tolstoy, *War and Peace,* 1154–57.
79. Ibid., 1153.
80. *Tolstoy's Letters,* vol. 1, 221.

Chapter Four: A Shadow Passed between Us

1. SA letter to LN, September 4, 1869.
2. *Tolstoy's Letters,* vol. 1, 222.
3. *The Diaries of Sophia Tolstoy,* 846.
4. LN letter to Fet, October 21, 1869.
5. Sophia Tolstoy, "My Life," part 2.
6. *The Diaries of Sophia Tolstoy,* 844.
7. Ibid., 845.
8. Ibid.
9. Ibid., 846.
10. Leo Tolstoy, *Anna Karenina,* 414.
11. *The Diaries of Sophia Tolstoy,* 46–47.
12. LN letter to SA, July 8–9, 1871.
13. Leo Tolstoy, *Anna Karenina,* 10.
14. SA letter to LN, June 10, 1871.
15. SA letter to LN, July 19, 1871.
16. SA letter to LN, July 1, 1871.
17. *Tolstoy's Letters,* vol. 1, 234.
18. Ibid., 235.
19. Tribesmen's tent.
20. SA letter to LN, July 14, 1871.
21. SA letter to LN, July 10, 1871.
22. Sophia Tolstoy, "My Life," part 2.
23. Ibid.

24. *The Diaries of Sophia Tolstoy,* 46–47.
25. Now Kutaisi, second biggest city of Georgia.
26. SA letters to TA, August 30 and October 10, 1871.
27. *Tolstoy's Letters,* vol. 1, 240–41.
28. SA letter to TA, April 23, 1872.
29. *The Diaries of Sophia Tolstoy,* 847.
30. SA letter to TA, September 20, 1871.
31. SA letter to TA, January 4, 1873.
32. *The Diaries of Sophia Tolstoy,* 47.
33. *Tolstoy's Letters,* vol. 1, 245–46.
34. Tatyana Tolstoy, *Tolstoy Remembered,* 110.
35. SA letter to TA, March 1872.
36. Tatyana Tolstoy, *Tolstoy Remembered,* 110–11.
37. *The Diaries of Sophia Tolstoy,* 847.
38. LN letter to SA, July 14, 1872.
39. *Tolstoy's Letters,* vol. 1, 248.
40. Ibid., 262.
41. SA letter to TA, November 14, 1872.
42. Sophia Tolstoy, "My Life," part 2.
43. SA letter to Stepan Behrs, November 19, 1872.
44. *Tolstoy's Letters,* vol. 1, 230.
45. *The Diaries of Sophia Tolstoy,* 847.
46. SA letter to TA, March 20, 1873.
47. *The Diaries of Sophia Tolstoy,* 845.
48. Ibid., 848.
49. Ibid.
50. Sophia Tolstoy, "My Life," part 2.

Chapter Five: Observing the Artist

1. *The Diaries of Sophia Tolstoy,* 50.
2. SA letter to TA, April 26, 1873.
3. LN letter to TA, May 18, 1873.
4. SA letter to TA, May 18, 1873.
5. LN letter to TA, May 18, 1873.
6. Tatyana Tolstoy, *Tolstoy Remembered,* 138.
7. SA letter to TA, June 22, 1873.
8. The center of Mordovia is Saransk, a city on the Volga. The Mordovian language belongs to the Finno-Ugric family.
9. Finno-Ugrian peoples.
10. Tatyana Tolstoy, *Tolstoy Remembered,* 169.
11. SA letter to TA, July 8, 1873. Quoted in Tatyana Tolstoy's memoir, *Tolstoy Remembered.*
12. SA letter to TA, July 8, 1873.
13. Ibid.
14. Sophia Tolstoy, "My Life," part 2.
15. SA letter to TA, August 25, 1873.
16. *Tolstoy's Letters,* vol. 1, 264.
17. Sophia Tolstoy, "My Life," part 2.
18. *The Diaries of Sophia Tolstoy,* 46.
19. SA letter to TA, September 14, 1873.
20. Sophia Tolstoy, "My Life," part 2.

21. Ibid.
22. Tatyana Tolstoy, *Tolstoy Remembered,* 50.
23. SA letter to LN, July 27, 1871.
24. *The Diaries of Sophia Tolstoy,* 50.
25. Sophia Tolstoy, "My Life," part 2.
26. Leo Tolstoy, *Anna Karenina,* 607.
27. *Tolstoy's Letters,* vol. 1, 268.
28. SA letter to TA, December 19, 1873.
29. SA letter to TA, January 9, 1874.
30. SA letter to TA, December 19, 1873.
31. *Tolstoy's Letters,* vol. 1, 271.
32. SA letter to TA, February 23, 1875.
33. Sophia Tolstoy, "My Life," part 2.
34. Leo Tolstoy, *Anna Karenina,* 265.
35. *Tolstoy's Letters,* vol. 1, 272.
36. SA letter to TA, November 8, 1874.
37. SA letter to Stepan Behrs, November 20, 1874.
38. SA letter to TA, November 26, 1874.
39. SA letter to TA, December 10, 1874.
40. Ibid.
41. SA letter to TA, December 28, 1874.
42. *Tolstoy's Letters*, vol. 1, 275.
43. Ibid.
44. SA letter to TA, February 23, 1875.
45. SA letter to TA, February 27, 1874.
46. Leo Tolstoy, *Anna Karenina,* 607.
47. *Tolstoy's Letters,* vol. 1, 275.
48. Ibid., 277.
49. SA letter to TA, February 23, 1874.
50. Tatyana Tolstoy, *Tolstoy Remembered,* 49.
51. Sophia Tolstoy, "My Life," part 2.
52. SA letter to TA June 27, 1875.
53. LN letter to N. Strakhov, August 25, 1875.
54. LN letter to Fet, November 8–9, 1875.
55. *Tolstoy's Letters,* vol. 1, 283.
56. Sophia Tolstoy, "My Life," part 3.
57. *The Diaries of Sophia Tolstoy,* 51–52.
58. SA letter to TA, January 1877.
59. SA letter to TA, December 12, 1875.
60. *Tolstoy's Letters,* vol. 1, 293.
61. SA letter to TA, early March 1876.
62. Ilya Tolstoy, *Tolstoy, My Father: Reminiscences,* trans. Ann Dunnigan (Chicago: Cowles Book Company, 1971), 97.
63. *Tolstoy's Letters,* vol. 1, 293.
64. LN letter to SA, September 4, 1876.
65. Sophia Tolstoy, "My Life," part 3.
66. Ibid.
67. *The Diaries of Sophia Tolstoy*, 849.
68. SA letter to TA, January 9, 1874.
69. SA letter to TA, December 9, 1876.
70. Strakhov's letter to LN, February 1877.
71. Botkin was also a brother of Maria Petrovna Fet.

72. Alexandrine's letter to LN, January 18, 1877.
73. LN letter to SA, January 16, 1877.
74. *The Diaries of Sophia Tolstoy*, 850–52.
75. Sophia Tolstoy, "My Life," part 3.
76. SA letter to TA, September 28, 1877. The multicolored carpet is in Sophia's bedroom at the Yasnaya Polyana house, covering a table.
77. LN letter to Vladimir Islavin, December 10, 1877.
78. *The Diaries of Sophia Tolstoy,* 851.

Chapter Six: At a Crossroads

1. *The Diaries of Sophia Tolstoy,* 852.
2. SA letter to LN, March 5, 1878.
3. *The Diaries of Sophia Tolstoy,* 853.
4. Ibid., 64.
5. Ibid., 62.
6. SA letter to TA, March 4, 1878.
7. *Tolstoy's Letters,* vol. 1, 320.
8. LN letter to SA, June 22, 1878.
9. Sophia Tolstoy, "My Life," part 2.
10. *Tolstoy's Letters,* vol. 1, 319.
11. Sophia Tolstoy, "Reminiscences about Turgenev," *Oryol Herald,* no. 224, 1903.
12. *The Diaries of Sophia Tolstoy,* 857.
13. "Let anyone who is afraid of death raise his hand."
14. "Well yes, I don't want to die either."
15. Sophia Tolstoy, "Reminiscences about Turgenev."
16. SA letter to TA, March 5, 1879.
17. SA letter to LN, March 7, 1878.
18. *Tolstoy's Letters,* vol. 1, 335.
19. Sophia Tolstoy, "My Life," part 3.
20. SA letter to TA, March 5, 1879.
21. SA letter to TA, March 23, 1879.
22. Nikolai Gusev, *Chronicle of L. N. Tolstoy's Life and Work,* vol. 1, 513.
23. Ibid., 516.
24. SA letter to TA, November 1879.
25. Sophia Tolstoy, "My Life," part 4.
26. SA letter to TA, November 29, 1879.
27. Sophia Tolstoy, "My Life," part 3.
28. *The Diaries of Sophia Tolstoy,* 66.
29. SA letter to TA, April 12, 1879.
30. SA letter to TA, February 15, 1879.
31. *The Diaries of Sophia Tolstoy,* 69.
32. SA letter to TA, February 6, 1880.
33. SA letter to TA, January 9, 1880.
34. SA letter to TA, January 30, 1880.
35. Sophia Tolstoy, "My Life," part 4.
36. Turgenev's letter to LN, January 1880.
37. Sophia Tolstoy, "My Life," part 3.
38. SA letter to TA, February 19, 1880.
39. LN letter to Stasov, May 1, 1881.
40. Italics are by the author.
41. *Tolstoy's Letters,* vol. 2, 340.

42. Ibid., 339.
43. LN letter to SA, August 2, 1881.
44. Polner, *Tolstoy and His Wife,* 134.
45. Sophia Tolstoy, "My Life," part 3.
46. SA letter to LN, August 28, 1880.
47. SA letter to TA, October 1880.
48. SA letter to TA, November 28, 1880.
49. Sophia Tolstoy, "My Life," part 3.
50. Ibid.
51. SA letter to TA, December 8, 1880.
52. Hysteria is arguably the oldest neurological disorder in medicine; yet, there is still no agreement about its nature and causes. Some describe it as a cry for help, inspired by a sense of powerlessness.
53. Sophia Tolstoy, "My Life," part 3.
54. LN letter to SA, November 10, 1883.
55. *The Diaries of Sophia Tolstoy,* 854–55.

Chapter Seven: Life with a Religious Philosopher

1. SA letter to TA, March 3, 1881.
2. Tatyana Tolstoy, *Tolstoy Remembered,* 193.
3. Ilya Tolstoy, *Tolstoy, My Father,* 175.
4. *The Diaries of Sophia Tolstoy,* 1000–1001.
5. LN letter to M. Engelhardt, December 1882.
6. Tolstoy's doctrine of nonresistance was inspired by his study of the Sermon on the Mount, particularly by the Gospel of Matthew, chapter 5, verses 38–44. Beginning with: "Ye have heard that it hath been said, An eye for an eye, and a tooth for a tooth: But I say unto you, That ye resist not evil: but whosoever shall smite thee on thy right cheek, turn to him the other also" (King James Version).
7. See more on this in Aylmer Maude, *The Life of Tolstoy: Later Years,* vol. 2 (London: Oxford University Press, 1930), 249–65.
8. *Tolstoy's Diaries,* vol. 1, 196.
9. Ilya Tolstoy, *Tolstoy, My Father,* 169.
10. *Jubilee Edition,* vol. 83, 100.
11. *Tolstoy's Diaries,* May 4, 1881. Quoted in Aylmer Maude, *The Life of Tolstoy,* 70.
12. SA letter to TA, April 22, 1881.
13. Pointed out in Leo Tolstoy, *Plays: Volume Three,* trans. Marvin Kantor with Tanya Tulchinsky (Evanston, Ill.: Northwestern University Press, 1998).
14. Sophia Tolstoy, "My Life," part 3.
15. Leo Tolstoy, *Plays,* vol. 3, 65.
16. Ibid., 39.
17. About one hundred miles west of Tula, near the ancient town of Kozelsk.
18. Polner, *Tolstoy and His Wife,* 129.
19. *Tolstoy's Letters,* vol. 2, 352.
20. LN letter to SA, June 11, 1881.
21. SA letter to LN, June 12, 1881.
22. The house no longer exists.
23. Sophia Tolstoy, "My Life," part 3.
24. SA letter to LN, August 6, 1881.
25. *Tolstoy's Diaries,* vol. 1, 198.
26. LN letter to SA, July 22–23, 1881.
27. LN letter to SA, August 6, 1881.

28. LN letter to SA, August 2, 1881.
29. SA letter to LN, August 26, 1881.
30. *Tolstoy's Letters,* vol. 2, 347.
31. SA letter to TA, March 12, 1881.
32. SA letter to TA, March 3, 1881.
33. SA letter to TA, April 22, 1881.
34. Sophia Tolstoy, "My Life," part 3.
35. SA letter to TA, September 20, 1881. Quoted in Tatyana Tolstoy, *Tolstoy Remembered.*
36. Sophia Tolstoy, "My Life," part 4.
37. Ibid.
38. SA letter to LN, April 1885.
39. SA letter to TA, October 14, 1881.
40. Sophia Tolstoy, "My Life," part 4.
41. *Tolstoy's Diaries,* vol. 1, 199–200.
42. Ibid., 199.
43. LN letter to SA, February 4, 1882.
44. SA letter to LN, February 4, 1882.
45. SA letter to LN, February 3, 1882.
46. SA letter to LN, February 6, 1882.
47. SA letter to LN, February 7, 1882.
48. Sophia Tolstoy, "My Life," part 4.
49. SA letter to TA, January 30, 1882.
50. Sophia Tolstoy, "My Life," part 4.
51. Anton Rubinstein was the founder and first director of the Petersburg Conservatory.
52. Sophia Tolstoy, "My Life," part 4.
53. Ibid.
54. SA letter to TA, January 1882.
55. Sophia Tolstoy, "My Life," part 4.
56. Ibid.
57. SA letter to LN, March 3, 1882.
58. Sophia Tolstoy, "My Life," part 4.
59. SA letter to LN, March 5, 1882.
60. LN letter to SA, February 27, 1882.
61. SA letter to LN, March 3, 1882.
62. LN letter to SA, March 5, 1882.
63. LN letter to SA, March 4, 1882.
64. SA letter to LN, March 5–6, 1882.
65. *Tolstoy's Letters,* vol. 2, 358.
66. Russian game babki, or knucklebones.
67. SA letter to LN, May 18, 1882.
68. *Tolstoy's Letters,* vol. 2, 355.
69. SA letter to TA, May 2, 1882.
70. Sophia Tolstoy, "My Life," part 4.
71. SA letter to LN, September 28, 1882.
72. Ilya Tolstoy, *Tolstoy, My Father,* 113–14.
73. *The Diaries of Sophia Tolstoy,* 71.
74. Ibid.
75. *Tolstoy's Letters,* vol. 2, 362.
76. *The Diaries of Sophia Tolstoy,* 71.

77. Tatyana Tolstoy, *The Tolstoy Home, Diaries*, trans. Alec Brown (London: Harvill Press, 1950), 29.
78. Ibid., 30.
79. SA letter to TA, November 9, 1882.
80. A realist artist, member of the Wanderers or the Itinerants group.
81. *Jubilee Edition,* vol. 23, 316.
82. Sophia Tolstoy, "My Life," part 4.
83. *Tolstoy's Diaries,* vol. 1, 201.
84. *Tolstoy's Letters,* vol. 2, 363.
85. *Jubilee Edition,* vol. 63, 127.
86. Polner, *Tolstoy and His Wife,* 133.
87. Sophia Tolstoy, "My Life," part 4.
88. *The Diaries of Sophia Tolstoy,* 75.

Chapter Eight: Separate Lives

1. SA letter to TA, January 9, 1883.
2. Prince Shcherbatov would go down in history as a brilliant city administrator who did much for the public good and was recognized as Moscow's first honorary citizen.
3. Sophia Tolstoy, "My Life," part 4.
4. SA letter to TA, January 3, 1883.
5. *The Diaries of Sophia Tolstoy,* 72.
6. Ibid., 73.
7. Sophia Tolstoy, "My Life," part 4.
8. SA letter to LN, June 23, 1883.
9. *The Diaries of Sophia Tolstoy,* 73.
10. SA letter to TA, February 10, 1883.
11. SA letter to TA, January 30, 1883.
12. *Jubilee Edition,* vol. 83, 579.
13. Sophia Tolstoy, "My Life," part 4.
14. LN letter to SA, June 8, 1883.
15. SA letter to LN, June 15, 1883.
16. SA letter to LN, June 21, 1883.
17. LN letter to SA, June 15, 1883.
18. LN letter to SA, May 25, 1883.
19. SA letter to LN, June 2, 1883.
20. SA letter to LN, May 29, 1883.
21. LN letter to SA, June 8, 1883.
22. LN letter to SA, June 2, 1883.
23. SA letter to LN, June 7, 1883.
24. SA letter to LN, June 2, 1883.
25. SA letter to LN, June 7, 1883.
26. SA letter to LN, June 2, 1883.
27. SA letter to LN, June 7, 1883.
28. SA letter to LN, June 2, 1883.
29. SA letter to LN, June 7, 1883.
30. Sophia Tolstoy, "My Life," part 4.
31. *Jubilee Edition,* vol. 23, 550.
32. SA letter to LN, October 1, 1883.
33. SA letter to LN, September 28, 1883.
34. LN letter to SA, November 13, 1883.

35. SA letter to LN, November 14, 1883.
36. SA letter to TA, January 1884.
37. LN letter to SA, November 10, 1883.
38. SA letter to LN, November 12, 1883.
39. LN letter to SA, November 15, 1883.
40. SA letter to TA, October 9, 1883.
41. Tatyana Tolstoy, *The Tolstoy Home, Diaries,* 56.
42. SA letter to LN, January 31, 1884.
43. SA letter to LN, February 5, 1884.
44. SA letter to TA, February 5, 1884.
45. SA letter to LN, October 23, 1884.
46. Ibid.
47. *Tolstoy's Diaries,* vol. 1, 208.
48. SA letter to TA, March 22, 1884.
49. *Tolstoy's Diaries,* vol. 1, 203–5.
50. Sophia Tolstoy, "My Life," part 4.
51. *Tolstoy's Diaries,* vol. 1, 206.
52. GMT; the letter was first quoted by Tatyana Komarova.
53. *Tolstoy's Diaries,* vol. 1, 208.
54. Ibid., 211.
55. Ibid., 212.
56. SA letter to LN, December 9, 1884.
57. *Tolstoy's Letters,* vol. 2, 395.
58. Ibid., 368.
59. SA letter to LN, February 22, 1885.
60. Sophia Tolstoy, "My Life," part 4.
61. SA letter to LN, January 30, 1884.
62. M. V. Muratov, *L. N. Tolstoy and V. G. Chertkov,* trans. Scott D. Moss (Tenafly, N.J.: Hermitage Publishers, 2002), 33.
63. Ibid., 48.
64. LN letter to Chertkov, July 24, 1884.
65. *Tolstoy's Diaries,* vol. 1, 218.
66. Sophia Tolstoy, "My Life," part 4.
67. LN letter to Chertkov, June 24, 1884.
68. Sophia Tolstoy, "My Life," part 4.
69. *Tolstoy's Diaries,* vol. 1, 222.
70. SA letter to LN, October 31, 1884.
71. *Tolstoy's Diaries,* vol. 1, 221.
72. Sophia Tolstoy, "My Life," part 4.
73. *Tolstoy's Diaries,* vol. 1, 223.
74. SA letter to TA, September 23, 1884.
75. LN letter to SA, October 26, 1884.
76. SA letter to LN, October 27, 1884.
77. LN letter to SA, October 27, 1884.
78. SA letter to LN, October 29, 1884.
79. LN letter to SA, October 27, 1884.
80. SA letter to LN, October 29, 1884.
81. SA letter to TA, December 4, 1884.
82. Sophia Tolstoy, "My Life," part 4.
83. LN letter to Chertkov, May 13–14, 1885.
84. SA letter to TA, January 9, 1885.
85. SA letter to LN, October 29, 1884.

86. LN letter to SA, October 24, 1884.
87. SA letter to LN, October 25, 1884.
88. Sophia Tolstoy, "My Life," part 4.
89. SA letter to TA, January 1885.
90. Tatyana Tolstoy, *Tolstoy Remembered,* 211.

Chapter Nine: The Money Brought Me No Joy

1. Anna Dostoevsky, *Dostoevsky: Reminiscences,* trans. Beatrice Stillman (New York: Liveright, 1975), 363.
2. Ibid., 362.
3. SA letter to LN, February 24, 1885.
4. Sophia Tolstoy, "My Life," part 4.
5. Ibid.
6. *The Diaries of Sophia Tolstoy,* 77.
7. *Tolstoy's Letters,* vol. 2, 378.
8. SA letter to LN, March 9, 1885.
9. SA letter to TA, April 12, 1885.
10. SA letter to LN, March 15, 1885.
11. *Tolstoy's Diaries,* vol. 1, 226.
12. *Tolstoy's Letters,* vol. 2, 383–84.
13. Sophia Tolstoy, "My Life," part 4.
14. Tatyana Tolstoy, *Tolstoy Remembered,* 210.
15. Sophia Tolstoy, "My Life," part 4
16. Ibid.
17. Sophia Tolstoy, "My Life," part 5.
18. LN letter to SA, August 19, 1885.
19. SA letter to LN, October 13, 1885.
20. LN letter to SA, October 18, 1885.
21. SA letter to LN, October 23, 1884.
22. SA letter to LN, October 13, 1885.
23. *Tolstoy's Letters,* vol. 2, 386–87.
24. Sophia Tolstoy, "My Life," part 4.
25. LN letter to SA, November 20, 1885.
26. SA letter to LN, November 24, 1885.
27. SA letter to LN, November 25, 1885.
28. Sophia Tolstoy, "My Life," part 4.
29. SA letter was first published by Tatyana Nikiforova in 2004.
30. *Tolstoy's Letters,* vol. 2, 392.
31. SA letter to TA, fall 1885.
32. *Tolstoy's Letters,* vol. 2, 397.
33. SA letter to TA, December 20, 1885.
34. Tatyana Tolstoy, *Tolstoy Remembered,* 202.
35. SA letter to TA, December 20, 1885.
36. Tatyana Tolstoy, *Tolstoy Remembered,* 204.
37. LN letter to SA, December 21–22, 1885.
38. SA letter to LN, December 26, 1885.
39. SA letter to LN, December 24, 1885.
40. SA letter to LN, December 23, 1885.
41. SA letter to LN, December 24, 1885.
42. SA letter to LN, December 26, 1885.
43. SA letter to TA, January 9, 1886.

44. *The Diaries of Sophia Tolstoy,* 75.
45. Sophia Tolstoy, "My Life," part 4.
46. SA letter to TA, January 20, 1886.
47. LN letter to Chertkov, January 18, 1886.
48. SA letter to TA, March 2, 1886.
49. SA letter to TA, February 13, 1886.
50. SA letter to TA, March 2, 1886.
51. Strakhov's letter was first published in *Yasnaya Polyana Almanach* (Tula: 1978).
52. *Tolstoy's Letters,* vol. 2, 402.
53. SA letter to Strakhov, June 21, 1886.
54. *The Diaries of Sophia Tolstoy,* 75.
55. Ibid., 80.
56. Ibid., 75.
57. Sophia Tolstoy, "My Life," part 4.
58. *The Diaries of Sophia Tolstoy,* 77.
59. Ibid., 78.
60. SA letter to LN, January 10, 1887.
61. Ibid.
62. Feoktistov letter to SA, January 9, 1887.
63. *The Diaries of Sophia Tolstoy,* 79.

Chapter Ten: The Martyr and the Martyress

1. Initially called "On Life and Death."
2. Sophia Tolstoy, "My Life," part 5.
3. SA letter to TA, November 18, 1887.
4. *The Diaries of Sophia Tolstoy,* 79.
5. Ibid.
6. Sophia Tolstoy, *Letters to Tolstoy,* 383.
7. SA letter to LN, January 10, 1887.
8. *The Diaries of Sophia Tolstoy,* 78.
9. Among the executed conspirators was Alexander Ulyanov, a member of the notorious organization People's Will and brother of Vladimir Ulyanov (Lenin), future head of the Socialist state.
10. *The Diaries of Sophia Tolstoy,* 82.
11. Ibid.
12. Ivan Bunin, *The Liberation of Tolstoy* (Evanston, Ill.: Northwestern University Press, 2001), 42.
13. *The Diaries of Sophia Tolstoy,* 85.
14. SA letter to LN, April 14, 1887.
15. *The Diaries of Sophia Tolstoy,* 80.
16. SA letter to TA, January 5, 1888.
17. Sophia Tolstoy, "My Life," part 5.
18. SA letter to TA, May 6, 1887.
19. *The Diaries of Sophia Tolstoy,* 79.
20. LN letter to SA, April 7, 1887.
21. SA letter to LN, April 13, 1887.
22. SA letter to LN, April 4, 1887.
23. SA letter to LN, April 3, 1887.
24. SA letter to LN, April 4, 1887.
25. *The Diaries of Sophia Tolstoy,* 86.
26. Ibid., 111.

27. Ibid., 84.
28. Ibid., 82.
29. Sophia Tolstoy, "My Life," part 5.
30. Ibid., 5.
31. SA letter to TA, January 25, 1888.
32. Tatyana Tolstoy, *The Tolstoy Home,* 130.
33. SA letter to TA, April 11, 1888.
34. Polner, *Tolstoy and His Wife,* 84.
35. Sophia Tolstoy, "My Life," part 5.
36. Ibid.
37. Tatyana Tolstoy, *Tolstoy Remembered,* 23.
38. LN letter to SA, May 5, 1888.
39. Sophia Tolstoy, "My Life," part 5.
40. SA letter to LN, May 1, 1888.
41. *Tolstoy's Diaries,* vol. 1, 212.
42. Sophia Tolstoy, "My Life," part 4.

Chapter Eleven: Who's to Blame?

1. Bunin, *The Liberation of Tolstoy,* 55.
2. Sophia Tolstoy, "My Life," part 5.
3. Strakhov's letter to Tolstoy, May 21, 1890.
4. Sophia Tolstoy, "My Life," part 5.
5. SA letter to TA, March 13, 1889.
6. SA letter to TA, October 12, 1888.
7. SA letter to LN, May 11, 1888.
8. Sophia Tolstoy, "My Life," part 5.
9. SA letter to TA, December 8, 1888.
10. Sophia Tolstoy, "My Life," part 5.
11. *Tolstoy's Diaries,* vol. 1, 244.
12. SA letter to LN, March 28, 1889.
13. *Tolstoy's Diaries,* vol. 1, 233.
14. Ibid., 238.
15. Sophia Tolstoy, "My Life," part 5.
16. *Tolstoy's Diaries,* vol. 1, 237.
17. SA letter to LN, March 28, 1889.
18. SA letter to LN, March 31, 1889.
19. Kuzminskaia, *Tolstoy as I Knew Him,* 269.
20. Sophia Tolstoy, "My Life," part 5.
21. Strakhov's letter to Tolstoy, November 6, 1889.
22. *The Kreutzer Sonata,* in *Tolstoy's Short Fiction,* ed. and trans. Michael R. Katz (New York: Norton, 1991), 206.
23. Sophia Tolstoy, "My Life," part 3.
24. Ibid., part 5.
25. *The Kreutzer Sonata,* 189.
26. Ilya Tolstoy, *Tolstoy, My Father,* 217.
27. *The Kreutzer Sonata,* 191.
28. *Tolstoy's Diaries,* vol. 1, 271.
29. Sophia Tolstoy, "My Life," part 5.
30. *The Diaries of Sophia Tolstoy,* 371.
31. Sophia Tolstoy, "My Life," part 5.
32. Leo Tolstoy, *Plays,* vol. 3, 96.

33. Tatyana Tolstoy, *The Tolstoy Home,* 146.
34. *Tolstoy's Diaries,* vol. 1, 261.
35. SA letter to TA, March 1889.
36. SA letter to TA, December 7, 1889.
37. *Tolstoy's Diaries,* vol. 1, 273.
38. Strakhov's letter to Tolstoy, April 24, 1890.
39. *The Diaries of Sophia Tolstoy,* 144.
40. *Jubilee Edition,* vol. 51, 85.
41. *The Diaries of Sophia Tolstoy,* 123.
42. Sophia Tolstoy, "My Life," part 5.
43. SA letter to TA, February 7, 1891.
44. *The Diaries of Sophia Tolstoy,* 94.
45. Ibid., 95.
46. Ibid.
47. Ibid., 92–93.
48. Ibid., 122.
49. *Tolstoy's Diaries,* vol. 1, 304.
50. *The Diaries of Sophia Tolstoy,* 889.
51. Ibid., 132.
52. SA letter to TA, April 15, 1891.
53. *The Diaries of Sophia Tolstoy,* 141.
54. Ibid., 157.
55. Ibid., 155.
56. SA letter to LN, October 25, 1891.
57. Sophia Tolstoy, "My Life," part 5.
58. *The Diaries of Sophia Tolstoy,* 107.
59. See more in Peter Møller, *Postlude to the Kreutzer Sonata* (New York: E. J. Brill, 1988.)
60. Bunin, *The Liberation of Tolstoy,* 64.
61. Sophia Tolstoy, "My Life," part 6.

Chapter Twelve: The Brotherhood of People

1. *Tolstoy's Letters,* vol. 2, 480–81.
2. One pood equals about thirty-six pounds.
3. *The Diaries of Sophia Tolstoy,* 168.
4. Ibid., 164.
5. Ibid., 167.
6. SA letter to LN, November 6, 1891.
7. LN letter to SA, November 7, 1891.
8. *The Diaries of Sophia Tolstoy,* 169.
9. SA letter to LN, November 20, 1891.
10. LN letter to SA, November 28, 1891.
11. *Tolstoy's Letters,* vol. 2, 489.
12. SA letter to TA, January 8, 1892.
13. *Tolstoy's Letters,* vol. 2, 487.
14. *Tolstoy's Diaries,* vol. 1, 316.
15. SA letter to LN, December 17, 1891.
16. *Tolstoy's Diaries,* vol. 1, 317.
17. The episode is drawn from *The Diaries of Sophia Tolstoy,* 173.
18. Sophia Tolstoy, "My Life," part 6.
19. Ibid.

20. *Tolstoy's Diaries,* vol. 1, 315.
21. LN letter to SA, November 25, 1891.
22. *The Diaries of Sophia Tolstoy,* 895.
23. SA letter to TA, February 28, 1892.
24. SA letter to TA, March 4, 1892.
25. SA letter to LN, February 6, 1892.
26. SA letter to LN, February 11, 1892.
27. SA letter to LN, February 16, 1892.
28. SA letter to TA, February 28, 1892.
29. LN letter to SA, July 19, 1892.
30. Chertkov letter to LN, April 16, 1892.
31. Ibid.
32. SA letter to Chertkov, May 14, 1892.
33. Chertkov letter to LN, March 18, 1892.
34. Strakhov letter to LN, March 27, 1895.
35. *Tolstoy's Letters,* vol. 2, 488.
36. SA letter to Strakhov, January 13, 1893.

Chapter Thirteen: I Long to Be Alone with My Family

1. SA letter to TA, April 21, 1891.
2. *The Diaries of Sophia Tolstoy,* 125.
3. *Tolstoy's Diaries,* vol. 1, 318.
4. *The Diaries of Sophia Tolstoy,* 146.
5. SA letter to LN, November 9, 1892.
6. SA letter to LN, February 21, 1892.
7. SA letter to LN, November 8, 1892.
8. Sophia Tolstoy, "My Life," part 6.
9. An illegitimate son of a German mother and a Russian nobleman, Fet had struggled for much of his life to attain legitimacy and this change of name.
10. Sophia Tolstoy, "My Life," part 6.
11. SA letter to Strakhov, January 13, 1893.
12. SA letter to LN, February 25, 1893.
13. SA letter to Strakhov, February 23, 1893.
14. Strakhov letter to SA, September 24, 1893.
15. LN letter to SA, November 17, 1898.
16. SA letter to LN, October 23, 1893.
17. *Tolstoy's Diaries,* vol. 1, 327.
18. Ibid., 331.
19. Strakhov's letter to SA, April 27, 1893.
20. SA letter to LN, September 16, 1893.
21. *The Diaries of Sophia Tolstoy,* 175.
22. Sophia's translations were often not credited to her, like this book. Her correspondence with Tolstoy establishes that she translated it.
23. Paul Sabatier, *Life of St. Francis of Assisi* (New York: Charles Scribner's Sons, 1916), 13.
24. *The Diaries of Sophia Tolstoy,* 895.
25. Her official name was Anna.
26. Tatyana Tolstoy, *The Tolstoy Home,* 248.
27. Ibid., 207–8.
28. Ibid., 256.
29. *Jubilee Edition,* vol. 88, 108–9.

30. *The Diaries of Sophia Tolstoy,* 315.
31. Lev had surplus money because Sophia had paid him fifty-eight thousand rubles as settlement for their Moscow house, his share of the inheritance.
32. Maude, *The Life of Tolstoy: Later Years,* 202.
33. Alexandra Tolstoy, *The Daughter* (Moscow: Vagrius, 2000), 43.
34. *The Diaries of Sophia Tolstoy,* 177.
35. SA letter to TA, July 12, 1894.
36. LN letter to SA, October 25, 1894.
37. *Tolstoy's Diaries,* vol. 1, 338.
38. SA letter to LN, September 11, 1894.
39. LN letter to SA, September 18, 1894.
40. The Yalta Conference was held there in 1945.
41. Tatyana Tolstoy, *The Tolstoy Home, Diaries,* 259.
42. SA letter to LN, October 28, 1894.
43. *Tolstoy's Diaries,* vol. 1, 342.
44. SA letter to TA, October 16, 1894.
45. SA letter to LN, October 31, 1894.
46. Tolstoy's diary, November 14, 1909. In *Jubilee Edition,* vol. 57, 171.
47. *The Diaries of Sophia Tolstoy,* 180.
48. *Tolstoy's Diaries,* vol. 1, 343.
49. SA letter to LN, January 9, 1895.
50. *The Diaries of Sophia Tolstoy,* 184.
51. Shock therapy was used in the second part of the nineteenth century to treat patients with "nervous diseases." Several electrodes were applied to different parts of the body. Patients claimed the tingling sensation relieved their symptoms.
52. *The Diaries of Sophia Tolstoy,* 182.
53. *Tolstoy's Diaries,* vol. 2, 399–400.
54. LN letter to SA, May 19, 1897.
55. *The Diaries of Sophia Tolstoy,* 190.
56. Ibid., 191.
57. Sophia Tolstoy, "My Life," part 7.

Chapter Fourteen: A Song without Words

1. *Tolstoy's Letters,* vol. 2, 517.
2. *The Diaries of Sophia Tolstoy,* 861.
3. SA letter to TA, March 7, 1895.
4. *The Diaries of Sophia Tolstoy,* 860.
5. *Tolstoy's Diaries,* vol. 2, 401.
6. Ibid., 404.
7. *The Diaries of Sophia Tolstoy,* 861.
8. It was published in her collection of prose poems, in the *Monthly Journal for All,* no. 3, 1904.
9. SA letter to LN, October 24, 1895.
10. SA letter to TA, November 27, 1894.
11. Sophia Tolstoy, "My Life," part 3.
12. Ibid., part 7.
13. Sophia Tolstoy, "Song without Words," GMT.
14. SA letter to TA, December 10, 1895.
15. Sophia Tolstoy, "My Life," part 3.
16. See more about this in Oliver Sacks, *Musicophilia* (New York: Alfred A. Knopf, 2007).

17. SA letter to LN, October 12, 1895.
18. *Tolstoy's Diaries,* vol. 2, 418.
19. Ibid., 419.
20. LN letter to SA, October 25, 1895.
21. SA letter to LN, October 26, 1895.
22. SA letter to Leonila Annenkova, fall 1896.
23. LN letter to Chertkov, March 11, 1897.
24. *Tolstoy's Letters,* vol. 2, 440.
25. SA letter to TA, October 24, 1896.
26. *The Diaries of Sophia Tolstoy,* 291.
27. Sophia Tolstoy, "My Life," part 3.
28. *Tolstoy's Letters,* vol. 2, 555.
29. SA letter to Annenkova, February 19, 1897.
30. SA letter to TA, May 15, 1897.
31. *Tolstoy's Letters,* vol. 2, 557.
32. *Tolstoy's Diaries,* vol. 2, 439.
33. *The Diaries of Sophia Tolstoy,* 267.
34. *Tolstoy's Letters,* vol. 2, 559.
35. *Jubilee Edition,* vol. 84, 284–85.
36. *The Diaries of Sophia Tolstoy,* 211.
37. *Tolstoy's Letters,* vol. 2, 564–65.
38. *The Diaries of Sophia Tolstoy,* 233.
39. Ibid., 256.
40. Ibid., 226.
41. Ibid., 258.
42. Ibid., 254.
43. Sophia Tolstoy, "My Life," part 7.
44. *The Diaries of Sophia Tolstoy,* 243.
45. Ibid., 391.
46. Sophia Tolstoy, "Song without Words."
47. *The Diaries of Sophia Tolstoy,* 321.
48. Ibid., 379.
49. Ibid., 411.
50. Ibid., 274.

Chapter Fifteen: In Life's Whirlpool

1. *Tolstoy's Letters,* vol. 2, 561–62.
2. *Tolstoy's Diaries,* vol. 2, 418.
3. *The Diaries of Sophia Tolstoy,* 355. Unless otherwise specified, information and quotations in this chapter come from *The Diaries,* 1898–1902.
4. SA letter to LN, May 9, 1898.
5. *Tolstoy's Diaries,* vol. 2, 465.
6. Ibid., 444.
7. SA letter to TA, January 10, 1900.
8. SA letter to LN, October 29, 1895.
9. Sophia Tolstoy, "My Life," part 7.
10. LN letter to SA, November 3–4, 1899.
11. SA letter to TA, January 10, 1900.
12. Now the Great Hall of Columns.
13. Sophia Tolstoy, "My Life," part 8. Also see *The Diaries,* 916.

14. Maxim Gorky, *Collected Works in Ten Volumes,* vol. 9, *Literary Portraits* (Moscow: Progress Publishers, 1982), 159.
15. Now Myanmar.
16. It was published unaccredited and abridged in 1911, in Tolstoy's collection *A Cycle of Reading*. This fact was established by Tatyana Nikiforova at GMT.

Chapter Sixteen: The Line Has Been Drawn

1. *The Diaries of Sophia Tolstoy,* 470–71. Unless otherwise specified, all information and quotations in this chapter come from *The Diaries,* 1901–8.
2. Maude, *The Life of Tolstoy: Later Years,* 427–28.
3. Alexandra Tolstoy, *The Daughter,* 103.
4. *Tolstoy's Diaries,* vol. 2, 403–4.
5. SA letter to TA, April 28, 1903.
6. SA letter to TA, July 2, 1903.
7. SA letter to TA, May 16, 1904.
8. SA letter to TA, September 27, 1903.
9. SA letter to TA, February 10, 1906.
10. *Tolstoy's Diaries,* vol. 2, 517.
11. SA letter to TA, February 1, 1904.
12. SA letter to TA, March 24, 1904.
13. SA letter to TA, March 28, 1904.
14. SA letter to TA, May 16, 1904.
15. Alexander Goldenweiser, *Lev Tolstoy: Reminiscences* (Moscow: Zakharov, 2002), 166.
16. *Tolstoy's Diaries,* vol. 2, 555–56.
17. SA letter to TA, November 26, 1906.
18. SA letter to Annenkova, September 21, 1907.
19. SA letter to TA, May 20, 1907.
20. *Tolstoy's Diaries,* vol. 2, 570.
21. SA letter to TA, January 10, 1907.

Chapter Seventeen: In the Name of Universal Love

1. Alexandra Tolstoy, *Tolstoy: A Life of My Father* (London: Victor Gollancz Limited, 1953), 465.
2. *Tolstoy's Diaries,* vol. 2, 580.
3. SA letter to TA, March 10, 1908.
4. *The Diaries of Sophia Tolstoy,* 491–92.
5. Ibid., 649.
6. LN letter to Evgeny Popov, January 17, 1908.
7. LN letter to Vasiliev, March 7, 1909.
8. *Tolstoy's Diaries,* vol. 2, 585.
9. Quoted in Nikolai Gusev, *Chronicle of L. N. Tolstoy's Life and Work* (Moscow: State Literary House, 1960), vol. 2, 634.
10. *Tolstoy's Diaries,* vol. 2, 572.
11. Goldenweiser, *Lev Tolstoy: Reminiscences,* 184.
12. Ibid., 182.
13. *The Diaries of Sophia Tolstoy,* 494.
14. Ibid., 492.
15. Tolstoy's letter to Alexandra, May 1910.
16. *The Diaries of Sophia Tolstoy,* 584.

17. Ibid., 486.
18. SA letter to TA, July 27, 1908.
19. *The Diaries of Sophia Tolstoy,* 494.
20. Ibid., 633.
21. Ibid., 644.
22. SA letter to TA, June 15, 1908.
23. Alexandra Tolstoy, *Out of the Past,* ed. Katharine Strelsky and Catherine Wolkonsky (New York: Columbia University Press, 1981), 96–97.
24. *The Diaries of Sophia Tolstoy,* 519.
25. Maude, *The Life of Tolstoy: Later Years,* vol. 2, 478.
26. *Tolstoy's Diaries,* vol. 2, 589.
27. *The Diaries of Sophia Tolstoy,* 640.
28. Ibid., 643.
29. Ibid., 646.
30. Ibid., 647.
31. *Tolstoy's Diaries,* vol. 2, 633.
32. SA letter to TA, December 4, 1909.
33. *Tolstoy's Diaries,* vol. 2, 664.
34. Ibid., 638.
35. Ibid., 636.
36. *Jubilee Edition,* vol. 57, 163.
37. *Tolstoy's Diaries,* vol. 2, 643.
38. Ibid., 646.
39. Valentin Bulgakov, *The Last Year of Leo Tolstoy* (New York: Dial Press, 1971), xxiv.
40. Dushan Makovitsky, *The Yasnaya Polyana Notes,* vol. 1 (Moscow: Nauka, 1979), 438. Translation is by the author.
41. *The Diaries of Sophia Tolstoy,* 664.
42. Goldenweiser, *Lev Tolstoy: Reminiscences,* 306–7.
43. *The Diaries of Sophia Tolstoy,* 672.
44. Ibid., 676.
45. From unpublished portions of Sophia Tolstoy's diaries kept at The L. N. Tolstoy State Museum.
46. *The Diaries of Sophia Tolstoy,* 498.
47. Ibid., 536.
48. Ibid., 924–25.
49. Alexandra Tolstoy, *The Daughter,* 158.
50. *The Diaries of Sophia Tolstoy,* 502.
51. Ibid., 537.
52. Ibid., 505.
53. Bulgakov, *The Last Year of Leo Tolstoy,* 158.
54. Ibid., 167.
55. *Tolstoy's Diaries,* vol. 2, 678.
56. *Tolstoy's Letters,* vol. 2, 703.
57. Ibid., 704.
58. *The Diaries of Sophia Tolstoy,* 498.
59. Alexandra Tolstoy, *Tolstoy: A Life of My Father,* 496–97.
60. Goldenweiser, *Lev Tolstoy: Reminiscences,* 423.
61. *The Diaries of Sophia Tolstoy,* 529.
62. Bulgakov, *The Last Year of Leo Tolstoy,* 171.
63. *Tolstoy's Letters,* vol. 2, 705.
64. SA letter to LN, July 24–25, 1910.

65. *The Diaries of Sophia Tolstoy,* 529.
66. Bulgakov, *The Last Year of Leo Tolstoy,* 185.
67. *Tolstoy's Diaries,* vol. 2, 683.
68. An epileptic seizure may occur in the wake of a stroke.
69. *The Diaries of Sophia Tolstoy,* 570.
70. Ibid., 577.
71. Ibid., 586.
72. *Tolstoy's Diaries,* vol. 2, 687.
73. *Jubilee Edition,* vol. 89, 231.
74. *Tolstoy's Diaries,* vol. 2, 676.
75. *The Diaries of Sophia Tolstoy,* 586.
76. *Tolstoy's Letters,* vol. 2, 710–11.
77. Quoted in the almanac *Dni Nashei skorbi [Days of Our Mourning],* collection of articles and reports about L. N. Tolstoy's final days (Moscow: Student Life, 1911), 72.
78. *Jubilee Edition,* vol. 58, 573.
79. *Tolstoy's Letters,* vol. 2, 713.
80. SA letter to LN, October 29, 1910.
81. SA letter to LN, November 1, 1910.
82. Bulgakov, *The Last Year of Leo Tolstoy,* 228–29.
83. Quoted in the almanac *Days of Our Mourning,* 112–13.
84. Makovitsky, *The Yasnaya Polyana Notes,* vol. 4, 420.
85. Ibid., 426.
86. Sophia Tolstoy, "Autobiography," 53.
87. Makovitsky, *Yasnaya Polyana Notes,* vol. 4, 431.
88. Sophia Tolstoy, "Autobiography," 53.
89. Makovitsky, *Yasnaya Polyana Notes,* vol. 4, 432.
90. Sergei Tolstoy, *Tolstoy Remembered By His Son,* trans. Moura Budberg (London: Weidenfield and Nicolson, 1961), 147.

Chapter Eighteen: And the Light Shineth in Darkness

1. *The Diaries of Sophia Tolstoy,* 679. Unless otherwise specified, all information and quotations in this chapter come from *The Diaries,* 1910–19.
2. Vladimir Snegirev letter to SA, April 10, 1911.
3. Boris Svadkovsky, "Sophia Tolstaia: The Unpublished Letters from the 'Steel Room' in *Sovershenno Sekretno,*" no. 3, 1992.
4. SA letter to Snegirev, April 1911.
5. Tatyana Komarova, "On the Flight and Death of L. N. Tolstoy" (Yasnaya Polyana Yearbook, 1992).
6. Tatyana Tolstoy letter to SA, January 29, 1911.
7. See more in Tatyana Komarova, "The Guarding Angel of Yasnaya Polyana" in *Pamyatniki Otechestva,* no. 28, 1992.
8. Sophia Tolstoy, "The Autobiography," 55.
9. Alexandra Tolstoy, *The Daughter* (Moscow: Vagrius, 200), 226.
10. Alexandra Tolstoy, *Tolstoy: A Life of My Father,* 524.
11. During World War I, the name of the Russian capital was changed from St. Petersburg to Petrograd. The old name sounded German to contemporary Russians.
12. Alexandra Tolstoy, *Tolstoy: A Life of My Father,* 524–25.
13. Alexandra Tolstoy, *Out of the Past,* 85.
14. Ibid., 88.
15. Ibid., 97–99.

16. Alexandra Tolstoy, *I Worked for the Soviet* (New Haven: Yale University Press, 1934), 40–45. Sergeenko's name is not revealed in the book so as not to compromise Tolstoy; however, good clues are provided.
17. Sergei Tolstoy letter to SA, February 13, 1918.
18. Tikhon Polner, *Tolstoy and His Wife* (Moscow: Nash Dom—L'Age d'Homme, 2000), 195–96. Translation is by the author.
19. SA letter to Varya Nagornova, September 24, 1919. First published by Tatyana Komarova.
20. Alexandra Tolstoy, *Out of the Past,* 111.

Epilogue

1. Vladimir Chertkov, *The Last Days of Tolstoy* (London: Heinemann, 1922), ix.
2. Ibid., 58.
3. Ibid., 19.
4. Maxim Gorky, *Literary Portraits,* 147–63.
5. *Jubilee Edition,* vol. 85, 17.
6. In 1920, this place became the national museum and the center for preserving Tolstoy's manuscripts.
7. Lev Osterman, *The Battle for Tolstoy* (Moscow: Grant, 2002), 29. Translation is by the author.
8. See more in Alexandra Tolstoy, *I Worked for the Soviet.*
9. Vladimir Chertkov, *The Last Days of Tolstoy,* 14, 21.

Bibliography

Works by Sophia Tolstoy

"The Autobiography of Countess Sophia Tolstoy" in *The Two Wives: Tolstoy and Dostoevsky.* Edited by Yu. Aikhenvald. Berlin: Izdatelstvo Pisatelei, 1925.

Children's stories for *ABC,* unaccredited and included in Tolstoy's *Jubilee Edition,* vol. 21: "Masha and the Guests," "It Was in Winter but It Was Warm," "The Children Went Mushrooming," "A Hazelnut Branch," "How I Learned to Sew," "A Tamed Sparrow."

A Cookbook. Tula, 1991.

Count L. N. Tolstoy. Edited by L. N. Tolstoy. Vol. 9. St. Petersburg: Russian Library, 1879. Also in *Literaturnoe Nasledstvo* 69 (1), 1961.

The Diaries of Sophia Tolstoy. Translated by Cathy Porter. New York: Random House, 1985.

From the Life of Tolstoy: Photographs Exclusively by Countess S. A. Tolstaia. Photo album. Moscow: Scherer, Nabholz & Co., 1911.

Groans. Collection of Poems in Prose, under pseudonym "A Tired Woman." *Monthly Journal for All,* no. 3, 1904.

Letters to Tolstoy: 1862–1910. Moscow-Leningrad: Academia, 1936.

"My Life." Memoir, parts 1–8. L. N. Tolstoy State Museum (GMT).

Skeleton Dolls and Other Stories. Moscow: Kushner Printing Works, 1910.

Novellas

"Natasha." 1861–62. Not preserved.

"Song without Words." GMT (L. N. Tolstoy State Museum) Unpublished.

Who's to Blame? Oktyabr, no. 10, 1994.

Reminiscences

"L. N. Tolstoy's Marriage." *Russian Word,* 1912.

"The Power of Darkness." Tolstoy Yearbook, 1912.

"Reminiscences about Turgenev." *Oryol Herald,* no. 224, 1903.

"Tolstoy's Four Visits to the Optina Monastery." Tolstoy Yearbook, 1913.

Public Appeals

An appeal for donations to help the starving. *Russian Gazette,* no. 303, November 3, 1891.

Letter to the chief procurator of the Holy Synod and the Metropolitans in response to Tolstoy's excommunication. Supplement to no. 17 of the unofficial part of the *Church Gazette,* March 24, 1901.

Translations

Life of St. Francis of Assisi, by Paul Sabatier, into Russian. Moscow: Intermediary, 1895.

On Life, Leo Tolstoy, into French. Paris: C. Marpon et E. Flammarion, 1889.

Sydney Sprague, a year with the Bahais in India and Burma, into Russian. Included in Tolstoy's collection of wise sayings *A Cycle of Reading* and published abridged and unaccredited, 1911.

Works by Tolstoy

Anna Karenina. Translated by Richard Pevear and Larissa Volokhonsky. New York: Penguin Books, 2002.

Childhood, Boyhood & Youth, in *The Works of Leo Tolstoy.* Translated by Aylmer and Louise Maude. London: Oxford University Press, 1928–37.

Complete Collected Works in 90 volumes: Jubilee Edition. Edited by V. G. Chertkov. Moscow-Leningrad: Goslitizdat, 1928–58.

Plays. 3 vols. Translated by Marvin Kantor with Tanya Tulchinsky. Evanston, Ill.: Northwestern University Press, 1998.

Tolstoy's Diaries. 2 vols. Edited and translated by R. F. Christian. Vols. 1–2. London: Anthlone Press, 1985.

Tolstoy's Letters. 2 vols. Edited and translated by R. F. Christian. London: Anthlone Press, 1978.

War and Peace. Translated by Richard Pevear and Larissa Volokhonsky. New York: Alfred A. Knopf, 2007.

Tolstoy's Short Fiction. Edited and translated by Michael R. Katz. New York: Norton, 1991.

Books about the Tolstoys

Behrs, Stepan. *Recollections of Count Leo Tolstoy.* Translated by Charles Edward Turner. London: Heinemann, 1893.

Biryukov, P. I. *Leo Tolstoy, His Life and Work. Autobiographical Memoirs, Letters and Biographical Material.* London: Heinemann, 1906.

Bulgakov, Valentin. *The Last Year of Leo Tolstoy.* New York: Dial Press, 1971.

Bunin, Ivan. *The Liberation of Tolstoy.* Evanston, Ill.: Northwestern University Press, 2001.

The Cambridge Companion to Tolstoy. Edited by Donna Tussing Orwin. New York: Cambridge University Press, 2002.

Chertkov, Vladimir. *The Last Days of Tolstoy*. Translated by Nathalie A. Duddington. London: Heinemann, 1922.

Dostoevsky, Anna. *Dostoevsky: Reminiscences*. Translated by Beatrice Stillman. New York: Liveright, 1975.

Edwards, Anne. *Sonya: The Life of Countess Tolstoy*. New York: Simon & Schuster, 1981.

Fet, A. A. *Moi vospominaniya*. Munich: Wilhelm Fink Verlag, 1971.

Goldenweiser, Alexander. *Lev Tolstoy: Reminiscences*. Moscow: Zakharov, 2002.

Gorky, Maxim. *Collected Works in Ten Volumes*. Vol. 9, *Literary Portraits*. Moscow: Progress Publishers, 1982.

Guide to the Great Kremlin Palace. Moscow: Synod Press, 1914.

Gusev, Nikolai. *Chronicle of L. N. Tolstoy's Life and Work*. 2 vols. Moscow: State Literary House, 1958–60.

Komarova, Tatyana. "The Guarding Angel of Yasnaya Polyana." In *Pamyatniki Otechestva,* no. 28, 1992.

———. "On the Flight and Death of L. N. Tolstoy." Yasnaya Polyana Yearbook, 1992.

Kuzminskaia, Tatyana. *Tolstoy as I Knew Him: My Life at Home and at Yasnaya Polyana*. Translated by Nora Sigerist. New York: Macmillan, 1948.

Makovitsky, D. P. *The Yasnaya Polyana Notes*. Vols. 1–4. Moscow: Nauka, 1979.

Mandelker, Amy. *Framing Anna Karenina: Tolstoy, the Woman Question, and the Victorian Novel*. Columbus: Ohio State University Press, 1993.

Maude, Aylmer. *The Life of Tolstoy: Later Years*. London: Oxford University Press, 1930.

Møller, Peter. *Postlude to the Kreutzer Sonata*. New York: E. J. Brill, 1988.

Muratov, M. V. *L. N. Tolstoy and V. G, Chertkov*. Translated by Scott D. Moss. Tenafly, N. J.: Hermitage Publishers, 2002.

Nabokov, Vladimir. *Lectures on Russian Literature*. New York: Harcourt Brace Jovanovich, 1981.

Nikiforova, Tatyana. "The Beginning of Sophia Tolstoy's Publishing Activity." In *Tolstoy Is a Complete World* (almanac). Moscow: Pashkov Dom, 2004.

Osterman, Lev. *The Battle for Tolstoy*. Moscow: Grant, 2002.

Polner, Tikhon. *Tolstoy and His Wife*. New York: Norton, 1945.

Polyakova, Tamara. "On the History of the Tolstoy Home in Khamovniki." In Yasnaya Polyana Yearbook. Tula, 1984.

Puzin, Nikolai. *Yasnaya Polyana, the Lev Tolstoy Estate Museum*. Moscow: Progress Publishers, 1965.

Safonova, O. Yu. *The Behrs Ancestry in Russia*. Moscow: Village Encyclopedia, 1999.

Svadkovsky, Boris. "Sophia Tolstaia: The Unpublished Letters from the 'Steel Room.'" In *Sovershenno Sekretno*, no. 3, 1992.

Tolstoy, Alexandra. *The Daughter*. Moscow: Vagrius, 2000.

———. *I Worked for the Soviet*. New Haven: Yale University Press, 1934.

———. *Tolstoy: A Life of My Father*. London: Victor Gollancz Limited, 1953.

———. *Out of the Past*. Edited by Katharine Strelsky and Catherine Wolkonsky. New York: Columbia University Press, 1981.

Tolstoy, Ilya. *Tolstoy, My Father: Reminiscences*. Translated by Ann Dunnigan. Chicago: Cowles Book Company, 1971.

Tolstoy, L. N. *Documents, Photographs, Manuscripts*. Moscow: Planeta, 1995.

Tolstoy, S. L. *Tolstoy Remembered by His Son*. Translated by Moura Budberg. London: Weidenfeld and Nicolson, 1961.

Tolstoy, Tatyana. *The Tolstoy Home, Diaries*. Translated by Alec Brown. London: Harvill Press, 1950.

———. *Tolstoy Remembered*. Translated by Derek Coltman. New York: McGraw-Hill Book Company, 1977.

The Tolstoys' Correspondence with N. N. Strakhov. Edited by A. A. Donskov. Ottawa: Slavic Research Group, 2000.

Wilson, A. N. *Tolstoy*. London: Penguin Books, 1989.

Yasnaya Polyana Almanac. Tula: 1978.

Zhdanov, Vladimir. *Love in Leo Tolstoy's Life*. Moscow: Planeta, 1993.

Other Sources

Ackroyd, Peter. *Dickens*. London: Sinclair-Stevenson, 1990.

Alexander, John. *Catherine the Great: Life and Legend*. Oxford: Oxford University Press, 1989.

Maugham, W. Somerset. *The Moon and Sixpence*. New York: Penguin Books, 2005.

Micale, Mark S. *Approaching Hysteria: Disease and Its Interpretations*. Princeton: Princeton University Press, 1995.

Micklem, Niel. *The Nature of Hysteria*. London: Routledge, 1996.

Orwell, George. *Collected Essays*. London: Secker & Warburg, 1961.

Sabatier, Paul. *Life of St. Francis of Assisi*. New York: Charles Scribner's Sons, 1916.

Sacks, Oliver. *Musicophilia*. New York: Alfred A. Knopf, 2007.

Schapiro, Leonard. *Turgenev: His Life and Times*. Oxford: Oxford University Press, 1978.

Shenk, Joshua Wolf. *Lincoln's Melancholy: How Depression Challenged a President and Fueled His Greatness*. Boston: Houghton Mifflin, 2005.

Index

About the Author

ALEXANDRA POPOFF was born and educated in Moscow. A journalist and writer, she has published her work in the Russian national newspapers and magazines. As an Alfred Friendly Press Fellow in 1991, she wrote for the *Philadelphia Inquirer*. After marrying a Canadian journalist in 1992, she settled in Saskatchewan, which is where the Russian Doukhobors, her husband's ancestors, had originally migrated and settled.

Popoff lives in Canada. She earned postgraduate degrees in literature in Moscow, Toronto, and Saskatchewan.